blue
rider
press

ALMIGHTY

ALMIGHTY

COURAGE, RESISTANCE, AND
EXISTENTIAL PERIL
IN THE NUCLEAR AGE

Dan Zak

BLUE RIDER PRESS
New York

blue
rider
press

An imprint of Penguin Random House LLC
375 Hudson Street
New York, New York 10014

Blue Rider Press gratefully acknowledges permission to reprint
Daniel Berrigan's poem "Hymn to the New Humanity" © 1984. Permission
granted by John Dear, S. J., literary executor of the Berrigan estate.

Library of Congress Cataloging-in-Publication Data
Names: Zak, Dan.
Title: Almighty : courage, resistance, and existential peril in the nuclear age / Dan Zak.
Description : New York : Blue Rider Press, an imprint of Penguin Random
House, 2016. | Includes bibliographical references and index.
Identifiers : LCCN 2016011566 (print) | LCCN 2016013992 (ebook) | ISBN 9780399173752
(print : alkaline paper) | ISBN 9780698189232 (ePub)
Subjects: LCSH: Antinuclear movement—United States—History—21st century. |
Pacifists—Tennessee—Oak Ridge—Biography. | Y-12 National Security Complex (U.S.) |
Courage—United States. | Government, Resistance to—United States. | Nuclear weapons—Moral
and ethical aspects—United States. | Nuclear weapons—Social aspects—
United States. | Nuclear weapons—United States—History. | Nuclear weapons industry—
United States—History. | United States—Military policy. |
BISAC: POLITICAL SCIENCE /International Relations / Arms Control. | HISTORY /
Military / Biological & Chemical Warfare. | HISTORY / Military / Nuclear Warfare.
Classification: LCC JZ5584.U6 Z34 2016 (print) | LCC JZ5584.U6 (ebook) |
DDC 327.1/7470973—dc23
LC record available at http://lccn.loc.gov/2016011566

Printed in the United States of America
1   3   5   7   9   10   8   6   4   2

Book design by Meighan Cavanaugh

For my teachers

The seed of our destruction will blossom in the desert, the alexin of our cure grows by the mountain rock, and our lives are hunted by a Georgia slattern, because a London cutpurse went unhung. Each moment is the fruit of forty thousand years. The minute-winning days, like flies, buzz home to death, and every moment is a window on all time.

THOMAS WOLFE, *Look Homeward, Angel* (1929)

CONTENTS

PART III

RELATIVITY/UNCERTAINTY

PROLOGUE

The zero hour approached but time seemed at a standstill. There was no cell service out there in the bramble, off a state highway named for a U.S. senator, past the point where brick estates gave way to matchstick shanties, past where foothills overtook steeples, where civilization faded down tangles of switch-backs. Off one sudden turn, a gravel drive hitched into the dim heather and got narrower, until it was just a mud lane rutted with tire tracks that wormed between warped barns. And there was the grove of sycamore, the rows of grapevine and corn, the handsome country house. A sanctuary. On the wraparound porch facing the vegetable garden, especially at night, it was possible to pretend that this was all there was—that the world was made only of tranquil enclaves under ancient starlight.

They knew the world was not this way, so they retrieved three Red Cross blood bags from the refrigerator, snipped their corners, and began to funnel the blood into baby bottles on the porch.

The blood was human, and until very recently had been frozen for some time, so at first it appeared almost black and was cool to the touch. In the afternoon light, as it hit the thick midsummer oxygen of East Tennessee, the blood became cherry red. One man, who had done this type of thing several times before, funneled the blood over a ceramic bowl on a Ping-Pong table. He thought, *God, let this all be to the good, in some way or another.* The voice of a departed friend, who had first demonstrated this process for him 30 years earlier, was also in his ear: "This is sacred stuff. This is the stuff of life."

The solemnity of the ritual kept it tidy. The funneling of the blood was one of many practical chores on the checklist, but it was also a private preparation for public prayer. To mark an object of scorn with blood was both symbolic and literal. It was a sacrament.

Nine people were at the house, including three who would put the six bottles of blood in their backpacks for illicit transport later that night. One was a Roman Catholic sister, 82 years old. One was a Vietnam veteran, age 63, who had no earthly possessions. One was a housepainter, 57, who knew that this could be his last day as a free man, or perhaps his last day alive. The remaining six at the house were the support team. The mission was initially scheduled for early Sunday, but on Thursday the group felt ready enough to go a day early. The sister in particular was anxious. Her life had been building to this moment.

Using box cutters, they scraped the peacenik bumper stickers from the drop-off car, which they would send to the junkyard afterward, just to be safe. A woman unrolled a long ribbon of red caution tape, wrote NUCLEAR CRIME ZONE in black marker after each DANGER, then rolled it back up. The sister, the vet, and the painter had the bolt cutters, the hammers, the flashlights, their typed statement of intent. They had observed one another over the week for hesitation, for spiritual disquiet. The man who funneled the blood remembered what his friend had told him years ago, before a similar mission: "Don't macho bullshit your way through it." A young man in the support group had decided just that week not to go the distance. He was not as ready as the sister was, or as steadfast as her companions.

Now another woman was inside the safe house making two loaves of bread from scratch. One would be broken over dinner. The other would go into the backpacks with the bolt cutters and the blood. After the dough rose a second time, she used a kitchen knife to carve a cross atop both circular loaves. She herself was not a believer—not in Jesus Christ, anyway, but certainly a believer in the spirit of the night's mission. If carving crosses into loaves of bread was in the service of peace, then doing so would be her pleasure.

The sister, the veteran, and the housepainter rehearsed likely scenarios out in the yard, which they imagined was the fenced perimeter of their target. Supporters played the role of armed guards who might discover them at any point in the mile-long hike over a wooded ridge. The possibilities ranged from the pedestrian to the fatal: What if one of them turns an ankle? What if the guards open fire, as they were authorized to do? What if they were thwarted before they got anywhere near their target? Would they be satisfied with their mission even if it was stopped early? What was their definition of victory?

The bread baked in the oven.

Afternoon unwound into evening.

Supper was salad and potatoes. A liturgy followed in the living room. One of the supporters, a Catholic priest, consecrated bread and wine near an unlit woodstove. Then there was nothing to do but lie down and wait.

Around 1 a.m. they gathered in the living room and held hands. They drew a collective breath. They prayed for success.

Then they walked out of the house, light of head, heavy of heart.

The sister, the veteran, and the housepainter embraced their supporters, shouldered their backpacks, and piled into the car after the driver.

Then they were moving through the night, back to civilization, toward their target, armed with a weapon whose power they believed was unmatched.

PART I

ACTION

I do not know how to teach philosophy without becoming a disturber of the peace.

BARUCH SPINOZA

1.

MANHATTAN

Gargoyles ruled the island at the turn of the century, but in 1910 the new building at 35 Claremont Avenue had angels peering from its third story. They were archangels, not cherubs, with stern stone faces and sleek wings flared upward, bodies protected by stone shields—a biblical squadron rendered in medieval style, as if summoned from the pages of Milton to the building's Italian Renaissance facade. They looked ready for battle.

In the spring of 1926, one floor above the angels, a man of science moved into apartment 4B.

Selig Hecht was 34, with a wife named Cecelia and a two-year-old daughter named Maressa. He was fresh from Cambridge University and was now Columbia University's newest associate professor of biophysics. Selig's academic and scientific bona fides were prodigious for his age, especially given his lower-class upbringing. He was born in the village of Głogów, in what was then Austria, and journeyed at age six with his family to the Lower East Side, a grimy warren of poor European expats. The oldest of five, Selig ran errands after Hebrew school to support the family, and during high school and college he kept the books at a wool business. His father fancied friendly arguments about history and philosophy. He raised Selig on a diet of Schopenhauer, who believed the world was godless and meaningless, and Spinoza, who believed the world was inherently divine and perfect, though man's blundering prevented him from realizing it. Philosophy and ethics would later inform Selig's work and writings, but first he pursued a formal education in the hardier fields of mathematics and zoology. He graduated with a biology degree from the City College of New York and got a job as a chemist in a fermentation research laboratory, where he studied the effect of light on beer. Selig then worked as a chemist at the Department of Agriculture in Washington, D.C., to raise money for graduate school. The subject of his dissertation at Harvard University was the physiology of a marine invertebrate called a sea squirt, which he studied at the Bermuda Biological Station. His life's work, though, would be the study of human vision and its adaptation to darkness.

It took him years to get an academic appointment worthy of his talents. "You yourself may safely ignore the stupidity and even brutality of our times," the biologist Jacques Loeb wrote to Selig in 1922, in a note of encouragement. Loeb told him to "keep that serenity which is required of a man who wishes to do his best work. The future needs you and belongs to you."

Now here he was in that future, on Claremont Avenue, back in his adoptive hometown of New York City, albeit far uptown from his youth in terms of geography and class. Riverside Drive was visible from the Hechts' west-facing windows. To the east, following the gaze of the stone archangels, was Columbia's campus, with its handsome new physics building three blocks away at West 120th Street and Broadway. A brick structure crowned with copper cornice, the Pupin Hall physics building was in some ways a monument to Albert Einstein's special theory of relativity, which had hurled physics into its modern era 21 years earlier by describing the relationship between energy and mass in the equation $E = mc^2$. Energy (E) and mass (m) are essentially the same thing, because all mass is bound together by energy. Because the speed of light (c) is such a massive number whose value remains constant, a small amount of mass multiplied by c can transform into a disproportionately massive amount of energy. Pupin Hall would also be an investment in the application of Werner Heisenberg's recently introduced "uncertainty principle," which argues that both the position and velocity of an atomic particle cannot be precisely measured at the same time. The more an observer knows about the particle's position, the less he knows about its velocity, and vice versa, and the observation itself affects the particle's location or speed.

"We cannot know, as a matter of principle, the present in all its details," Heisenberg wrote in 1927, packaging quantum mechanics into a neat maxim. Quantum mechanics is the study of the universe's smallest parts: atoms, the basic component of an element, and the protons, electrons, and neutrons inside—the invisible whirling ingredients of all things.

By the time Selig became a full professor in 1928, he was the sovereign of the physics building's 13th floor, with an expansive lab and views of the southern sweep of Manhattan and sunsets over the Hudson River. During the next decade, Pupin Hall welcomed younger academic stars whose expertise was the atom. These scientists, shaggy and eccentric, were known in academia as "longhairs."

Selig Hecht wasn't a longhair. His black hair was short, wiry, and wavy, and would later turn steel-colored. He kept his mustache trimmed to his upper lip. He wore woolen three-piece suits with a white handkerchief peeking from his jacket pocket. Tea was served every afternoon in his lab, which became a salon for lively discussions of art, music, literature, and politics. He was known for drawing diagrams at lightning speed on his blackboards while providing a run-

ning commentary that was as clear as it was fast. One evening a week
Selig hosted students, faculty, and other peers at his apartment on
Claremont Avenue. Near Selig's own vibrant watercolor paintings, in
a dining room of dark oak wainscoting, they would discuss books
like *The Logic of Modern Physics* by P. W. Bridgman. In his first chapter Bridgman asked bracing questions that enlivened cocktail hours
shared by men of science:

Why does time flow?

Why does nature obey laws?

Are there parts of nature forever beyond our detection?

Was there ever a time when matter did not exist?

May time have a beginning or an end?

Selig's salons were typical of bohemian Manhattan in the first decades of the 20th century. The Great Depression, its pall blanketing
the city in the year after Selig became a full professor, transformed
such academic discussions into social engagement and activism. By
1930 the Lower East Side, Selig's childhood neighborhood, had de-
volved into a festering slum with 50 breadlines serving 50,000 meals
a day. By 1932 half the city's factories were closed, one-third of the
population was unemployed, and the plight of the worker was a favorite cause of progressive New Yorkers. Selig and other professors
signed a protest that year against the state of Kentucky's mistreatment
of industrial workers.

In January 1935 Selig published an essay in *Harper's Monthly Magazine* titled "The Uncertainty Principle and Human Behavior," in
which he suggested that Heisenberg's work had opened physics to
philosophy. Heisenberg "apparently destroyed the pure and inevitable relations of cause and effect," Selig wrote. The German physicist
had discovered "a natural limit to knowledge" and that "there is a
distinct limit to the total precision with which such an event may be
described." Uncertainty frees biological behavior from predetermi-
nation, allowing for the existence of free will, which in turn imbues

mankind with godlike powers. Despite this feeling of freedom, Selig wrote, humans are still guided by an unseen hand.

> To his own mind, the behavior of a man seems to be free and of his own choosing, and all the accumulated moralities of the world exhort him to choose the good and to act righteously on the assumption that he is capable of free choice and action. . . .
>
> If free-will means that we can choose our good behavior and be rewarded for it, it means also that we can choose our evil behavior and be punished for it. . . .
>
> [All behavior] is determined by the complicated series of conditions and circumstances which enter into the composition of an event.

Selig, by applying an atomic principle to the wider world, arrived at a social dictum: Man must act as if he were free to choose, while remembering that the origins of his behavior are complex and steered by forces long forgotten and not immediately understood.

The uncertainty of the present, in other words, is the product of a certain past.

The *Harper's* essay drew excitement and blowback from readers who were tantalized by the notion of scientific and moral uncertainty. When a reader from West Point wrote to *Harper's* to criticize Selig's validation of both free will *and* determinism, Selig responded with a typewritten note. Free will and determinism are as mutually exclusive as reason and instinct, Selig wrote. That is to say: They are not.

"I think that we can have both," he wrote to the West Point reader, "since they are each a partial view of the world."

The essay burnished his reputation as a technician of nuance with a refined social conscience, which would soon be inflamed by the buildup to World War II.

The United States, as yet unprovoked by the Japanese attack on

Pearl Harbor, was already engaged in World War II from an experimental standpoint. Thirteen floors below Hecht's lab, in the basement, was a 30-ton, seven-feet-tall hunk of metal known as a cyclotron, which used a giant electromagnet to propel atomic particles at up to 25,000 miles per second. On January 25, 1939, a team at Columbia used the cyclotron to split an atom of the element uranium for the first time on American soil. This was fission, the process by which neutrons serve as projectiles that shatter atoms. Fission releases the energy that binds matter together, and is therefore the most efficient way to actualize Einstein's famous equation involving E and m.

"Believe we have observed new phenomenon of far-reaching consequences," the Columbia physicist John R. Dunning wrote in his diary that night.

In the minds of scientists, this discovery had two practical applications, both at odds with each other: as a peaceful source of energy and as a godlike force of destruction. "Complementarity" was the word that the physicist Niels Bohr used to describe the contradiction inherent in quantum physics—and, philosophically, in life itself.

A nuclear reaction could light a city.

A nuclear reaction could level a city.

It was all a matter of how the energy was used.

Over in Europe a madman was planning invasions of neighboring countries. His scientists were seemingly out in front with this new science.

WITH A URANIUM ATOM SPLIT in the basement, the Italian physicist Enrico Fermi settled into his office on Pupin Hall's seventh floor. His family had just arrived from Italy that month on the ocean liner *Franconia*. In early March, Columbia scientists discovered that fission ejected "secondary" neutrons that could split other nuclei, which would eject other neutrons, starting a chain reaction of splits that could grow instantaneously and exponentially. In Pupin Hall, physicists worked seven days a week researching gaseous diffusion, a process by which uranium could be enriched and concentrated to a point where a chain reaction was possible. With both the means and the ends quickly coming into focus, Fermi looked out over the island of stone and steel, cupped his hands, and said, "A little bomb like that, and it would all disappear."

On March 15, Adolf Hitler took Czechoslovakia.

Upstairs in his penthouse laboratory, Selig Hecht focused on the human eye, its adaptation to darkness, and its response to flickering light. He was not involved with atomic work but heard chatter about its progression. He hosted longhairs at his apartment and made those short walks home with them. He understood what the scientific community, and the United States, was working toward. He hoped they would never succeed.

On a Wednesday morning that July, Selig's Columbia colleague Leo Szilard and theoretical physicist Eugene Wigner drove to Einstein's cottage on Long Island. Over iced tea, Szilard and Wigner persuaded the famous 60-year-old physicist to sign a letter of warning that would be sent from his cottage to the White House. Einstein, in Szilard's words, told President Roosevelt of "extremely powerful bombs of a new type" that were fueled by uranium, to which the United States had little domestic access.

"I understand that Germany has actually stopped the sale of uranium from the Czechoslovakian mines which she has taken over," Einstein wrote.

A month later Hitler took Poland.

The secrecy was on, Szilard thought. Over the next two years, a vast administrative effort kicked into gear to develop an atomic bomb before the Nazis did. Columbia physicists began assembling four tons of graphite bricks. The "pile," as they called it, would be used to conduct and moderate a nuclear chain reaction on a small scale. After long, exhausting days they trudged home through the neighborhood of Morningside Heights smudged with graphite, looking like wayward coal miners. A month and a half before Pearl Harbor, 2,000 American scientists were engaged in "defense research" for the government at a cost of millions of dollars per month. Three out of four physicists in the United States were working on military projects. It was a "concentrated attack upon a problem," said electrical engineer Vannevar Bush, the director of the government's Office of Research and Scientific Development, at a joint luncheon of scientific societies at the Hotel Pennsylvania in Midtown Manhattan in October 1941. This was as much as Bush would say on the matter. He was already asking scientists involved in uranium research for a pledge of secrecy that prohibited them from even uttering the word "uranium." Just several miles away, in warehouses on Staten Island, sat 1,100 metric tons of the stuff in 2,000 steel drums labeled URANIUM ORE. It had been shipped from the Congo the year before by a Belgian miner who worried that Hitler's annexation of Belgium might extend to its African colonies. That night, at the same hotel, the Optical Society of America presented its highest honor to Selig Hecht for "distinguished work in the field of optics."

By then Fermi and other Columbia professors were meeting at the Men's Faculty Club on the first day of each month to forecast the future, just for kicks. As they lunched, this "Society of Prophets," as they called themselves, would come up with ten yes-or-no questions concerning events that might occur that month.

Would German ships attack a neutral American convoy?

Would Hitler give the order to land in Britain?

Would the British hold the strategic Libyan port city of Tobruk?

The "prophets" would write down their answers, check them against current events at the end of the month, and keep score. When the informal society disbanded after Pearl Harbor, Fermi held the highest score: 97 percent of his predictions were accurate. His wife,

Laura, attributed this success rate to his conservative belief that situations change more slowly than people expect them to.

After the United States entered the war in December 1941, Selig was tapped by the Army and Navy to devote his laboratory to military work. He and his assistants refined night-vision equipment for the Allies and visited military installations to troubleshoot equipment problems. In the fall of 1942 Selig taught a course at Columbia on night vision and camouflage. Aware of both the flight of Jewish academics from Europe and the breathless race to develop the bomb, he had a strong sense of urgency about the war. His plain speech and blunt wit endeared him to military officers. Selig didn't speak about his wartime work at home and only vaguely alluded to his colleagues' dance with the atom. Tight lips were the fashion.

"I learned to ask no questions," Laura Fermi wrote in her memoir. "No more 'What have you done today?' nor 'Are you pleased with your work?' nor 'Who is your collaborator?'" When her husband returned from mystery trips, she was left to speculate about the dust on his suit and the mud on his shoes. "Other women's husbands also went on frequent travels," she wrote. "It would have been bad taste indeed to ask where."

Nuclear physicists from various countries, alarmed by the theoretical power of a chain reaction, attempted to cloak themselves in secrecy. This was unnatural, even antithetical, to the standards of modern science. State control of knowledge was a hallmark of autocracies like the Third Reich, and yet it was fear of the Nazis that compelled U.S. scientists into self-imposed censorship. "A conspiracy," as Leo Szilard called it. History would call it the "Manhattan Project."

This aura of secrecy pervaded the Columbia campus and drifted out into neighborhood gossip in Morningside Heights, a village unto itself, where many professors and their families lived above tearooms, Chinese laundries, and small grocery stores that were just beginning to stock pudding powders and frozen foods for the first time. Secrecy found its way down the gentle slope of Claremont Avenue from West 119th to 116th, up the marble steps of the stately apartment buildings, to wives commiserating in steamy galley kitchens, to eavesdropping children.

Across the tiled hallway from the Hechts, apartment 4A belonged to Frederick W. Rice, an obstetrician at Bellevue Hospital, and his wife, Madeleine Newman Hooke Rice, a graduate student at Columbia. The Rices were progressive Catholics. They had three daughters, one of whom was the same age as the Hechts' daughter, Maressa. The children played together on the fourth floor, often shouting through the apartments' shared wall, and sneaking through a door off the Rices' kitchen that connected the homes. The adults visited regularly at night to socialize with guests, who included longhairs, "prophets," and academic refugees from Nazi Germany.

Megan, the Rices' youngest daughter, would overhear the adults alluding to the secret work of the men of Morningside Heights. She asked why Dr. Hecht's work was hidden, even from his own wife, especially when it was conducted only blocks away from their homes.

"Well, Dr. Hecht understands the Einstein theory," Megan's mother said, implying that scientific knowledge was the key to the mystery in their midst.

THEN ALL OF A SUDDEN the newspapers, in hulking black headlines, announced the atomic bombing of Japan on August 6, 1945. Secret sites, spread out across the United States, had collaborated at breakneck speed to theorize, assemble, and test bomb components. The physics building at Columbia University was one such site. The buzz around campus and out in Morningside Heights was hypothetical and experimental in nature, while the sweaty industrial work was done in those secret cities farther west. The effort was called the

Manhattan Project, and it was credited with ending the war by devastating two major cities.

The men of science whose intellect had underpinned the project recoiled at the devastating military use of atomic power over Hiroshima and, three days later, Nagasaki. They viewed this as a kind of original sin, a Rubicon crossed, Pandora's box now opened.

Selig Hecht tried to wrangle the unthinkable into words by writing an essay titled "Science and Moral Values," which was in the spirit of Niels Bohr's concept of complementarity. Selig typed some of the essay, revising by hand in blue ink, and wrote some of it in elegant cursive on unlined paper. While editing, he grafted typewritten passages onto handwritten ones. It was not a polished academic editorial. It was an emotional treatise of philosophy—less Schopenhauer, more Spinoza. On a handwritten page headlined with the Roman numeral "I," he wrote:

> Everything that happens, from the composition of a symphony to the eruption of a volcano, involves an intricate and interlocking pattern of sequences in the movement of matter and the transformation of energy. When wheels rotate and water flows, when muscles contract and nerves conduct, when bells ring and pianos play, when grass grows and wheat is mown, there is an incessant and vast interplay between energy and matter.

He wrote that "every advance in civilization seems to bring its quota of disturbance" and that the intersection of science and morality often leaves us with a paradox. Human intellect had progressed far enough to leverage science for ultimate power.

> But of what avail is this knowledge if we use it to destroy cities and people, to devastate the countryside, and to shatter the very

structures and men that made possible this knowledge and civilization?

The contrast is humiliating: on the one hand, clear knowledge and precise control of natural forces; on the other, spiritual anarchy and devastating ruin. Why is this? Why has man learned to understand and to dominate the forces of nature, and why has he failed to understand himself so that his control of nature serves to destroy himself? This is the modern paradox: the more we know of nature, the more easily we wreck our lives with the knowledge; order in natural knowledge and chaos in social behavior. Why?

Natural law is fixed and describes what *will* happen, he thought, while moral law is voluntary and prescribes what *should* happen. Morality "can be brought into concrete form by social mechanism," wrote Selig, who had demonstrated this theorem in his own life. The essay was at once hopeful and frightened. "In a few years this war has ruined much of what we have built in centuries of patient history," he said. "The next war may be of an entirely different order of magnitude and destroy us completely." To drive his point home, he wondered if every supernova explosion in deep space was actually evidence of an extraterrestrial civilization that was not a careful steward of its atomic power.

Perhaps we can still achieve a happy moral order before it is too late. In order to do so let us not rely only on social mechanisms, or only on personal virtue and responsibility.

Each is necessary, but neither is sufficient. With the two actively combined we may yet emerge from our moral barbarism and achieve that spiritual integrity which our great teachers and prophets had the genius to recognize ages ago.

Selig, because of this reputation for extolling the social obligations of science, was named the honorary vice president of the Emergency Committee of Atomic Scientists, created in 1946 by Szilard and Einstein to educate the public about the dangers of atomic energy, to encourage its use for peaceful matters, and to curb military control over it. In its first letter asking for public donations, the committee wrote that a "new type of thinking" is "essential if mankind is to survive." The committee thought that atomic power necessitated a world government, that building bombs meant forever postponing peace.

"I do not believe that we can prepare for war and at the same time prepare for a world community," Einstein wrote in the *New York Times*. "When humanity holds in its hand the weapon with which it can commit suicide, I believe that to put more power into the gun is to increase the probability of disaster."

Even Leslie Groves, the towering gung-ho Army general who was in charge of the Manhattan Project, admitted the dangers in stark tones. "Modern civilization might be completely destroyed" if other countries produced their own atomic weapons, he and Secretary of War Henry Stimson wrote to President Harry S. Truman a couple of months before they were used on Japan. The following year, during a closed Senate hearing, the head physicist of the Manhattan Project was asked whether a nuclear bomb could be smuggled into Manhattan and detonated by enemies of the United States.

"Of course it could be done," replied J. Robert Oppenheimer, "and people could destroy New York."

Selig was the only member of the committee who wasn't a nuclear physicist, but he proved his expertise the following year by publishing *Explaining the Atom*, a layman's guide to quantum physics. The book's epigraph invokes the British physicist Lord Rayleigh: "There is no possibility of telling whether the issue of scientists' work will prove them to be fiends, or dreamers, or angels."

In the prologue to *Explaining the Atom*, Selig wrote about "public men"—congressmen, presidents, appointees—who have no understanding of the basic principles of atomic energy and yet make decisions about this ultimate weapon. His book was essentially dedicated to these elected officials, and to citizens of the world who'd been shielded from knowledge by the secrecy of the Manhattan Project. The Atomic Energy Act of 1946, passed by "public men" in Congress that summer, reassigned the stewardship of nuclear energy from the military to civilians. The act also prescribed the death penalty or life imprisonment for anyone guilty of stealing or sharing atomic secrets. The language of this law, Selig thought, implied that the release of atomic energy was a sudden development triggered by isolated data— something that could be stolen and used as easily as a loaded handgun resting beside a cash register.

Really, though, the atomic bombing of Japan was a culmination of a half century's work between thousands of people whose "intellectual drama" (as Selig put it) eventually yielded both the understanding and the technology to unlock the energy of matter. The bomb was "merely the latest impact of the wave of physical science that began about fifty years ago on the ocean of knowledge," Selig wrote at the end of his prologue. Ernest Rutherford had imagined the existence of neutrons 25 years before Hiroshima, Einstein had published his special theory of relativity 15 years before that, and "radioactivity" entered the lexicon nine years prior. In his 1914 novel *The World Set Free*, the science-fiction writer H. G. Wells envisioned how any "scrap of solid matter in the world would become an available reservoir of concentrated force."

A chain reaction of thinking over many years at a macro level, in other words, led to a chain reaction at the nuclear level.

Explaining the Atom was Selig's way of rendering the complexities of nuclear physics in clear terms. Energy and mass are "different aspects of the same basic cosmic stuff," he wrote, and a small change in mass releases a comparatively large amount of energy. Uranium is a heavy, radioactive and unstable element, and thus breaking down an atom of uranium releases enough energy to pulverize other uranium atoms. The first fissioned nucleus frees 170 million electron volts and two neutrons, which are absorbed by two other atoms, which each release two more neutrons. Thus, the 30th generation of fission causes the splitting of more than a billion atoms. The energy release grows instantly into a self-sustaining torrent, into an explosion, into a fireball that can flatten and ignite a metropolitan area. By destroying the smallest parts of matter, mankind could destroy the largest parts.

And it was all accomplished by "a staggering project," as Selig called it, that was now public knowledge. Manhattan dreamed up the atomic bomb. Secret industrial cities around the country helped to make it. Selig Hecht wanted to teach it. He stated his goal—almost a plea—in the preface to *Explaining the Atom*, which he prepared in the late summer of 1946 at his summer home in Bridgewater, Connecticut:

> My purpose is to supply a background against which people can think and act intelligently on the problems of atomic energy. So long as one supposes that this business is mysterious and secret, one cannot have a just evaluation of our possession and security. Only by understanding the basis and development of atomic energy can one judge the legislation and foreign policy that concern it. I hope that this book will help make intelligent voters.

The man of science who lived in a building of angels, who believed not in God but in humanity's potential for grace and goodness, was concerned about the future. He foresaw the abuse of atomic power and worried about society's ignorance of what it possessed. Selig felt that good citizenship required a good understanding of science. Knowledge was important, but so was the application of knowledge for the betterment of the world. Science was nothing without synthesis. "There is no end to the cataloguing of interesting phenomena," he once told a Columbia colleague. "The problem of putting the interesting phenomena into a meaningful context is a much more difficult story, and the success which attends the effort is the mark of a true scientist."

NOW THAT THE SECRET was out, the United States needed a bureaucracy to formally and publicly handle it. Through the National Security Act of 1947, Congress created a thicket of management to shield and shepherd the atom-powered defense of the United States in the postwar world: the National Security Council, the Central Intelligence Agency, the Joint Chiefs of Staff, and the National Military Establishment, which would later become the Department of Defense. Congress had already established the Joint Committee on Atomic Energy, with nine members each from the House of Representatives and the Senate, to deal with nuclear matters. Unlike all other congressional committees, the Joint Committee on Atomic Energy had the power to both "authorize" *and* "appropriate," meaning it approved policy and funneled the money to carry it out, giving a group of 18 lawmakers unprecedented control over the evolution of the country's nuclear-weapons complex. Eventually the complex would grow into a series of laboratories and plants, run chiefly by private contractors, all over the United States.

Because this "new source of energy must remain under state control," it increased "enormously the power of the state over the citizen," wrote E. L. Woodward, an Oxford professor of international relations, in the *New York Times*. The ultimate power would belong to a powerful few.

The bureaucracy that was supposed to run the nuclear-weapons complex, coupled with the Manhattan Project's vanguard classification system, would make meaningful context hard to come by in this cascade of dollars and secrets. Public men had classified information from the public, and would continue to do so for generations. President Harry S. Truman was fully aware that atomic bombs went beyond war games and organizational charts.

"You have got to understand that this isn't a military weapon," Truman said in a meeting with officials from the Atomic Energy Commission and the Department of Defense. "It is used to wipe out women and children and unarmed people, and not for military uses. So we have got to treat this differently from rifles and cannon and ordinary things like that."

By the new millennium, the United States would spend ten trillion dollars on nuclear-weapons programs—more than any other government expense except Social Security and non-nuclear defense—and begin spending a trillion more on modernizing the arsenal for the 21st century. Nukes, in other words, would be America's third-highest national priority, ever. Along the way, the weapons would evolve from a strategy into a policy into a faith. They would hasten doomsday, and also be credited with delaying it. They would be detonated in experiments all around the planet, in desolate expanses out West and on remote islands in the Pacific. They would be attached to missiles on high alert that were buried in the ground or loaded into submarines that roamed the oceans. They would create economies, inspire movements, and destroy lives. They would survive accidents and budget cuts, and outlast presidents and wars. They would number in the tens of thousands, spread to other countries, and then recede from view, but they would remain the pinnacle of human ingenuity and insecurity, a force that binds American power and threatens to blow it apart, a paradox to be pondered and maybe, one day, resolved.

All the while, a counterforce pushed back. Men and women of science, and of faith, believed that humanity was too frail to tangle with the almighty. The mere possession of nuclear weapons, to them, was a wish for death. Before a nuclear weapon was even detonated, movements to abolish them were underway. The anti-nuclear campaign would draw energy from every corner of the Earth, and it would grow and shrink, triumph at times and fail at others. It would propel people into noble lunacy—to lay down in front of trains and trucks, to scale fences and climb onto submarines, to march in the streets and through the desert, to plunge into the technicalities of warhead design and congressional budgeting, to spend years in court and prison with no hint of reward or promise of victory.

They would seek nothing less than the transformation of the American identity.

It would seem impossible. But every now and then, the impossible would occur.

ALMOST EXACTLY one year after he finished the final chapter of *Explaining the Atom*, in September 1947, Selig Hecht died of a heart attack in apartment 4B at 35 Claremont Avenue. He was 55. A fellow professor had noted that Selig seemed unwell during a visit to Cambridge University earlier that summer. The hustle and strain of the war years had left a mark, not only on him but also on the army of scientists who had aided the war effort.

Selig's body was cremated and his ashes were scattered around Columbia's physics building, just a short walk from his home.

By this time, Megan, the youngest Rice daughter who used to live across the fourth-floor hall—the girl so captivated and unnerved by those secretive conversations about the atom—was 17 years old and had decided to become a Roman Catholic sister.

2.

THE FIELD

The car eased into the parking lot beside a brick Baptist church on the edge of town. Sister Megan Rice stepped out into the amber floodlight alongside the veteran and the painter. At the back of the lot, just past the moss-covered parking curbs, was a carpet of clover in front of a curtain of flora. Beyond that: darkness.

Step one of the mission was actually 600 steps, from the parking lot across an open field to the base of Pine Ridge. The trio brushed aside thorny branches and hanging vines at the edge of the lot. They were on the move. Slowly. Deliberately. It was just past 2 a.m. on July 28, 2012.

The ridge was a black shadow under a deep-gray sky. The waxing moon, nearly three-quarters full, had just dipped below the horizon to their right, beyond a Frisbee golf course and a new subdivision called Groves Park Commons, which was named after the Army general in charge of the Manhattan Project. Einstein Avenue and Oppenheimer Way intersected about 500 feet from where the trio were now plodding over soft marsh. Lightning bugs drifted, signaled, vanished. In front of them was lumpy terrain and pools of brown water.

Behind them was Oak Ridge, Tennessee, a sleeping city of 30,000 people 30 minutes west of Knoxville.

The Catholic sister had a mild heart condition, so she set the pace. She wore a multicolored madras tunic. The grass got higher as they walked. Wet red mud slowed their footsteps. They pushed aside stalks of Queen Anne's lace and avoided black corrugated drainage pipes whose runoff had carved a deep scar in the earth. They passed a second Baptist church on their left. Deer pogoed away, their white tails lagging in the air with each hop.

The grass was mowed short near the base of the ridge. In front of them was a wall of forest. The only noise ahead was the eerie knock of acorns as they fell through oak branches. The trio pushed into the dark, into the smell of moss. Bullfrogs whined like tripped alarms.

The ridge began to tilt into a 40-degree angle. To lessen the strain, they snaked their way up, back and forth in long, slow turns. The sister had trained for this part, building up her endurance by going on long walks, but the incline was still a challenge. She was short of breath.

Their first man-made impediment was a six-foot chain-link boundary fence bordering a gravel patrol road. It ran out in either direction, forming a 19-mile oblong perimeter around their target. Strung along the fence were yellow No Trespassing placards threatening a $100,000 fine and up to one year in prison, "By Order of the United States Department of Energy."

The housepainter gripped a pair of bolt cutters, fixed the jaws around a link, and squeezed. He cut vertically, then opened the new flap. No alarm. No patrol cars. The sister went through first. After the two men followed her, they closed the breach with twine, crossed the patrol road, and then continued the steep ascent to the dark crest of the ridge. The crime had started, which meant they were one step closer to justice.

This was the last and perhaps hardest stretch of a long and winding journey Sister Megan Rice had started 67 years earlier, in a high-school jumper and high-top basketball shoes, in Manhattan.

GEORGE BARRY FORD'S first big decision after becoming pastor of Corpus Christi Church was to build it a new and bigger home. On West 121st Street rose an eight-story Georgian revival structure, complete with school, auditorium, and convent. It was a clean, gleaming monument to liberal Catholicism—as uncluttered by classic ornamentation on the outside as it was free of draconian doctrine inside. The windows were plain. The columns and pilasters inside were white. It was simple.

Morningside Heights was a neighborhood on a vast plateau above the city. In the 1800s it was pure pasture, then the seat of a sprawling insane asylum, then the riverfront perch of a few wealthy men around the turn of the century. The neighborhood clotted with middle-class apartment buildings as quick, affordable rail wormed its way up from downtown business centers. Upper-middle-class families settled on Claremont, Broadway, and Riverside. The lower-middle class lived in row houses on Amsterdam Avenue. Columbia's campus became the cornerstone of this new Morningside Heights, with Corpus Christi Church going up one block north of the Pupin Hall physics building.

Nearly 50 years old when he took the reins of Corpus Christi in 1935, Father Ford was a tall man from Utica, New York, with thin lips and elfin ears. He was counselor to Columbia's Catholic students and as savvy in the classroom as he was from his pulpit. Over the next several years he inspired the conversion of a Columbia student named Thomas Merton, who was baptized at Corpus Christi in 1938. Merton eventually became a monk, renowned thinker, and best-selling author, as well as the conscience of the 1960s peace movement.

Father Ford's charisma was both a magnet and a propellant. His homilies were earnest, not scolding. He wanted to nourish both the souls and the brains of his congregation. The parish hosted discussion groups on world affairs and partnered with neighboring social organizations to ease the poverty that plagued Manhattan. Father Ford wanted to bring the church out of the sanctuary and into the public square. He thought that women should be priests and that popes should be elected in a more democratic manner. If anything radical needs to be done, he thought, a Catholic organization should do it.

It was the thriving progressive spirit of the neighborhood that lured Frederick and Madeleine Rice to Morningside Heights. In 1937 they moved with their three daughters to 35 Claremont Avenue, into the apartment across from the Hechts', so they could attend Mass at Corpus Christi and enroll in its parochial school. Father Ford had cleared out the diocesan sisters from the faculty and recruited a more liberal order of Dominican nuns from Wisconsin. With the Depression giving way to World War II, Corpus Christi middle schoolers were encouraged to grapple with the subjects of isolationism and racism—things they saw and felt every day outside the classroom. Struggling first-generation Irish Catholic immigrants were filling the pews and desks, though the neighborhood as a whole was diverse: Italian enclaves overlapped with Spanish-speaking territory, and lively lower-class Harlem was mere blocks away. Germans and Italians fleeing Hitler and Mussolini sought refuge in Manhattan's patchwork of ethnic villages and were welcomed into congregations like Corpus Christi's. It was a spirited, enriching landscape in which to raise a family.

Frederick Rice was a professor of obstetrics at New York University's medical school and an obstetrician at Bellevue Hospital along the East River. He co-authored the introduction to a 1922 guidebook called *Getting Ready to Be a Mother*, which was dedicated "To the baby, upon whose wellbeing depends the future of the race." Having seen how the Depression beset impoverished new mothers, he spoke about birth control despite his religion's strict opposition to it. He was known for waiving the cost of delivery for poor mothers, and for spiriting away distressed newborns from a home delivery—in his coat pocket—to medical facilities that could properly care for them.

His wife, Madeleine, who was half his age, had attended Barnard College in the 1920s—the anthropologist Margaret Mead was one of her classmates—and was thus acquainted with Morningside Heights and Father Ford before the family moved there. The Rices' oldest daughter was Alessandra, tall and lanky; she was followed by Madeleine, who was nicknamed Maddy to distinguish her from her mother. Madeleine liked the name Megan after seeing it in the newspapers in reference to British politician Lloyd George's youngest daughter, who in 1929 became the first female member of Parliament to represent a Welsh district. When their third daughter was born the following year in their East 86th Street apartment, they called her "*Mee*-gan." Her parents had never heard the name pronounced out loud.

As a girl, Megan wore her hair short, swept to the side and boyish, which set off her high cheekbones. She and her sisters called their parents "Mummy" and "Daddy." In 1939, she was learning reading, writing, and human rights at Corpus Christi on 121st. And Madeleine was beginning her master's and PhD work in history at Columbia, a couple of blocks south. Physicists in the neighborhood who understood the Einstein theory were at work on the atom. Selig Hecht and his family were five paces across the hall from the Rices. War was beginning to rage across the Atlantic. The Rices got a dog, a half papillon, half spitz. In a small show of solidarity with the United Kingdom—which was under assault by the Third Reich's air force—they named the dog Brit, after the patriotic British song "Rule, Britannia!"

Secrecy was in fashion on the home front, except in the pages of a one-cent newspaper that would land on the stoop of 35 Claremont once a month.

First distributed in Union Square on May 1, 1933, as the Depression raked the city, the *Catholic Worker*'s circulation grew from 2,500 to 35,000 in six months. The newspaper featured stories about politics, labor, war, and peace. It was written in a friendly and intimate style, with the aim of awakening the public to the progressive potential of the church, which had the reputation of being stern and conservative. Its co-founder Dorothy Day penned columns that both decried social injustices and dished out a taste of life in New York.

"Late fall is here," she wrote in the November 1933 issue. "A haze hangs over the city. Fogs rise on the river, and the melancholy note of the river boats is heard at night." She then segued into a description of the mournful sight of struggling neighbors who were being evicted from their homes into the oncoming winter.

Dorothy's socialist adolescence and newfound religious fervor made her a target of the FBI, which described her in its reports as five feet ten and 120 pounds, with "long straight black hair streaked with gray," "dark eyes," a "pronounced stoop," and "ideas radical compared to those generally accepted today." Church leaders were barraged by complaints about the *Catholic Worker*, from the activist tenor of its articles to the political nature of its very name.

"We confess to being fools," Dorothy said, "and wish that we were more so."

Co-founder Peter Maurin's "easy essays" ran in a thin front-page column almost every issue. They were poetic, repetitive reminders of life's simple truths, chief among them society's responsibility to care for the destitute and homeless:

> Although you may be called
> bums and panhandlers
> you are in fact the Ambassadors of God.

Peter and Dorothy set up a shelter in the West Village. It would be a model of charity that would proliferate across the country in the following decades. The pair hosted "clarification of thought" meetings at their headquarters in the East Village to share thoughts on scripture and politics. Frederick and Madeleine Rice, devoted fans of Franklin and Eleanor Roosevelt, attended and couriered this communal energy back uptown to share with their daughters, whom they taught to view life as a journey toward fulfilling one's purpose for the benefit of society. Dorothy occasionally visited the Rices' summer home in Wilton, Connecticut, talking gravely with Madeleine about current affairs as the girls took turns on the swing that hung from the tulip tree.

The *Catholic Worker*'s rise was meteoric. Circulation hit 110,000 by 1936, with the name "Mahatma Gandhi" reportedly among its subscribers. Even though it lost thousands of subscribers by refusing to beat the drum for U.S. entry into World War II, the *Catholic Worker* had spawned a movement that transcended its pages. Two of its major wellsprings of support were Corpus Christi Church and greater Morningside Heights. The July–August 1940 issue opposed the compulsory military training bill. Dorothy and Peter delivered speeches around the country that urged young men to become conscientious objectors. She wrote that working in a weapons factory—or in the service of war making in general—was contrary to the teachings of Jesus Christ.

"We love our country and we love our president," Dorothy wrote in the *Catholic Worker* a month after the attack on Pearl Harbor, but "we have failed as Americans in living up to our principles."

"I saw a bit of Germany on the west coast," Dorothy wrote on the front page in June 1942, referring to Japanese internment camps in California.

During this time the FBI routinely monitored her "subversive" behavior. FBI director J. Edgar Hoover wrote that her "activities should be restricted." He received a letter from a citizen asking for an investigation of Dorothy, who was "doing Hitler's work for him" under "the false name of 'Freedom of the Press.'" For a while, Hoover entertained the false rumor that Dorothy was a Russian spy. He sought counsel on whether the *Catholic Worker* could be charged with sedition after it published an article headlined "Forget Pearl Harbor" in December 1942. To the FBI, the movement was operating a flophouse for bums and using the church as a front to finance and spread communist propaganda.

In reality, the Catholic Worker movement was inspiring a generation of nascent activists.

MEGAN FIRST SAW THE WORD "pacifism" in the pages of the *Catholic Worker*. Objecting to war, even to a just war, was a concept in stark contrast to the patriotism in the streets. Neighborhood kids ran lemonade stands in support of the British war effort. Navy plebes were marching on Columbia's campus and kneeling in Corpus Christi's pews. Newsreels of the war unspooled before feature films at Trans-Lux movie palaces. Though they were preteens sheltered in Manhattan's upper-middle class, Megan and her friends saw war up close on the big screen, in stark black-and-white film shipped from disputed Pacific islands and crumbling European cities. On Saturday trips to the movies, Megan closed her eyes and ears to the staccato artillery, the groaning aircraft. Swayed by the strong sentiment of pacifism on her stoop and in dinner-table conversation, Megan concluded that the images of total war and the murmurs of secret work at Columbia signaled that an evil was pervading the world. She was in sixth grade when the Japanese attacked Pearl Harbor. The United States barreled into the war, though at Columbia it had already begun its hurried, hush-hush work on uranium. Gold-star banners began to appear in windows across the city, signaling a family's grief for a son lost in combat.

In 1942 the Rices moved about 300 feet, from Claremont Avenue to the stately brick building at 468 Riverside Drive, at West 119th Street. The girls went to high school 20 blocks up in Harlem Heights, at the all-female St. Walburga's Academy. The school was five stories of heavy stone facing the Hudson, with Gothic finials and a gabled roof. It was known as "the castle." The school was run by the Society of the Holy Child Jesus, an order of sisters founded in 1846 by Cornelia Connelly, a Catholic nun who chafed against the cloistered lifestyle. She wanted her new order of sisters to engage the world, minister to the needy, and "meet the wants of the age" through direct intervention. The motto of the Sisters of the Holy Child Jesus was "actions not words." The sisters expanded the society to Africa in 1930, setting up schools in Nigeria.

The Holy Child sisters at St. Walburga's wore heavy black robes and habits, their faces peeking out of tight white coifs. Wooden rosaries clacked from their waists. Despite their imposing presence, they were not scary disciplinarians.

"Trust the children," Cornelia Connelly had said. "Confidence begets confidence."

The sisters' gentle trust in their students inspired self-discipline. The worst kind of punishment was being sent home after school instead of being allowed to linger around the castle for socializing and extracurriculars. Nothing was more humbling than Mother Mary Laurentia's soft expression of disappointment. She had been the first American sister of her order to go to Nigeria. A look of longing crossed her face when she spoke about her time in Africa. It was clear she loved the continent, and this wistful passion made a deep impression on the students, especially Megan.

Classes were tiny at St. Walburga's, usually around 30 students per grade, and some girls lived as boarders on the third floor of the academy alongside the sisters. The school uniform was a maroon jumper that went past the knees, a tan button-down shirt with a maroon tie, and lace-up Oxfords. The girls learned to dance by partnering up in the gymnasium and hitching around to the records of Harry James and his big band orchestra. Basketball was the sport of choice among all-girls academies in New York.

In 1943, as Megan was beginning high school, her mother, Madeleine, finished her dissertation at Columbia. It was titled "American Catholic Opinion in the Slavery Controversy." The church did not stake out a clear position on slavery during the era of its practice, Madeleine wrote, deferring to the concept of "just servitude" instead of decrying its blatant immorality. Animated by both the timidity of the 19th-century Catholic Church and the intensity of 20th-century racism, Madeleine would take her daughters to Friendship House, a missionary outpost in Harlem dedicated to interracial justice. Thomas Merton, the protégé of Father Ford, volunteered there. On field trips with Ford, the Rice girls heard the poet Langston Hughes speak at the Catholic Interracial Council.

"I just can't wait until everybody in the world is tan," Madeleine would say to her daughters, dreaming of a world without racism, or race in general, and making sure they were aware of the atrocities endured by blacks through history.

The Rice girls played all around the city in tunics with matching bloomers and high-top sneakers. The only mischief they'd get into with friends was sneaking a cigarette here or there, or trespassing in the sisters' quarters. They were good girls, ensconced in meaningful Manhattan living, aware of the less fortunate and the war-torn but given every opportunity to learn and thrive as the rest of the world quaked.

And then the atomic calculations at Columbia were secretly made manifest in the desert of New Mexico, with the first-ever explosive test of the bomb in July 1945.

And then three weeks later the bombs were dropped on Japan.

And then Megan's uncle Walter, a 32-year-old Marine, was sent into the smoldering ruins of Nagasaki.

WALTER G. HOOKE was born in Westchester County in 1913, a decade after Madeleine. Their parents were staunch adherents to papal encyclicals that upheld the rights of the working class and prescribed an economic "third way" between totalitarian communism and dehumanizing capitalism. They considered the crossing of a picket line to be wrong in any circumstance. Walter was educated by Jesuit priests, first at Loyola High School on the Upper West Side and then at Fordham University in the Bronx. He lived with and cared for his mother in an apartment on Amsterdam Avenue in Morningside Heights, a few blocks from Madeleine and his three nieces, and was enraptured by Father Ford's sermons at Corpus Christi Church. In 1936 his brother-in-law Frederick took him to one of Dorothy Day's downtown lectures. The experience would inform his thoughts and actions for the rest of his life.

Walter took a leave from his labor job at a five-and-dime retail chain to join the Marine Corps in 1942. Exempt from the draft because he was caring for his ailing mother, Walter voluntarily enlisted as a private because he felt it was the most direct and sincere way to defend democracy. He thought that if one truly believed in the concept of democracy—and its binding force of truth—then one must demonstrate a commitment to it in every walk of life. He reported to Parris Island for boot camp, then Camp Pendleton for artillery training, and then Hawaii, where after a couple of years he began to feel guilty that he wasn't being sent into the fight.

Germany abandoned its own atomic-bomb project in 1942—the same month that Roosevelt okayed the transition from atomic research to bomb production—and surrendered in May 1945. Japan refused to comply with the U.S. demand for unconditional surrender, despite the relentless firebombing of Tokyo, Kobe, Osaka, and other major cities. Thousands of American B-29 bombers had swarmed Japan that year, igniting firestorms that fed on acreages of bamboo homes and thatched roofs. By early August about 190,000 Japanese civilians had died in the air raids, which incinerated entire metropolitan areas. *Time* magazine called the raids a "dream come true," a celebratory remark born of the era's climate of existential crisis. *Harper's* declared that World War II was "a life and death struggle for national survival" and that the United States is "therefore justified in taking any action which will save the lives of American soldiers and sailors." The Empire of Japan was also ruthless in its war making: 37 percent of American POWs in Japanese captivity died—on death marches, in forced labor, after torture and medical experiments— compared with 1 percent of those in Nazi and Italian custody. If hundreds of thousands of civilian deaths by conventional bombing didn't shock Japan into submission, then the United States needed a trump card to avoid an amphibious assault on the mainland, which military commanders thought would cost at least half a million American lives. That trump card was the atomic bomb, constructed in secret cities around the United States over several years of around-the-clock work.

A few months after Pearl Harbor, Roosevelt had ordered the internment of more than 100,000 Japanese Americans. "In Europe we felt our enemies, horrible and deadly as they were, were still people," the legendary war correspondent Ernie Pyle had written from the Pacific. "But out here I gathered that the Japanese were looked upon as something subhuman and repulsive; the way some people feel about cockroaches or mice." The "Jap is a savage and cares little for human life," Arthur W. Page, the vice president of marketing at AT&T, wrote in a July letter to the U.S. War Department, for which he was managing public relations in advance of the bomb's deployment. Using the bomb would convince the empire that the United States was not "soft-hearted and tired," he said, and then force it to "capitulate to the power of the universe." To Secretary of War Henry Stimson, this "deliberate, premeditated destruction was our least abhorrent choice." It would stop the air raids and the blockade at sea. It would preclude an overland clash of armies that might be bloodier than the previous year's invasion of France. It might even prevent all future war, which would thereafter have apocalyptic undertones. It would justify the expense and effort of the Manhattan Project, whose momentum could not be stopped. Most practically, though: It would send a message to the Soviet Union, which was readying to enter the war, that there would be only one superpower in the 20th century.

In the end, General Groves wrote the orders—"as weather will permit" after August 3—which were sent by the Army chief of staff to the Pacific theater. There is no record of formal authorization by Truman, who knew the Japanese emperor was asking for peace. Groves described the president's role as "one of non-interference." The Manhattan Project, started and conducted in secret, was coming to its climax without the firsthand knowledge or direct authorization of the president of the United States.

At 8:15 a.m. on August 6, a U.S. B-29 dropped toward Hiroshima an untested 9,700-pound atomic bomb that looked like a long garbage can with fins. The bomb was named Little Boy. Many Japanese citizens looked skyward as they heard the airplane's sharp evasive maneuver, its wings gleaming in the morning sun as it trailed a thin line of wispy exhaust in its swift retreat. The crew members counted 43 seconds. Then, around 1,900 feet above the courtyard of Shima Hospital, one mass of uranium inside the bomb was fired like a bullet at another. The impact set off the nuclear chain reaction that Columbia physicists had experimented with years earlier in Manhattan using Einstein's theory as their guide.

Energy equals mass times the speed of light squared.

Inside the bomb, billions and billions of invisible atoms ruptured. In a nanosecond the smallest of particles created the biggest of booms. The light from the explosion reached the Japanese first. Its blinding heat energy carbonized anyone within a half mile of ground zero. Thousands of pedestrians crumpled into crisp black husks. Birds in flight burst like fireworks. Then came the blast wave, which steamrolled houses and ripped off human flesh that had already been broiled by the flash. Then came the fireball itself, which set five square miles of rubble ablaze and created a firestorm that chased the maimed into the delta city's tributaries, which were soon clogged with floating corpses. If a Japanese citizen survived all that, he became his own ticking time bomb. His cells stopped dividing because of the intense dose of radiation, which meant organ decay, hemorrhage, and death in the hours and days afterward. All told, 160,000 people were dead, dying, or injured in the aftermath. Expanding over the city was a massive cloud of "boiling dust," as bomber pilot Paul Tibbets Jr. described it. A black rain of radioactive ash began to fall within 30 minutes of the detonation. The firestorm's gale-force winds raged for six hours. The effect was so profound that survivors meandered, away from the epicenter, zombie-like and without panic, in complete silence. Some were convinced that they had died and gone to hell.

About 141 pounds of highly enriched uranium were in the bomb. Only two pounds of it underwent fission, and the rest fizzled. Hiroshima had been erased by an amount of uranium that weighed no more than a human fetus at 28 weeks.

"This is the greatest thing in history," Truman said upon hearing confirmation of the detonation.

"One of the greatest blunders in history," wrote physicist Leo Szilard.

Truman's official public summation was both euphemistic and majestic, and harked back to the science behind it all: The atomic explosion, "a harnessing of the basic power of the universe," had "destroyed [Hiroshima's] usefulness to the enemy." The United States had taken "the greatest scientific gamble in history. And we have won. But the greatest marvel is not the size of the enterprise, its secrecy or its cost, but the achievement of scientific brains in making it work."

The suddenness of the news did not numb the public to the sheer import of the event. Right away there was a sense that the world had changed in an instant, even though information was scarce and the smoke hadn't cleared. There was also an aura of fear and danger— that what happened to Japan could happen to the United States. "For all we know, we have created a Frankenstein," NBC radio commentator H. V. Kaltenborn said on that evening's broadcast. "We must assume that with the passage of only a little time, an improved form of the new weapon we used today can be turned against us."

While the world was still trying to grasp the extent of the event, the United States readied another atomic bomb for deployment. Instead of enriched uranium, this bomb would use another heavy element called plutonium, which had been manufactured at a secret plant in Washington state. On the Pacific island of Tinian, where the first bomb had been fully assembled, the Catholic military chaplain George B. Zabelka blessed the 13-man crew of the B-29 bomber that would deliver the second bomb to Nagasaki, home to Japan's largest population of Christians and to the Mitsubishi factory that made the torpedoes that had sunk American battleships in Pearl Harbor. The crew had stayed up overnight playing poker in their Quonset hut. Father Zabelka had never preached against the killing of civilians during wartime, though he knew very well it was happening. He had ministered to young men on Tinian who were losing their minds.

One hospitalized airman told the priest that he was haunted by the image of a young Japanese boy on a city street who looked up in wonder, during a raid, at his low-flying plane. The airman had already released a shower of napalm, which hit the boy seconds later.

On August 9 at 11:02 a.m., as the Soviet Union moved into Manchuria, the second atomic bomb, named Fat Man, exploded more than a mile off target and almost directly over the Urakami Cathedral, where parishioners were waiting to give confession. The yield of Fat Man was greater than that of Little Boy, though the hills outside Nagasaki deadened its impact. Still, 70,000 were dead or dying, and many were asking to be killed to escape the miserable pain of their injuries. Another 70,000 would die from the effects over the next five years. In the realm of body-count statistics, during a world war that claimed tens of millions of lives, the atomic bombings were a pittance. What was shocking was the *mode* of these two mini-holocausts: quick, efficient, concentrated, and almost robotic in execution, requiring zero American boots on the ground.

"It is an awful responsibility which has come to us," Truman said on the radio the next day, after ordering that no more bombs be dropped on the list of targets devised by the military. "We thank God that it has come to us instead of to our enemies, and we pray that He may guide us to use it in His ways and for His purposes."

The newspapers were quick to pivot from shock to victory, as Japan surrendered within a matter of weeks. The world heaved a sigh of relief. The bloodiest, costliest war in human history was officially over after six years of butchery by the hands of the world's great powers, and the atomic bombs were credited with its cessation.

The mood in Washington, though, did not match the elation in the rest of the country. D.C. residents went about their business with dour expressions and a "sense of oppression," the *New York Sun* correspondent Phelps Adams wrote. The capital was bedeviled by a "curious new sense of insecurity," the *New Republic* reported.

"The use of the atomic bombs in Japan has created an unfavorable impression on the Vatican," declared the press office of Pope Pius XII, while the Vatican privately affirmed the need for U.S. atomic superiority.

Dorothy Day was sharper in her critique:

[They] are vaporized, our Japanese brothers—scattered, men, women and babies, to the four winds, over the seven seas. Perhaps we will breathe their dust into our nostrils, feel them in the fog of New York on our faces, feel them in the rain on the hills of Easton.

Megan's uncle Walter no doubt read this. That fall, his Marine unit was ordered to help occupy the Japanese island of Kyushu, specifically Nagasaki, where the devastation was more "spectacular and startling" than that in Hiroshima, according to an Army report. Everyone in a half-mile radius of ground zero was killed instantly. Glass windows shattered 17 miles away.

A delegate from the International Committee of the Red Cross made it to Hiroshima at the end of August and sent back a telegram: "Conditions appalling . . . city wiped out . . . eighty percent all hospitals destroyed or seriously damaged . . . conditions beyond description."

Uncle Walter spent October 1945 to February 1946 in Nagasaki, where the breeze carried the smells of scorched flesh and stone. As a transport officer, he drove a Jeep through the wasteland. He climbed on the ruins and helped collect and catalog the belongings of the dead. He played in an impromptu "atomic bowl" football game in the flattened blast area on New Year's Day 1946. The U.S. military never told the occupying forces about the radiation in the air, ground, and water.

Walter met Catholic bishop Paul Yamaguchi, whose Urakami Cathedral was decimated by the explosion while his family members were inside praying. One of the few items left intact at the cathedral was the charred head of a wooden statue of the Virgin Mary, its benevolent face turned into a horrified mask by the fire. Over several months Walter drove the bishop to meet with surviving members of his congregation. On Christmas Day parishioners sang "Silent Night" in the cathedral, surrounded by the remains of the collapsed ceiling. Walter also met Takashi Nagai, a Catholic doctor of radiology who was a half mile away from the detonation. After recovering from his own severe injuries, Nagai treated other survivors and became known as "the saint of Urakami." He balked at American generals and leaders who played down the effects of the atomic bomb.

"We carry deep in our hearts, every one of us, stubborn, unhealing wounds," Nagai wrote in *We of Nagasaki*, published in 1951, the year of his death from leukemia. "When we are alone we brood upon them, and when we see our neighbors we are again reminded of them; theirs as well as ours. It is this spiritual wreckage, which the visitor to Nagasaki's wastes does not see, that is indeed beyond repair."

Though it did nothing to protect American soldiers from radiation, the U.S. military tried mightily to protect the American people from the truth. It prohibited the publication of Nagai's book *Bells of Nagasaki* until he added information about Japanese atrocities in Manila, where the empire enslaved and murdered scores of Filipinos. This censorship was common. Much of what Uncle Walter saw was never communicated by American media back to the United States. The Australian journalist Wilfred Burchett transmitted a report from Hiroshima via Morse code to the *London Daily Express*. More than a month after the bomb, he reported, people uninjured by the blast were "still dying, mysteriously and horribly . . . from an unknown something which I can only describe as the atomic plague." Meanwhile, the *New York Times* reported that no radiation sickness resulted from the bombs.

Back in Washington, at the annual dinner of the Gridiron Club in December, Truman told attendees, "It occurred to me that a quarter of a million of the flower of our young manhood was worth a couple of Japanese cities, and I still think they were and are."

IN THE NEW YEAR, Walter returned to the States a changed man. His mood, once exuberant, was tempered by an unseen force.

That summer, a report from the War Department concluded that even if the atomic bombs had not been dropped, Japan probably would have surrendered prior to November 1, 1945—the date considered for a land invasion by the United States—given the force of American air supremacy and the entry of the Soviet Union into the war. Nevertheless, the American men waiting on ships and in submarines, their nerves jangling, credited the atomic bombings with saving their lives. Parts of the Pacific were so crowded with American seacraft, lying in wait, that you could almost walk from deck to deck.

Paul Fussell, a 21-year-old second lieutenant readying to lead a rifle platoon in the land invasion of Japan, wrote years later, "When the bombs dropped and news began to circulate that [the invasion] would not, after all, take place, that we would not be obliged to run up the beaches near Tokyo assault-firing while being mortared and shelled, for all the fake manliness of our facades we cried with relief and joy. We were going to live."

This sentiment, that the war was ended and lives were saved by the bomb, would root itself in American culture going forward—in diary entries, in casual conversation, in schoolbooks, in feature films, in official speeches by presidents.

Uncle Walter refused a commission as a first lieutenant. After seeing the ruin of total war firsthand, he wanted nothing more to do with the military.

For most of his life, Walter rarely spoke about his experience in Nagasaki. He spent his career at United Parcel Service as a personnel manager and worked with Veterans for Peace. All four of Walter's children were born prematurely, and his wife had three miscarriages. He never claimed that this was related to his time in Nagasaki. He had seen fellow veterans endure much worse, which is why he devoted his retirement to advocating for atomic veterans, who numbered in the hundreds of thousands. Their exposures ranged from July 1945, when the very first atomic test was conducted in the New Mexico desert, to the end of atmospheric testing in 1963 and beyond. During that time span the United States conducted 235 aboveground explosions on Pacific islands and in the Nevada desert. Between May and July 1956 there were 17 tests in the Marshall Islands that were hundreds of times as powerful as the Hiroshima bomb. Five different B-57B planes made 27 passes through the mushroom clouds to obtain radiation-dose information. For the pilots and crew, there was no medical follow-up. Naval officers aboard battleships ingested more plutonium in a bite of contaminated ham in the mess hall than is considered acceptable exposure over the entire lifetime of a nuclear-plant worker.

Walter had seen them lose hair and teeth in the short run. In the long run: thyroid problems, multiple myeloma, slow and agonizing deaths in their 50s and 60s. The veterans felt like guinea pigs.

In the 1980s Uncle Walter traveled often to Washington, D.C., to lobby for legislation that would win benefits for these veterans. The Pentagon withheld its own radiation reports and routinely pushed back against findings that showed veterans were overexposed to radiation and exhibited higher instances of cancer. By 1986 the Veterans Administration had granted only 16 of 4,000 atomic claims. Another "occupation veteran" who had been in Nagasaki with Walter went on a hunger strike to call attention to the issue. Five thousand vets filed a class-action lawsuit against the VA, which responded by destroying thousands of documents related to radiation surveys and claims. About

12,000 atomic-veteran claims were filed by 1992, with no more than 10 percent fulfilled.

Walter wished he could testify against government officials in a Nuremberg-style trial. All he could do, though, was remain committed to the national associations of Atomic Veterans and Radiation Survivors. Healthy and free of serious post-traumatic stress disorder, Walter was one of the associations' most respected and articulate voices. He and others lobbied Congress over many years.

Walter was also a letter writer. He wrote to bishops and judges and presidents from his home in Cambridge, New York. He quoted Dorothy Day. He stamped the back of each envelope with the word "peace." In July 2002, with the cleanup of the demolished World Trade Center ongoing, he wrote to George W. Bush to repudiate the president's statement "You're either with us or against us," which he viewed as pernicious. Six months later, on his 90th birthday, Walter sent another letter to Bush to object to the administration's "belligerent" nuclear-weapons policy and its withdrawal from the Anti-Ballistic Missile Treaty with Russia. Noting his time in Nagasaki, Walter wrote that "from that experience I am fully aware of the consequences of the action you seem willing to initiate" by using nuclear weapons. In May 2003, Walter wrote to the archbishop of Denver, concerned that the confluence of the White House's nuclear-weapons policy and the invasion of Iraq increased the chances of nuclear war:

> I saw enough in Nagasaki to convince me that the use of the Bomb then or at any time in the future is indeed a sin of murder. Over 150 million people have died from war during my lifetime and still we spend billions on weapons and research but seldom a word about the struggle for peace.

He could never get Nagasaki out of his mind.

In 2010, as her 97-year-old uncle Walter was dying, 80-year-old

Sister Megan moved in to care for him in upstate New York. She had been living in Las Vegas, engaged in anti-nuclear civil disobedience that was inspired in part by her uncle's life story. She gave him Holy Communion every day. She prayed with him.

Whenever she was back East, Megan's family would ask her to stop winding up in jail. That was a promise she couldn't make.

In February 1946, Walter was just one of tens of thousands of military men returning home after an epic and costly struggle in the name of democracy. To 16-year-old Megan, her uncle seemed under a peculiar kind of strain—what she would describe many years later as "the terrible weight of knowing." He had peered into the abyss. She absorbed whatever he was feeling and stored it away.

Megan's eyes were turned toward Africa. By her senior year in 1947 she was ready to follow her oldest sister, Alessandra, into the Society of the Holy Child Jesus. That way she could devote her best years to teaching and ministering on the continent that she'd heard so much about from her teachers. After being raised by a mother whose chief academic interests were slavery and racism, and after being taught by sisters who made social justice and equality part of the curriculum, Megan saw a commitment to Africa as one small way to repair what America had done to black people for generations.

The work of the church was not in the pews and confessionals, after all. It was out in the field.

Actions not words, Cornelia Connelly had said.

If anything radical needed to be done, Father Ford said, a Catholic should do it.

Before she could get to Nigeria, Megan had to complete her schooling while also learning to become a teacher herself. Nigeria needed science teachers, so she took courses in biology at Villanova and Fordham universities and in Rosemont, Pennsylvania, the headquarters of her order. She enrolled at Boston College for her master's in biology, where she studied the expanding field of radiation biology. During lab work, she wore a lead vest over her black habit while handling samples of tritium, a radioactive form of hydrogen that is produced during nuclear fission and used to boost the yield of a bomb. She worked on autoradiography in the darkrooms at Harvard Medical School, dipping slides into liquid photographic emulsion in total darkness, using gamma radiation to map the development and division of cells. She was studying the science behind the forces of the universe.

In 1953 President Dwight D. Eisenhower, an Army general who had opposed using the bombs on Japan, gave a pair of speeches that were in the tradition of Dorothy Day. One was to the American Society of Newspaper Editors on the occasion of Joseph Stalin's death. "Every gun that is made, every warship launched, every rocket fired signifies, in the final sense, a theft from those who hunger and are not fed, those who are cold and are not clothed," Eisenhower said. The other speech was to the United Nations General Assembly, advocating that the world take its nuclear arsenal and "strip its military casing and adapt it to the arts of peace."

The largest-ever U.S. nuclear test, called Castle Bravo, was conducted the following March in the Pacific and was equal to 1,000 Hiroshima bombs. A vast storm of radioactive fallout poisoned both American military men and the people of the Marshall Islands, a smattering of atolls in the infinite blue halfway between Hawaii and Australia.

Three months later on June 14, 1954, the United States conducted a mock detonation in its own cities. During the drill, air-raid sirens in Washington, D.C., blared at 10:01 a.m. Cars pulled over and pedestrians hustled into buildings and basements. President Eisenhower, his wife, and his top advisers filed into an underground shelter at the White House for 25 minutes. A 75-kiloton bomb (about five times the power of Hiroshima's) was "dropped" at 11th and F streets NW. Emergency responders were to imagine that the explosion instantly killed 137,000, injured nearly 400,000, destroyed everything within a mile radius—including the White House—and knocked out all public utilities and two-thirds of hospital services. After the exercise many Washingtonians complained that they hadn't heard the sirens. The siren on top of a Senate office building didn't even go off, but that didn't matter: Congress chose not to participate in the drill. Congressmen were busy approving a joint resolution that amended the pledge of allegiance and codified the way to say it. The resolution requested that civilians place their right hand over their heart when reciting it.

Dorothy Day and a posse of pacifists protested another drill the following year in New York, where 679 sirens wailed for three minutes starting at 2:05 p.m. on June 15, 1955. The protesters distributed 1,000 yellow leaflets outside city hall. At the top in large black letters was written IN THE NAME OF JESUS. Below, smaller:

> We will not obey this order to pretend, to evacuate, to hide. In view of the certain knowledge the administration of this country has that there is no defense in atomic warfare, we know this drill to be a military act in a cold war to instil [sic] fear, to prepare the collective mind for war. We refuse to cooperate.

The protesters had a point. New York's blast scenario included a total loss of life within a 2.3-mile radius of the detonation point, so what sense did it make to take shelter? Regardless, failing to do so was a misdemeanor. In court, Day vowed "loyalty to God even at the risk of disobedience and subversion to a coercive state." In retaliation, Hoover tried to get the Department of Justice to charge the *Catholic Worker* with sedition.

During congressional testimony in 1956 and '57, an Army general recommended that the United States build and maintain a stockpile of 151,000 warheads for his branch alone, even though Operation Alert revealed that just one would flatten a metropolis. The potential fury of such an arsenal was unfathomable, though many tried to put it into words.

"You can't have this kind of war," Eisenhower said. "There just aren't enough bulldozers to scrape the bodies off the street."

While the U.S. stockpile would never come close to the Army's recommendation, the tally of warheads had risen from several hundred to nearly 20,000 by the time Eisenhower left office in 1961.

"Only an alert and knowledgeable citizenry can compel the proper meshing of the huge industrial and military machinery of defense with our peaceful methods and goals, so that security and liberty may prosper together," Eisenhower said in his farewell address, which popularized the term "military-industrial complex."

Yet the potential explosive yield of the stockpile he oversaw far exceeded all the firepower expended during World War II. Eisenhower, despite his peace-minded speeches, left belligerent policies: "First-strike capability" meant nukes were not just a retaliatory option, and "massive retaliation" described a nuclear response that far outweighed an enemy attack. One of Eisenhower's legacy programs, Atoms for Peace, would deliver about 22,600 kilograms of highly enriched uranium over the years to 35 countries, including Iran and Pakistan. The seeds of proliferation were sown just as the Cold War was coming to a boil.

Meanwhile, Dorothy Day protested the civil-defense drills every year until it was discontinued. During the last protest, in 1961, 2,000 people were outside city hall. Many were mothers pushing strollers or holding hands with their children.

In 1962, the year Megan Rice finally moved to Africa, the United States went crazy with testing. It set off 97 nuclear bombs in an expanse of desert called the Nevada Test Site, north of Las Vegas, and in the Pacific. Even though 5,000 students picketed the White House around the clock in February, 66 percent of Americans supported the testing. In July the United States rocketed an atomic bomb into space from Johnston Island, 860 miles southwest of Hawaii, and detonated it at an altitude of 250 miles. It created an enormous, cherry-red aurora that hung in the sky for seven minutes. The electromagnetic pulse of the blast short-circuited streetlights in Honolulu. The fallout from this atmospheric testing prompted mothers to picket the White House with signs that worried about strontium 90, a radioactive byproduct of the explosions. Tests were conducted underground after 1963, out of sight and out of mind of the American public, after the Limited Test Ban Treaty was signed with Russia and others.

Having traded in her black wardrobe, Megan—now Sister Frederick Mary, in honor of her father—arrived in rural Nigeria in a flutter of white: a white habit whose brim shielded her eyes from the sun, a white wimple that descended into a flowing white veil. Between the tan dirt and the blue skies, she was a peculiar and luminous vision.

The sisters of the Holy Child Jesus had built schools in remote villages in Nigeria. Megan arrived at one in Abakaliki, a village in the south. There was no electricity and no running water. She and the other sisters taught in the classroom during the day and slept in the classroom at night. She helped build her own biology lab. She spent the next 40 years of her life in Africa as a teacher.

Back home in the United States, major social movements ebbed and flowed around the nuclear threat. The Cuban Missile Crisis in October dragged the world to the brink of nuclear catastrophe, drew 10,000 peace demonstrators to the doorstep of the United Nations, and made a generation of students develop a duck-and-cover reflex.

"Nuclear weapons must be banned," Pope John XXIII wrote six months later in his encyclical *Pacem in Terris*.

The Reverend Martin Luther King Jr., in his 1964 Nobel Prize lecture, spoke of "ancient habits" and "vast structures of power" that perpetuate war. In 1967, at Riverside Church in Megan's old neighborhood, King said that "the U.S. is the greatest purveyor of violence in the world today," a line that would echo in protests into the next century.

The energy of the civil rights movement fueled opposition to the escalating Vietnam War, which catalyzed the new Catholic Left movement. The movement's leaders were the brothers Philip and Daniel Berrigan, priests who were inspired by the social-justice crusade of Dorothy Day and carried King's vision of civil disobedience into raids on military draft offices.

Megan would hear about their exploits from her mother, who visited Africa three times over the years. Madeleine was now a history professor at Hunter College, on the East Side, and was as attentive to social justice in the 1960s as she was in the 1930s. Her onetime neighbor Thomas Merton called his own conscience more authoritative than any institution. Merton abandoned the Catholic Church's "just war" theory—an echo of the church's "just servitude" concept that Madeleine had researched—and equated conventional war with nuclear war. Vietnam was "an overwhelming atrocity," he wrote, and "a bell tolling for the whole world." The "American policy of escalation makes peace and order impossible" there, though the existence of nuclear weapons made peace impossible anywhere. Merton looked at the U.S. nuclear-weapons complex and saw a "bureaucratization of homicide" comparable to that in Nazi Germany, with its secrecy, compartmentalization of work, and technical language that turned sane, normal people into lever-pullers on a machine of death.

None of these complications were part of Megan's austere life in Nigeria, but in the United States more and more young men were being drafted into the service of war. As a 38-year-old Megan was finishing her sixth year on the continent, a teenager from Michigan named Michael was preparing to ship off to Vietnam. Their experience with war—his firsthand, hers through Uncle Walter—would bring them together 44 years later on a hike over a ridge in East Tennessee.

3.

THE PROPHET

The first fence was behind them. The crest of Pine Ridge was ahead, upward, through darkness. They had duct-taped their flashlights to reduce the beams to slivers. The veteran hiked in front of the sister, clearing her path of rocks and branches. Michael Walli believed that he was a frail earthen vessel and that Sister Megan was a child of God. He thought of himself as her lowly protector. He prayed: *Lord, make me an instrument of your peace, for all the glory is yours, and on the last day Jesus will come like this, like a thief in the night, and the warmongering United States will fulfill Isaiah's prophecy by beating its swords into plowshares, by abandoning militarism. It is foreseen. And this is part of its happening.*

Michael wore a light blue construction hat, with "UN" marked on the front, and a blue-and-red plaid shirt buttoned all the way to the collar. His breath smelled of Top brand tobacco. In their backpacks, he and Megan carried twine, matches, candles, a tattered copy of the New Testament, three hammers, two pairs of bolt cutters, six cans of spray paint, three protest banners, copies of a letter they planned to deliver to people they met on the other side of the ridge, and two emblems of sustenance: a packet of cucumber seeds and the fresh-baked loaf of bread with a cross molded into the top. They also carried the six baby bottles of human blood. Each item would play a role in their mission.

The housepainter was ahead, leading the hike. They reached the crest of the ridge shortly after 3:30 a.m. From there, at an elevation of 1,190 feet, they could see lights winking through the ivy-wrapped trees. That was their target: the Y-12 National Security Complex, by some measures the last remaining full-scale production facility for nuclear weapons in the United States. It had made parts that were currently in every warhead in the U.S. arsenal. Michael considered it a bastion of the fascist U.S. war machine, terrorism incarnate, the antichrist itself. It was here, in a valley between two ridges, that the United States had processed uranium and machined bomb components for decades.

A dog barked in the distance. It was hard to tell if the sound was coming from a guard post inside the complex or from someone's backyard behind them in the city of Oak Ridge. Sister Megan, so committed to nonviolence, had told herself that if she was attacked by guard dogs, she would not raise her hands in self-defense. She was tired after the climb, but it was all downhill from here.

As they made their slow, careful descent on the other side of the ridge, the complex emerged between the trees, lit bright as day. Hundreds of buildings filled Bear Creek Valley, many dating to the Manhattan Project and in need of repair. Rusty piping snaked through the site, exhaling steam. Fences angled this way and that. Concrete barriers lurked in long rows. Concrete dragon's teeth, pyramid-shaped, encircled certain buildings.

In front of the trio, the tree line gave way to an embankment of rocks, a manicured knoll, and clusters of black-eyed Susans. And then, past a paved patrol road, past one of those concrete barriers, past three ten-foot-tall fences, was a bright white castle of a building, taking up two football fields' worth of the valley. Inside was perhaps the largest single inventory of fissile material on the planet. There was enough storage space inside for 400 metric tons of highly enriched uranium, contained in drums secured on racks, though the exact total was classified. This was the Highly Enriched Uranium Materials Facility, or the HEUMF, which is what gave Y-12 its nickname: the Fort Knox of Uranium. It was their target. The painter had thought they might have to search for the building, but there it was, right in front of them. To the left, near the base of the ridge, were two fat water reservoirs. The painter recognized them from Google Earth. This was exactly where they wanted to be. From the edge of the woods, they watched a security SUV roll by on the patrol road. They saw the same vehicle double back several minutes later.

All three were worn out from summiting the ridge. They had to maintain forward momentum.

Michael, now leading the way, tossed aside the UN hard hat, his symbol for international weapons inspection. He had performed acts of civil disobedience like this many times before. He had trespassed on federal property and served jail time. He had even trespassed on this very site two years ago, in broad daylight and in full view of law enforcement. After a protest outside the front entrance of Y-12, Michael and 12 others had walked across railroad tracks, through a swing gate, and over the blue boundary line that distinguishes a lawful protest from a crime. They had formed a circle on Department of Energy property and prayed as a helicopter circled overhead. One of Y-12's security officers raised a bullhorn and started to read a warning. After a three-day jury trial the following year, the activists were convicted of trespassing. During the proceedings, the senior federal manager of Y-12 was called by the government as a witness.

"Y-12 is a very secure facility," said Ted Sherry, a former Navy officer. "It is, and will always be, one of the most secure facilities in this country and in the world."

Michael had gotten out of prison for that trespass less than seven months before this present action. If this mission continued to progress smoothly, it was about to become much more serious. Michael was ready for that. He always said he had one foot in the grave.

The trio, having now reached flat ground in the valley, crossed the two-lane patrol road and stepped around the vehicle barriers. Thinking that cutting the fences would instantly summon security, Michael uncapped a bottle of white spray paint and wrote two instructions on the concrete base of the first fence in thin capital letters.

**DISARM
TRANSFORM**

Then, a smaller addendum:

**PEACE
NOT
WAR**

Michael took one of the baby bottles from his backpack and dribbled blood over DISARM. Then they hung one of the banners on the outside of the first fence. Its black lettering spelled out the biblical prophecy of Isaiah:

**SWORDS INTO
PLOWSHARES
SPEARS INTO
PRUNING HOOKS**

If they were caught soon, at least they accomplished this much. But no one was coming for them. So the painter fixed one of the bolt cutters around a link of the first fence. It looked just like the perimeter fence, except that it was topped with three taut strands of barbed wire, angled outward. The painter squeezed the red handles.

No alarms. No shouts. Just the buzz of the white floodlights.

He continued cutting, making a small flap. Above him a sign with a skull and crossbones was fixed to the fence. It said DANGER: HALT! DEADLY FORCE IS AUTHORIZED BEYOND THIS POINT.

One fence down. Two to go. The painter opened up the flap.

Megan ducked and crawled through, entering the kill zone first.

Vigilant and praying, Michael followed her.

HUNDREDS OF MILLIONS OF YEARS AGO, the planet's tectonic plates collided and heaved earth upward into the peaks and valleys of Appalachia. Ridges rippled between the Great Smoky Mountains and the steep escarpment of the Cumberland Plateau. This washboard-like topography prevails in East Tennessee: ridges of sandstone and dolomite, valleys of shale and limestone. Ridge, valley, ridge, valley—frustrating hurdles for early Caucasian pioneers headed farther west, ideal shelter for self-contained homesteads. The Cherokee natives were driven out in the 18th and 19th centuries as Scotch Irish settlers planted farming communities in the valleys. On either side of Pine Ridge grew the outposts of New Hope, hardly more than a church and a cemetery, and Robertsville, a cluster of stores, a school, and a blacksmith shop that operated as a gristmill on the weekends. Nearby was a natural spring where travelers rested their horses on the journey between the growing towns of Clinton to the east and Kingston to the west.

Around 1900 the area's most famous resident was a certified lunatic.

John Hendrix was born in Bear Creek Valley and by the turn of the century lived with his wife, Julia Ann, and four children in a worn, ramshackle home with an off-kilter porch. Hendrix had a habit of taking long walks in the woods and returning with prognostications that seemed crazy but tended to come true. He told his wife that a railroad would be built from Knoxville through their homeland,

and within a few years construction began on the Louisville and Nashville Railroad. He voiced his predictions at a country store at a crossroads near his home. Customers and passersby laughed him off. Hendrix's wife blamed him when their two-year-old daughter died of diphtheria, and she fled with the other children to Arkansas. Wracked by grief and guilt, Hendrix turned to religion to ascribe meaning to his ruined world. He became a wandering indigent. His devotion to Christianity fueled his sense of prophecy. His ravings got him committed to a hospital for the insane, but he escaped and told lawmen that God would destroy the hospital. A few weeks later, as the legend goes, lightning struck the hospital and it burned to the ground. He eventually got married again, to a woman named Martha Jane, and spooked her children with his soothsaying babble. During one jaunt into the woods, he claimed to have heard a voice as big and bold as thunder. The voice told Hendrix to sleep with his head on the ground for 40 nights. In exchange, he would be granted more visions. So Hendrix went to the woods and slept outside, gratefully accepting the dry blankets that townspeople would drape over his shivering body as his hair froze to the dirt. On the 41st day, he returned to town and described a vision with confounding specificity.

"And I tell you," Hendrix said to people at the crossroads store. "Bear Creek Valley some day will be filled with great buildings and factories and they will help toward winning the greatest war that ever will be. . . . Big engines will dig big ditches and thousands of people will be running to and fro. They will be building things and there will be great noise and confusion and the earth will shake."

Whenever he related this vision, townsfolk would dismiss or ridicule him.

"I've seen it," Hendrix would reply with frustrated confidence. "It's coming."

Then he would retreat to the crest of Pine Ridge and look across

the valleys on either side, imagining the future. When he raved outside the town courthouse, people gave him dimes and shook their
heads. Others invited him to dinner when it was clear he had nowhere
else to go. They called him the "prophet of Oak Ridge." He died in
1915 of tuberculosis. Over the next 30 years, his visions came true.

IN THE 1920S, electricity found its way to public buildings in East
Tennessee. Telephone and radio service connected the ridges and
valleys to the outside world. In 1933 the Tennessee Valley Authority
(TVA), an epic social experiment envisioned by Franklin D. Roosevelt
and established by Congress, began to salvage the region from the
Great Depression by commissioning the construction of dams along
the Clinch River to halt flooding and harness hydroelectric power.
Industry flocked. Jobs proliferated. Wages rose. After the United
States entered World War II in 1941, aluminum factories sprang up in
the region to make parts for airplanes. Around the same time, the government was scouting locations that were suitable for a more secretive round of military construction projects. East Tennessee, with its
contained valleys and abundance of water and power, was on the list.

Roosevelt summoned to the Oval Office one of Tennessee's senators, Kenneth Douglas McKellar, a powerful member of the Senate
Appropriations Committee. McKellar, a bombastic presence in a bow
tie and pinstriped trousers, was the king of patronage, an ill-tempered
logroller prone to cursing and fistfights. Once, after reading unsavory
press reports about himself, he slugged the publisher of the *Nashville
Tennessean* in the lobby of the Mayflower Hotel in Washington. With
the purse strings of Congress in his fist, McKellar could launder some
of the Manhattan Project's funding through conventional legislation.
Roosevelt asked if he could discreetly fund a big construction effort
for the war.

Well of course I can, Mr. President, McKellar allegedly replied, aware that a huge haul of money was at his fingertips. *And where in Tennessee are we going to hide this facility?*

It was settled: The uranium needed for the atomic bomb would be enriched in East Tennessee. An entire city and several factories would be built in a cluster of valleys in between ridges, which would provide natural protection if there was an accident. The project's immense thirst for water and power would be quenched by TVA's network of dams. Its inland location would insulate it from any Axis incursion from the coasts. On September 19, 1942, General Leslie Groves, the Manhattan Project chief, ordered the purchase of nearly 60,000 acres of rivers, ridges, and valleys that had been home to the prophet of Oak Ridge. Not even the governor of Tennessee was informed about the plan. Roosevelt deemed the site a federal military reservation, which meant it was not subject to state or local laws.

"It now appears almost certain that what we have called the 'mystery plant' will be built in this immediate vicinity, a plant of considerable size producing a mysterious product for war purposes," wrote TVA chief David E. Lilienthal in a journal entry a week later. His colleagues called it "the Shangri-la plant." The undersecretary of war called it "a very important project." Lilienthal had heard that it would use twice as much power as the city of Memphis consumed, which prompted him to jot a disclaimer in his journal: "Without TVA, by the way, that would be impossible."

Men with survey rods began puttering through the valleys and ridges. Soon after, letters of eviction from the War Department appeared at homes across the region. Three thousand farmers and homesteaders, some pocketing $25 per acre, skedaddled to Clinton and farther afield. Some had been dislocated by the government once or twice before, when the Great Smokies National Park was established or when TVA built the Norris Dam in the 1930s. "The only difference is when the Yankees came before, we could shoot at them," said one older resident who had endured his share of outside incursion during the Civil War.

The son of the prophet of Oak Ridge received his eviction letter on November 11, 1942. Curtis Allen Hendrix, 33, had been a heavy-boom operator on TVA's construction of the Norris and Douglas dams. The letter that arrived at his home on Gamble Valley Road said, "The War Department intends to take possession of your farm Dec. 1, 1942. . . . Your fullest cooperation will be a material aid to the War Effort." The government paid him $850 for his 60 acres, and was so eager to take the land that it burned a stack of new cedar fence posts before Curtis could remove them. Curtis, his wife, and their children relocated northeast to a farm dotted with sugar maples in Union County. Paid off but aggrieved, Curtis wrote a peculiar little poem, calling it "my tale of woe." His verse described government men with "big shining badges" who "read a lot of great big words" and seized "our hills." A couple of stanzas seemed possessed by the spirit of his legendary father.

> But I've done seen me a vision,
> And it's one I understand.
> In the none to distant future,
> Working folks will own no land.
> There will be a bunch of planners.
> Everyone will live by plan.

The plan was even more ambitious than that for the TVA: Build a city from scratch to jump-start the biggest industrial project in history, which would manifest the science conducted at universities in New York and Chicago and win World War II. Oak Ridge would be only one part of the Manhattan Project, an effort that would cost around $2 billion and involve 5,600 distinct inventions and a half million citizens at hundreds of labs, plants, universities, and corporations from over half the states in the union. The Manhattan Project was conducted behind the backs of all but seven congressmen, who barely questioned the under-the-table appropriations of hundreds of millions of dollars a year. For the small cadre of scientists and Army men who knew everything, the painstaking creation of factory infrastructure was really a lofty quest to defeat fascism. A few years before, Niels Bohr had said that the bomb could not be built "unless you turn the United States into one huge factory." That's what happened, at a staggering speed.

The government hired engineering contractors to pave the East Tennessee valleys with 200 miles of road and construct 44,000 dwelling units and "victory cottages" in ordered rows. It interviewed 400,000 workers and imported 75,000 of them over a couple of years: steel men from Pennsylvania, machinists and woodworkers from Michigan, riveters and physicists and stenographers and chemists from coast to coast. The area was referred to officially as the Kingston Demolition Range, then "Site X," then the Clinton Engineer Works.

A road was paved between Knoxville and this new city eventually named Oak Ridge after one of the surrounding geological ripples. Country stores became guard posts. Barns became parking garages. The next valley over—Bear Creek Valley, nestled between Pine and Chestnut ridges—became a cradle for a plant composed of 268 buildings made with 38 million board feet of lumber: laboratories, electric substations, water-cooling towers, pump houses, employee cafeterias and locker rooms, and a million square feet of calutron buildings. Similar to the atom-smashing cyclotrons used in Columbia University's basement, the calutrons were 15-foot-high curved machines that used electromagnetism to isolate U-235, the rare isotope of uranium that's unstable enough to break apart and start the chain reaction of fission necessary to create a nuclear explosion. It is the only isotope found in nature that can sustain such a reaction.

The plant was named Y-12. Neither the letter nor the number had any meaning, and the rest of the 14-square-mile "secret city" of Oak Ridge was similarly opaque. Billboards said, "Keep mum about this job" and "We will win in '44 with your help." Oak Ridge was fenced off from the outside and required a badge for admittance. Residents inside didn't know what they'd been drafted for. They knew only that the mission was complex and off the record.

An Eastman Kodak subsidiary was hired by the Army to manage and operate the Y-12 plant and its 4,800 workers. By the time calutrons were operational at the end of 1943, a fleet of East Tennessee high school girls were being trained to operate the machinery at the Y-12 plant. Some were told that they were manufacturing ice cream. They didn't know that each flick of their wrists conducted the painstaking gram-by-gram separation of U-235. The girls, seated on backless wooden stools at a bank of switches and dials, followed instructions blindly and completely. Grams of enriched uranium were spirited from Y-12 to a concrete bunker next to a farmhouse in town. The land, still roamed by cattle, had belonged to an evicted East Tennessean. Now that farmer's home was a base for security guards. His silo had been remodeled into a machine-gun tower. General Groves stored the uranium on the farm until bomb design was completed at a laboratory in New Mexico. Meanwhile, in southern Washington state, another secret city was producing plutonium, which could also undergo fission.

The government thought Y-12 would cost $30 million to build. The actual cost was $427 million, equal to several billion dollars in 21st-century money. More than half of the Manhattan Project's entire cost would be spent in Oak Ridge. Groves didn't want to gamble all his money on the electromagnetic-separation method at Y-12, so he commissioned the building of a backup plant that isolated U-235 through gaseous diffusion, a process envisioned by Columbia University physicists. The "K-25" gaseous diffusion plant took up 44 acres on the west end of Oak Ridge, tucked in another valley. The plant was four stories high and a mile long, cost $512 million to construct, and employed 9,000 workers. There, uranium in gas form was guided into a barrier; U-235 atoms passed through minuscule holes in the barrier, which stopped larger U-238 atoms. By late 1944 Oak Ridge had two massive plants that enriched uranium through different methods. The operation was like trying to find needles in a haystack while wearing boxing gloves, said George T. Felbeck, who captained the K-25 process for contractor Union Carbide.

Around the clock for 18 months, the secret city of Oak Ridge hummed and hustled, the muscle to Columbia University's brain. It used around 14 percent of all the electricity in the United States.

Oak Ridgers found themselves settled in a place that was both a utopia and a prison. Residents lived in small prefabricated "alphabet" houses made of cement and asbestos. An A-house, the smallest, was reserved for laborers, many of whom were natives of the surrounding hills. PhDs from out of town lived in D-houses, which were larger, had dining rooms, and were perched on winding roads up the ridges, on or near a crest called Knob Hill. "Snob Hill" was how the A-house crowd referred to it. Men outnumbered women 20 to 1. Unmarried residents lived in dormitories segregated by gender but mingled with the fervor of college students away from home for the first time. They built new, blended families in a place that had few before.

In Scarboro, the section of town closest to Pine Ridge, African American workers were crammed into rickety wooden hutments, 16 feet by 16 feet, without private bathrooms or glass on the windows. The city bus system, which was free to ride, soon became the ninth largest in the United States. Two hundred private businesses were recruited to serve a population that materialized overnight. Workers commuted to sites in the morning on barren roads that had been lined with houses by the time they returned home. Movie theaters were built before churches, so Mass was said in front of a screen, and Catholic children started thinking that posters of Clark Gable and Betty Grable depicted Jesus Christ and the Virgin Mary.

The massive construction effort to build the city stirred up a sea of sticky mud that caked everything, and it was all enclosed by fencing, guard posts, and barbed wire salvaged from former farms. Births and deaths inside Oak Ridge were registered elsewhere. There were no names on the jerseys of the high school's sports teams.

There was zero unemployment, top-notch schools, and universal health care. Badges were an essential accessory for residents.

Talking about the work, or guessing about the mission, was forbidden. Workers found life and knowledge to be totally compartmentalized in the name of security. An Army psychiatrist determined in a March 1944 report that isolation and secrecy created a "personality disturbance" in Oak Ridge's population, which was beset by tension and exhaustion. Counselors were assigned to dormitories, whose residents were troubled by alcoholism and a rash of suicides. Recreational activities such as bowling and badminton tournaments were intended to distract and relieve the populace. Many employers required sedatives to sleep, even though they worked more than 70 hours a week. There was no tangible result from all the effort, nothing in which they could take pride. The Y-12 plant, for all its machinery, didn't seem to be producing anything other than stress.

The same month as that Army report, Oak Ridge's first sample of enriched uranium was sent for testing to a laboratory in the New Mexican desert. The lab was run by J. Robert Oppenheimer in another secret city, named Los Alamos. Its mission was to design the actual bomb and integrate the fuel made in Oak Ridge. A year later, Oak Ridge was producing several hundred grams of bomb-grade uranium per day and sending it west, in leather suitcases handcuffed to armed couriers, who would board express trains in Knoxville and start a hand-off relay that would end near Santa Fe. Inside the suitcases were small wooden boxes of nickel cylinders about the size of coffee cups. In the cylinders was the uranium, in a form that looked like green salt. This was the magic fuel for the bomb. This was Oak Ridge's secret pride. Eventually there would be enough of it to form a critical mass—the amount of fissionable material necessary to sustain a chain reaction and cause an explosion.

By 1944 Manhattan Project expenses reached $100 million per month, and General Groves ordered that all bomb-related work be designated with a new label: "top secret." Roosevelt died on April 12, 1945, and Germany surrendered one month later, but the bomb project barreled ahead as Y-12 operated at peak force, with 22,482 employees. There was a momentum to the project, and the demise of neither a president nor the Third Reich would stop it.

TRUMAN FIRST LEARNED of the bomb within hours of taking the oath of office, but details were remarkably scarce for the commander in chief. Just four months removed from the Senate at the time of Roosevelt's death, Truman had been the chairman of the Committee to Investigate the National Defense Program. As the Pentagon watchdog on the Hill, he had dipped his toes in the river of money flowing toward the Manhattan Project, but his inquiries had been stymied by Secretary of War Henry Stimson. Now Stimson was dictating a memo to Truman on War Department letterhead, the word "secret" stamped above: "I think it is very important that I should have a talk with you as soon as possible on a highly secret matter."

Less than two months later, just before dawn on July 16, the first-ever atomic bomb was detonated in New Mexico, on Apache land 180 miles south of the Los Alamos lab, in the form of a bulbous "gadget" atop a 100-foot tower. The gadget was built around a heavy core of plutonium made in the secret city in Hanford, Washington. Oppenheimer called the remote test site Trinity, perhaps because he had John Donne and the *Bhagavad Gita* on the brain. In verse, both had pondered the notion of a God made of three elements.

Father, Son, and Holy Spirit.

Creator, preserver, and destroyer.

Inside the gadget, a shell of conventional explosives detonated inward, compressing the plutonium core from the size of an orange to the size of a lime. This compression of a critical mass triggered a nuclear chain reaction and an explosion of tens of millions of degrees—a temperature comparable to that of supernovas. The explosion came first as a white light that filled the whole desert sky, a light that "blasted," that "pounced," that "bored its way right through you," in the words of physicist I. I. Rabi, who was watching ten miles away. It was an extraterrestrial light, a light that had never before originated on Earth.

"The enormity of the light and its length quite stunned me," wrote Harvard University president James Conant, who was also ten miles from ground zero. "The whole sky suddenly full of white light like the end of the world."

The light faded to reveal an orange fireball crowned with a bright purple cloud. Groves's deputy, General Thomas Farrell, spoke of the "strong, sustained, awesome roar which warned of doomsday and made us feel that we puny things were blasphemous to dare tamper with the forces heretofore reserved to The Almighty."

Windows shattered 125 miles away. The light was seen from El Paso. Oppenheimer, who watched the test from 5.7 miles out, was relieved, emboldened, and humbled, all at once. "Terrifying," he told the *New York Times* reporter in attendance. "Lots of boys not grown up yet will owe their life to it."

Assembled scientists and military men danced and cheered.

Harvard physicist Kenneth Bainbridge, was less celebratory in his remark: "Now we're all sons of bitches."

"I no longer consider the Pentagon a safe shelter from such a bomb," wrote General Groves, who had now captained both the construction of the War Department's immense fortress in Washington and the creation of a weapon that could erase it.

For the first time in history, humanity had achieved a power that could incite its own extinction. The men at the top of the chain of command were relieved. The bomb was usable, and it would be used in war, in part to justify the hidden effort and vast expense. Its detonation, in other words, would validate its existence.

"I have been responsible for spending two billions of dollars on this atomic venture," Secretary of War Stimson said. "Now that it is successful I shall not be sent to prison in Fort Leavenworth."

The men of science, though, were troubled. By this point, a petition was circulating around Los Alamos, Oak Ridge, and Columbia University. Leo Szilard had written it and dozens of scientists had signed it. It was titled "A Petition to the President of the United States" and it read in part,

> a nation which sets the precedent of using these newly liberated forces of nature for purposes of destruction may have to bear the responsibility of opening the door to an era of devastation on an unimaginable scale.
>
> If after this war a situation is allowed to develop in the world which permits rival powers to be in uncontrolled possession of these new means of destruction, the cities of the United States as well as the cities of other nations will be in continuous danger of sudden annihilation. All the resources of the United States, moral

and material, may have to be mobilized to prevent the advent of such a world situation.

The U.S. Army threatened to charge Szilard with espionage. Robert Oppenheimer used his authority to quell this uprising of opposition. He delayed the petition's bureaucratic journey to the White House, where it would arrive too late to be effective.

THE FINAL SHIPMENT of enriched uranium for the Little Boy bomb left the secret city on July 23, 1945, with Oak Ridge courier Nicholas Del Genio, an Army lieutenant. In Los Alamos, Del Genio was instructed to accompany the bomb's uranium components in a C-54 aircraft to the Pacific island of Tinian, the staging ground for the bomber flight to Japan. Tinian, 6,000 miles from the West Coast near Guam, was now home to the largest airport in the world: six wide runways, each two miles long and lined with B-29 bombers glinting in the sun. The island was roughly shaped like Manhattan and its roads were named appropriately. There was a 125th Street, an 8th Avenue, a Riverside Drive.

In his diary after hearing about the successful Trinity test, President Truman wrote that he was certain the Japanese would surrender "when Manhattan appears over their homeland." On the steel frame of the bomb Lieutenant Del Genio wrote a message to the Japanese emperor: "From us in Oak Ridge to Tojo."

News from Hiroshima reached Oak Ridge first through breathless but vague rumor, then by radio reports, then by residents calling one another on the telephone to swap facts and suspicions. The city had been working on a bomb—or, rather, the radioactive heart of a bomb—and the investment in money and manpower had paid off. Suddenly they could talk about it, as surely as President Truman was talking about it on the radio. Residents converged on the town square, whooping and screaming. The co-founder of the Oak Ridge Symphony drove around town crying, "Uranium!" over and over again from the open window of his car. At least one housewife confronted her husband about his work at the plant, which had resulted in the deaths of many innocent civilians, but the city as a whole was celebrating.

"We know now that when man is willing to make the effort, he is capable of accomplishing virtually anything," General Groves would write in his memoir.

The quickness of this accomplishment was, by all accounts, miraculous—especially because Groves, a strict hard-nosed military man, and Oppenheimer, a rebellious progressive physicist, had surmounted personal and political differences to engage in one of mankind's great collaborations in virtual secrecy: three atomic bombs designed, produced, delivered, and detonated in just a few years.

The banner headlines on two "extra" editions of the *Knoxville Journal* swiftly categorized the bomb as a salvation. The first proclaimed WAR ENDS. The second said, PEACE. A headline in the *Oak Ridge Journal* localized the watershed event: OAK RIDGE ATTACKS JAPANESE. Japan, one city writhing in flames while another was being targeted, would not surrender for three more weeks.

TVA chief Lilienthal foresaw trouble in peacetime. "The effect of this research, as it moves into non-military fields, upon our government and economic life, may be very great," he wrote in his journal the day after Hiroshima. "Industry will try to get control, and at first will be successful. But as it goes on, it will be clear that no such control over the destinies of us all can be left in the hands of private corporations." He co-wrote a report advocating for international control of atomic energy, a concept buoyed by the movement for global government, which swelled in reaction to the catastrophic world war and the new threat of nuclear war.

The Federation of American Scientists, founded by the brains behind the Manhattan Project, published a book titled *One World or None* that sold more than 100,000 copies. The federation's Oak Ridge affiliate found that 90 percent of its members supported the creation of a world government. Three years into his job as director of the U.S. Atomic Energy Commission (AEC), Lilienthal's endorsement of globalized control and his distrust of private corporations had apparently switched.

"Contractors" is not the right word, Lilienthal told the Joint Committee on Atomic Energy in June 1949. "Partners" was more appropriate.

"We are trying to develop a new kind of setup in industrial affairs, a hybrid of public and private," he testified. "And it is good if the public does not sit on the necks of the private, or the private is not completely unaware of its public responsibilities. The alternative is that every step taken by the operator should be checked by government supervisors. This we do not believe is right."

That summer he was dragged in front of hearings in the name of accountability, even as he argued for a longer leash. Congress was upset about cost overruns and lax security. Congress wanted to know: How did 31 grams of uranium go missing from a lab in Illinois? Why did the landscaping of one Los Alamos cottage cost $10,000? And why did the concrete slabs under trash cans in Oak Ridge cost $90 each? By the end of his tenure, Lilienthal despaired that he was the very thing he had dismissed: a mere contractor for the Pentagon.

Oak Ridge, its founding prophecy fulfilled and its wartime goal achieved, continued to separate and stockpile U-235, now at a more efficient clip of 1.063 kilograms per day. There was no short-term military application for it, so General Groves ordered it put into a long-term reserve. The Y-12 workforce dropped to 1,450 by 1947.

The city gates came down in 1949 with a fitting ribbon-cutting ceremony: The ribbon was laced with chemicals and charged with electricity that was generated from a minor uranium reaction. It caught fire, belched a tiny white mushroom cloud, and twirled to the road. The secret city was now an open secret, though many aspects of it would remain classified. For years, even the amount of toilet paper delivered to Y-12 was hush-hush, lest the Soviets extrapolate the number of employees at the site.

Five months after the gates came down, and just over four years after Hiroshima and Nagasaki prompted Joseph Stalin to jump-start a Soviet nuclear program, Moscow tested its first nuclear bomb. Oak Ridge, which had achieved its first objective in 18 months, now had a second mission that would last for generations: Stay ahead of the Soviets.

A pilot plutonium plant called X-10, west of Y-12, became the Oak Ridge National Laboratory, which ensured that the city would serve an open-ended purpose related to national security. Enrichment operations increased at the K-25 gaseous diffusion plant, but construction and production were ongoing at Y-12 through the 1950s and '60s. The plant took the lead in separating lithium isotopes for the hydrogen bomb project, which would use both fission and fusion to produce a thermonuclear explosion many times greater than those in Hiroshima and Nagasaki.

Alvin Weinberg, who in 1955 became the director of the Oak Ridge lab, likened fission to "burning the rocks" and fusion to "burning the sea." The rocks, of course, were uranium and plutonium atoms, which are heavy with neutrons and can be split. The sea was a reference to deuterium, an isotope of hydrogen (the lightest element) that is abundant in the ocean. Atoms of deuterium, which have only one proton and one neutron each, can produce energy by uniting instead of splitting. One gram of deuterium, undergoing fusion, can release eight times as much energy as one gram of uranium undergoing fission. But fission energy is needed to initiate fusion, which is possible only at extremely high temperatures comparable to those on the sun. So the thermonuclear bomb had two main parts: the primary and the secondary. The "primary" was a spherical plutonium trigger, a Nagasaki-like component that imploded, underwent fission, and ignited a "secondary" canister of uranium, lithium compounds, and two isotopes of hydrogen (deuterium and tritium). The energy from the first "bomb" would cause the hydrogen isotopes to fuse and create a second more powerful "bomb," all in one device, all in one instant. Y-12 would produce and refurbish secondaries. Its modern mission was to turn atomic bombs into *super* atomic bombs.

Fusion bomb, hydrogen bomb, thermonuclear bomb—these were all different terms for the same device, which was first tested in 1952 in the Marshall Islands, out in the Pacific. The ensuing decade would see a mad buildup of them, culminating in two heart-stopping events.

In the early days of the John F. Kennedy administration, Daniel Ellsberg was a 30-year-old consultant to the Department of Defense. The Pentagon had worked up the Single Integrated Operational Plan (SIOP)—a massive nuclear first strike against Soviet and Chinese targets—and Ellsberg queried the Joint Chiefs of Staff about how many global fatalities would be expected if such a plan were carried out. He received his answer on a single sheet of paper marked TOP SECRET.

Six hundred million.

This piece of paper should not exist, thought Ellsberg, who would later leak the Pentagon Papers. *Not in America. Not anywhere, ever. It depicts evil beyond any human project that has ever existed.*

At the United Nations, Kennedy himself would refer to "a nuclear sword of Damocles, hanging by the slenderest of threads, capable of being cut at any moment by accident or miscalculation or by madness. The weapons of war must be abolished before they abolish us."

And yet the United States was barreling toward a confrontation where the SIOP might be executed. In October 1962 the Cuban Missile Crisis brought the United States and the Soviet Union to the brink of nuclear war. Even schoolchildren understood that they were awaiting annihilation. A month later, the Atomic Energy Commission produced a report that said, "the ultimate limits of nuclear weapon technology are not known and are highly speculative." The world had gotten within a hair's breadth of all-out war using weapons whose effects were largely mysterious. In the anxious aftermath of the crisis, an overwhelming majority of Americans said they would choose total war over Communist rule, though Kennedy declared in a June 1963 speech that "total war makes no sense" in a nuclear world.

Let us "examine our attitude toward peace itself," Kennedy said in the speech, delivered outdoors at American University in D.C. "Too many of us think it is impossible. Too many think it is unreal. But that is a dangerous, defeatist belief. It leads to the conclusion that war is inevitable, that mankind is doomed, that we are gripped by forces we cannot control."

That same year, with the help of Oak Ridge, Kennedy added about 2,500 nuclear bombs to the U.S. stockpile, bringing the total to 28,133. By 1963 the Y-12 plant was operating 55 specialized machine shops, pledging an 18-day turnaround for orders from the weapons labs in Los Alamos and Livermore, California. The secret city was still very much at work, its gates opened but its activities still cloaked.

In 1964 the world's most famous anthropologist, a graduate of Columbia University, came to visit and started asking too many questions.

"I was very interested in this town with no grandmothers," said

Margaret Mead, referring to the young population of a city with no past. She arrived in Oak Ridge on a spring day in May, wearing a green cape with gold fringe and carrying her typewriter and a wooden staff. She wanted to grasp the fishbowl anthropology of a city founded in secrecy, built behind fences, and committed to military science. She riled up the townspeople during a talk titled "Children in a Scientific Community," which she delivered on a Friday night in the Oak Ridge High School auditorium. Science was hollow without the humanities, she said. PhDs who move to Oak Ridge are like colonialists, she said, taking land and resources but keeping themselves at a distance from the "natives" and "service community": the Scarboro neighborhood of blacks and the Appalachian lower class, impoverished and uneducated in the surrounding valleys. She saw in Oak Ridge a microcosm of a socioeconomic caste system taking root around the country.

"We must think of the point where we can take *everyone* side by side into the future," Mead said.

"Is stratification characteristically human?" asked an engineer from Oak Ridge National Laboratory.

"No," Mead replied, "it's not human in the sense that it's universal, but it is one thing man is good at. . . . We can sit on one hill and turn people on the next hill into the most horrible creatures."

Life and work in Oak Ridge continued as normal. The rest of the country began to forget nuclear weapons, even as they accounted for 10 percent of the gross national products of both the United States and the Soviet Union. In 1965, as the U.S. stockpile was reaching its historical high, just 16 percent of Americans viewed nuclear war as the nation's No. 1 problem. When the States signed the Nuclear Non-Proliferation Treaty with the Soviet Union and 60 other nations in 1968, pledging to begin disarmament negotiations at "an early date," Y-12 was working on eight types of nuclear warheads, under a new kind of secrecy created by inattention. The Vietnam War, then at its bloodiest, had pulled the nation's focus to a more immediate threat.

THE SKY WAS CLEAR of clouds but the thunder kept rumbling. The sound of carpet bombing would echo in Michael Walli's skull long after he completed his present mission.

Hauling a briefing board into Cambodia required four men. The boards were made of heavy plywood and contained military information and mapping. VINI VIDI VICI was printed at the top of each board. As teams carried the boards onto and off helicopters, American B-52 bombers flew overhead to incinerate Vietcong havens. The incursion created a distant, unearthly roar.

Michael was a 21-year-old Army clerk typist, although in some ways he was just a farm boy with big round glasses who was lost in the jungle. It was April 1970. Back home, opposition to the Vietnam War was reaching its ugly peak. In the thick of it, though, there was only the noise from above.

He was the 12th of 14 children, born in 1948 at St. Joseph's Hospital in Menominee, Michigan, on the lower flank of the Upper Peninsula. The hospital was run by Franciscan sisters, who had opened it in 1891 after traveling on foot between lumber camps to solicit building materials. The Wallis lived to the north, in the village of Stephenson, between two family farms 30 miles apart. Michael was baptized by a French immigrant priest at the Church of the Precious Blood. The family walked to Mass every Sunday. There was no parochial school in Stephenson, so the Walli children attended the local public school and weekly catechism classes. The county library was only a mile from home, and Michael immersed himself in books. He was a poor student but had a vague desire to become a writer. When he wasn't working on the farm and enjoying the animals, he was in the woods, exploring, getting lost. He wasn't college material, so when he turned 18, he enlisted in the Army. Michael knew that there was a war under way, and that it was getting worse, so he asked for a noncombat role. After being inducted into the Army in Milwaukee in September 1967, he boarded an airplane for the first time and flew from Mitchell Field to Chicago O'Hare to Nashville, where he hopped a bus to Fort Campbell, on the border between Tennessee and Kentucky. After a hardscrabble upbringing, basic training came relatively easy. It felt like camp, but with foulmouthed counselors. Michael qualified as a sharpshooter for M14 and M16 rifles. Company commanders gave speeches about helping the South Vietnamese exercise self-determination. Michael stepped in line and chanted in time.

I wanna be an airborne ranger.
I wanna be an airborne ranger!
I wanna live a life of danger.
I wanna live a life of danger!
I wanna go to Vietnam.
I wanna go to Vietnam!

He took a typing course at Fort Leonard Wood in the Missouri Ozarks and then, within five months of enlisting, he arrived in Vietnam, a week after the Tet Offensive began and five weeks before U.S. soldiers massacred hundreds of unarmed civilians in the village of My Lai. Michael was assigned to U.S. Army Support Command in Da Nang, just below the demilitarized zone, not far from the shoreline of the South China Sea. It was a pretty spot. Soldiers nicknamed the area China Beach and surfed its breakers while on leave. On his half day off every week, Michael swam and hung around the seaside R&R center. He worked in the military police office, which was just a portable tent with floors made of plywood from Texas. One of his duties was to burn classified material in a barrel out back. Another duty was typing up reports on base security and its components: fences, razor wire, guards, lights. He was at his typewriter on April 5, 1968, when the radio crackled with news that Martin Luther King Jr. had been gunned down the previous day on a motel balcony in Memphis. This was the man who had said, regarding Vietnam, that "our scientific power has outrun our spiritual power," that "we have guided missiles and misguided men." The latter phrase lodged in Michael's brain.

BACK IN THE STATES, antiwar priests Philip and Daniel Berrigan were igniting a mini-revolution against the government's commitment to Vietnam. The brothers and seven others raided a draft office in Catonsville, Maryland, on May 17, 1968, in broad daylight. They confiscated hundreds of draft files while holding clerks at bay, then heaped the papers into a pyre made with homemade napalm in the parking lot. They were praying, ashes swirling, when law enforcement arrived. "We are Catholic Christians who take our faith seriously," their statement read. Dan Berrigan said they acted "to make it more difficult for men to kill one another." Tom Lewis, an artist from Baltimore, had helped choreograph the action like a work of art and made sure the media arrived in time for a photo op. The group happily accepted the designation of the "Catonsville Nine" as they were indicted for conspiracy and destruction of government property. The archbishop of Baltimore rebuked the group's "damaging" actions and hindrance of government affairs. In public, Dorothy Day commended them for their "acts of witness," saying that the "one way to end this insane war" was to "pack the jails with our men." In private she distanced the Catholic Worker movement from the concept of burglary as resistance, and worried that the Catonsville Nine's aggressive tactics subverted pacifism and would do more harm than good. A week later, while at a sentencing hearing for a previous act of civil disobedience conducted with Tom Lewis, Philip Berrigan made a statement to the court: "The American power structure is, by and large, lawless and it must, very simply, be made lawful."

Federal judge Edward Northrop accused them of arrogance and showing "no remorse but rather a determination to bend society" to their will. "You will not tolerate the views of others," the judge said. "You hide behind words."

Phil Berrigan and Lewis were sentenced to six years in prison. Their crime was pouring blood on draft files at another selective service office, in Baltimore. Their statement at the time included this sentence: "We pour it upon these files to illustrate that with them and with these offices begins the pitiful waste of American and Vietnamese blood 10,000 miles away."

TEN THOUSAND MILES AWAY, the war intensified, and opposition to it eclipsed the civil rights and anti-nuclear movements, the latter of which was mollified by the Nuclear Non-Proliferation Treaty. Michael Walli finished his first tour in February 1969, a couple of weeks after Richard Nixon took office, and started his second that September with the First Calvary Division. By October he was at Fire Support Base Buttons, a sprawling outpost that buttressed offensive forces, 20 miles from the Cambodia border. Tents were surrounded by pale green sandbags and circled by concertina wire. An extinct volcano lurked over the scrubby earth less than a mile southeast. Meanwhile, in Washington, President Nixon was playing with fire.

From October 13 to 30, Nixon ordered a worldwide nuclear alert that triggered military operations from the Middle East to the Sea of Japan. The purpose of this alert was to intimidate Moscow into softening its support for Hanoi and to bear out Nixon's "madman theory," in which the president believed that the appearance of recklessness would cow his foes.

The North Vietnamese Army didn't get the message. Incoming fire was routine. Whenever the warning sirens wailed, Michael grabbed his flak jacket, helmet, and M16 rifle and raced to his post alongside a helicopter revetment. Cowering behind sandbags, he would hear bits of shrapnel ping off the tin roof of a nearby outhouse. In the early-morning hours of November 4, the Vietcong pummeled Michael's base with rockets and mortars as they attempted to breach the perimeter from all sides. Rangers had spotted the incoming ambush hours earlier, so the base was ready to defend itself. Michael was assigned to guard an entrance to the defense bunker and to hand out illumination flares. American helicopter gunships and transport planes—armed with Gatling guns that spat 100 rounds per second—routed the enemy by dawn. Several dozen Vietcong corpses were buried that morning in a mass grave dug by a Caterpillar just outside the base. Two Americans were dead and 26 were wounded.

When he wasn't taking cover, Michael typed reports on body counts and received disciplinary updates on terrified soldiers who had refused to board helicopters. He spent time in the base's morgue, making sure soldiers' remains were sorted and identified. From helicopters he flung propaganda that urged defection among North Vietnamese insurgents, and watched the leaflets corkscrew toward the dense jungle.

Around Christmas, Michael saw Bob Hope perform at a nearby base on a rubber-tree plantation. In between wisecracks, Hope told the crowd of GIs that Nixon had personally assured him that the White House was working on an exit strategy. "This time I believe our president has the answer," Hope said. His straight man for part of the show was Neil Armstrong, five months removed from his moonwalk, who was asked on the tour if people would eventually live on the moon. "Yes," Armstrong replied from the stage at Camp Eagle on Christmas Day, "but more important than if man will inhabit the moon is: Will man be able to live together down here on Earth?"

The U.S. incursion into Cambodia began May 1, 1970. The front line was so close that the men could hear it on Fire Support Base Buttons. Gunboat flotillas braved the Mekong River, which was lined with Vietcong sanctuaries, and mowed down water buffalo that were carrying cargo for the enemy. Michael carried those heavy briefing boards, hearing the rumble of B-52s overhead and the thunder of their payload as it hit Cambodian soil.

Antiwar demonstrations erupted across U.S. college campuses. The governor of Ohio called student protesters at Kent State University "the worst kind of people" and dispatched the National Guard, which shot 13 of them, killing four. A few days later, construction workers from the World Trade Center site wrapped tools in American flags and attacked student protesters in downtown New York City, injuring 70. At the White House, Nixon honored 22 of the construction workers for their patriotism.

J. Edgar Hoover, reaching the end of his epic reign over the FBI, dismissed the protesters as hippies and hoodlums. "Let us treat them like the vicious enemies of society that they really are, regardless of their age," he said at a dinner with congressmen. Operation Chaos, a CIA scheme to spy on and disrupt peace activism, targeted 1,000 American groups and 200,000 individuals.

Meanwhile, American soldiers in Cambodia were run ragged by this second front. They were unshaven, glassy-eyed, and often buzzed on beer, and they "would have gladly traded the compulsory violence of Vietnam and Cambodia for the elective violence of America," reported James P. Sterba for the *New York Times*. "They did not choose this violence; they were chosen for it."

A month into the incursion, the U.S. military had killed 9,658 enemy soldiers and captured 10 hospitals, 5,000 tons of rice, and

12,000 individual weapons. The mission ended on June 30, with soldiers from the First Calvary Division tumbling out of helicopters back on Vietnam soil, their uniforms torn and splattered with mud. Preliminary reports tallied 337 American dead and 1,524 wounded.

This violence is evil, Michael began to think, and his aversion to it was growing into an allergy, into a cause, into a way of life.

MICHAEL SURVIVED HIS SECOND TOUR, and at the end of August 1970 he left Vietnam through Saigon. He was discharged September 1, reenlisted March 2, 1971, and spent the ensuing three and a half months drinking beer, being disciplined, going AWOL, and living on the streets between assignments at forts Eustis and Belvoir in Virginia. He was discharged for good on June 16, 1971. For his service he had been awarded five medals, including a Bronze Star, but he was beginning to feel like he had been an accomplice to war crimes. Like soldiers before him who survived their own wars, Michael was a different man when he left the Army. He wanted to get as far away from himself as possible.

He moved to Chicago and earned a wage at a Christmas-card factory. In 1972 he started working on bulk carriers on the Great Lakes that shipped salt, coal and sand, but post-traumatic stress dogged him even out on the water. He voluntarily entered the psychiatric wing at Hines VA Hospital in suburban Chicago in the summer of '73, and was transferred to Downey VA Hospital near Lake Michigan, where he was given the antipsychotic drug Thorazine. He went to Alaska, arriving in the autumn of 1974, became a merchant seaman and sailed into the Pacific. Still, he could not escape his conscience. He spent the autumn of '76 and two weeks of '78 at the St. Cloud VA Hospital in Minnesota, relying on counseling instead of pills. He didn't check in with his family for years at a time.

He read the Bible. Life began to organize itself in tiny miracles and supernatural signs. On July 15, 1978, after reading the Gospel of Matthew's passage about how God cares even for a lowly fallen sparrow, he stepped outside his apartment in Wisconsin and there was a dead bird on the stoop. Michael would spend the rest of his life seeing divinity in happenstance.

He returned to Chicago in January 1979 and would spend most of the next decade there, volunteering at churches, working and living in homeless shelters and food warehouses. The Bible brought order to his scattered world. In the Gospel of Luke, Jesus said, "No one who puts his hand to the plow and looks back is fit for the kingdom of God." So he destroyed all his memorabilia from Vietnam and dedicated his life to serving the poor and crusading against war. He protested Morton Salt, whose plant was on the Chicago River, because its parent company provided fuel propellant for intercontinental ballistic missiles that carried nuclear warheads.

In April 1987 he arrived in Washington for a protest against the CIA. Before the demonstration, he visited the Vietnam War Memorial on the National Mall. In the reflective surface of the memorial, he saw a 38-year-old man free of earthly entanglements and consumed by purpose, a man who had hollowed himself out to exist purely as an instrument to hasten the coming of the day of God. Many names were carved into the black granite of the memorial, one after the other, in columns that grew taller as he walked down the sloping sidewalk. *War is evil*, he thought, *and these names are proof.*

So he thronged the gates of the CIA in McLean, Virginia, from which President Ronald Reagan was running a secret war against Nicaragua's Sandinista government by funneling aid to rebels. About 1,500 protesters blocked the gates and snarled traffic on April 27, and Michael was one of them. He was fined for "obstructing free passage." He felt that D.C. was the belly of the beast, the heart of the

war-making machine, and decided it would be his new home. He
moved into the Dorothy Day Catholic Worker house, a roomy old
Victorian in Northwest D.C. In the spirit of their namesake, the community embraced this strange man, who was high-strung but gentle,
kind but haunted, and who was given to rambling prophetic statements about heaven and hell, the devil and Jesus.

While volunteering at the Center for Peace Studies at Georgetown University, Michael became friends with its founder, Father
Richard T. McSorley, a rebellious Jesuit and pacifist who had tried
to run the ROTC off campus. His views were black and white, and
they were forged during his four-year detention in a Japanese prison
camp in the Philippines during World War II. Father McSorley was
starved, tortured, and terrorized by mock executions until the Allies
liberated the island in 1945. He joined the Georgetown faculty in
1961, marched with Martin Luther King Jr. in Selma, and provided
the Catonsville Nine with the recipe for homemade napalm from a
Special Forces handbook in the Georgetown law school library. He
found his most challenging foe—the biggest threat to peace and to
life itself—in the form of nuclear weapons.

"The taproot of violence in our society today is our intent to use
nuclear weapons," he wrote. "Once we have agreed to all that, all
other evil is minor in comparison."

His Center for Peace Studies was in a small white building on the
edge of Georgetown's campus, the office door pasted with antiwar
bumper stickers and an illustration of Jesus holding a cross made of
atomic bombs. He was arrested at both the Capitol building and
the Soviet consulate in New York while protesting the Cold War
arms race.

Father McSorley kept a mailing list of prisoners of conscience, including those who had taken civil disobedience to an intrepid and
dangerous level by breaking into nuclear-weapons sites. He encour-

aged Michael to write to the prisoners, strike up a correspondence, learn something from their boldness and sacrifice. One of the prisoners Michael wrote to was named Greg Boertje. He had broken into nuclear-weapons sites with the Berrigan brothers. He was a house-painter by trade.

4.

THE MIRACLE

The second fence was intimidating. The one on the backside of the ridge was just a perimeter fence, but the three fences surrounding the target were clearly integrated into the site's electronic security system. The first and third fences were topped with angled rows of barbed wire. The second fence, about 20 feet from the others, was threaded with fiber-optic motion sensors crowned with taut sensor cables that shimmered in the floodlight. The fences were made only of chain link. They had cut through the first one with ease. This second one, though, might be electrified. A single cut could trip an alarm. There were cameras watching them. It was around 4:15 a.m., and now it was only a matter of time.

They had paused in an avenue of small white rocks between the first and second fences. Michael had hung a cloth banner on the backside of the first fence. On it they'd painted a fat black bomb that looked like the one dropped on Nagasaki. It was falling into red flames. NEVER AGAIN was painted below it in small capital letters. Now Greg was facing the second fence, bolt cutters in hand, his heart sinking.

This is not going to work, he thought. *We are not going to get through this.*

As his hopes deflated, an inner voice piped up: "Well, you won't know unless you try."

Through the years, other activists had faced similar obstacles at weapons sites and had somehow made it through. Greg had been arrested more than 40 times for civil disobedience, and had seen some remarkable things in his previous five break-ins at weapon sites. So he started cutting with his $25 red-handled bolt cutters from True Value, making sure to avoid the sensor wiring that he could see. The cutters bit down on the metal, one link at a time.

Crack. Release.

Crack. Release.

Crack. Release.

No alarms. No team of armored men. No vehicles screeching around the corner. Inside the castle-like turrets on the corners of the Highly Enriched Uranium Materials Facility were guards and guns, but they did not stir. Somewhere on the premises were armored cars mounted with six-barreled Gatling guns that could fire 50 finger-size bullets per second, a fusillade that could down an airplane. In terms of artillery, Y-12 was prepared for an armed assault by multiple intruders.

While he pulled back the flap of fencing for Megan, Greg was moved by the silence and the ease of their mission.

God is with us, he thought. *This is grace.*

Each step they had taken felt ordained, as if they were being led by a force, by a voice that said, "Take this step, take that step." Greg felt summoned. He felt protected.

They had prepared as much as they could. They had learned that the Department of Energy spent 42 percent of its money on the nuclear-weapons complex. They had schooled themselves on both the history and the future of Y-12, which was planning the $6.5 billion construction of a facility to process uranium. They had learned that the new facility would continue the assembly, recertification, and storage of secondaries, those dense stainless steel cases of uranium that turn a fission bomb into a fusion bomb. There were at least 5,000 secondaries stored at Y-12, some of which were being disassembled and refurbished for the W76 warhead, which would be attached to Trident missiles on submarines patrolling the oceans. The trio had learned about life-extension programs for the weapons, which Pentagon officials referred to as "patients" who needed to be kept "alive," who deserved "better ways to heal" from maintenance issues.

Sister Megan, Michael, and Greg had scouted from above using Google Earth, where the uranium storage facility was visible like a white bull's-eye in the scrubby green hills. They had consulted loved ones. They had measured all good things against this one necessary thing, and they were prepared to die. They believed in the resurrection. Death was not a specter but an inevitability. They did not overplan, though. They had left room for the Spirit.

And now they were feeling its presence. The third and final fence was no problem. Cut, pull, duck. It was 4:29 a.m. They were in the inner sanctum, well inside the lethal-force zone, with nothing between them and the nation's storehouse of weapons-grade uranium but 75 feet of asphalt and a haze of bright floodlight. The facility's walls, towering and white, were so colossal that they could allegedly withstand the impact of a jet—a scenario that had a probability of occurring once every 100,000 years, according to a government report.

The most powerful tools they had were three hammers, scuffed from previous use. One was a household hammer, its wood handle inscribed with lettering in red permanent marker: SWORDS INTO PLOWSHARES, TRANSFORM NOW INTO LIFE FOR ALL, and the names of two deceased men. One was Corbin Harney, a leader of the Western Shoshone Indians in Nevada, and the other was Walter Hooke, Megan's uncle, who never forgot Nagasaki. A small sledgehammer had an instruction from the Gospels burned into its handle: "Repent! God's kingdom is at hand!" The third hammer, a ball-peen, was tied with strands of cloth inscribed with quotations, including ones from Father Richard McSorley ("It is a sin to build a nuclear weapon") and Eisenhower ("Every dollar that is spent on armaments is a theft from the poor"). The hammers were the tools to carry out the prophet Isaiah's command to end war, to transform swords into plowshares and spears into pruning hooks. With the hammers, the trio would symbolically disarm the facility and start its transformation.

But first they pulled three cans of spray paint from their backpacks. Along the north face of the building, near a turret, Greg wrote two-foot-tall red letters as he moved along the wall. His graffiti was inspired by the Old Testament Book of Nahum, who scolded the ancient Assyrian city of Nineveh, a bastion of war located in what is now northern Iraq.

WOE TO AN EMPIRE OF BLOOD, Greg wrote.

Michael used the pentagonal base of the northwest turret for his canvas. On one side he spray-painted in black, THE FRUIT OF JUSTICE IS PEACE. Megan strung the red DANGER: NUCLEAR CRIME ZONE tape between yellow concrete bollards. They were labeling the building with truth—the truth as they saw it—and this part of the mission wasn't complete until they italicized the words with real human blood, which would make visible the invisible. Blood served two purposes here. It symbolized both the waste of human life and the gift of eternal life. Most of the men and women who worked on weaponry, or who fought wars at 10,000 feet or from 10,000 miles, did not see bloodshed. This was a way to make that real.

They took the six baby bottles out of the backpacks and began to streak the white walls with blood, which dribbled down to the asphalt in dark-red rivulets. The blood had been drawn from fellow activists, including Tom Lewis, one of the Catonsville Nine. Years after burning draft files with the Berrigans, on the 60th anniversary of Hiroshima in 2005, Lewis and 14 others blocked the road into Y-12 to protest the ongoing operations of the site that had enriched the uranium for Little Boy. Lewis died in 2008, but his blood was frozen so that he might participate in one last action from beyond the grave. It was now pooling on the asphalt outside Y-12's uranium-storage facility in the early hours of July 28, 2012.

Now the hammers. They took turns hitting the base of the turret. The small chunks of concrete that crumbled away honored the biblical command to hammer tools of death into tools of life. Greg was filled with joy.

They thought they heard voices from up in the guard turret, but the trio made no move to hide or escape. Part of the mission was their arrest, and that was the one thing that wasn't going according to plan. They could hear faint conversation above them, up a tower of white concrete at the top of the guard turret, which was perforated by five small rectangular windows. Because they had time, Michael began to spray another message on the base of the turret—PLOWSHARES PLEASE ISAIAH—until Greg alerted him to the lights of a vehicle. Michael didn't quite finish the "H."

The trio watched as a Chevy Tahoe SUV slowly approached them from the east at 4:35 a.m. This was it. The final part of the action had begun.

THE TOWN OF PELLA was founded by several hundred Dutch Christians who broke from the national church in 1847, boarded four large sailboats in Rotterdam, and took trains and riverboats westward from Baltimore to their new home on 18,000 acres of farmland in the belly of Iowa. "Pella" means "city of refuge," and that's what it was for those Dutchmen looking to escape religious persecution in the Netherlands. Pella's most famous son, Wyatt Earp, was born shortly after the town itself. Its first tulip festival in 1935 was a last-minute affair, so a local cabinetmaker whittled 125 wooden tulips, each four feet tall, and placed them around the town square. A tulip committee was formed to plant 85,000 bulbs in preparation for the following year, and the tradition continued annually except in 1946, when the town focused instead on an auction that raised $100,000 for the war-torn people of Holland. Gregory Irwin Boertje was born near Pella in 1955, a week after the 20th tulip festival.

The Boertjes bounced around the state for much of Greg's childhood: Ames so his father could complete his PhD in biology, then Denison so his father could teach at the college. The first book Greg bought with his own money was a guide to identifying birds. He collected butterflies. The Boertjes were churchgoing Christians. Greg memorized Bible verses from an early age. In Denison, the family house abutted a golf course, and as a child Greg wanted to be a professional golfer. The family moved to Louisiana when Greg was in high school so his father could teach at the Southern University of New Orleans. The Vietnam War draft ended before Greg turned 18. An older cross-section of baby boomers had bled out before Greg became politically aware of it. Nevertheless, he hopped on a military track while still a teenager. His scholarship to Tulane University was through the ROTC, which paid for tuition and textbooks and gave him a stipend.

In graduate school he studied social and organizational psychology at Louisiana State University in Baton Rouge. There, his social conscience was awakened by nuclear weapons. He attended a Lutheran church on campus that hosted evening forums on the weapons. He subscribed to national peace publications like *Sojourners* and the magazine of the pacifist group Fellowship of Reconciliation, though to join this group you had to sign a vow that you would not kill someone. Because Greg was in the military, he had vowed to do the exact opposite if called upon.

It was 1980. The meltdown at the Three Mile Island nuclear reactor the previous year—on the heels of the nuclear-accident blockbuster *The China Syndrome*—had reignited public anxiety about the awesome power of the atom. NATO decided to install intermediate-range U.S. missiles in western Europe, which meant Moscow could be obliterated within six minutes of launch. The Senate Foreign Relations Committee had in its possession a new 154-page report called *The Effects of Nuclear War.* Appendix C was a fictional narrative of the deterioration of Charlottesville, Virginia, in the months after Washington and Richmond were nuked by the Soviets.

> Though less than perfect, the [radio] relay was able to bring limited news from outside, most of that news being acutely distressing. From the limited report, it was clear that there was little left in the coastal cities. . . . In time, the sorrow of loss would affect almost everyone. Although they had survived themselves, still they had lost.

The public was nevertheless dismayed with the apparent timidity of U.S. foreign policy, given the Iran hostage crisis and the collapse of contentious arms-control talks with Moscow when the Soviets invaded Afghanistan. A hawkish and conservative political tide was lifting presidential nominee Ronald Reagan toward the White House.

A movement was forming in opposition to Reagan's call for increased defense spending and an aggressive upgrade of nuclear forces to keep pace with the Soviets—an effort that would cost $240 billion. An MIT student named Randall Forsberg published a proposal titled "Call to Halt the Nuclear Arms Race," in which she argued that a total freeze on the testing, production, and deployment of nuclear weapons would be safer and easier than complex and incremental international treaties, especially when the United States and Soviet Union had ten-year plans to add 20,000 warheads to a combined arsenal that had already reached a mind-boggling 50,000.

"The weapons programs of the next decade, if not stopped, will pull the nuclear tripwire tighter," Forsberg wrote. The proposal became the manifesto for the nuclear-freeze movement, which would gain steam over the next two years with the help of a peace conference in D.C. and a band of rogue Catholics just outside Philadelphia.

Eight activists, including the Berrigan brothers, were meeting that summer for prayer and discussion as they planned an act of civil disobedience directed at nuclear weapons. They were a Catholic sister, a history professor, a lawyer, a former divinity student, a mother of seven, and three Catholic priests (Philip had been excommunicated seven years prior but still considered himself a man of the cloth). They prepared themselves for prison, for abandoning their families. Dan Berrigan wondered if their action would be a one-off, or if its daring would trigger a series of awakenings. The group had trouble deciding what to call their action, but they knew its name had to be more intentional and prophetic than the mundane "Catonsville Nine." They settled on the "Plowshares Eight," which referenced the Book of Isaiah's verse on the cessation of war.

And they shall beat their swords into plowshares,
And their spears into pruning hooks;
Nation shall not lift up sword against nation,
Neither shall they learn war anymore.

On September 9, 1980, after several days of prayer together, they acted in King of Prussia, Pennsylvania. Their target was a General Electric plant that made reentry systems for Minuteman missiles, which could be launched from ground-based silos and carry nuclear warheads across oceans. The plant was a vast industrial park with a series of anonymous buildings. The group found the huge facility that reportedly contained the nose cones for the missiles, but they didn't know exactly where to go once inside. They slipped by a security guard. In two minutes, without interference, they found the nose cones, hammered them, and lashed them with blood. Their written indictment read in part:

> We commit civil disobedience at General Electric because this genocidal entity is the fifth leading producer of weaponry in the U.S. To maintain this position, G.E. drains $3 million a day from the public treasury, an enormous larceny against the poor.
>
> We wish also to challenge the lethal lie spun by G.E. through its motto, "We bring good things to life." As manufacturers of the Mark 12A re-entry vehicle, G.E. actually prepares to bring good things to death.

A polling group had determined two years before that the public was largely unaware of the dangers of nuclear weapons because most people felt military issues were beyond their control, and forbidding in their complexity. Participation in peace groups had declined accordingly.

"In the 1960s they called us crazy," Dan Berrigan told the *New York Times* after the action in King of Prussia. "Now they say we are passé. . . . All great things have small beginnings."

The Plowshares Eight had unwittingly started a movement within a movement: a strain of bold civil disobedience that defied the law, flirted with violence, and added urgency and energy to the wider nuclear-freeze campaign. From jail, Dan sent a letter to Dorothy Day. The letter was a call to arms, against arms. It was also a goading of the public:

> No wonder that today Americans find it more plausible, more conducive to sanity, to ignore our nuclear plight, to fight survival in areas where the facts are less horrid, the cards less stacked. Economic woes, job layoffs, inflation—we have enough trouble draw-

ing the next breath. And you with your little hammers and bottles of blood, go out against Goliath? Thanks, good luck. But no thank you.

Print this, Dorothy told her staff. Two months later, on November 29, she died of congestive heart failure at her shelter for the homeless in the Bowery. She was 83 and survived by a daughter, 9 grandchildren, 14 great-grandchildren, and 40 Catholic Worker houses around the country. At her wake, the homeless and destitute kneeled at her pine-box coffin, adorned with a single long-stem red rose.

OVER REAGAN'S first term there were 11 more Plowshares actions, each carrying forward Day's rebellious spirit into territory between courage and foolishness. Each had a name.

Trident Nein: At the General Electric shipyard in Groton, Connecticut, four activists canoed to the 560-foot-long USS *Florida* submarine, which was armed with 24 missiles equipped with nuclear warheads. They hammered its missile hatches and spray-painted "USS Auschwitz" on its hull. It took security a half hour to notice and apprehend them, while five other activists spent three hours wandering inside the shipyard, hammering sonar equipment.

Griffiss Plowshares: Seven activists entered Griffiss Air Force Base in Rome, New York, hammered and poured blood on a B-52 bomber, then turned themselves in after several unimpeded hours on-site.

Pershing Plowshares: Eight activists slipped into the Orlando aerospace division of Martin Marietta, the manufacturer of Pershing II missiles, and hammered and poured blood on missile components and a launcher.

Throughout the 1980s and beyond, the Plowshares movement enfleshed the word of God and bedeviled the American justice system. Judges and juries were often tangled in the line between peaceful protest and disruptive crime, as activists leveraged courtrooms to spread their message and indict the U.S. government even as they themselves were being convicted.

"I've had about 1,500 major felony cases, and this isn't a major felony case," Judge Seymour L. Hendel said during the sentencing of the Trident Nein activists in New London, Connecticut. "Yet in all these cases there was no case, except maybe one, that I've felt more sympathy than I do here."

The Reagan administration, continuing the U.S. government's tradition of tracking and hampering dissent, had been targeting the Plowshares and nuclear freeze movements from the start. The FBI sent moles into disarmament groups like Physicians for Social Responsibility. Before Reagan even took the oath of office, the Heritage Foundation delivered a security report to his transition team that said, "individual liberties are secondary to the requirement of national security and internal civil order."

GREG BOERTJE became an active-duty Army man the day after July 4, 1981—a time when nearly half of all Americans thought nuclear war was imminent. Greg was a shy, 26-year-old Midwestern boy with full lips, droopy eyelids, and a love of nature—the antithesis of the typical grunt in his Fifth Infantry Division. He took an eight-week basic-training course at Fort Polk to become a field medical assistant with the 588th Engineer Battalion. He managed a medical aid station in exercises that simulated nuclear, chemical, and biological warfare. During one such exercise at Fort Sam Houston in Texas, a large fireball was set off and the men were told it was a nuclear explosion. They were instructed to answer certain questions about the explosion and report to headquarters.

Was it an air burst or did it detonate on the ground?

In which direction and at what velocity was the wind blowing?

The soldiers were instructed to wear protective vests, pants, and masks for increasingly long time periods: first for 15 minutes, at which point Greg would have a splitting headache, then 30, then an hour, then two, three, four, five. It was unbearable. While ministering to mock casualties with a gas mask squeezing his head for hours on end, Greg began to have doubts about the mission. His current study of the Bible went beyond rote memorization; he was now taking its verse seriously and applying it to real life. Military activity and nuclear weaponry seemed like the height of idolatry. Do not put your trust in horses and chariots, the Book of Psalms advised, and that is exactly what the United States seemed to be doing. He knew that a gas mask wouldn't protect anyone from radiation.

In October, during a press conference, President Reagan called for a modernization of each leg of the 20-year-old nuclear "triad": the sea-based Trident missiles on submarines, the airborne gravity bombs on B-52s, and the land-based intercontinental ballistic missiles (ICBMs) in silos across the interior of the United States. The existing ICBM force would be supplemented by MX missiles, which would carry ten warheads each.

The MX was nicknamed "the Peacekeeper." Two weeks after the press conference, Reagan issued a presidential directive: that the most fundamental national-security objective was to deter a direct nuclear attack, and that the United States "must prevail" if deterrence failed and nuclear war began. Yet in the years following, Reagan would often repeat: "A nuclear war cannot be won and must never be fought." The president, in public, was saying that nuclear war was unwinnable while, in private, he was establishing a national policy that the United States must prevail during one. It was a paradox. Reagan was also readying to approve a $4.3-billion program that would evacuate two-thirds of the U.S. population to 3,040 rural sites during nuclear war.

Greg, a cog in the military response to such an event, sought refuge by driving an hour from Fort Polk to a Bible study group. He gave a presentation there on loving one's enemy, a notion that was both threaded throughout the Bible and in direct opposition to the preparation for war with the Soviets. While riding in a Jeep after one military exercise, Greg read a passage from Dorothy Day's journals that addressed people who earned a living by building weapons.

"One can get by if one's wants are modest," Day wrote on March 11, 1948. "One can withdraw from the factory, refuse to make munitions, airplanes, atom bombs."

He thought this applied to him. He wasn't building weapons but he felt like he was promoting them. His Bible study group taught him that he was a vessel of God's work on Earth, that the Holy Spirit could speak through him and guide what he was meant to do. By the summer of 1982, Greg felt God was saying, "Don't cooperate anymore with this preparation for war."

What if instead of preparing for killing, he tried to prevent it?

So Greg talked to his commanding officer, who recommended that he apply to be a conscientious objector. During the process, Greg was interviewed by both a psychiatrist and a chaplain, whose job was to determine whether Greg was sincere about his pacifism. The chaplain told Greg that the Army had difficulty getting Catholic priests to enlist, because many of them opposed the military. This was news to him, and further validated his feelings. Greg was honorably discharged from the Army as a first lieutenant and conscientious objector on July 28, 1982, just over a year into his active duty, exactly 30 years to the day before he would find himself crossing a wooded Tennessee ridge in the middle of the night.

NINETEEN EIGHTY-TWO was a banner year for the revived antinuclear movement. Jonathan Schell, a *New Yorker* staff writer, published *The Fate of the Earth* in April. It was a warning. With grave scientific and moral authority, Schell ticked off the effects of nuclear weaponry and the risks of the arms race. A one-megaton explosion—equal to a million tons of TNT, or 60 Hiroshimas—above the Empire State Building, he wrote, would flatten everything between the toe of Manhattan and 125th Street, and set at least 280 square miles on fire. He then noted that the Soviet Union was more likely to strike with a 20-megaton bomb, which, if detonated at 30,000 feet, would incinerate people who were outdoors on the Jersey Shore. He argued that Heisenberg's uncertainty principle, conceived at an atomic level, could apply at a macro level: Mankind's knowledge of its ability to cause its own extinction is limited by extinction itself. The suddenness of the event would prohibit both observation and intervention. Though the possibility of such a holocaust may be small, he wrote, the stakes are infinite—therefore, in Schell's mind, there was no difference between possibility and certainty.

> Once the "strategic necessity" of planning the deaths of hundreds of millions of people is accepted, we begin to live in a world in which morality and action inhabit two separate, closed realms. All strategic sense becomes moral nonsense. . . . By threatening life in its totality, the nuclear peril creates new connections between the elements of human existence—a new mingling of the public and the private, the political and the emotional, the spiritual and the biological.

The nuclear-freeze movement reached a zenith on Saturday, June 12, 1982, when hundreds of thousands of people amassed outside the United Nations at sunrise. They clogged Fifth and Seventh avenues, brushing against storefronts on either side of the streets on a march that trailed for more than three miles. People had walked on foot from places like Montreal and Maine to be part of the event. Marchers included victims from Hiroshima, Nobel Prize winners, veteran activists of the 1960s, newlyweds who had just exited St. Patrick's Cathedral after exchanging vows, great-grandmothers, congressmen, Joan Baez, and a little girl wearing a sign around her neck that said, "Ray guns . . . Yucchy!" The two northbound marches funneled onto the Great Lawn of Central Park from both its east and west sides, where they were met by Susan Sarandon, Bella Abzug, Coretta Scott King, Jill Clayburgh, New York mayor Ed Koch, and Orson Welles, who was ferried through police barricades in a Cadillac and proclaimed from the rally stage in his baleful baritone, "This world has never known a single moment of such deadly jeopardy."

Greg Boertje didn't have the money to travel to New York, but Sister Megan Rice, 52 years old and on break from her ministry in Africa, was there with her mother, Madeleine. The NYPD estimated the crowd size in Central Park at between 550,000 and 700,000, besting the park record set the previous year at a Simon and Garfunkel concert. In time, the volume of people in and around Central Park would be estimated at one million strong—the largest political demonstration in U.S. history.

"We've done it," said Randall Forsberg, only two years removed from the publication of her freeze paper. "The nuclear-freeze campaign has mobilized the biggest peacetime march in United States history."

"To those who march for peace, my heart is with you," Reagan said in Bonn, as part of his peace-through-strength tour in Europe. "I would be at the head of your parade if I believed marching alone could bring about a more secure world."

The Monday after the march, as a special session on disarmament continued at the United Nations, protesters blocked the entrance to the U.N. missions of the five countries that acknowledged their nuclear stockpiles: the United States, the Soviet Union, the United Kingdom, France, and China. No less than 1,600 people were arrested, a city record for an act of civil disobedience.

"I think the time has come, especially for religious people, to consider breaking the human law in favor of a higher law," said seminary teacher Paul Mayer, who was arrested outside the Soviet mission. The Berrigan brothers, out of prison, were also arrested. Crowds gathered at the curved wall across from the U.N. headquarters that was engraved with the prophet Isaiah's words about beating swords into plowshares. "More nukes! Less kooks!" an NYPD officer shouted from a police bus, as his compatriots sang "God Bless America" to drown out the protesters' rendition of "We Shall Overcome."

The weekend was a greater show of peaceful force and energy than any antiwar demonstration of the Vietnam era. The look and backgrounds of the marchers were different, too. In contrast to the stereotypical flower children and long-haired extremists of the 1960s, the anti-nuclear crowd of the freeze movement was mostly mainstream, rooted in the middle class or in academia. They were less likely to burgle and burn government property than they were to publish papers and give lectures. Hawks still called them "freezeniks."

The midterm elections in November 1982 were a de facto referendum on Reagan and the nuclear-arms race. Twenty-three state legislatures and 370 city councils passed nuclear-freeze resolutions. Rep. Ed Markey (D–Mass.) believed the freezeniks were replacing Reagan's "moral majority," and the House passed his congressional freeze resolution in May 1983.

Freeze language found its way into the platforms of Democratic presidential candidates. Sen. Gary Hart (D–Colo.) locked arms with anti-nuclear activists at a march in New Jersey. Former vice president Walter Mondale said he would unilaterally stop underground nuclear tests in Nevada.

"Do not be deceived by a hawk in sheep's clothing," the Reverend

Jesse Jackson said after accusing his primary rivals of wanting to raise the military budget.

The Reagan administration perceived the movement as a serious threat to his reelection and to the nuclear-modernization program. Reagan himself was consumed by the specter of "evil, godless" Communists armed to the hilt. "You know, over there, they're not even human beings like we are," the president said privately of the Russians.

Now out of the military, Greg went back to graduate school but was more interested in studying the Bible than in completing a degree. He took Bible- and peace-studies courses at Louisiana State University for a year. He was introduced to the writing of Dan Berrigan, whose words vibrated with passion and conviction. A Christian is obligated to make public witness, Berrigan said, and to resist unjust laws.

Berrigan taught summer classes at Loyola University in New Orleans. Greg attended them and was enthralled. Berrigan, to Greg, seemed very human, very caring, and invested in his students' lives. He would join students for dinners at their apartments. Berrigan taught the Book of Revelation in the summer of 1983. He spoke about communities that were built around shared living and civil disobedience. He described the Plowshares actions, which fused together a deep understanding of the facts, an aggressive sense of moral outrage, and the tactics of civil disobedience born of Vietnam. This was more than a way of life, Berrigan said. It *was* life. He encouraged his students to write to Plowshares activists in prison. Greg heard an inner voice growing louder: "Go in this direction."

Berrigan sensed in Greg an unrealized transformation and encouraged him to find direction in his book *The Dark Night of Resistance*, a polemic of fiery words and verse: "the human quantum," "the murderous realities of public policy," the "systems" that "captivate man" and lead to "new enslavement," the "Brooks-suited investor" who's "infinitely removed from the bloodletting his manicured fingers set in motion." Berrigan summoned Margaret Mead's work on the American family, Thomas Merton's letters about being dead to society, J. Edgar Hoover's deceptions.

"Leaving the house" is how Berrigan described the move toward resistance:

> It has to do with the beginnings, the first stirrings of conscience, the first serious step as a consequence, the first march, the first legal jeopardy, the first trial attended. And everything serious after; the first trial, as defendant now; in the docks, the new play of relationships, the rupture of old safety devices, the cutting loose. Then too, the decision to refuse to pay the piper. . . . To go underground. To join that vast network of the unborn and the dead. To resign from America, in order to join the heart of man.

Greg had already read the book. He took this as a sign that his next move, his transformation, was surely nonviolent resistance.

THE WORLD TEETERED on the brink. In the fall of 1983, the fear of nuclear war invaded both secret military facilities and prime-time television.

In the first minutes of Monday, September 26, alarms went off as a 44-year-old lieutenant colonel named Stanislav Petrov was monitoring Soviet satellites from the commander's chair in a bunker 50 miles outside Moscow. One of the satellites, part of the USSR's early-warning system for incoming U.S. missiles, was sending word of a nuclear attack: Five ICBMs were streaking toward the homeland. In front of Petrov was a button flashing red, like a prop out of *Dr. Strangelove*. His choice was between reporting the data up the chain of command—which might trigger a nuclear war even if one was not actually under way—and following his hunch that this was a false alarm. A first strike from the United States, after all, would aim at decapitating Soviet command. That would require more than five missiles. A phone in one hand and an intercom in the other, Petrov declared the alarm to be false. He was right. The satellite in question had interpreted the sun's reflection off clouds as a missile launch.

It would be years before the world learned Petrov's story, but less than two months later the public had another frightening scenario beamed directly into their living rooms. The TV movie *The Day After*, inspired by Jonathan Schell's book, premiered on ABC at 8 p.m. on November 20, mere weeks before NATO began deploying U.S.-made Pershing II missiles in Europe. A whopping 100 million viewers saw the actor Jason Robards, burned and haggard, stumbling through a decimated Kansas town, having abandoned patients who were beyond help after a nuclear exchange with the Soviets. Directly after the program, as candlelight vigils were held by activists in Kansas, Secretary of State George Shultz appeared on ABC's *Viewpoint* to assure the American public that the government was working to prevent such a scenario from becoming reality.

The Day After was preceded by weeks of controversy, as the White House quietly panicked, the Pentagon sought script alterations, and disarmament campaigns scrambled to capitalize on the attention. Not since the Cuban Missile Crisis 20 years earlier was the American public so fixated on nuclear weapons and their effects. The Matthew Broderick thriller *WarGames*, about a high schooler who accidentally launches a simulated Soviet attack that the United States believes is real, had opened in theaters fives months earlier but ended happily. *The Day After*, so bleak and omnipresent, left Reagan "greatly depressed," according to his diary.

"My own reaction was one of our having to do all we can to have a deterrent," Reagan wrote, "and to see there is never a nuclear war."

Reagan would eventually pursue the Intermediate-Range Nuclear

Forces Treaty with the Soviets, eliminating a whole class of nukes in 1987, but the United States maintained a thicket of forward-deployed warheads surrounding the USSR: 7,200 in Europe alone, a few thousand around Asia.

After the end of Dan Berrigan's second summer of classes in 1984, Greg moved to Jonah House, a peace community in a narrow row house in West Baltimore founded by Phil Berrigan and his wife, Liz McAlister, who in 1972 were both charged with conspiracy after corresponding about kidnapping National Security Advisor Henry Kissinger and blowing up heating tunnels in Washington, D.C. McAlister and Berrigan wanted to nurture a community that was strong enough to sustain people in a life of resistance. Berrigan was adamant that Jonah House wasn't a Catholic Worker house, that its primary function was serving as a launchpad for nonviolent resistance. From Jonah House, Greg began planning his first Plowshares action with others, including a grandmother and a Vietnam veteran who lived in the house, a social worker from Ithaca, New York, a former college professor from Medford, Pennsylvania, and a poet-musician from D.C.

The group picked a submarine production facility run by General Dynamics in North Kingstown, Rhode Island. The subs would eventually be outfitted with Trident II missiles, which Reagan put into development in his first term. The Trident IIs would have increased accuracy and a range of 4,000 miles, and carry warheads that could destroy hardened targets in the Soviet Union. The action would be called Trident II Pruning Hooks. The actual intrusion was only part of the Plowshares process, which started with months of prayerful discernment and self-examination among a wider group.

Am I doing this for the right reasons? the group members asked themselves. *Is this for my own glory or the glory of God? Am I at peace with how this will affect my spouse, my children, my religious order? Do I fully accept*

that this path might lead to imprisonment, injury, or death? Will we collec-
tively refuse bail? Will I represent myself in court?

The logistical planning was minimal compared with the spiritual investigation. On a series of retreats they read the Bible, studied international law, held a mock trial, and prepared to get the most out of their impending "jail ministry." During one of the retreats, the group also devoted a whole session to fear. Greg's fear was that the mission would be a failure, that they would be stopped early and denied the chance to bear witness. Others feared spending years in prison.

As the Trident II group was winnowing itself to six members and finishing its planning in March 1985, four other Plowshares activists were given the movement's longest sentences to date for an action the previous November: initially a total of 54 years in prison between them. As part of Silo Pruning Hooks, they infiltrated a Minuteman missile site near Whiteman Air Force Base in Missouri and used a pneumatic jackhammer and air compressor to damage the lid. They were convicted of conspiracy, trespassing, destruction of government property, and intending to endanger the national defense.

"The true verdict in this case will be rendered by God, not by man," said Helen Woodson, a 41-year-old mother of 11, in court after her conviction. Woodson then filed an affidavit saying she would return to the site upon her release, jackhammer in hand. This promise, plus future violations of her parole, would keep her in prison until 2011.

Whenever Plowshares candidates got nervous about acting—about the armed men they'd face, about the profound legal repercussions— Phil Berrigan's refrain would be, "They are not in charge. They are not in charge." This had a brazen logic to it. The ability to imprison someone for any amount of time did not convey authority, which ultimately rested with God, and carrying out a Plowshares action was carrying out God's will.

"The push of conscience is a terrible thing," Dan Berrigan had written, and Greg and his compatriots, undaunted, were feeling it. Greg engraved "In God We Trust" on the handle of the household hammer he planned to use.

They bailed on their first attempt when a security van began following their vehicle near the drop-off point. A few weeks later, just after midnight on April 18, 1985, the members of Trident II Pruning Hooks cut through General Dynamics' shipyard fence and then split up into two groups of three, to maximize their chance of success. The groups moved to different parts of the shipyard. They hammered, poured blood, and spray-painted "Dachau" on the missile launch tubes. They brought with them an indictment of General Dynamics titled "Call to Conscience," which equated preparing for war with committing a war crime. The fact that the action achieved success without interruption was proof, in Greg's mind, that this was God's will. Greg's group was confronted by a single security guard. They were all arrested at 1:20 a.m. and charged with breaking and entering and malicious destruction of property.

Greg was exhilarated. God's will had been articulated in a concrete way.

After a two-week trial, the members of Trident II Pruning Hooks were convicted on all counts. Four jurors, despite voting guilty, asked the judge to read aloud a statement of support.

Greg was out by the summer, with time served, and began planning his next Plowshares action.

In January 1987, he and three others entered Willow Grove Naval Air Station in Horsham, Pennsylvania, hammered and poured blood on aircraft, and hung banners that said, SEEK THE DISARMED CHRIST and SWORDS INTO PLOWSHARES. They left a written indictment of the U.S. government's first-strike policy, which permitted preemptive nuclear attack. After three mistrials (two from hung juries), Greg was convicted that September of conspiracy, trespass, and destruction of government property. Instead of appearing for his sentencing, Greg issued a statement that he was going underground to plan another action.

He reappeared in the public spotlight on Easter Sunday 1988, just after 3 p.m., on board the USS *Iowa* at the Norfolk Naval Station in Virginia. With Phil Berrigan and two others, Greg blended into a public tour of the battleship. On the upper tier of the ship, they scaled a metal staircase to pour blood and hammer on two cruise-missile launchers. The clanging echoed across the shipyard. When personnel realized they weren't doing repairs, Marines with automatic rifles swarmed the deck. Tourists murmured with surprise.

"I'm just glad we live in a country where people can express their opinions," one said.

"Not like that," another replied. "Not like that."

The station was put on lockdown. Greg, a fugitive, was convicted of trespassing and served 27 months. During his prison time, Greg received a letter of support from Michael Walli, who lived at the Dorothy Day Catholic Worker house in Washington.

The writing was eccentric and passionate. Greg replied with his thanks, and Michael continued the correspondence, updating Greg about Father McSorley's activities at the peace center at Georgetown. Not long after Greg's release, the two met in D.C. at a faith and re-sistance retreat for members of the Jonah and Dorothy Day houses. Greg met and married his wife, Michele Naar, in Baltimore in 1993. Onto their last names they tacked "Obed," which is Hebrew for "servant." The two lived together at Jonah House with Phil Berri-gan, Liz McAlister, and others who were in and out of jail. It was an intense community of loving and volatile personalities. Three weeks after their wedding, Greg and Michele participated in a Plowshares action together. Throughout their marriage, they took turns breaking into weapons sites so that one of them was always out of jail to take care of their daughter, Rachel.

In June 2006, 15 years after the end of the Cold War and 35 years after leaving the Army, Michael conducted his first Plowshares action, with Greg by his side. The two men and septuagenarian Catholic priest Carl Kabat—one of the original Plowshares Eight in 1980—traveled to North Dakota, where ICBMs were tucked in underground silos across 8,500 square miles of prairie. Dressed as circus clowns, they broke a lock at one of the sites outside the town of Garrison and painted DISARM NOW and NUCLEAR WEAPONS ARE A SIN on the lid of a silo. They hung a large banner on the front gate that said, WEAPONS OF MASS DESTRUCTION HERE. They banged on the silo with a hammer that had "Repent! The Kingdom of God is at hand!" burned into its handle. After 45 minutes, during which they spray-painted a dozen messages on the grounds, a helicopter began circling overhead and 20 armed guards hustled into the site. The trio kneeled, joined hands, and began singing "Peace Is Flowing Like a River." Guards positioned them facedown on the ground and handcuffed them.

Six years later, Greg and Michael would find themselves in the same position together, on the ground, restrained and singing, with a Catholic sister instead of a Catholic priest.

WHILE GREG AND MICHAEL were in prison for their North Dakota action, Sister Megan was living in a former Air Force barracks in Las Vegas, driving a 1980 station wagon that ran on vegetable oil. It belonged to the Nevada Desert Experience, an anti-nuclear interfaith collective. She had contracted malaria and typhoid fever one too many times in Africa and in 2003 decided to return to the United States, get healthy, and commit herself full-time to anti-nuclear activism.

After seeing doctors in New York City, she decamped to a scrubby plot on the outskirts of Las Vegas to live a life on the margins with other activists at the Nevada Desert Experience.

Fifty miles north was the Nevada Test Site, where the government had detonated hundreds of test bombs over the years. Every Holy Week, activists walked from the National Atomic Testing Museum in downtown Vegas, onto the shoulder of Highway 95, into the desert, and eventually onto the property of the test site for ritual arrests. Megan had protested at the site in the 1980s by crossing the property line and blocking traffic. During a March 1988 protest, 2,065 people were arrested for crossing the boundary line. By the new millennium, though, interest in nuclear weapons had faded with the memories of the Cold War. Whatever work continued at secretive sites around the country—the missile silos in North Dakota, the uranium facilities in Tennessee, the shipyards of Rhode Island—was off the public's radar.

Then, in November 2009, there was news of two Jesuits and an 83-year-old Catholic sister breaking into a nuclear-weapons facility in Washington state. Megan, then 79, perked up. This was the latest Plowshares action, preceded by a full year of prayer and planning. In the middle of the night under a full moon, the priests, the sister, and two others cut their way through fences at Naval Base Kitsap–Bangor, across Puget Sound from Seattle. The activists were seen at the north end of the base by civilian workers, who did not report them because an intrusion seemed impossible. After finally tripping an alarm around 6:30 a.m., the group was surrounded. They unfurled a banner that revealed the name of their group and their message: DISARM NOW PLOWSHARES. TRIDENT: ILLEGAL + IMMORAL. They were handcuffed by Marines and hooded so that they couldn't see more of the secure area, then kept on the base for hours.

Megan attended their trial in Tacoma, Washington, the following year. They were charged with the usual battery of crimes—conspiracy, trespass, destruction of government property—and continued the

Plowshares tradition of admitting to their actions but pleading not guilty. They petitioned the judge to use two kinds of arguments in court: the justification defense, in which they'd argue that nuclear weapons are illegal under international law, and the necessity defense, in which they'd state that they *had* to act in order to save lives that were at risk because of the warheads' mere existence. They were barred from using either tactic, but the Disarm Now Plowshares group managed to sneak some messaging into the courtroom.

During jury selection, 67-year-old Jonah House resident Susan Crane, representing herself, asked every potential juror if they would have convicted Rosa Parks. Sister Anne Montgomery, also representing herself, stated the intention of Disarm Now Plowshares in her opening remarks.

"We felt that we could show a way for people who feel isolated and helpless, show that we are vulnerable, too," said Sister Anne, who was one of the original Plowshares Eight three decades before. "We are afraid, but we had hope, and walked through that to find freedom from the prison of fear and isolation."

During a cross-examination of a naval petty officer, Sister Anne asked, "In any of your training were you given military regulations that prohibit the indiscriminate killing of civilians?"

The U.S. attorneys objected, saying that the question was irrelevant.

"Well, it was very important to us," Sister Anne replied.

The trial lasted four days.

"Our intent was to keep the law," said Sister Anne, in her closing remarks. "To protect our lives as human beings and the lives of others."

Sitting on a courtroom bench, Megan was tantalized. "Who's going to do the next one?" she repeated in the courthouse during breaks. Plowshares veterans urged her to keep quiet.

The five members of Disarm Now Plowshares were convicted on all counts. In March 2011 they were sentenced to between 2 and 15 months in prison. This did not deter Megan. After hearing about them for 30 years, after witnessing the drama and emotion and frustration of a trial, she wanted to do the next Plowshares. Another one should come soon, she thought. This is urgent.

Sister Megan asked Sister Anne how to make this happen.

"Call Greg Boertje-Obed," Sister Anne suggested.

5.

SECURITY

Something is not right in zone 63."

The alarm-station operator at Y-12 was puzzled. Zone 63 was a cross section of the PIDAS, the perimeter intrusion detection and assessment system, which encircled the HEUMF, the Highly Enriched Uranium Materials Facility. No one was allowed inside the PIDAS unless they had a Q clearance. This top secret clearance from the Department of Energy required regular medical and psychological evaluations as part of a "human reliability program," to make sure that the people working around nuclear material were stable and reliable. All of these policies and acronyms were designed to form an unbreakable barrier around some of the most dangerous material ever known to man.

It was early in the morning on July 28, 2012, and alarms from zone 63 kept pinging. The first alarms came from the PIDAS's microwave sensors, which detect movement, and popped up in tiny font on the control panel at the alarm station, a cramped room located in the guard building about 1,000 feet from the HEUMF.

Two microwave sensors in zone 63 were tripped at 4:21 a.m.

Two more sensors were tripped one second later.

Fourteen seconds after that, the alarm-station operator acknowledged the alerts, assessed them as false, and cleared them. Y-12 had an average of 2,170 alarms every day, many caused by wildlife, weather, foliage, or a breeze. An alarm—even a series of alarms—did not raise any concern in a work environment that was swamped by false ones. Because of the frequency of false alarms, guards were directed not to respond in person unless multiple alarms were going off simultaneously. The operators normally would have checked the area through closed-circuit television cameras, but none of the cameras that covered zone 63 were operating. Six other cameras trained on the PIDAS were also broken and awaiting repairs. Ten percent of the cameras site-wide were kaput.

Eight seconds after the alarms were cleared, the zone's electromagnetic detectors reported movement. With two types of alarms pinging in the same zone, perhaps an intrusion was proceeding along a specific pathway.

Next came a series of alerts that the middle fence's fiber-optic cables were being severed one by one. These alerts also went out to officers inside the HEUMF. Up in the facility's turrets, guards soon heard banging and hammering, which they dismissed as construction work without looking out their gun ports. If the sharpshooters on site had spied intruders, they might have taken them out.

Y-12's alarm system placed the continuous alerts on "auto-bypass" status, meaning they were not sounding with urgency in the alarm station.

Something had reached the nation's storehouse of weapons-grade uranium, and Y-12's brand-new $150-million-a-year security apparatus was missing it.

There were two parts to the apparatus: the physical security infrastructure (the fences, the fiber optics, the sensors) and the human protective force (the camo-clad guards with 9mm handguns holstered at their hips and M4 rifles in their vehicles). The former was the responsibility of Babcock & Wilcox Technical Services Y-12, the private contractor that managed and operated the site for the Department of Energy. The latter was provided by WSI Oak Ridge, a subcontractor, which was owned by a company called G4S. Y-12 had a force of 850 security and emergency personnel to provide a 24/7 response to any manner of threat or accident. The on-duty workforce was preoccupied with a shift change at the time the alarms started cascading through the central station.

"Level 4, PIDAS, zone 63, no camera coverage," the alarm-station operator finally radioed to the supervising lieutenant, who was distracted by both the shift change and by another alarm in a different area of Y-12. Something was also amiss at Building 9995, which was built during the Manhattan Project and still housed the site's analytical chemistry labs, a few thousand feet east of the HEUMF.

A security officer named Kirk Garland had just rotated from a guard tower to a patrol vehicle, a Chevy Tahoe, to cover an officer who was on a break. Kirk was a sturdy and soft-spoken man, with a cinnamon-colored mustache, and had worked in security at nuclear-weapons sites for 30 years. There were two hours left in his overnight shift, which had begun just before 6 p.m. the day before with a half-hour briefing called a "guard mount." The briefing was quick and simple: Nothing doing.

A three-second beep had just sounded over his radio, which meant a level-4 response was under way. His lieutenant called Kirk's cell phone to dispatch him to Building 9995, but as he arrived at 4:31 a.m. to make an assessment, the phone rang again. The lieutenant asked him to check on the PIDAS. There was no indication that it was anything other than the usual: alarms on the fritz that needed to be eyeballed.

We've already cleared it but it keeps bouncing in and out, his lieutenant said.

Kirk drove around to the HEUMF, idling his way along the north side of the facility at 4:35 a.m. Through the windshield he surveyed zone 63, ahead and to his right. He braked, put the car in park, and turned to exit the vehicle to make an inspection on foot. Outside the driver's window, to his left, three people were coming toward him. Though maintenance work was done at all hours at Y-12, Kirk was surprised that there would be a painting crew at the HEUMF, especially because there had been no briefing to that effect.

Then his eyes darted to the graffiti behind them.

"Empire."

"Blood."

"Justice."

"Peace."

"Plowshares."

The individuals came into focus, their hands up and out in a gesture of supplication. Two middle-age men on either side of an old woman. She bowed.

Bible verses.

Blood.

He had seen all this before.

SOON AFTER THE END of the first race for the bomb—which began in a basement in Manhattan, accelerated in Oak Ridge, and ended a few thousand feet over Japan—the second one started on a windswept mesa 16 miles northwest of Denver. There were more Soviet targets to destroy than atomic bombs in the U.S. arsenal, so production had to accelerate, particularly on the plutonium front. The United States needed to add another plant to its weapons complex. Colorado's senators, Edwin Johnson and Eugene Millikin, were both on the Joint Committee on Atomic Energy and steered the project to their state, much like Senator McKellar had done with Y-12. The Atomic Energy Commission (AEC) took about 2,600 acres of rocky soil from farmers and ranchers, as the War Department had done in East Tennessee eight years earlier. The AEC contracted Dow Chemical to build and manage a plant that processed plutonium into primaries—referred to as "triggers" or "pits"—that started the first stage of a thermonuclear explosion. State government officials were not consulted on the project, and no one seemed to know exactly what the plant would be for, but the community welcomed the influx of jobs.

THERE'S GOOD NEWS TODAY: U.S. TO BUILD $45 MILLION A-PLANT NEAR DENVER was the headline in the *Denver Post* on March 23, 1951.

"In a matter of months men of intelligence and purpose, patriotism and ambition, will begin tinkering with the scientific version of Russian roulette—right in our own backyard," wrote columnist Pasquale Marranzino in the *Rocky Mountain News*.

As Y-12 processed uranium and manufactured secondaries over in the valleys of Tennessee, Rocky Flats began milling plutonium for primaries in the shadow of the Continental Divide starting in 1953. Together, the sites made the reactive hearts of thermonuclear bombs throughout the Cold War.

The plutonium was black like coal and hot to the touch. It was constantly emitting radiation. It could ignite spontaneously. The pits were grapefruit-size spheres, hollow and weighing seven to nine pounds each, and encased in stainless steel. Plutonium, like uranium, could sustain a nuclear chain reaction, but it was far more efficient. Plutonium was also more radioactive, volatile, and toxic. The Denver area was now home to a government-owned, contractor-operated site that handled one of the most dangerous materials on Earth but the Joint Committee on Atomic Energy reported that the operation was safe enough to locate near the White House. Senators Johnson and Millikin believed there was no danger to their constituents in the nearby suburbs of Arvada, Westminster, and Broomfield. The company hired to assess the location collected its wind data from Stapleton Airport, 20 miles east of Rocky Flats, and concluded that high winds blew north, into the foothills, when in fact they blew southward to Denver and its suburbs. Two creeks flowed through Rocky Flats and into the Great Western Reservoir and Standley Lake, both of which supplied drinking water to the metropolitan area.

Rocky Flats, like Oak Ridge, had a mystique born of secrecy. The children of plant workers didn't know their fathers spent weekdays with their hands in lead-lined gloves, shaping plutonium in glass boxes, but they nonetheless enjoyed an elevated social caché among their peers. In November 1957, a month after the Soviet Union launched Sputnik, the Pentagon raised hell about a "missile gap" between the Soviet and American arsenals.

"The evidence clearly indicates an increasing threat which may become critical in 1959 or early 1960," the report stated, noting that "increased defense spending" helped the economy and could stave off recessions.

The report's claim of a missile gap was inaccurate, but it turbocharged the rate of U.S. warhead production. At the same time, the Pentagon was diversifying the delivery vehicles for the warheads, primarily because each military branch wanted a piece of the action. By the early 1960s the military had a nuclear triad of delivery systems, a trinity of methods to bring a warhead to its target:

1. The Air Force's bomber planes, ready to be loaded with gravity bombs. Bombers could disperse, complicating an enemy's effort to engage, and be recalled if necessary before reaching enemy territory. The value of this air-based leg of the triad was flexibility.

2. Intercontinental ballistic missiles spread out in underground silos. The advantages of ICBMs were their protected placement across the interior of the country and their ability to travel thousands of miles quickly. An ICBM could hit a tar-

get anywhere in the world in 30 minutes, but once launched, it could not be recalled.

3. U.S. Navy submarines, undetectable and therefore unhittable. If the Soviets destroyed or thwarted U.S. bombers or ICBMs, the submarines could launch their fatal reply without even surfacing. The value of this sea-based leg was its survivability.

Throughout the 1960s, defense analysts articulated a retroactive rationale for the triad that would persist into the 21st century. Each leg of the triad had strengths and weaknesses. Combined, they complicated Soviet offensive strategies. A Soviet first strike might lay waste to U.S. ICBM fields, but Washington still had airborne bombers and hidden submarines on call. The concept of strategic deterrence hinged on assuring an enemy that a nuclear strike would be answered by devastation, which led to the notion of "mutually assured destruction." The triad gradually became an indispensable part of deterrence, and deterrence worked only if Rocky Flats did.

Its plutonium triggers were shipped to test sites in Nevada or the Marshall Islands, or to the Pantex Plant in Amarillo, Texas, where they were assembled with Oak Ridge's secondaries and other weapons components into full-scale warheads, which in turn would be stored or deployed into the triad. This Cold War assembly line trundled along for decades in the name of deterrence and national security. The survival of the world hinged, paradoxically, on the ease and imminence of its destruction. An unofficial policy of "extended deterrence" widened the American nuclear-defense umbrella to other countries like Japan, Australia, and members of NATO, which then refrained from pursuing their own nuclear programs.

The Atomic Energy Commission and Congress's Joint Committee on Atomic Energy worked together to funnel money to Rocky Flats. The Denver area boomed. Its overall population nearly doubled

between 1950 and 1960. The proliferation of federal offices and bureaucrats won Denver the nickname Little Washington.

Rocky Flats, with its white-clad workers and assembly line of steel
machines, looked like both a hospital and an automobile factory.
Only a handful of the plant's 3,000-plus employees had clearance to
enter more than one of the site's several dozen structures, which were
dedicated to nasty tasks like solvent burning and scrap-metal disposal. The site was pocked with landfills, ash pits, and burial grounds
for contaminated soil. The pit-milling process produced a flood of
radioactive waste, which was eventually shipped by the trainload to a
disposal site in Idaho.

Problems plagued Rocky Flats from almost the moment it opened.
As early as 1959, thousands of storage drums were leaking waste
into an open field, polluting soil that was picked up by winds and
dispersed over Denver. On Mother's Day 1969, scraps of plutonium
combusted in a glove box and started a large fire, which turned the
element to powder and spewed it through roof vents in black plumes.
It was the costliest industrial accident in the United States to date. It
shut down the nationwide production of warheads and required AEC
chairman Glenn Seaborg—the co-discoverer of plutonium—to beg
Congress for an extra $45 million just to reopen the plant.

Rocky Flats and the U.S. government were able to cover up incidents through the perpetual invocation of classification and national
security, but a PhD in radiochemistry nailed them after the 1969 fire
by conducting his own field tests for contamination. Ed Martell, who
in the 1950s studied radiation's effect on organic life in the Marshall
Islands, found that the concentration of plutonium in populated areas
east of Rocky Flats was higher than in Nagasaki after Fat Man detonated. As other whistle-blowers brought details of accidents and leak-
ages to the public in the ensuing years, activists mobilized.

The Rocky Flats Action Group held its first demonstration in 1975,
and 25 people showed up. The following year's demonstration drew

6,000. In the spring of 1978 and 1979, hundreds of autopsies showed plutonium in the bodies of people who lived near Rocky Flats. Scores of protesters were arrested for blocking entrances, including Allen Ginsberg and Daniel Ellsberg, who sat on the train tracks leading into and out of the site. As a train idled toward them, Ginsberg recited his poem "Plutonian Ode."

> Destroyer of lying Scientists! Devourer of covetous Generals,
> Incinerator of Armies & Melter of Wars!
> Judgement of judgements, Divine Wind over vengeful nations,
> Molester of Presidents, Death-Scandal of Capital politics!
> Ah civilizations stupidly industrious!

The surge of activism at Rocky Flats came on the cusp of both Reagan's arms buildup and the nuclear-freeze movement. In 1980, after a decade of handling plutonium for an extra 15 cents an hour of "hot pay," a 31-year-old worker named Don Gabel died from the first case of cancer linked to radiation exposure at Rocky Flats. After his death, the Los Alamos lab asked to study his brain. Gabel's widow agreed, provided that it would release a written report of its findings. The brain went missing at the lab before any report could be made.

Three years later, after a million people marched in Manhattan against the bomb, 22-year-old Kirk Garland became the fourth member of his family to work at Rocky Flats.

KIRK'S UNCLE JIM KELLY, a staunch Irish Catholic and Navy veteran, was president of the steelworkers union at the site. Kirk's father, Ronald, was a metallurgist and an inspector working in the machining buildings. His older brother, Kevin, worked in security, and Kirk joined him in June 1983 as the youngest officer on the protective force. Their job was sacrosanct, especially in the tense Reagan years.

They were Cold Warriors protecting America's nuclear deterrent, which in turn protected the American people. They safeguarded the power that kept the United States safe. It was a patriotic family calling.

Kirk grew up the youngest of three children in Westminster, a town between Denver and Rocky Flats. The Garlands lived in a house across the street from the elementary school in a new middle-class development. The kids skipped back home for hot lunches. Their father, a volunteer firefighter and former airman, had a lively sense of humor and a keen respect for authority. Their mother was a homemaker with a gentle spirit. The family attended a nondenominational Christian church and, one by one, the children accepted Jesus as their savior. They were raised to be humble, to respect the law, to be loyal to one another, to stand up for themselves. Ronald was a motorcycle enthusiast, and Kirk grew up in the saddle of Norton hogs.

Rocky Flats was technically owned by the Department of Energy, which was created several years before to replace the Atomic Energy Commission and consolidate bureaucracy during the energy crises of the 1970s. As at Y-12 and its other weapons sites, the DOE contracted private companies to manage Rocky Flats. When Kirk reported for duty, he was working for Rockwell International, an aerospace manufacturer that built the B-25 bombers used in the firebombing of Tokyo. His father had been a B-25 crew chief during the Korean War.

The site was still very much under siege by activists, especially now that the nuclear-freeze movement was under way. Less than a year before Kirk started, two Catholic sisters used fake security badges to gain access to the site. They hoisted a flag that said, "Death Factory." They were arrested as they tried to hang a sign comparing Rocky Flats to a Nazi concentration camp. Their goal was to alert the public to the purpose of the site: to make bombs that could kill large numbers of people.

"If the law is not for the common good of the people," Sister Anne Marie Nord said in court, "then you must break it."

"You cannot take the law into your own hands," said federal district judge Zita Weinshienk during sentencing, "and if you do, you must be prepared to face the consequences."

Three months later, two more Catholic sisters accomplished a similar feat without bothering to forge badges. Their vehicle was simply waved through security. They had to wait to be arrested after pouring blood on crosses that they had hung on a fence.

Four months after Kirk started, 12,000 demonstrators held hands and tried to encircle Rocky Flats, causing a mass disruption. His first seven years at the site were defined by handling and arresting protesters, especially when he was promoted to the special response team, whose members were trained to deal with everything from hostage situations to an activist who refused to move. Sometimes it was Greenpeace activists. Sometimes it was Buddhist monks, sometimes Catholic clergy. They were always nonviolent, always just looking to be heard, and sometimes as combative as possible without resorting to actual violence. Sometimes they'd secure their heads together with U-locks, so that to pick one up you'd have to pick them all up. Sometimes they'd urinate once you did. They were fiendish in their single-mindedness. Every Sunday, the special response team was dispatched to monitor protesters who were holding their weekly vigil at the west gate.

By this time Rocky Flats had 6,000 employees, many of whom were suffering from illnesses related to exposure to plutonium and beryllium, which is used in nuclear weapons to reflect and slow neutrons, making fission more efficient. Every month there were dozens of contamination incidents, and yet the Department of Energy paid millions of dollars in bonuses to Rockwell. When it came to safety standards, the DOE governed itself. Its mission was too sensitive and specialized to be governed by the Occupational Safety and Health Administration, insiders argued. Activists and whistle-blowers thought otherwise, and accused the DOE of dodging responsibility so contractors could secure their bottom line.

Things started to go south in the mid-1980s, when environmental and safety violations became too serious and numerous to hide from public scrutiny. In 1989, under the code name Operation Desert Glow, the FBI raided the site and began carting off evidence. It was the first and only time in the history of the United States that one federal agency raided another. Allegations against Rockwell and the DOE included the dumping of toxic waste into the two creeks. Residents began digging ditches to divert water from their neighborhoods. A DOE memo surfaced that called the waste-disposal methods at Rocky Flats "patently illegal." Rockwell sued the U.S. government, claiming that the Environmental Protection Agency imposed laws that made it impossible to honor the production requirements set forth by the Department of Energy.

National-security policy was jeopardizing environmental safety, in other words.

The philosophy in the nuclear-weapons complex "was that this was a secret operation, not subject to laws," and "everybody else butt out," admitted W. Henson Moore, deputy secretary of the Department of Energy.

The Berlin Wall fell that autumn, and with it the contest that fueled the Cold War. The mission at Rocky Flats morphed from weapons production to an even bigger project: cleanup, which would cost $7.7 billion. It would be the biggest public-works project in Colorado history. In 1992 Rockwell pleaded guilty to ten environmental crimes, and the Department of Justice concluded that "a prevailing DOE 'culture' allowed Rocky Flats' crimes to occur."

At the dawn of the Clinton administration, new DOE secretary Hazel O'Leary launched an "openness initiative," stripping away the secretive nature of the weapons complex and ordering the declassification of millions of Cold War documents that revealed radiation experiments on humans over decades—from the Marshall Islands, where exposed islanders were studied instead of treated, to laboratories in Oak Ridge, where subjects were injected with plutonium. In 1947, for example, an Army colonel wrote to Oak Ridge to recommend the classification of documents related to human experimentation, so they wouldn't have an "adverse effect on public opinion or result in legal suits."

Now, nearly half a century later, the general public was getting its first look at how people were exposed, accidentally and deliberately. Exposure was ongoing, though, during cleanup at Rocky Flats, and the Garland family was in the middle of it.

KIRK'S BROTHER, KEVIN, transferred out of the protective force to supervise radiation monitoring. Crews combed the mesa, dredged contaminated trenches, and dug up more than a million rotting drums of radioactive green sludge—all by-products of building 70,000 plutonium pits over decades. Sometimes the sludge ignited when it was exposed to the air. To keep the unearthed elements from hitching a ride on the breeze, cleanup crews erected tents around the site. Kevin worked under these tents, breathing the most toxic air on Earth.

The Department of Energy called the site's plutonium-processing center, known as "the Hole," the nation's most dangerous building. The cleanup process was laborious, dangerous, and expensive. About 600 pits were sent down to the panhandle of Texas, to be stored in bunkers at the Pantex Plant.

In the mid-1990s, Kirk and Kevin's father, Ronald, developed most of the signs of berylliosis, a chronic lung disease caused by exposure to beryllium, but he was diagnosed with farmer's lung.

Contractors blamed Ronald's condition on pigeon droppings that may have accumulated on the outside of a trailer where he worked. He went on oxygen. Fluid was pumped through his nose into his lungs to flush out toxins and heavy metals. He developed pneumonia, then sepsis. His lungs hemorrhaged. Ronald died in 2001 at the age of 66.

Kirk's mother took the family on an overdue vacation in 2003. At their hotel in Hawaii, Kevin repeatedly had trouble figuring out how to get from their room to the downstairs lobby. It wasn't the only bizarre behavior he had exhibited. With cleanup finished at Rocky Flats, he had recently returned to the protective force but found it difficult to handle and operate his pistol. The fact that Kevin had trouble putting bullets in his handgun was troubling to Kirk. Kevin was laid off in 2004, as he continued to exhibit signs of what doctors presumed was early-onset Alzheimer's. He was 48.

The Garlands' troubles were no surprise to Jim Kelly, Kirk and Kevin's uncle, who had been at Rocky Flats since the '50s. He worked mostly in the Hole, which had safety incidents every day. In 1957 he helped scrub it after a glove-box fire scattered plutonium more than 8.5 miles away. During the Mother's Day fire in 1969, he spent 20 hours at Rocky Flats directing cleanup and praying that smoldering flecks of plutonium never caused a chain reaction. He led his union into battles against contractors, which cut corners on safety, and long ago concluded that the paramount concern of contractors and federal officials was production at any cost. Uncle Jim had once told his family that Rocky Flats wasn't the only unsafe part of the Denver area; a woman shopping downtown was a health risk, too. At Bikini Atoll in the Marshall Islands, some of his co-workers had witnessed Castle Bravo, the largest-ever American test, at 15 megatons—or 1,000 times the power of the Hiroshima bomb.

"To have a guy telling you what it was like, how unimaginable one of those things was, made you go home and not even talk to your family about it," Uncle Jim told journalist Len Ackland in 1996, describing the "terrible worry" of raising kids while working to prepare the country for nuclear war. "I always hid behind the fact that I was not the guy who would make the decision. Somebody out there had to be pulling the trigger, but that would never be me."

In 2003 Uncle Jim sat for an interview with the Boulder Public Library's oral history project on Rocky Flats. He was asked his opinion of the site's mission.

"I always looked at that as part of whatever the political geniuses at the time, in the world, decided the rest of us were gonna live with," Jim said, the plastic tube of his oxygen tank running up through his shirt, around his ears, to his nostrils. "I looked at that as something that was dictated by people far distant from any of us. I looked at it like I was looking at my counterpart in China or Russia or the U.K.: They're all in these plants doin' what I'm doin' because their country has decided that's what they're gonna do. And, you know, everybody decided we were gonna have a Cold War."

Kevin's condition worsened over the years. He forgot how to work the TV remote. He got lost on drives. He eventually needed help getting dressed. "Oh, I'm so stupid," he'd say, and his sister, Kim, hitching up his pants, would reply, "No, you're not. You just need a little help." Kevin's wife, Misti, swamped by raising three children while caring for her faltering husband, moved him into a succession of nursing homes. Kevin retreated into a fog. He wasn't the only Rocky Flats worker in his age group to deteriorate this way.

When Kevin was in the hospital, he pantomimed motions from work. He would pull a nonexistent trigger while aiming at the wall, as if he were at target practice. He would lather his limbs with air, as if he were back in the decontamination room. He was a smart man, but near the end he was playing with toy blocks on his hospital bed.

He had played semi-pro football when he was a young 270-pound man, and now his wife could nearly pick him up. Kevin died of acute neurotizing pneumonia in 2008 at 52 in a nursing home in Commerce City, Colorado. An autopsy showed that his brain had atrophied.

Kim delivered the eulogy at Kevin's funeral. "I believe his job cost him his life," she said from the pulpit, and his Rocky Flats co-workers—many of whom were on oxygen or had walkers—applauded.

Misti tried and failed three times to wrest money from the Department of Labor under a compensation act passed by Congress to pay out sick DOE workers or their surviving family members. There was no evidence that linked Kevin's demise with exposure to toxic chemicals.

Ronald, Kevin, and Jim were added to a running list of hundreds of Rocky Flats employees who had died prematurely of various cancers and ailments. Many had been smokers, which often sabotaged their compensation cases. A group called the Cold War Patriots formed to honor the service of nuclear workers at two dozen sites and to help them untangle the paperwork and bureaucracy once they got sick.

Why did the Garlands and many other families keep working at Rocky Flats and other sites, where the question was not *if* you'd get sick but *when*?

Simple: the money. It was a good job. It paid well, particularly if you did "hot pay" work with plutonium or other special nuclear material. There were benefits. Misti and Kevin had a five-bedroom house and brand-new cars. Kirk thought of it as similar to coal mining: You know you'll probably get black lung or be crushed in a collapse, but people still descend into the depths. People sacrifice and take the risk to serve their country and provide a good life for their families. Since the launch of the Manhattan Project, at least 700,000 Americans worked to create and maintain the U.S. nuclear arsenal.

And Kirk knew that the country needed nuclear weapons. They were a part of the world, and if the bad guys had them, then the good guys needed them. Simple as that. It wasn't a religious issue. And for those who objected to them on religious grounds, there was ample opportunity to protest lawfully and engage in the democratic system in a responsible manner.

In the spring of 2004 Kirk followed the route of the pits he'd helped protect. He left his home state for a new job in Amarillo, Texas, where he would rediscover God and come one step closer to the activists who claimed to be doing His work.

THE PANTEX PLANT outside Amarillo was the only non-military site in the United States that housed full-scale nuclear weapons. In neat, boxy bunkers across 16,000 scrubby acres of the tightest stretch of the Bible Belt, bombs were either awaiting dismantlement or awaiting reassembly and shipment in armored convoys to Air Force bases, naval bases in Washington state and Georgia, or ICBM silos in Montana, Wyoming, Nebraska, Colorado, and North Dakota. Each warhead was composed of thousands of individual parts that had been manufactured across the weapons complex: uranium from Oak Ridge, tritium from the Savannah River Site in South Carolina, electrical components from Kansas City, Missouri. All these parts reached communion at Pantex, inside short, gray-paneled circular structures called "gravel gerties," where the uranium and plutonium were married to the rest of the weapon underneath a heap of graded rocks and earth designed to deaden an accidental explosion. From the air, Pantex was a dense cropping of squat silver buildings surrounded by the brown and green geometry of North Texas agriculture. The site had dismantled thousands of warheads since 1991. It had also chucked nuclear waste in unlined landfills and burned it in open pits. Toxins had leached into aquifers that provided drinking water to the

Great Plains and nourished one-fifth of the corn, cattle, and wheat in the United States. Nearly 14,000 plutonium pits, made at Rocky Flats, were stored at Pantex.

There were always fewer protesters at Pantex than at Rocky Flats, even during the nuclear-freeze movement. The most visible agitator at that time was a Catholic bishop who visited parishioners by riding a white horse in his clerical garb. Leroy "Matt" Matthiesen, once pastor of St. Francis Church two miles from the weapons site, was unaware of the work going on in his backyard until a troubled Pantex employee sought his counsel. From his pulpit, Bishop Matt urged Pantex workers to quit their jobs. He stirred up trouble in a town that didn't talk about the nature of its job base.

"It made me realize that a man who loves God's creation must look for other work," one parishioner said after quitting.

Amarillo is where Kirk found his way back to God, more than two decades after Bishop Matt galloped along the perimeter of Pantex. A friend invited him to an enormous 7,000-person church with three Amarillo campuses, a Christian rock band, jumbo TV screens, and a state-of-the-art lighting system. Services were electrifying. You could feel the Holy Spirit at work in the thrum of singing and swaying, the faithful legion awash in baptismal blue light. One of the founding mantras of the congregation was "Whatever God says, we will do it."

The church even had a name that evoked both the central mystery of Christianity and the name of the first-ever atomic detonation: Trinity.

Despite the rewarding experiences at Pantex and Trinity, life in Amarillo didn't suit Kirk, his wife, Joann, or their young daughter, Kodie. It was flat, treeless, and smack-dab in Tornado Alley, so he jumped when a job opened at Y-12 in the lush, rolling hills of East Tennessee. He had followed the plutonium route from Rocky Flats to Pantex, and now he was following the route of uranium to Oak

Ridge. He moved there to pursue opportunity, just like the generation of young people during wartime more than half a century before. The Garlands eventually settled in a two-story brick home in Lake City, a patch of exurbia 20 miles north of Y-12 near the Norris Dam, that seminal creation of the Tennessee Valley Authority. They had room out back to build a stable for Kodie and Joann's horses and a kennel for German shepherds, which Kirk trained and sold to law-enforcement K9 units. He started as a security police officer at Y-12 on April 1, 2007. It didn't take long to see that the Fort Knox of Uranium was falling apart.

MORE THAN HALF the infrastructure in the nation's nuclear-weapons complex was 40-plus years old, and many of Y-12's wooden buildings were in the roughest shape. Building 9212—where workers wore protective clothing head to toe while processing uranium—had warped steel floors, interior walls scarred with rust, and a roof that leaked when it rained. After the floors of 9212 were scrubbed, the mop heads were incinerated. Indoor sprinkler systems were 50 years old. Nearly 300 structures at Y-12 were demolished in the first years of the 21st century, which eliminated about 1 million square feet of the site's footprint. The one brand-new, state-of-the-art building was the Highly Enriched Uranium Materials Facility, the 300-by-475-foot behemoth made of 400 tons of steel and 91,000 cubic yards of concrete. The previous uranium storage facility had been made of wood.

Upon the HEUMF's completion in September 2008, 1,000 people gathered at Y-12 to dedicate the $549-million building, whose construction cost had doubled since ground was broken four years earlier. Some of the congressional guests on the program had to remain in Washington—the economy was collapsing into the Great Recession—but the replacement speakers were effusive. The facility was impervious to any force, natural or man-made, they said.

"Fort Knox is the nation's Y-12 for gold," said the chief of staff for Rep. Zach Wamp (R), whose district included Y-12. Wamp, the only Tennessee congressman on the House Appropriations Committee, had for years sought extra funding for Y-12 over proposed budget levels. The government wanted smaller, smarter, more efficient buildings. The HEUMF, despite its cost overruns and chaotic construction, was a poster child for the modernization of the nation's complex. It was situated in a protected area that included Building 9212 and what would be that building's eventual replacement: the Uranium Processing Facility, then in its design stages.

Some of Y-12's streets were named after elements: Barium, Boron, Beryllium. The guard force at Y-12 was headquartered on Carbon Lane in Building 9710, a sad-looking bunker that was too small for the force. The job was high paying and not particularly strenuous. Security police officers—or SPOs, as they were called—could make nearly $100,000 a year by racking up overtime on 12-hour day or night shifts, rotating between patrols, fixed posts, and tower duty. Instead of working the usual four days on and four days off, Kirk routinely worked more than 60 hours a week.

He had spent his whole career in the service of the DOE and its private contractors. Over the years he had repeatedly passed countless trainings and courses, many specially tailored to nuclear security: shooting while moving, shooting at night, bomb-threat recognition, crime-scene preservation, vehicle stops, the legal implications of deadly force, counter-ambush techniques, beryllium awareness, radiological training, demonstrator control, terrorism indicators, and both daytime and nighttime uses of handguns, automatic rifles, and grenade launchers. After 30 years of this, he considered himself a model employee, with the DOE's standards and practices fused to his bones. So he was surprised by a certain laxness at Y-12.

Aggressive training regimens instituted after September 11 outpaced contractor personnel systems, leading to fatigue and cynicism in the ranks. "Police officer" was in the title, but an SPO couldn't actually make an arrest. There was none of the sudden danger or unpredictability of municipal police work, though SPOs were equipped with heavy-duty tactical technology like Gatling guns and BearCats, a steel-armored vehicle that could fit ten people and go off-roading. SPOs were worn out by preparing for war but spending their days in a kind of purgatory. It was both tedious and scary: "an endeavor of chilling monotony," as a report would describe the task. The job required both a readiness for the unthinkable and the knowledge that you could live out your entire career without seeing one minute of action. SPOs sometimes worked 17-hour shifts. About once a year, a guard was dismissed or suspended for sleeping on the job.

There was a peculiar contrast between Y-12's mission and Y-12's vibe. The site handled category 1 nuclear material, the most serious kind, and it was helping to build and take apart weapons that could destroy the world. It was also helping to reduce the global stocks of fissile material by accepting highly enriched uranium from countries like Libya and Mexico and down-blending it for use in power reactors and medical diagnostics. A contractor "vulnerability assessment team" created computer models of the facilities to determine the likelihood that certain plans would work against certain threats, from a band of armed insurgents to a 747 aimed at the HEUMF. It was all fantastically complicated in theory and fantastically boring in practice. There was a sense that none of the plans would ever be seriously tested in the real world.

Working at Y-12 was sometimes like guest-starring in a British sitcom, with all that a farce entails.

One week there would be electricians and carpenters renovating a building, the next week bulldozers would be flattening it.

Only parts of Y-12's fencing had razor wire.

Heavy concrete chunks fell from the ceilings of buildings.

Termites chewed through wooden beams.

Toxic-waste drums were used to catch rainwater leaks.

Employees were judged more on paperwork compliance reviews than on actual work performance.

There was the story of how, in June 1995, an employee flew a prop plane over Y-12 only a couple of hundred feet off the ground—near the old wooden storehouse of the nation's stockpile of highly enriched uranium—and dropped dozens of nude photos of his mistress, who was also an employee.

For every bizarre story, though, there was a tragic tale. Every now and then you'd hear that so-and-so had lung cancer. Medical-screening trailers emblazoned with the words "Detect Lung Cancer Early" were often parked near Oak Ridge churches. The Oak Ridge Beryllium Support Group met twice a month at Y-12's visitors center. If you worked at the site, you had tremendous pride in the mission, but you couldn't rub the fear away.

Y-12 also gave public tours, which made Kirk nervous. *So what if Y-12 was historically significant?* Kirk thought. *You don't let unauthorized people see your operation.* During the annual Secret City Festival in June, busloads of Oak Ridgers and tourists came through the site, driving along Bear Creek Road past the HEUMF, close enough to count the number of fences and the paces between them.

All these factors nurtured a culture of complacency. Most individual SPOs and Y-12 workers were patriotic, duty-bound Americans who were serious about the nature of their mission. The system they worked in, however, was lax and wobbly. It focused on the bottom line rather than the high bar.

In the words of one SPO who left Y-12 before the July 28, 2012, break-in: "The IRS fucks up and somebody loses their home. The DOE fucks up and you lose cities."

In the tradition of the Manhattan Project, Y-12 was very compartmentalized. There were 80 federal employees from the Department of Energy on site, but most of Y-12's workforce of 7,400 people, from the machinists to the janitors, was employed by B&W Y-12—a partnership between Babcock & Wilcox and Bechtel National, which combined had $6.6 billion in government contracts. The arrangement of government-owned, contractor-operated nuclear facilities was the norm, and had been since the Manhattan Project. Over decades, an inherent trust developed between the government and its contractors. It was termed "faith-based management." Management contractors came and went over the years as corporate conglomerates bid and lost the contract. There was ever-present instability. The top leadership of both Y-12 and the Department of Energy was always turning over, but the vast majority of workers continued in their normal jobs without much interference from their new overlords. These workers, secure in their ability to ride out management storms, called themselves "WeBe's."

As in, "We be here when you come, we be here when you go."

Relations could be frosty between the WeBe's—many of whom had worked at the site for decades—and the protective force. Federal officials were viewed as meddlesome Washington assholes who didn't know the first thing about protecting and processing special nuclear material. "DOE," to some of the guard force, stood for "Department of Evil." Distrust spread like a cancer. Y-12 and the other sites in the complex felt as far away psychologically from Washington as they did physically. The WeBe's and the SPOs were guided by different rules imposed by different bosses and monitored by different unions. Sometimes management conflicts triggered work stoppages, which meant that SPOs abandoned their posts in the name of union solidarity.

Money was paramount. Pointing out flaws in the system was not only secondary but also potentially harmful to a status quo that kept the paychecks coming and the profits up. Safety was considered "nonproductive" work and took a backseat to operations that produced product, progress, and profit. The result was little fiefdoms, spread over the country, containing nuclear material and managed by for-profit enterprises. Performance bonuses were tied to scores received during a training scenario, but the bonuses were divided up at the management level. The SPOs, if they scored well, would get a turkey or a honey-baked ham at Thanksgiving, or a pizza party where they were allowed two slices each. Hearing about a manager buying a 90-foot boat with his bonus wasn't much incentive to give 110 percent during the normal course of work.

At a March 2012 threat meeting attended by security officials from the DOE and their counterparts from the United Kingdom, B&W Y-12 announced the downgrading of perimeter resources. Forget the fences and the PIDAS, said B&W's manager of risk assessment. "We will accept risk in detection. The fight begins at the skin of the MAA," or material access areas, he said—meaning the HEUMF itself. The primary initial defense would be its white concrete walls, which were allegedly impenetrable.

And five days before the 2012 break-in, WSI confirmed that it was cutting as many as 34 security police officers from Y-12.

"WILL YOU LISTEN to our message?"

The old woman had spoken first, after bowing to him. She was holding a single piece of white paper.

Kirk's driver's-side window was down. He ordered them to stop, keep their hands out. "How did you get in here?" Kirk asked.

"God led us here," said one of the men, who was wearing glasses, with a peculiar matter-of-factness. They began to take turns reading from the paper, which was titled in bold capital letters A STATEMENT FOR THE Y-12 FACILITY and signed with their names, followed by the name of their action: TRANSFORM NOW PLOWSHARES.

"Brothers and sisters, powers that be, we come to you today as friends, in love," the intruders said.

Kirk's cell phone rang and he answered it from inside the car. It was his supervising lieutenant. "I've got three individuals here who have appeared to have breached our system," Kirk said, "and they've written graffiti all over the walls."

His lieutenant thought he was kidding.

"I'm not. I'm telling you what I got. They're peace protesters. You better send some backup."

The intruders asked Kirk if he wanted to read the message out loud, and continued when he declined: "A loving and compassionate creator invites us to take the urgent and decisive steps to transform the U.S. empire, and this facility, into life-giving alternatives which resolve real problems of poverty and environmental degradation for all."

Kirk exited his vehicle but didn't move to restrain the intruders. He was outnumbered. They appeared non-threatening and identical to the activists he had dealt with at Rocky Flats. There were a couple of backpacks behind them, some papers blowing in the early-morning breeze, a pool of floodlight encircling them. Kirk's mind was racing. He turned around, reached back into the car, and turned off the engine. He didn't pull his gun. Neither his life nor nuclear material felt at risk, and he knew the guys in the towers now had him covered with heavier artillery.

"We bring our life symbols: blood, for healing and pouring out our lives in service and love," they said. "Our very humanity depends on lives given, not taken. But blood also reminds us of the horrific spilling of blood by nuclear weapons."

One of the men went to a backpack. He withdrew candles and lit them and gave one to the other man. Then they wanted to break bread with Kirk. They had a loaf with a cross carved into the top. It had been four minutes since Kirk had called for backup. He paced, scanning the area, as they continued to recite their indictment.

At 4:40 a.m., another Tahoe pulled around the northeast corner of the HEUMF and approached the scene. Sergeant Chad T. Riggs flipped on the emergency lights and exited the driver's seat almost before his vehicle had come to a complete stop. He drew his gun but kept it aimed at the ground as he ordered the intruders to show their hands, lie on the ground, and crawl away from their backpacks. It appeared to him to be an act of vandalism, but he wasn't taking any chances. He had never seen this type of thing in his eight years at Y-12, and Kirk seemed too relaxed for the circumstances. Riggs called their supervisor for more ground units. SPOs were trained to anticipate an unseen sniper in intruder situations, so Riggs asked Kirk to cover him as he donned his body armor and retrieved a rifle from his truck. Then Riggs covered Kirk as he did the same. Two more SPOs arrived and they restrained the trio with plastic handcuffs and leg cuffs. The intruders began to sing "This Little Light of Mine."

"Shut up," barked one of the officers.

Other vehicles arrived over the next few hours carrying grim-faced managers and officials. Repeated announcements echoed between the HEUMF and Pine Ridge: This site is under lockdown. BearCats and special response teams were sent on patrol. Additional guards with M4 rifles and body armor were deployed with vehicle-borne Dillon Aero mini-guns to the site entrance. Dawn was breaking over Bear Creek Valley.

The activists sang "Down by the Riverside" and "Peace Is Flowing Like a River" as they waited.

K9 tracking units sniffed out the pathway of incursion and searched the woods for other intruders. The officers retrieved folding chairs and sat the trio near the defaced wall of the HEUMF. Special agents from the Department of Energy arrived to make the actual arrests. The agents started asking questions.

What are your names? Did you act alone?

Site workers duct-taped blue tarp over the graffiti, which would be power-scrubbed away by the following day by workers wearing booties, coveralls, gloves, and face shields. Y-12 spent the rest of Saturday trying to determine whether there were further threats, if these kooky activists were merely a diversion for something bigger. They wouldn't find Michael's UN hard hat until a few weeks later. They wouldn't repair the boundary fence over the ridge until December.

Just past 10 a.m., a full five hours after they had first been detained, the intruders were restrained with metal handcuffs, patted down, herded into a van, and taken to Blount County jail. There, Greg called one of their supporters. After so much radio silence, the support group didn't know if something had gone very right or very wrong.

"And we went right through the perimeter lethal zone," Greg said on the phone. "And we are lucky to be alive."

Sister Megan made her own call.

"We did everything we wanted to do," she told a supporter. "It's a miracle."

The government would have another word to describe the incident: "catastrophe."

PART II

REACTION

===

War is too important to be left to politicians.

BRIG. GEN. JACK D. RIPPER, *Dr. Strangelove, or:
How I Learned to Stop Worrying and Love the Bomb*

6.

WASHINGTON

Appalling."
"Bizarre."
"Incredible."
"Keystone Cops."
"Mind-boggling incompetence."

The congressmen were in a contest of indignation. One leaned into his microphone and peered over his glasses at the old woman in the gallery. It was six weeks after she had snuck into the Fort Knox of Uranium.

"Would you please stand up, ma'am?" said Rep. Joe Barton (R-Texas).

Sister Megan rose from her seat next to Michael.

"We want to thank you for pointing out some of the problems in our security," Barton said. "While I don't totally disa—don't totally agree with your platform that you were espousing, I do thank you for bringing up the inadequacies of our security system, and thank you for being here today. Mr. Chairman, that young lady there brought a Holy Bible. If she had been a terrorist, the Lord only knows what could have happened."

Another Republican congressman from Texas, Michael Burgess,

was alarmed at the presence of Plowshares activists in the Rayburn House Office Building on Capitol Hill.

"I don't understand why these individuals are free to be here in the hearing room today," Burgess said. "Why are they not incarcerated? My understanding is they've been charged with both criminal trespass, which is a misdemeanor, and destruction of federal property, which is a felony. . . . Why are they not being held in detention somewhere? What is to prevent them from doing the very same thing tomorrow night or the night after?"

Rep. Edward Markey (D-Mass.), who had begun introducing nuclear-freeze resolutions 30 years prior, addressed Sister Megan later on in the hearing.

"Thank you, Sister Megan Rice, for being here," said Markey, a product of 20 years of Catholic schooling in the Boston area. "Thank you for your actions. Thank you for your willingness to focus attention on this nuclear weapons buildup that still exists in our world and how much we need to do something to reduce it. We don't need more nuclear weapons. We need fewer nuclear weapons. We don't need more hostility with Russia. We need less hostility with Russia. We thank you. We thank you for your courage."

Megan and Michael watched the hearing with compassionate contempt. Their presence in Rayburn 2123 was an act of bearing witness. They looked more attentive than the congressmen themselves, who arrived late—if they arrived at all—and left early, after delivering a statement of general outrage. The lack of attendance and vigor at these hearings was typical of Congress's relationship to nuclear weapons. On Capitol Hill, there are never formal debates about strategy and doctrine: Why do we have nukes and what are we doing with them? The focus is instead on budgets and operations in a fiscal environment hobbled by caps and "continuing resolutions," which are passed to fund the government while Congress bickers over the debt and the deficit.

Rep. Jeff Fortenberry (R-Neb.), who had organized a nuclear-security caucus in the House, had a favorite anecdote to describe Congress's inattention to the weapons. One day, during his first years in office, he was dashing between two simultaneous hearings—one on nukes in North Korea and one on Iran's nuclear ambitions. Both had only a handful of members in attendance, yet there was a long line to get into a hearing on the merger between Sirius and XM Satellite Radio.

"Congress reacts to crisis and urgency," Fortenberry would say at various nuclear panels and conferences around D.C. "And with this we *can't* have a crisis. We *can't* respond to it. Look what happened when planes flew into buildings." Two wars. The USA Patriot Act. A tectonic shift in American society, and in America's relationship to the rest of the world. And only buildings were lost, not cities. There were government officials on September 11 who were relieved that the attacks were not nuclear in nature, that they involved only jets and gasoline, given that Osama bin Laden had called for a Hiroshima in the United States. "As unfathomable as this was," said Vice President Dick Cheney as debris from the collapsed World Trade Center billowed through the canyons of Manhattan, "it could have been so much worse if they had weapons of mass destruction."

The break-in at Y-12, while far from terrorism, summoned disturbing what-ifs.

"It is simply fucking unbelievable," said the Project on Government Oversight's Peter Stockton, who called it the only serious penetration of a weapons plant in his 30-plus years watchdogging nuclear security. He claimed that with the same uninterrupted access to the secure area, terrorists could have blown through the doors or walls of the HEUMF with an explosively formed penetrator. They could have rigged a dirty bomb or an improvised nuclear device using highly enriched uranium and conventional explosives. And although the chances of success are tiny, a terrorist could drop one properly shaped 100-pound chunk of highly enriched uranium from a height of six feet onto another 100-pound chunk, and perhaps trigger a blast of five to ten kilotons.

A ten-kiloton detonation at Y-12—roughly two-thirds the strength of the one at Hiroshima—would kill an estimated 18,000 people and injure 42,000 in East Tennessee. Radiation would sicken people within 40 miles. It was the type of scenario that the commander in chief had been worrying about for years, ever since he began writing about nuclear war as a college student in Manhattan.

A 21-YEAR-OLD BARACK OBAMA, in his final semester at Columbia University in 1983, wrote an article titled "Breaking the War Mentality" for a student newspaper.

"Most students at Columbia do not have first hand knowledge of war" was his first sentence.

Obama wrote about campus activism and "military-industrial interests" and "their billion dollar erector sets." He expressed opposition to the arms race. He endorsed the nuclear-freeze movement. He referenced the previous year's million-person march in Central Park. The "most pervasive malady" in both college culture and the world at large, he wrote, "is that elaborate patterns of knowledge and theory have been disembodied from individual choices and government policy." Student activists are "adding their energy and effort in order to enhance the possibility of a decent world" so "they may help deprive us of a spectacular experience—that of war. But then, there are some things we shouldn't have to live through in order to want to avoid the experience." His last sentence envisioned a peace "that is genuine, lasting and non-nuclear."

Obama's senior seminar paper, for which he got an A, was about the Cold War and disarmament prospects. The reduction and elimination of nuclear arsenals made sense to Obama, who had been exposed to Christian ethics in grade school.

During World War II his grandfather was deployed to France in the weeks after the invasion of Normandy. In Wichita his grandmother worked as an inspector on a Boeing assembly line for B-29s, which were used to firebomb Japan. Obama's childhood teachers had marched in the movements for civil rights and against the Vietnam War. He was a product of those parallel fights but a student of the Reagan years, when a whole range of Americans mobilized against an out-of-control arsenal.

When the Cold War ended, America's understanding of the world's balance of power ended, too. George H. W. Bush and Mikhail Gorbachev signed the Strategic Arms Reduction Treaty (START) in 1991 to lower the number of deployed warheads, and Bush's follow-on presidential initiatives curbed the U.S. arsenal even more. The Soviet Union declared a moratorium on testing that year, and the United States followed suit, conducting its last underground explosive test in September 1992, at the Nevada Test Site. Closing and cleaning contaminated sites like Rocky Flats was a top priority. Nuclear weapons weren't dismantled alongside the Berlin Wall, but they were consigned to history anyway.

This alarmed the Department of Energy's labs and contractors, who were suddenly facing their own obsolescence.

Around the same time, an international push was afoot for a treaty that would outlaw any kind of nuclear testing. The labs and contractors, whose political power stemmed from arming the Pentagon with the ultimate weapon, would make way for the treaty only if they received a second lease on life. The DOE obliged by recasting its nuclear mission around the concept of "science-based stockpile stewardship," which was a fancy way of saying that any testing would be simulated in labs or on computers, or conducted subcritically—that is, just short of a nuclear chain reaction. The program would certify the reliability and safety of the stockpile without actual testing. President Bill Clinton and Congress determined the ongoing need for nuclear weapons, and in 1996 Y-12 was ordered to continue its weapons-production mission. The complex had found a reason to work ambitiously beyond the Cold War, just as it had after World War II.

As Obama taught constitutional law in Chicago, wave elections in 1992 and '94 flushed institutional knowledge and nuclear memory out of both houses of Congress. Clinton's first secretary of energy, Hazel O'Leary, had no experience with the weapons complex, which in 1993 took up 68 percent of the department's budget. The sword of Damocles was still hanging, though, as was made clear by a breathtaking incident in 1995.

At dawn on January 25, NASA launched a research rocket from a Norwegian island to study the northern lights. Such launches were routine, but Norway's letter of advance notice had gotten lost in Moscow's bureaucratic shuffle. The rocket was bigger than normal, and on Russian radar it looked like a nuclear missile from a U.S. submarine. Unlike the 1983 incident, when the bogey was sunlight and the call was made by a lieutenant colonel in a bunker, this situation reached the Kremlin. An alert was sent to Boris Yeltsin's nuclear-command suitcase, from which the president could authorize a launch. Yeltsin had about eight minutes to approve a retaliatory attack before Russia's own command system was devastated. It was a Cold War tension in the post–Cold War age. The incident that triggered the first major restructuring of the U.S. nuclear-weapons complex was more mundane but made bigger headlines.

In December 1999, while Obama was in the Illinois Senate writing legislation on guns and racial profiling, a Taiwanese American nuclear scientist named Wen Ho Lee was indicted on 59 counts for the "intent to injure the United States." He was accused of leaking to China classified nuclear information on the W88 warhead, the most sophisticated American nuclear bomb. At Los Alamos National Laboratory, where he had worked since 1978, Lee modeled simulations of nuclear detonations—an artificial version of the work that Robert Oppenheimer had performed at the same location during the Manhattan Project. When the FBI found illegally downloaded weapons data on Lee's desk at Los Alamos, he was held in solitary confinement for nine months.

A presidential advisory board had recently issued a scathing investigation of the Department of Energy titled *Science at Its Best; Security at Its Worst*. The weapons complex had been set up to fail, the report concluded, ever since the Atomic Energy Commission was dissolved and its work eventually reassigned to the newly created DOE in 1977. And it had since failed time and time again.

The report itemized the screwups: Thousands of pounds of nuclear material were unaccounted for, classified computing practices were wobbly, security officers failed basic tests like firing weapons, lag times for site repairs were epic. At weapons facilities with sensitive information, it took nearly three years for the DOE to replace a broken lock. The department was "saturated with cynicism, an arrogant disregard for authority, and a staggering pattern of denial," the report said. The DOE's main role was just writing checks that were then cashed without oversight by labs and contractors. The advisory panel recommended that the weapons complex be restructured, that it be placed in a "semi-autonomous" agency within the DOE that had "a clear mission, streamlined bureaucracy, and drastically simplified lines of authority and accountability."

The government's solution to a bureaucratic problem was more bureaucracy.

Now, in the Wen Ho Lee case, there was a scandal to bear out the panel's findings and fast-track a restructuring. Leading the charge were Republican officials who had DOE sites in their districts. Rep. Mac Thornberry (R-Texas), who represented Amarillo and the Pantex Plant, wanted to make the sites more accountable to Washington. Pete Domenici, the Republican senior senator from New Mexico, wanted to protect the independence of DOE's Albuquerque office. Domenici was nicknamed "Saint Pete" for his pork-barrel power. The DOE was one of the largest employers in New Mexico, and Saint Pete was chairman of the Senate subcommittee on energy and water appropriations. With Rep. Ellen Tauscher (D–Calif.) and senators Jon Kyl (R–Ariz.) and Frank Murkowski (R–Alaska), they compromised and drew up plans for the National Nuclear Security Administration (NNSA), which would be within the Department of Energy but semi-autonomous—akin to the FBI and the Department of Justice.

"To set up a new fiefdom in the department of fiefdoms is not what I need," DOE secretary Bill Richardson told Congress.

The National Nuclear Security Administration Act of 2000 listed under its auspices three national security laboratories, including Los Alamos in New Mexico, and five nuclear-weapons production facilities, including Y-12 in Tennessee. The act also absolved contractors of any responsibility to the DOE except to the secretary himself. Critics saw this as brilliant bureaucratic sleight of hand, an attempt to circle the wagons as the Cold War receded into the past.

In an outside assessment of the NNSA a dozen years later, its semi-autonomy would be described as "a birth defect."

AS THE UNITED STATES invaded Iraq in 2003, on the hunt for weapons of mass destruction, the 10,000 nuclear weapons at home were an afterthought. Commanders were focused on overseas missions. Military units, including those that oversaw warheads at home, were sapped by repeated deployments. The importance of strategic deterrence was obscured by more pressing tactical worries.

Obama, now in his sixth year as an Illinois state senator, was fashioning himself as an antiwar politician with an asterisk. He was not opposed to all wars; he was opposed to "dumb wars." And Iraq was a dumb war, he said in a speech. Obama disqualified Iraq as an imminent threat. Instead, he said, America should be worried about al-Qaeda and the security of nuclear material.

When Obama was elected to the U.S. Senate in 2004, his top three priorities were energy, education, and nuclear nonproliferation. With fellow senator Richard Lugar (R-Ind.), Obama inspected Russian weapons facilities and visited former Soviet sites in Ukraine and Azerbaijan, where security was weak and munitions were splayed around.

"Many of these aging research facilities have the largest, least-secure quantities of highly enriched uranium in the world—the quickest way to a nuclear weapon," Obama said in 2005. "For a scientist or other employee to simply walk out of a lab with enough material to construct a weapon of mass destruction is far too easy, and the consequences would be far too devastating."

A year and a half later he was running for president. Obama and his team envisioned their campaign as something broader and deeper. It was a movement, with "change" as its theme. The goals were to exorcise Washington of its partisanship and reestablish the United States' moral standing in a world that had recoiled from its conduct in Iraq. Nuclear weapons weren't a national topic of conversation, and candidate Obama wanted to change that.

He had a quartet of political mandarins on his side: former Georgia senator Sam Nunn, former secretary of defense William Perry, and former secretaries of state Henry Kissinger and George Shultz. In January 2007, a month before Obama declared his candidacy, the bipartisan quartet co-authored an editorial in the *Wall Street Journal* titled "A World Free of Nuclear Weapons." It was a rare marquee moment for nuclear weapons in the 21st century. It had extra resonance because Kissinger, as Nixon's right-hand man, had pondered using nuclear weapons in Vietnam and Shultz, in Reagan's State Department, was party to the last big arms buildup.

Unless "urgent new actions are taken, the U.S. soon will be compelled to enter a new nuclear era that will be more precarious, psychologically disorienting, and economically even more costly than was Cold War deterrence," wrote "the four horsemen of the nuclear apocalypse," as they would be called henceforth. They anticipated a "new and dangerous nuclear era" defined by terrorism. They quoted Eisenhower, Kennedy, and Reagan, each of whom preached against nukes but deepened the United States' commitment to them.

Candidate Obama wanted to be the president who broke that cycle. A little more than a year later, a full generation after the fall of the Soviet Union, the peace-minded former community organizer was elected to be the person who commands the arsenal. Between his election and inauguration, Obama said that the threat of nuclear weapons was "just as grave" as the economic crisis then roiling the United States. Protecting the American people was his foremost responsibility, and the foremost threat was the spread of these weapons.

One of Obama's first major priorities as president of the United States was to deliver a watershed speech on the topic. The writing of that speech was entrusted to a 31-year-old whose first memory of nukes was the movie *WarGames*.

BEN RHODES GREW UP in Manhattan during the last decade of the Cold War. From a young age he knew that the city was a target, just by virtue of its size and prominence in American life. His family's apartment building had those little yellow-and-black fallout-shelter signs. He saw *WarGames* on VHS and it made an impression on him. Here was a young character who exploits a vulnerability in the high-tech systems that govern the most dangerous tools on the planet, sending phantom Soviet missiles arcing over the North Pole. It was terrifying.

After college, Ben worked for Lee Hamilton, a former congressman who was a member of the Iraq Study Group and the 9/11 Commission, which noted that two dozen terrorist groups were pursuing weapons of mass destruction. The commission envisioned a nuclear version of September 11 involving a grapefruit-size amount of plutonium or highly enriched uranium.

"A little bomb like that," Enrico Fermi had said 60 years prior, "and it would all disappear."

Hamilton was one of those old Washington hands who wanted to rid the world of nuclear weapons, and Ben got to know the real-world issues that underpinned the Hollywood entertainment of his youth. He joined the Obama campaign in its early days as the go-to guy for foreign policy. Then he was the go-to guy for the president's first overseas speech, which would be delivered in Prague. Whatever Obama said would set the tone for his first year as leader of the free world.

Not even four months into his presidency, Obama was riding a wave of goodwill, and the White House wanted to capitalize on it. The staff settled on nuclear weapons as the topic. The policy had already been fully shaped during the campaign. It applied to the whole world and it would resonate with the Czechs, who had shaken off Communist rule through a nonviolent revolution. The plan was to focus on nuclear weapons but open with the lessons of Prague politics: how people can do the impossible, without firing a shot, if they are willing to make the effort and keep their eyes on the prize. Ben had a week to write the speech, and he was still editing it as the staff was departing London for Prague. The morning of the speech, word came that North Korea had fired a rocket over Japanese airspace. It was a reminder that the president's utopian vision needed a healthy dose of realism.

Hours later, in Hradčany Square, with the dome and belfry of the baroque Church of St. Nicholas behind him, Obama delivered his soaring oratory to tens of thousands. Nearly half the 3,200-word speech focused on nuclear weapons:

> Today, the Cold War has disappeared but thousands of those weapons have not. In a strange turn of history, the threat of global nuclear war has gone down, but the risk of a nuclear attack has gone up. More nations have acquired these weapons. Testing has continued. Black-market trade in nuclear secrets and nuclear materials abound. The technology to build a bomb has spread. Terrorists are determined to buy, build or steal one. . . . Some argue that the spread of these weapons cannot be stopped, cannot be checked—that we are destined to live in a world where more nations and more people possess the ultimate tools of destruction. Such fatalism is a deadly adversary, for if we believe that the spread of nuclear weapons is inevitable, then in some way we are admitting to ourselves that the *use* of nuclear weapons is inevitable. . . . [And] as the only nuclear power to have used a nuclear weapon, the United States has a moral responsibility to act. We cannot succeed in this endeavor alone, but we can lead it. We can start it. So today, I state clearly and with conviction America's commitment to seek the peace and security of a world without nuclear weapons.

The crowd cheered and waved small American flags. The rest of the speech contained a plan, a hedge, and a paradox. The plan was itemized and specific: Negotiate a new arms treaty with Russia before the end of the year, get the U.S. Senate to ratify the Comprehensive Nuclear-Test-Ban Treaty, strengthen the existing Nuclear Non-Proliferation Treaty, proceed with a missile-defense system to counter Iran's belligerence, and ensure that terrorists never acquire a nuclear weapon.

"I'm not naive," the president said after all this, delivering his hedge. "This goal will not be reached quickly—perhaps not in my lifetime."

Then came the paradox: "As long as these weapons exist, the United States will maintain a safe, secure, and effective arsenal to deter any adversary, and guarantee that defense to our allies."

To the White House, there was nothing paradoxical about this statement. It was something that needed to be said to an audience of Czechs, because their country, as a NATO member, relied on extended U.S. deterrence. The president couldn't stand in the geographical center of Europe and say that the United States was going to get rid of its nukes before Russia did.

Though the Prague speech made no promises beyond seeking a world without nuclear weapons, it branded Obama as an anti-nuclear president in the eyes of longtime activists.

That October he won the Nobel Peace Prize, chiefly for his vision of a "world without nuclear weapons." The following year, though, he made a political deal that ensured that the United States would indeed have nuclear weapons well past his lifetime.

To get the Senate's consent for the ratification of the New START treaty in 2010, Obama agreed to request $90 billion to modernize the nuclear-weapons complex. The Prague speech never promised disarmament, but peace activists and the nuclear-zero crowd saw this move as hypocritical, as a deal with the devil. The modernization plan would fund "life-extension programs," a euphemistic term for the refurbishment of warheads. The plan would build a new fleet of Ohio-class submarines, which carried Trident missiles armed with warheads capable of 100-kiloton blasts. These subs would be operational until at least the year 2080—a surprising investment given that a fundraising letter for Obama's Senate campaign said that he opposed "building a new generation of nuclear weapons." The plan would also continue sweeping up and tightening the weapons complex, which had sprawled all over the country since the Manhattan Project.

It was now simply too large, too dirty, and too faulty. The complex of the future would be lean and tight, with ever-lessening chances of accident or incident. That was the plan, anyway.

THE PHONE RANG at 7:25 a.m., but Neile Miller was already up and packing for a trip. Her family was in Europe for a two-week vacation and she was taking a flight that evening to join them. It was a Saturday—July 28, 2012—so when she heard her boss's voice on the other end, she thought someone had died.

"What's wrong?" she asked.

Fences had been cut at Y-12, Tom D'Agostino, the administrator of the NNSA, said to his deputy. There was graffiti on the HEUMF. Protesters.

Neile was stunned. This was bad. Tom was a former naval submarine officer, and Neile was a former budget analyst. They had years of experience in the trenches of national-security bureaucracy, so together they calmly outlined a short-term plan for gathering more information and alerting the Department of Energy and the White House. The rest of the day was a tense scramble for facts. The more Tom learned about the incident, the more concerned he became. The intruders were *how* old? *How* many cameras were broken? The security footage was sent to Washington. There, in grainy black and white, was an easy intrusion by three people whose average age was nearly 70. There was the slow and measured response by an officer named Kirk Garland. Watching the activists rummage through their bags and light candles, all while mere feet from the HEUMF—to veterans of nuclear security, it was like a horror film.

During World War II Neile's mother worked IBM machines for the military in New York City and assisted a professor at Columbia who was working on the Manhattan Project. When Neile was growing up in the Boston area during the Vietnam War, her parents tacked peace signage to their front door. She went off to study political science at Vassar in the late 1970s, when the energy crisis led to the creation of the federal department for which she'd eventually work. She was fascinated by the dual uses of nuclear science—energy and military—and got her graduate degree in international affairs at Georgetown. She started her Washington career analyzing nonproliferation issues at the Congressional Research Service, which serves as Congress's brain and memory, and then analyzed Department of Energy programs at the Office of Management and Budget as the Reagan arms buildup was ending. One stark difference between the departments of Defense and Energy was that the DOD had full-time analysts whose job was to follow the money, from a line item in a budget to every tool and widget that constructed a delivery system for a nuke. DOE didn't have that. Money flowed out of Washington to places like Y-12 and the Los Alamos lab, into the hands and pockets of contractors who were designing and machining the nuke. Decades after the Manhattan Project, obscurity was still the philosophy.

Neile was one of the few women in a male-dominated field. By the time she became deputy of the NNSA in 2010, she had seen all manner of sexism from the old guard, which wanted to preserve the complex as it was: well funded, privileged, with a surplus of warheads in various stages of storage and refurbishment—"a zoo of extremely wild animals," in the words of one former DOE policy adviser.

There were many people, of all ages, who wanted to reform the system. They wanted to bring the money out of the shadows, to wrest some control back from the labs and plants, which were accustomed to running the country's highest-priority mission. The reformers' mantra was "change or die," but this opposing ideological force thought "change *and* die." For two years Neile and others had tried to bring the weapons sites out of their own fiefdoms and into the same 21st-century mission. She had created an office of management and operations to do just that, several months before the break-in, but bureaucracy strives for stasis. Making change was a career-limiting gesture.

The secrecy of the Manhattan Project had given way over the years to a complicated operation that was just as compartmentalized but much clumsier. This bureaucracy was fueled by profit, out of step with geopolitics, off the radar of most of the American public, dizzied by a revolving door between feds and contractors, and hamstrung by the parochial concerns of a handful of congressmen.

The binding forces of this bureaucracy were inertia and chaos, and it was in charge of shepherding the ultimate power into the 21st century.

Its mission and its handicap were embodied in a spherical sculpture outside the Department of Energy building on Independence Avenue in downtown Washington. Made of granite, Robert Russin's *Chthonodynamis*—an ancient Greek word for the primal energy of the Earth—is an abstract representation of a humanoid figure trying to contain something powerful. The placard at its base says it "depicts man trying to hold together the immense forces of energy within the earth, energy that both nourishes and threatens all mankind."

Neile and Tom were of the same generation, born 18 months apart in the late 1950s—she a Jew from Boston, he a Catholic from D.C.— and in middle age their careers had led them both to this building.

Tom had spent part of his childhood in Las Vegas, the son of an engineer at the Nevada Test Site, which during the 1960s was the prime U.S. location for atomic detonations (the large-scale tests in the Marshall Islands had ceased in 1958). One evening after dinner, when he was about seven years old, his father placed a glass of water, filled to the brim, on the kitchen table.

Tomorrow morning come in here, he told his kids, *and if we shook the ground really hard, you'll see some water spilled out.*

Tom stayed up late that night and felt a quiet tremor from out in

the desert. The next morning, sure enough, there was water surrounding the base of the glass. It was a small manifestation of the
work being done to counter the Soviet threat.

At 16 he entered the Naval Academy, and at 21, in 1980, he found
himself training to work on submarines, which patrolled the oceans
on the propulsive power of a controlled chain reaction. Reagan was
ascendant. The Plowshares movement would soon go after subs in
port. It was irritating that activists were making a hard job even
harder, but Tom was focused on the task at hand: keeping his sub
operating and secure on seven-month deployments at 300 feet under
the ocean's surface. Down there, you would get no more than four
hours of sleep at any given time and couldn't tell if it was day or
night. Down there you learned to respect the machine that protected
you from the ocean, which was trying to get in all the time, any way
it could.

After eight years on active duty, Tom joined the Department of
the Navy to help oversee the design and production of new engines
for the submarine force, but then the Berlin Wall fell and the government reduced its order from 30 engines to five. Tom moved to the
DOE, where he would remain for the next 22 years. He was nominated by George W. Bush in 2007 to be the administrator of the
NNSA and stayed on when Obama took office and challenged government agencies to be more efficient. This was interpreted within
the NNSA as reducing the cost of the mission while increasing safety,
security, and performance.

Every morning after his workout, Tom read the Bible for ten minutes at his desk at DOE headquarters. He liked Isaiah 43. It reassured
him that in the throes of chaos, God was still in control: "When you
walk through the fire, you will not be burned; the flames will not set
you ablaze."

He liked Hebrews 12. Part of it encapsulated the mission of nuclear security: "No discipline seems pleasant at the time, but painful. Later on, however, it produces a harvest of righteousness and peace for those who have trained by it."

Do the job right and the right things would happen, Tom had told himself. He had spent five years working to eliminate the possibility of an incident like the one on July 28, 2012.

It could've been worse. No one was injured in the lethal-force zone. No nuclear material was ever at risk. The activists' hammers chipped off a few small chunks of concrete from a building that was designed to withstand the impact of a 747. The intruders could have been hostile. A guard could have shot one of the activists or been shot himself. But "the event," as contractors and officials referred to it, got nowhere close to danger.

Nevertheless, there was a flurry of secure video teleconferences between the site and Washington. The NNSA alerted Sen. Bob Corker's office by 9:50 a.m. that day. One Corker staffer responded, "Did these folks get close enough to touch HEUMF? This would be a big concern about security." Reporter Frank Munger, who thought he had seen it all while covering the DOE and Oak Ridge for 30 years for the *Knoxville News Sentinel*, called the breach "unprecedented." He asked Y-12's spokesman, Steve Wyatt, if the age of the intruders was an added embarrassment. Wyatt responded, "The protesters put themselves at a high risk of losing their life in performing the act. We are thankful that did not occur." Security officials knew that if the system had worked properly, these activists might have been killed in action.

The HEUMF was perhaps the most impenetrable building on the planet, site managers reminded their federal overlords during the days following. There was never a chance that intruders could've gotten *into* the building. No one thought this type of thing would ever happen at Y-12, so they weren't equipped to handle it once it did. Y-12 shut down its operations for 15 days. Production activities were halted

August 1 and the uranium undergoing processing was placed into vaults. More than 400 security police officers and supervisors were required to take refresher courses on basic security practices over four 12-hour days.

E-mails were traded about the feds' "eyes on, hands off" attitude toward the weapons sites. There were situational reports, two-week plans, batteries of camera tests, and discussions via BlackBerry on how contractors B&W and WSI operated on their own.

WSI blamed B&W for busted cameras and false alarms, and B&W blamed WSI for nonchalant alarm station operators and guards. The level of malfunction at Y-12 had been routine for at least two years, though the government's most recent performance evaluation gave WSI high marks in all performance categories. For the previous two years, B&W received more than 90 percent of the annual $53 million in award fees that it was eligible for.

WSI's contract was placed under B&W's, to straighten the lines of authority. The security force underwent two intensive training exercises and adopted a more paramilitary attitude. Union reps started complaining that management was "working people to death." Senator Bob Corker toured the area of the breach, received a classified briefing, and concluded that human error was the culprit.

Personnel were added to Y-12's central alarm station. False alarms were reduced by 80 percent. Repairs were now required to be made within 24 hours. NNSA officials deployed to Capitol Hill for contentious meetings with congressional committee staffers. In a call with NNSA staff, Sen. Dianne Feinstein (D-Calif.) proposed that a list of nuclear facilities be shared with Google so that they could be removed from Google Maps and Google Earth.

Secretary of Energy Steven Chu called the break-in "deeply troubling" and "unacceptable."

Congressional committees sent letters to Secretary Chu and Tom that began, "The committee is gravely concerned."

It wasn't, in fact, a catastrophe, but it could've been. And that was nearly as bad.

IN THE 48 HOURS after the event, Kirk Garland was praised by WSI for his steady reaction to an unprecedented security situation. By that Monday, when he was called in to give a statement, management's tone had changed. His superior asked him to surrender his handgun. His union said that they were starting an investigation, but Kirk felt that something was up. On August 10 he was summoned to WSI's Oak Ridge headquarters and handed a letter. Certain phrases hit him like punches to the gut.

". . . failed in your responsibilities . . ."

"Your blatant disregard for the seriousness of the situation . . ."

". . . failure to take immediate control of the intruders . . ."

". . . terminating your employment effective immediately . . ."

He began to protest to Steve Gibbs, WSI's deputy general manager, who over 34 years at Y-12 had worked his way up from a guard post to the security force's No. 2 guy. Gibbs's grandmother had worked at Y-12 during World War II. He had served in the Air Force and been called a baby killer by peace activists on his way back from Vietnam. He entered nuclear security a couple of years before Kirk did, and what Gibbs had seen on the video sickened him. This incident, in the twilight of his career, had cut him to the core.

The decision is made, Gibbs said to Kirk.

Kirk lost his job then and there, with his health insurance set to expire within a month. That same day, B&W's top two senior leaders were allowed to retire: Darrel P. Kohlhorst, president and general manager, and William R. Klemm, deputy general manager of operations. "Darrel is a great American and will be missed by me, and I'm sure all of you," said his replacement, Chuck Spencer, in a message to Y-12 employees on August 11 that quickly turned to a caution: "We must become more focused than ever before, because another lapse in focus would be devastating." When he arrived on site, Spencer saw a workforce plagued by sorrow and denial. Y-12 employees had their heads down. The security event was devastating to morale. Local talk radio and social media crackled with anger and ridicule.

B&W's vice president for safeguards and security retired after being relieved of his duties. The top two guys at WSI were removed from their positions and reassigned. Steve Gibbs retired by the end of the year. Two operators in the central alarm station, a security police officer in one of the HEUMF's towers, and the supervising lieutenant were temporarily reassigned. Tom D'Agostino's multiple offers to resign from the NNSA were rebuffed by DOE higher-ups.

Kirk knew that if he'd shot or killed someone, especially an activist, he'd be on his own—maybe even arrested and charged. The Code of Federal Regulations said that deadly force was authorized only in self-defense or to prevent the theft or sabotage of special nuclear material. But to be hung out to dry for resolving a pacifist situation with arrests? The fault was with contractor management, which was more focused on cutting patrol jobs than on fixing cameras. B&W had rushed a new alarm system into operation so it could collect a "performance-based incentive" bonus, never mind that it wasn't properly integrated with the old system. Y-12 was also gummed up by paperwork. Repairs took three to four months. There was widespread cheating on written exams for guards, and managers looked the other way because bad grades meant missed bonuses. The fault was with a system that had gotten lazy and complacent and money-hungry, that had misread a clumsy hybrid alarm system and then dispatched a single officer to an area where there was clearly a pathway of intrusion. Kirk had been an alarm system operator at Rocky Flats for 12 years, and if there was a camera out, you'd put a guard on the zone and get a technician to fix the device pronto, even during the middle of the night in a blinding snowstorm. He was trained to assess a threat, and three people carrying Bibles and bread did not require him to pull his weapon. In his mind, there *was* no threat.

The week after the breach, the NNSA prepared a background briefing for White House press secretary Jay Carney that emphasized that the trio had been "detected and caught," a definitive statement repeated throughout internal communications between Y-12 and NNSA staffers in the days following the event.

The activists were detected and caught.

And yet these reckless ideologues, who could have easily protested lawfully outside the front gate, were now complicit in the unraveling of a 30-year career devoted to the defense of the United States. Kirk was three years away from enjoying a retirement that his brother and father were robbed of. He felt he was due the same respect as a soldier who had served in Iraq or Afghanistan. Members of his family had protected the nation's nuclear assets going back to 1956 and had already paid a price. Because he was technically an employee of a private company, he could be fired quickly and cleanly. Federal employees were protected from such a fate.

A little reorganization at the manager level, a couple of retirements and reassignments, a quick termination letter for the first man on the scene. Case closed.

Suspicions lingered in the guard force. Did the intruders know which section of the fence had incomplete camera coverage? Did they know it was a shift change on the guard force? It was all too easy, too perfect. The more Kirk learned about the breach, the more he thought there had to be an insider who helped them. How else could they have exploited each weakness in the system? Perhaps one of the officers who was scheduled to be laid off decided to stick it to WSI one last time.

Kirk gave interviews asserting that he was a scapegoat for a humiliated management system. "Thank God Kirk didn't shoot" the protesters, his union rep Randy Lawson told the *Knoxville News Sen-*

tinel. "He would probably be in jail and being sued. . . . He was in a no–win situation."

Sister Megan, meanwhile, was telling the press that Kirk was mature and poised during their encounter, that he presented himself as a "thinking person" who never took his eyes off them and treated them with dignity.

In an e–mail to an NNSA colleague, Y–12 federal manager Steve Erhart referred to "the new post 7/28 world we now all live in," and "the assortment of risks that now present themselves that are above and beyond what we are accustomed to."

By October, Y–12 had detailed its improvements on a handout that included the site motto "Making the World Safer" and a photo of a security guard at the helm of a Gatling gun in the turret of a BearCat. Despite the two-week stand-down of operations, the handout said, Y–12 was having its most productive year delivering purified uranium metal for weapons and reserves.

In the week after the break-in, though, there were half a dozen incidents where officers failed in their duties, from abandoning posts without approval, to forgetting to set alarms, to allowing an Oak Ridge police cruiser without a DOE badge onto the site at night. Every officer involved was retrained and put back to work except one, who resigned voluntarily.

WSI's parent company, G4S, described itself as the largest security contractor in the world, and had already made headlines that summer by not providing the proper number of guards for the Summer Olympics in London. In January 2013, CEO Paul Donahue issued a statement on the break-in that was stinging in its starkness: "The enemy of today is not just organized Nation States, but vandals, activists and protesters looking not necessarily to harm material, or people, but clearly seeking to embarrass."

Adding to the embarrassment was the fact that Megan, Michael, and Greg seemed so anachronistic to government officials. These were activists from an earlier era who had decided decades ago that the root of all the world's problems was nuclear weapons. Their old-school tactics had breached a new-world order that had moved beyond nukes and grown more complicated. In the minds of some officials, the actions and arguments of Transform Now Plowshares were a kind of extremism. Their mental reasoning was not so far from that of jihadists, whose single-minded devotion to a cause climaxed in mayhem.

TWELVE DAYS AFTER THE BREAK-IN, while they were still in custody in Blount County jail, the intruders pleaded not guilty to charges of trespassing and destruction of property. Sister Megan didn't have her heart and thyroid medication in jail and was suffering from chills. Greg, who would spend a month in jail before being released, earned the nickname "Y-12" on the cell block. Michael and Megan were released within the week. They exited the jail wearing the same clothes they'd arrived in. Michael opened the door for Megan with a flourish. Megan bowed to the assembled supporters and journalists. The *Knoxville News Sentinel* was there with a video camera, and she addressed it:

> When I was 9 years old, I was aware that a huge secret thing was happening three minutes from where I lived in Manhattan. The man next door, a physicist and mathematician, professor, his name was Professor Selig Hecht. Next door. We knew he was doing something secret in his work and he couldn't even tell his wife what he was doing, nor his daughter. And to me that was the first message that there must be something very evil happening because how could a husband ever keep anything secret from his wife or his children, or vice versa? And secrecy has predominated this industry. This is why the whole country, the whole world,

have not stopped it. It's gone on for 70 years. We have the power and the love and the strength and the courage to end it and transform the whole project.

The press was interested in matters more granular than good and evil.

"Was it easier to get onto the property than you thought it would be?" a reporter asked outside the jail.

"Far," Megan responded. "We were led, miraculously."

"How does it feel to be free again today?" another reporter asked.

"More empowered to continue with the great people of humanity and all creation in transforming this into life-sustaining and -enhancing alternatives."

Then she, Michael, and two supporters embraced. "Nuclear weapons will be eradicated as an antichrist scourge from the Earth soon!" Michael said.

"Amen," said his supporters, but he wasn't done.

"Isaiah will be vindicated, weapons will be destroyed, war making will be abolished, and we will give peace a chance!"

The security event at Y-12 received brief mainstream media coverage outside Knoxville. On the day that Kirk Garland was fired, a profile of Megan appeared on the front page of the *New York Times*. The novelty of a felonious octogenarian nun was enough to grab people's attention for a second. Then it was easy to write off the trio as hippies who hadn't gotten the message that the Cold War was over.

ABOUT SEVEN MILES due north of the DOE headquarters is a house that Dorothy Day built. The Catholic Worker house in Washington, D.C., is named after Dorothy and sits on the paved-over hills that Abraham Lincoln once overlooked from his summer cottage. The paint on the Victorian house is a vibrant forest green. The colored tiles in the kitchen are arranged to depict the loaves and fishes. Out front is a garden with a white cross and a green NO WAR IN AFGHANI-STAN sign. There are irises, yuccas, tulips. A magnolia tree. Herbs growing in cinder blocks. A flag of the first photo of Earth taken from space. The crepe myrtle was once crushed by a falling pine, but nine trunks grew back in its place. Michael Walli is always doing yard work, or picking up litter in the neighborhood. This has been his home base since he arrived in Washington to protest the CIA in the 1980s.

Normally around 12 to 20 people live in the 12-bedroom house. A handful of volunteers, including Michael, get a personal stipend of $10 a month, plus $10 for the Metro. Every Monday at 7 a.m. they're at the Pentagon to greet and shame arriving workers. Every Thursday they're parked on 16th Street NW serving food to the hungry and the homeless. Every Friday at noon they're at the White House, holding signs.

SWORDS INTO PLOWSHARES.

STOP DROPPING BOMBS IN PAKISTAN.

9/11: AN INSIDE JOB TO LEAD TO WAR.

IF WE CAN MOVE ONE PERSON IT WILL BE WORTH IT.

"We beg you, God," they pray there in a circle, "to forgive us for the actions of the U.S. government."

Catholic Worker residents oppose all killing—war, abortion, capital punishment—and live in accordance with Dorothy Day's example. The patron saints at the house are a diverse crew, and their likenesses and quotations hang on the downstairs walls: Martin Luther King Jr., Edward Snowden, Oscar Romero, Rachel Corrie, Daniel Berrigan, Daniel Ellsberg, Gandhi, Chelsea Manning. In the dining room is the quote from Father Richard McSorley about nuclear weapons being "the taproot of evil." Multiple members of the Plowshares movement live there, or have cycled through at some point, each with his or her own story of miraculous intrusion.

"To me, it goes to not only the overhype, the oversell of the whole security mythology, but it goes to what you can do with an act of faith," said Michael's neighbor Paul Magno, a Plowshares veteran, in the months after the Y–12 action. "God's people can be faithful, and the Red Sea parts and lets them through, when there's no reason to believe that should be possible."

Shortly after Michael was arrested in Tennessee, FBI agents and DOE investigators started showing up unannounced at the Dorothy Day house and the homes of other peace activists in D.C., hoping to suss out who was involved in planning Transform Now Plowshares. It was an unnerving experience. There was the feeling of being watched, now that Michael was back home and Sister Megan was just ten minutes away at a residence of the Sisters of the Holy Child Jesus. Surveillance did not deter Megan and Michael from continuing their Transform Now campaign. They attended the Dorothy Day house's weekly "clarification of thought," as Sister Megan's parents had done 80 years before. And they attended congressional hearings over the fall and winter following their action.

On the day of one particular hearing, they took the Metro toward Capitol Hill together. Michael used the commute to try to educate the unsuspecting public.

"What's your main reason for opposing antichrist nuclear weapons?" he loudly asked Megan, though other passengers ignored them.

"Common sense," said Megan, the bromide to Michael's brimstone.

"What do you think of your fellow sisters who are sitting out their retirement in the convent?"

"We're all doing our part."

"You don't feel morally superior to them?"

"No."

On each of their field trips to the Hill, they got off at the Capitol South Metro station, with its giant ads for defense contractors. "Any threat, any mission," said one billboard for Raytheon, which was about to win a $45 million Navy contract to produce lightweight torpedoes.

"The antichrist!" Michael said, pointing to the ad.

They walked together along the enormous congressional office buildings. Megan was a little short of breath but she moved with determination. She had another date with the people whose lives she had disrupted.

"EMBARRASSMENT."

"Catastrophe."

"Bureaucratic back-stabbing."

"The system is broken."

Congress uttered and re-uttered the phrase "wake-up call." "Peace through strength" became a refrain. Over four congressional hearings on the break-in, the word "culture" was used 72 times to explain how a complex, highly funded operation could be vulnerable to pacifist senior citizens. Federal officials at the witness table got turned around in a maze of their own jargon. Megan and Michael witnessed the hearings in sweatpants, lost in the navy scrum of young legislative assistants.

On February 28, 2013, a House subcommittee tried to sniff out blame.

"And as the chairman correctly pointed out," said Rep. Jim Cooper (D-Tenn.) at one point, "it's hard to find that anybody was punished except the lowest-level guard."

Sister Megan took detailed notes in a spiral notebook and dressed them with her own thoughts.

"Time to break the pattern!"

"'This terrible action of July 28'!"

"New culture! Changes! Hopes!"

At a break, Megan approached one of the expert witnesses, retired

Major General C. Donald Alston, a former Air Force assistant chief
of staff for strategic deterrence and nuclear integration.

"I'll give this to you," she said, handing him a folded sheet of
white paper. It was a letter calling for the immediate suspension of
funding for the design and construction of the Uranium Processing
Facility at Y-12.

"The whole thing can be solved by changing the mission," Megan
said to the major general. "Change the mission, brother."

"We have a lot of stability in the world because of" nuclear weapons, said Alston, smiling, towering over her in uniform.

"It's impossible to even secure *one*," Megan said. "We can change
the mission. It's *possible*."

"Okay," he said.

"We can have projects that *sustain* humanity."

"Okay," he said, starting to leave the witness table.

"This is the nun," Michael said, coming to her side.

"*Oh*," Alston said, before turning away.

Megan was not concerned with this slight. The world needs posi-
tive *and* negative charges, she said. You can't have energy without
both.

Seventy years after their creation, nuclear weapons are
still a Rubik's Cube in the capital, and a small community of wonks
is still trying to game out their needs and relevance. And with good
reason: Washington views itself as the biggest bull's-eye in the world.

In congressional testimony in 2008, Harvard professor Matthew
Bunn described a mathematical model that demonstrated that the
danger of nuclear terrorism is high enough to have a "significant"
effect on the life expectancy of anyone who lives or works in downtown D.C. or Midtown Manhattan.

"A terrorist cell of relatively modest size, with no large fixed facilities that would draw attention, might well be able to pull off" a nuclear attack, Bunn testified, "and the world might never know until it was too late."

On any given day in Washington, you can spend an hour hearing experts jabber about nuclear weapons. Nuclear panels are hosted regularly by think tanks, on the sixth or eighth floor of boxy office buildings around downtown D.C. There's always coffee and pastries and sometimes sandwiches from Potbelly or Au Bon Pain. White-haired Cold Warriors show up, as do young PhD candidates in smart suits.

There is a "Bomber Support Community" of lawmakers and manufacturers that meets on Capitol Hill to champion the valor and service of B-2 and B-52 aircraft.

At Nukefest, the nickname for a nuclear-policy conference hosted by the Carnegie Endowment for International Peace, attendees order specialty coffee drinks called Go Ballistic, which is a triple shot of espresso, and the Thermonuclear, a latte with brown sugar and cinnamon syrup.

The latest gizmos in defense technology are on display at the yearly Air and Space Conference and Technology Exposition, where the coffee breaks are sponsored by Northrop Grumman and military officials give speeches about fighting the "mythology of anti-nuclear folks" by partnering with "allies" in private industry.

There are regular 8 a.m. nuclear breakfasts in the prim banquet rooms of the National Republican Club of Capitol Hill, where DOE officials and Navy admirals extoll the virtues of the triad while employees of Lockheed Martin and Los Alamos eat bacon and eggs.

Every year the nuclear priesthood gathers at a D.C. hotel for the Nuclear Deterrence Summit, which is sponsored by defense contractors and opens with a benediction by the NNSA administrator. The summit is four days of banal PowerPoint, which reduces the awesomeness of nuclear weapons to inscrutable charts and budget forecasts that are projected two sizes too small.

The mood at these events is both complacent and anxious. Nuclear weapons are used every single day, attendees believe. They establish deterrence, minute to minute, which keeps large-scale war at bay over generations. And their importance grows as their numbers shrink, especially given a recalcitrant Russia and a rising China.

"We must recognize the world as it is, and not as we hope it might be," said Robert Joseph, the former top arms-control official in George W. Bush's State Department, at one deterrence summit.

The consensus in Washington is that the world is well into its second nuclear age. There are fewer warheads on the planet but more countries with stockpiles of weapons and undersecured material. The new nuclear-arms race is based not on numbers—or even on explosive yield—but on capabilities. The United States is in a race with itself to make warheads "interoperable," or able to accomplish many missions—not just the decimation of a city. Washington also agrees that the world is getting more dangerous. America is facing threats that are growing in number and complexity. That means the government and the military have to prepare for an infinite number of scenarios. With the rise of rogue non-state actors, warfare has become multilateral. There is no Germany to race, no Japan to burn, no Soviet Union to stare down. There is no front line. The enemy is everywhere. And the government's worst nightmare, as stated by both members of Congress and presidents, is a terrorist with a nuclear weapon.

Terrorists "will acquire weapons of mass destruction and mass disruption, and some will use them," said a January 2001 study titled "New World Coming: American Security in the 21st Century." "Americans will likely die on American soil, possibly in large numbers."

The second nuclear age will fully arrive when the age of terrorism intersects with it: A non-state actor will acquire the materials to detonate a dirty bomb, a non-nuclear explosion that disperses radioactive material, or an improvised nuclear device, which would achieve a small criticality and become the first non-experimental nuclear explosion since 1945.

The probability of a nuclear terrorist attack is often overstated. The consequences aren't.

All nine nuclear-armed nations are modernizing their arsenals. Vladimir Putin has restored a nuclear-tipped belligerence to relations, which frosted over with the annexation of Crimea. Iran is a perpetual source of anxiety, regardless of what deals or restrictions are in place. Israel's arsenal of about 80 warheads is the worst-kept secret in Washington, and viewed as both a guarantor of and an impediment to peace in the Middle East. Pakistan and India are viewed as combatants in the most likely scenario of nuclear war. North Korea, led by a succession of madmen, is the only nation to have tested nuclear weapons in the 21st century. All this adds up to an intractable doctrine in modern Washington: The United States still needs nuclear weapons to guarantee its security, and the security of its allies.

The problem is that most of Congress, which controls the money, knows nothing about nuclear weapons. Nuke work on Capitol Hill is "an enormous but somewhat opaque backwater," according to Ellen Tauscher, the former congresswoman from the California district that includes the DOE's Lawrence Livermore National Laboratory. So the weapons have become the province of those members who have plants, labs, bombers, silos, and shipyards in their districts.

There's an ICBM caucus—the senators and representatives from Wyoming, Montana, and North Dakota, whose states are stippled with launch sites and, therefore, jobs performed by voters. The town of Great Falls, Montana, wouldn't exist without Malmstrom Air Force Base, which monitors and operates 150 ICBM silos across the state. The land-based leg of the triad has always been considered the most outdated and expendable in the post–Cold War era, and getting rid of the silos would save $14 billion over ten years. But in its version of the 2015 National Defense Authorization Act, the House Armed Services Committee tried to require the Air Force to keep all ICBM silos regardless of future budget cuts, military recommendations, and arms-control deals. At the same time, the Vietnam-era helicopters that fly staff out to the missile fields were breaking down left and right because budget caps have delayed replacements.

The production rate of plutonium pits has also been insulated from logic and reason: The law requires Los Alamos to be able to manufacture 80 pits a year by 2030 regardless of the technical needs of the stockpile.

The NNSA allows its contractors to estimate budgets, which means that its construction projects—including the Uranium Processing Facility at Y-12—soar in cost and duration. Meanwhile, it pays millions of dollars to maintain old buildings that should be torn down because there isn't money *for* the teardowns.

The Pentagon exempted the nuclear arsenal from the automatic budget cuts. In a resolution to continue funding the government during these rolling budget crises, Congress inserted an exception to allow increased funding for the NNSA.

All this means that the 21st-century budget for nuclear weapons is higher than at any point in history, even though the volume of warheads has shrunk by 85 percent from its 1967 pinnacle. The modernization of this reduced weapons complex will probably cost more than $1 trillion through the 2040s. The share of Pentagon spending on a new generation of bombers, missiles, and submarines would rival that during the Reagan buildup. And the cost for those delivery systems would peak at the same time as the NNSA's life-extension programs for warheads.

The year-to-year appropriations of billions of dollars mean nothing in the unceasing cycle of federal budgeting, but they mean everything to people in places like Oak Ridge, where building the Uranium Processing Facility is priority No. 1.

Oak Ridge in the 21st century is a city of only 30,000 residents, and yet $4 billion flows through it every year from the federal government. That sum could cover the operating expenses of Philadelphia, which has 50 times as many people. At a yearly Capitol Hill confab between local DOE business partners and members of Congress, Rep. Chuck Fleischmann (R-Tenn.) had a succinct way to describe the secret city in the 21st century.

"Oak Ridge," Fleischmann told the room, "is a special place."

7.

OAK RIDGE

The prophet of Oak Ridge is buried in a grassy lot between two brick homes in a prim subdivision on a curvy street that bears his name: Hendrix Drive. The gravestone is made of knee-high gray granite. Down Hendrix Drive is Manhattan Avenue, which leads to Marietta Circle, named for a former management contractor of the Y-12 National Security Complex.

One of Oak Ridge's ice-cream trucks has "Top Secret Lab" painted on its exterior. St. Mary's Catholic Church hosts an Atomic Blast fundraiser; attendees are encouraged to dress in neon. An atomic symbol the size of an aboveground pool is on the facade of Oak Ridge High School. The symbol is rendered in stained glass inside the Oak Ridge public library. It is on the big green sign that heralds Y-12, just around Pine Ridge, where Bear Creek Road swerves off Scarboro Road. At the center of the symbol, in place of a nucleus, is an acorn from an oak tree.

At noon on the first Wednesday of every month, emergency sirens go off for 30 seconds around town. The siren closest to the public high school is so loud that some teachers usually stop midsentence and wait for it to pass—a compulsory moment of silence for what Oak Ridge was, and is.

History is like the red-clay mud that mucks up your shoes here. It gathers, sticks, slows you down—particularly during the Secret City Festival, held every June to celebrate Oak Ridge's contribution to "7 decades of international stability progress." Vendors and politicians set up tables in the parking lot of the public library. A room of the community center is reserved for '43ers, those first citizens of Oak Ridge who are still alive and sharp enough to answer questions about what it was like to be patriotic pioneers. Outside, the Cold War Patriots wave pamphlets on chronic beryllium disease and metastasized cancers. Candidates for sheriff and court clerk give away campaign buttons. The fountain in the library plaza is dyed patriot blue. Fake barbed wire made of rope is strung every which way.

The festival's main event used to be the Allied invasion of Normandy, which was reenacted in the town park with Jeeps, assault tanks, anti-aircraft guns, and 200 historical interpreters in military dress who died dramatic fake deaths in front of spectators eating funnel cake. For a few hours once a year, World War II made it to American soil. For miles around, it sounded like war had broken out in downtown Oak Ridge. The boom of anti-tank guns echoed between the ridges, drowning out the high-pitched karaoke of Taylor Swift fans near the food trucks. The invasion reenactment was eventually discontinued because it cost too much, and because some residents thought it glorified war.

More recently, the festival has settled for historical-interpreter stations and basic artillery demonstrations. In June 2014, following each demo, children ran into the park to scoop up smoking gold shells from the grass. Teenagers dressed in field jackets perched on top of M4 vehicles that were oven-hot in the sun. A Howitzer rested in the shade of an oak, its barrel pointed at the Oak Ridge Community

Center. An Army chaplain with Nashville's Historical Cadet Corps sat at a typewriter under a steeple of camouflage canvas, his paper spelling out "On Duty for God and Country, July August September 1943." It's you or him, chaplains would tell soldiers who were troubled by combat and killing. This was a just war, and the writings of St. Augustine and St. Thomas Aquinas provided the necessary absolution: It is possible for a Christian in battle to draw blood without committing a sin, provided the battle is to prevent further harm and advance the cause of peace.

The Secret City Festival is the only time of year when the public can tour the Manhattan Project facility that is still in operation. Tourists pile into coach buses at Y-12's visitor center, which is strung with a banner that says Y-12: PROTECTING AMERICA'S FUTURE, and are asked to turn off and stow their phones and cameras. The buses trundle through the site, where the vistas are framed by concertina wire and magnolia trees. If you're lucky, Ray Smith is your guide. Smith, Y-12's official historian, has mastered the geography of the cluttered site and the chronology of everything that happened there since the days of the prophet.

As the bus passed the Highly Enriched Uranium Materials Facility in June 2014, he mentioned the most high-profile incident of this young century. "We are well prepared for an armed assault," Smith said, standing at the front of the coach bus. "I'll tell you: I wouldn't want to be the *second* nun to cross Pine Ridge."

"The nun" was still inside the fences, in one way or another, two years after the fact. For a site nicknamed "the Fort Knox of Uranium" in a place known historically as "the Secret City," the intrusion by activists who described themselves as "bungling" was a profound embarrassment.

"We had this one event, and it paints the entire site in a very negative light—very unfairly, I think," said Ted Sherry, Y-12 site manager until 2011. "There are so many fine, fine professionals that work out there that do things for our country that are very patriotic, and it's just painful to watch."

When the *Knoxville News Sentinel*'s Frank Munger asked the president of the newest managing contractor, Consolidated Nuclear Security, about its first day on the job, July 1, 2014, the response was telling: "We haven't had any nuns crossing the fence or any major safety incidents."

Most outsiders hadn't heard of the security event, and most Oak Ridgers moved on from it quickly. The only approved prophecy in town is the one that foretold the winning of the greatest war. Peace activism in a bomb-making town makes people uncomfortable, and East Tennesseans don't like to make each other uncomfortable.

Except for a small group of people that sets up across the street from Y-12 every Sunday at 5 p.m.

THE WEEKLY VIGIL by the Oak Ridge Environmental Peace Alliance has been ongoing and uninterrupted since 2000. Its members used to meet by the flagpole near the Y-12 sign, in a designated First Amendment area underneath a security camera. After the break-in, another line of fencing was erected, and they were moved across Scarboro Road, onto a narrow patch of grass on the shoulder, near rusted railroad tracks. During the summer they have umbrellas to block the sun. During the winter they're bundled up, huddled in a tight circle, hopping in place to keep warm. They always begin with announcements and then move on to a discussion topic, like how violence is inculcated into a belief system. Every now and then a passing driver will call out, "Go home!" Sometimes the security officer assigned to the nearest post will crank up the country radio on his white SUV. In a town that still doesn't talk much, either because of secrecy or because of ignorance, the vigil stands out. The group always finishes by singing the old civil rights tune "Keep Your Eyes on the Prize."

Now the only thing I did wrong
Was stay in the wilderness too long.
Keep your eyes on the prize, hold on.

In the months before the Plowshares trial, a man named Ralph Hutchison shouted the names of Megan, Michael, and Greg during each chorus: "Hold on, Megan Rice, hold on!" A sprightly activist with a bone-dry sense of humor, Hutchison is the coordinator of the peace alliance, a small but fervent citizen effort to police the practices and expose the screwups of Y-12, with the ultimate goal of shutting it down. There's at least one informed citizen who watchdogs each DOE nuclear site around the country. Ralph is the man in Oak Ridge. He hears politicians talk about "perhaps not in my lifetime" and he shakes his head. That's admitting that it won't be done, even though he believes nuclear weapons pose as great a threat in the 21st century as they did at the height of the Cold War. About $300 million a year flows to the Uranium Processing Facility project, which Ralph views as the start of a second Manhattan Project, a new generation of war making that will last through the century.

"This community serves the DOE," Ralph said of the city. "It's the environment in which they live. It's the air they breathe."

Y-12 is the second-largest employer in East Tennessee and creates 24,000 indirect jobs. About 7,400 people go to work there, including contractors, small-business subcontractors, guards, and federal employees, all of whom commute from 28 counties in Tennessee. The National Nuclear Security Administration and Oak Ridge started calling Y-12 the "Uranium Center for Excellence" to attract and retain skilled labor, broaden the mission, and justify expenses. Y-12 is stockpiling secondaries in its HEUMF instead of dismantling the excess, partly in case of earth-bound asteroids. Someday the United States might need thermonuclear weapons to knock a killer rock off course, NNSA and Y-12 officials say—one extinction agent thwarting another.

The peak building phase of the Uranium Processing Facility (UPF), the largest federal construction project in the United States, will create 1,500 construction jobs and 5,000 support jobs, an economic boon that will ripple outward.

"This project is needed," Knoxville's deputy mayor said in a meeting of the Defense Nuclear Facilities Safety Board two months after the break-in. With "a significant chunk of UPF dollars going to goods and services, they'll be local, statewide economic impact and our local businesses will stand to benefit greatly."

Ralph Hutchison was also at the meeting. When it came time for public comment, he didn't pull any punches.

"In our opinion NNSA cannot be trusted to build and operate a safe, secure, functioning facility," he said. "What it can be trusted to do . . . is to add an additional layer of management between the contractors and Department of Energy. What it can be trusted to do is to get our tax dollars and give them away to corporate sponsors and weapons contracts by the billions."

In 2005 the UPF was expected to cost between $600 million and $1 billion. Then in 2012, seven years into the design process, managers discovered that the ceilings needed to be 13 feet higher to fit the proper equipment. This added $540 million to the design cost alone, and by 2014 the total estimated cost ranged as high as $19 billion. Additional public comment on the UPF arrived via hundreds of letters and e-mails.

Many of those in opposition cited the United States' commitment under the Nuclear Non-Proliferation Treaty to pursue the elimination of nuclear weapons.

"PLEASE do not make nuclear BOMBS in my backyard," e-mailed one Oak Ridger named Laura.

"We are tired of the endless news stories of leaks and lax security and dangerous conditions at the Oak Ridge bomb complex," e-mailed Carolanne from New Market, Tennessee.

Many of those in favor of it invoked the greatness of the United States and the solemn need to defend it.

My uncle "was fighting his way across the Pacific when the workers at Y-12 saved his life," wrote Gary from Knoxville. "There remain evil and dangerous people in the world."

"I believe Y-12 is essential to our national security and contributes significantly to our local community and economy," wrote James from Louisville, Tennessee. "I do believe that nuclear weapons play an important role as a deterrent and ensure our freedoms and the national security of our great nation."

Shut down Y-12, and shut down Oak Ridge.

Shut down Oak Ridge, and shut down America's might.

"WE LIVE KIND of in the past here."

Trina Baughn was sitting at Jefferson Soda Fountain, a quiet diner in a one-story brick plaza on the west edge of town. Her grandparents moved to Oak Ridge to work for the Manhattan Project. Her grandmother, who worked at Y-12, was told she was helping to make ice cream. Now Trina, a third-generation Oak Ridger, was a city councilwoman with a son in the Air Force in Afghanistan. She believed that Y-12 was a necessity but that Oak Ridge needed control of its land, and independence from the largess of the federal government.

"It's hard for me to relate to that [pacifist] opinion after 9/11," said Trina, who saw the special kind of panic in a town with a huge store of fissile material while terrorists were crashing jets into buildings. "We are hated as a country by other countries for nothing more than the freedom we enjoy. You have to be prepared."

Y-12 still certifies bomb components to be ready and effective should the president call on them, but Oak Ridge's nuclear legacy has been rebranded and diversified into a broader, vaguer mission that serves national security as a whole. Which, in a way, makes it more of a secret city than ever, even as it's been absorbed into the greater metropolitan area of Knoxville.

In the early days of Oak Ridge, you'd hear things like "My dad works at the plant." In the 21st century you hear things like "My dad is a project analyst."

Oak Ridge, while originally a creation of the federal government, is now an incorporated "host city" for the DOE, which means it has to act in its own best interest without discouraging the flow of money from Washington. The city retains a D.C. lobby shop on Connecticut Avenue NW that stays on top of issues such as land transfers—the slow clawing back of Manhattan Project land, now prime for development, from the DOE.

So there's a special tension in Oak Ridge. It's the only NNSA site where the entire federal operation is *inside* city limits, and this hampers the city from developing outward. Y-12 contains considerable quantities of special nuclear material, and sprawl and development have brought unknowing civilian populations closer to it than ever before.

"I'll be honest with you," said Oak Ridge's white-mustachioed mayor, Tom Beehan, who served from 2007 to 2014. "I was probably thankful it was the nun and the Catholic Workers than anyone else. In essence they probably did our community a big favor."

Beehan, a real estate agent, studied in Kentucky and Baltimore to be a Catholic priest and played the guitar at the county jail when the

Berrigan brothers were incarcerated. Forty years later, after deciding against the priesthood and starting a career in insurance, he found himself leading a city that played host to everything the Berrigans despised. He was the first mayor in the history of Oak Ridge who didn't come from the employee roster of DOE contractors. The city was trying to be something else, something more expansive.

Oak Ridge is part of Tennessee's "Innovation Valley," the state's branding effort to recapture the glory days of the Manhattan Project and prewar TVA. Oak Ridge National Laboratory (ORNL), located just up the road from Y-12, is a hub of research and a destination for some of the world's brightest minds. It's the home of Titan, one of the biggest and fastest machines in existence, made of 20,000 square feet of humming black boxes that require 18,000-volt transformers from TVA and 6,600 tons of coolant that chill the floor on which it sits. The Everest visualization facility has a billboard-size screen made of 35 million pixels that can model fusion reactions and supernovas in 4-D. The Spallation Neutron Source, with its million-dollar monthly electric bill, fires intense beams of neutrons to study materials. These machines are housed up in the ridges in giant buildings that look like sets for a sci-fi movie about time travel. A new experiment hall is being built for $1 billion. Oak Ridge may be innovating its way into the 21st century, but it's still a company town, and its business is the atom.

"These big facilities are answering fundamental questions about the matter of the universe," said ORNL director Thom Mason, a Canadian with a small gold hoop in his left earlobe. "The Spallation Neutron Source is not answering one big question; it's answering thousands of smaller questions about the structure and dynamics of atoms and how they move."

The city was born as a kind of utopia on the frontier, a brainy Brigadoon with zero unemployment and top-of-the-line social services, but over the decades since the gates opened, the population dropped by two-thirds. The city was stitched into a patchwork of urban sprawl. Unemployment among residents ages 16 to 44 was more than 10 percent in 2013. On the west side of town, the site of the former gaseous diffusion plant, K-25, has been torn down and renamed East Tennessee Technology Park. There's talk of a new regional airport on the old K-25 site, but 170 acres of federal land would have to be transferred first. There's also high hopes that carbon fiber and advanced manufacturing will gird the local economy as the Cold War recedes further into the past. Much of the lab's staff live outside Oak Ridge, in more upscale towns like Farragut and West Knoxville, and city dwellers these days are largely inattentive to what goes on at Y-12. In 1943 Oak Ridgers came for the promise of a decent job and a blind sense of patriotism. In the 21st century they come for the cheap real estate and the excellent school system, which has always been a top tax priority. The area has one of the country's highest concentrations of both PhDs and nuclear reactors. One in five Oak Ridgers over age 25 has a graduate degree or higher, which is quadruple the rate of Morristown, another city in East Tennessee with a similar total population, and double that of Knoxville.

"We do know that we need to diversify, and ORNL is a huge asset when it comes to that, but the reality is we don't have that yet," Mayor Beehan said over coffee at Panera Bread. As for Y-12, which is 5,000 feet away, just over Pine Ridge: "I just cannot believe that we don't need the deterrent. But this is insider stuff. If you were to walk around in here right now and start talking to people about [nuclear bombs], you'd get blank stares."

EVERY FRIDAY MORNING AT 7:30, the local nuclear crowd meets in a squat office building between the Taco Bell and the Applebee's. Over coffee and pastries, there's gabbing and cross talk between politicians, contractors, DOE officials who became contractors, contractors who became politicians, environmental consultants, housing developers, scientists from Oak Ridge National Lab, and academics from the University of Tennessee. Conversation is wide ranging, but it revolves around nuclear weaponry, nuclear research, and nuclear cleanup—the driving forces of the East Tennessee Economic Council, which hosts the meetings. A recent council vice chairman was Gerald Boyd, formerly DOE's top manager in Oak Ridge. A recent chairman was Darrel Kohlhorst, the general manager of B&W Y-12 who retired after the break-in. As in Washington, there's a revolving door in Oak Ridge.

This is all behind the scenes, though. The center of the city is mostly hotels and fast-food chains. Lines of cars snake around the Starbucks, the Sonic, the Chick-fil-A. There's a dead mall that senior citizens once used for daily walks in the winter. Historic Jackson Square has a community theater, a Saturday farmers' market, and Big Ed's, a cozy pizza joint that's decorated with Oak Ridge paraphernalia (including a few dozen security cameras that keep an eye on the kitchen, the cashier, the customers). The Alexander Guest House, built as an inn during the Manhattan Project, was renovated into an assisted-living center. With some scientists and federal folk opting for other suburbs, Oak Ridgers have become more blue-collar, working as painters, plumbers, roofers, or electricians, in the service industry, or in toolmaking.

The city gets prettier as you move outward from the center. Crepe myrtles stipple side streets. There are sheep and alpaca farms within the city limits. Roads twine up tree-laden ridges that go from lush green in humid summers to fiery red and yellow in the autumn. The landscape swells with oak, elm, and poplar and is swallowed in places by billowing kudzu. At twilight in summer, cicadas drone like jet engines. Handsome mid-century modern homes, bearded with English ivy, normally go for less than $400,000. There are still 4,500

alphabet houses sprinkled around town, though residents have renovated many of these cookie-cutter dwellings from the '40s into quirky
abodes with modern conveniences. There are cul-de-sacs of soulless
McMansions. The region's prescription-drug problem and meth epidemic have crept into the city.

Oak Ridge meanders. Both geographically and emotionally.

"We haven't done a good job of telling who we are," said Anne
Garcia Garland, a former city councilmember who lives in a converted A-house constructed during the Manhattan Project. "What I
want here is people who want to live in a sophisticated small Southern town. Who want to put down roots and have children here."

The neighborhood of Scarboro, in the shadow of Pine Ridge, was
and is the African American part of Oak Ridge. It's where blacks
were cordoned off in rickety hutments during the Manhattan
Project—"the first community I have ever seen with slums that were
deliberately planned," wrote *Chicago Defender* correspondent Enoch
P. Waters, who called Oak Ridge "as backward sociologically as the
atomic bomb is advanced scientifically." Scarboro is just off Tuskegee
Drive and Wilberforce Avenue, and it's the residential zone that's
closest to Y-12. Scarboro's Oak Valley Baptist Church was where
Sister Megan, Michael, and Greg were dropped off to begin their
hike up and over Pine Ridge. For decades Scarboro residents suspected that runoff from a Y-12 incinerator was contaminating their
gardens and livestock. Official studies weren't conducted and information wasn't released until there had been decades of contamination, which is still ongoing.

East Fork Poplar Creek burbles from a spring beneath Y-12 and
cuts through a notch in Pine Ridge, carrying contaminants from the
plant for 12 miles into the surrounding areas. About two million
pounds of mercury—which is used to enrich lithium for secondaries
and is poisonous to humans—was lost or unaccounted for by 1983.
The greatest potential health risk from mercury was to children in

Scarboro. It flowed through the creek into fishing waters and the Clinch River.

"You can find Oak Ridge in the Mississippi Delta," Ralph Hutchison is fond of saying.

Today, there are fish-monitoring sites along the creek as it skirts Scarboro. The DOE plans to build a mercury-treatment plant at Y-12, because the amount of mercury discharged from Y-12's storm-drain system is still above Tennessee guidelines. A 2011 study estimated that about 50,000 kilograms of uranium was released from Y-12 from 1944 to 1995—enough to fuel more than 3,000 nuclear weapons. In Scarboro, every instance of asthma and cancer is viewed as suspicious.

"We lived here for years and we didn't know what was going on—you still have that 'don't talk' mentality," said Scarboro native Rose Weaver, who didn't find out that her mother worked at Y-12 until after she died.

Weaver used to work as an administrator for WSI, but she lost her job when WSI lost its security contract after the Y-12 break-in. Ironically, the people who were trying to call attention to Y-12's impact on her community were the ones who indirectly caused her layoff.

Living near Y-12 was one thing, but working there was quite another. The U.S. Department of Labor has doled out around $1.5 billion in medical payments and compensation among 10,600 Y-12 workers (or surviving family members) who suffered from certain cancers, chronic beryllium disease, or any other ailment linked to toxic exposure.

Glenn Bell started working at Y-12 as a machinist in 1968, fresh out of vocational school in southwestern Tennessee, eager to serve his country after being deemed ineligible for the draft for medical reasons. The machine shops at the plant handled and shaped exotic metals and measured materials within two millionths of an inch, to create components precise enough for the nuclear bombs. Workers did not wear respirators. Localized vacuums were the only real safety precaution for many years. Six years before Glenn started, a report warned against having any food in the beryllium work areas at the Nevada Test Site, and yet coffee and doughnuts were laid out every day in Y-12's beryllium shop.

Over time Glenn realized that the good wages and benefits were actually veiled hazard pay. In his first several years at Y-12, three co-workers in their 30s died of brain cancer. By the early 1980s, Glenn developed symptoms that were first diagnosed as adult asthma and later identified as chronic beryllium disease. Breathing problems among employees were accompanied by anger, depression, and feelings of betrayal and alienation.

"I'm walking in like I got out of general math and y'all's talking calculus," said one Oak Ridge worker in a study of the psychosocial effects of beryllium diseases.

Since the early 1990s, Y-12 workers have absorbed more than 40 percent of the total internal radiation exposure among all DOE sites in the weapons complex. Glenn and others lobbied Washington in the late '90s for a compensation act for energy workers. More than 250,000 claims have since been made against the DOE nationwide from its network of plants, labs, and test ranges.

These atomic veterans outnumber the veterans of any modern U.S. war.

"If they had told us we're soldiers—that we're gonna be storming the beaches at Normandy and 'some of you are gonna get sick, but this is a risk we need you to take for the defense of the country'—we could've lived with that," said Glenn. "But they just told us everything was okay. . . . Especially since I retired, I have second and third thoughts about what we did out there, and I know it's the lesser of two evils. We really needed to maintain the stockpile. But at what cost?"

IN A ROOM on the second floor of the assisted-living facility on Laboratory Road, one entire wall was a scrapbook. Old newspaper clippings have been shellacked over one another, their headlines angling this way and that.

PEACE

OAK RIDGE ATTACKS JAPANESE

WORKERS THRILL AS ATOMIC BOMB SECRET BREAKS

Colleen Black slipped a large silver cross over her head, put on her magenta beret, and took the elevator to the ground floor. She strolled around outside the front entrance until her ride to church arrived. She had a flip phone, a fixed income, and stories to tell about being a pipe inspector at K-25, the gaseous diffusion plant on the edge of town, during World War II. Born in Nashville, she grew up during the Great Depression, in a Tennessee farmhouse without running water or electricity. When the United States entered the war, life's luxuries and essentials were rationed: butter, sugar, stockings (the nylon went to parachutes for the military). Americans dutifully siphoned off their own commodities for the war effort, sending pots and pans to scrap drives. When her older brother was drafted and deployed in 1942, her family moved to Oak Ridge to help the war effort and bring him back. Colleen, a teenager at the time, walked to her job at K-25 and lived in a trailer with her parents and eight siblings. Space was at a premium all around the new city, so her family would work in shifts, eat in shifts, sleep in shifts.

Now, at 89 years old, she sometimes spoke to young students.

They sometimes asked, "Why did you build that bomb?" and it made her heart flutter every time. She was glad the war was won, she told them, but "devastated" when she saw the ruin in Japan. All those hours in the early 1940s, crawling up and around pipes in that monstrous factory, the last remains of which were just now being hauled to the scrapyard in the autumn of 2014—did they add up to something more complicated than patriotism?

Colleen had married another Oak Ridger nicknamed Blackie and graduated from an A house to a D house as her family grew, to eight children in all. The war ended but she and Blackie remained in Oak Ridge. It was home in the truest sense. They had created a community out of whole cloth. In 2009, when Blackie died, she graduated to the Greenfield retirement home. She went to Mass every Sunday at St. Mary's, a short drive away up on a knoll. Just outside the church, the flag of the Vatican flies alongside flags from the branches of the U.S. military. Nearby, on the grassy slope down to the Oak Ridge Turnpike, is a six-foot marble statue of Mary herself. She's standing on a spheroid plinth that represents Earth. This Mary, like most Marys, has her foot on a serpent, but there's a curious nonbiblical icon embossed on the marble Earth: a nucleus framed by a whirl of electrons.

Catholics had broken into Y-12, but the Catholic congregation of St. Mary's didn't talk publicly about the break-in. There were no sermons about the rightness or wrongness of it, just like there were no sermons about the rightness or wrongness of receiving Holy Communion on Sundays and then showing up at a weapons plant Monday morning for work.

Colleen settled into a back pew.

The first reading was from the prophet Ezekiel, who spoke of a freshwater river flowing through a gated kingdom, bringing life to its banks, and emptying into a saltwater sea. The Gospel reading, from the Book of John, was the famous story about Jesus excoriating money-grubbing businessmen who had set up shop in the temple.

After Mass, Colleen always met her girlfriends in the restaurant at the DoubleTree hotel in town. The ladies, half of whom are nurses, are mostly longtime Oak Ridge residents whose husbands got jobs at the plant or lab. They gossiped and joked over steel decanters of decaf, with rolls and pastries on a big lazy Susan in the middle of the circular table. When one of them wanted to make an announcement, she would clink a fork against a water glass. There's a special spirit in Oak Ridge, they say, that carries down through generations. People who came from other places to this new place became one another's family. Their regular breakfasts were proof that this connection lasts.

At a stoplight after brunch, facing a Big Lots and a Pet Supplies Surplus, Colleen looked at the vista of plazas in this land of ridges and valleys. Before all this, back when Colleen had first moved here, there was just mud and trailers and secrets, and the feeling that everyone was working on something great. The Manhattan Project wouldn't be possible today, she said. Young people are too inquisitive. There isn't a blind love for country because there's nothing that unifies us.

"You couldn't keep a secret today," she said. "It'd be on Facebook and iPads and iPods. Back then we just did what we were told."

THE THREE MEMBERS of Transform Now Plowshares returned to Tennessee in February 2013 for a hearing on whether they could use morality to defend themselves in their May trial. They were going to face an uphill battle in court, but Megan, Michael, and Greg had other business first: spreading their anti-nuclear evangel all around Knoxville.

They told their story after a Sunday service at the Tennessee Valley

Unitarian Universalist Church in West Knoxville. A few years earlier a man had entered the church and fired a shotgun at the congregation, injuring seven and killing two, hell-bent on exacting revenge on the liberal ethos that he thought was corroding the country. Congregants, especially tuned to the sensations of indiscriminate violence, asked their guests how they could claim nonviolence when they destroyed property. Was there a bit of hypocrisy in their action?

"Maybe the triviality of that destruction comes from a truth that is monstrous," Sister Megan said, sitting in front of the altar. "Those very fences are illegal, and guarding lies and secrecy and corruption and great danger to the world."

"The six- and seven-year-olds killed by drone attacks are just as human as the six- and seven-year-olds killed in Newtown," Michael said. "Selective compassion is a form of hypocrisy, too."

A white-haired woman named Lillian Mashburn stood, arms crossed, in the back of the church. She was thinking of her father, who had been an infantryman stationed in the Pacific when Oak Ridge's uranium fell toward Hiroshima.

"He was saved by that bomb," Mashburn, a church board member, said after the discussion. "They were told when they landed they would be killed as part of the first wave. . . . There's a whole generation of people, most of whom would've been dead, who were saved."

Three days later, Megan, Michael, and Greg were guest speakers in a systems-theory class at the University of Tennessee. Greg talked about the diffusion of social responsibility and how he felt responsible for nuclear weapons because his taxes have paid for them. Michael, who was wearing a T-shirt that said GROUND THE DRONES, called Y-12 "a failed rogue terrorist state."

"I think there's a deafening silence about what's going on at Y-12," said a student named Rochelle Butler, "but I do know people who work there are good people. Why would I believe outsiders rather than people who work there, who I believe to be good?"

"We love these people in a deeply compassionate way," Sister Megan said of Y-12 employees. "Our motivation was in solidarity with people who spend their time making nuclear bombs to feed their children. . . . We are all so intertwined and empower each other. A thought creates its own energy. The quantum theory of physics is always at work."

The theory was at work a couple of days later at Maryville College, where the trio ate pizza with 15 students from a progressive Christian group. "They are each connected to 50 others," Sister Megan whispered before chatting with music student Chris Hickman.

"I know nothing about the anti-nuclear movement," Hickman told her. "I was born in '92, and it's kind of an afterthought for my generation."

The trio visited two dozen people at a potluck dinner of the Presbyterian Peacemaking Committee of East Tennessee.

"Prince of Peace, we thank you for your prophets who've spoken your word down through the ages, and we thank you for the prophets among us," said host Scott Brunger during his opening prayer.

The attendees chatted about the fallout from the break-in. Someone asked about what their intrusion has cost taxpayers—at least $15 million in security alterations by the NNSA, according to the *Knoxville News Sentinel*. Greg replied that they saved taxpayers $12.2 million that was docked from the management contractor's award fee.

Sister Megan brought up the first guard they encountered inside the facility and how he lost his job. She said how he saved their lives by not escalating the situation, how he was the scapegoat for a corrupt and criminal weapons enterprise.

"I feel very guilty not contacting him," Sister Megan said.

THE STICKER on the front door of Kirk's brick home in Lake City said, "This property has been determined to be vacant and abandoned." The backyard was scattered with cinder blocks and sodden heaps of pink insulation. When he popped back down to Pantex to make a quick buck doing short-term contract work, vandals hauled off the ten-stall kennel and stripped the small horse stable of its roof and most of its siding. The remaining frame still featured painted graffiti from his daughter, Kodie: purple crosses, the phrase "Protected by God."

The Garlands had moved into a rental home in nearby Clinton. Kirk's wife, Joann, couldn't stand to come back to Lake City, not with everything so torn apart. Kirk could save the house from foreclosure if he had $22,000. The guards at Y-12 passed the hat and collected $800 for him. Kirk had bought a lottery ticket every day for the past month.

"God's got a different plan for me," he said, as a truck that said JD's TIRE & SERVICE CENTER pulled into the gravel driveway.

"Here we go," Kirk muttered, as a fat man and a skinny man exited the truck and began walking toward him.

"You owe me a thousand dollars and you skip town?" the fat man asked. Kirk started to explain but the fat man kept saying, "Bullshit."

A 30-year career with the DOE and this was the result. He was unemployed and waiting for his union to schedule an arbitration with WSI. He had tried to hire a lawyer, but Tennessee was a right-to-work state, so no one would touch his case. Maybe there were answers at Faith Promise, the mega-church on a hill on the outskirts of Oak Ridge, which was similar to Trinity in Amarillo. The Garlands had attended on Sundays whenever Kirk didn't have a shift. Faith Promise was an enormous campus, like a Christian Disneyland, complete with a movie theater for kids, yearly baptism quotas, offertory ATMs called "giving kiosks," a sound system straight out of *American Idol*, and a pastor in casual dress who took the stage on a wave of theatrical fog, looking like he'd just come from a backyard barbecue in heaven.

"We don't get what we *deserve*," the pastor, Dr. Chris Stephens, said during a sermon. "We get *grace*."

Grace, the pastor said, was "God meeting us at the point of our greatest need."

The dirty socks all around Kirk's rental home were for training the German shepherds to bite and latch on. The sire's name was Goliath, and his siblings were working over in Iraq. One of the horses out back was named Genesis. Kodie was 16 and homeschooled. She had been training to be in the Women's Professional Rodeo Association, but it was an expensive endeavor. The Garlands had already sold one of the horses to make rent.

"We lost everything because they supposedly came from God," Kodie said of Sister Megan, Michael, and Greg. Kodie was up at dawn every day to care for the horses. Joann was often ill, so health insurance was crucial. Kirk scoured the Internet for jobs.

"I've got to sit down and ask a priest," Kirk said. "Doing the Lord's work is not protesting and getting arrested. You don't get to heaven on your works anyway. You get to heaven on salvation."

When told that Sister Megan thought he saved her life by not escalating the situation—that, in fact, *he* was her salvation—Kirk was speechless. His wife was not.

"That's amazing that she'd make that kind of statement," Joann said. "She is safe—because of him—to be able to go and do what she's doing. . . . The joke of it is they came in God's name. God does not say to break laws. Sorry. God does not say that."

THE MORNING OF their pretrial hearing on morality, on February 7, 2013, the trio ate an oatmeal breakfast and prayed with supporters at Riverside House, a rambling home across the Tennessee River from downtown Knoxville. The house hosted a rotating cast of visiting activists. It was the type of place that had a couch in the kitchen.

"What's the reading for today?" Michael asked.

It was from Hebrews 12, and Megan read it aloud.

> . . . you have come to Mount Zion, to the city of the living God, the heavenly Jerusalem. You have come to thousands upon thousands of angels in joyful assembly . . . to the sprinkled blood that speaks a better word than the blood of Abel.

Megan marveled that the reading included the symbolic application of blood. "Unbelievable that it would come today," she said. Michael then read the day's Gospel, from Mark.

> Take nothing for the journey except a staff—no bread, no bag, no money in your belts. . . . Whenever you enter a house, stay there until you leave that town. And if any place will not welcome you or listen to you, leave that place and shake the dust off your feet as a testimony against them.

Michael closed his eyes, feeling the validation of the Gospel, and said, "Let us proceed with joy and hope, knowing we are on the side of victory, even with temporary losses."

"Let us pray," Megan said, "for the many hidden, obscure, perhaps more powerful initiatives that sprout around this universe that's moving toward perfect harmony, healing, and growth. All of creation is the temple. We're all part of it. The courtroom I'm now going to look upon as a temple of the universe."

At U.S. District Court in downtown Knoxville, Megan had trouble getting through security.

"Any metal on you, Sister?" a guard asked during her third run through the metal detector.

"I have titanium in my wrists," Megan said. She gestured to the

X-ray machine. "Do you wear lead vests standing next to this all day? I think you should."

Their support group swelled to 25 people and filled all rows on the defense's side of courtroom 3B. Ralph Hutchison was there with folks from the Oak Ridge Environmental Peace Alliance. As they awaited the start of the hearing, the supporters began singing softly.

"Peace is flo-wing like a riiiii-ver," they warbled from their seats. "Flo-wing out into the de-e-sert."

Ralph chuckled. "Oh the judge *loves* it when they sing," he said.

Supporters in the room had been arrested while protesting the School of the Americas, or for crossing onto Y-12 property at the front entrance. They looked the part: peace-symbol earrings, court-issued hearing aids, shirts and hats that said VETERANS FOR PEACE. They were a stark contrast to the two assistant U.S. attorneys who entered the courtroom to represent the government. The pair, in business attire, walked down the aisle and through the wooden gate that separated the audience from the proceedings. Their faith was less in-your-face, but it was no less meaningful. They were the two Catholic lawyers in the Knoxville U.S. attorney's office.

8.

THE TRIAL

Over the years, Jeff Theodore had chances to hitch his wagon to a corporate law firm and make serious money. He felt called, though, to protect the community, to redress and discourage crime, to seek peace for victims, to work for stability through the rule of law. He moved from his home state of Michigan in 1998 to the Knoxville suburb of Farragut, after some locals dissuaded him from considering Oak Ridge because, well, "better safe than sorry." East Tennessee is not exactly Catholic country, but Jeff took his family to Mass on Sundays. He sometimes described himself as a "pantheistic, panentheistic Catholic-Christian agnostic," a hyper-specific term only a lawyer could fashion.

His portfolio at the district attorney's office was national security. Sometimes he'd find himself in court with activists who had performed ritualized civil disobedience at his district's marquee national-security site. He took no pleasure in charging peace activists. It was his own Catholic faith that first steered him to be a public prosecutor. On his desk was a pewter figurine of Catholic saint and lawyer Thomas More and a copy of a "lawyer's prayer," which began, "Give me the grace, good Lord, to set my mind fast upon Thee and not to hang upon the blast of men's mouths."

Before Transform Now Plowshares breached the Fort Knox of Uranium, Jeff had prosecuted the previous case of trespass at Y-12 involving Michael Walli and 12 others, including two Catholic sisters and a priest. In this instance, in 2010, they crossed the line in broad daylight, held hands in a circle, and ignored the bullhorn requests to vacate the premises. Everyone called the group the Y-13. Steve Baggarly, who co-founded the Catholic Worker house in Norfolk, Virginia, represented himself and testified on the third and last day of the trial. Over Jeff's objections, Steve prefaced his defense by talking about the "fiery inferno" and "excruciating pain" of Hiroshima and Nagasaki. He then talked about how Y-12 builds and maintains parts for weapons that are far more devastating than the bombs dropped on Japan. He then argued that laws are meant to be life-*giving*.

"It is precisely such laws and courts—which defend weapons capable of incinerating millions of children, women, and men in nuclear firestorms—that function to preserve the nation's state at the risk of all life on Earth," Steve said in closing, "and to use the law in service of sin and death."

To Jeff, there was something compelling about his delivery. Or maybe it was because both men were close in age. Steve wasn't an elderly priest or a Vietnam-era radical who seemed out of step with the present. He was a dad nearing 50 who had spent his life ministering to the poor, living humbly for others, shepherding Dorothy Day's legacy. Jeff prosecuted plenty of people with nefarious intentions, but these activists meant well. They had good hearts. Steve seemed especially sincere. A really decent human being.

Jeff was a worrier. He would turn a question over in his mind for hours, days, weeks, and these cases raised many questions. His co-counsel, Melissa Kirby, respected this, but tried to center him.

"You're letting your Catholic guilt get to you," she said knowingly. She herself had been educated by Catholic sisters in Chattanooga, and never thought her career would involve prosecuting them for walking onto a national-security site she had never heard of before. After law school she learned the ropes in the assistant district attorney's office in Spartanburg, South Carolina. Being a prosecutor was not about racking up convictions, she was told. It was about carefully considering every case on its own merits and using her job to nudge wayward souls back to law-abiding society. Sometimes, yes, there were criminals who did evil things and who had to be put away, but she was mentored to see the courtroom as an arena of redemption—which is what made the trials with activists so peculiar and compelling.

The sisters of her youth were rule-abiding educators. The ones who showed up at the courthouse in Knoxville were brazen rule-breakers. Melissa, like Jeff, respected the courage of their convictions. These people walked the walk. This walk, though, always took them to the wrong side of the law. Melissa sometimes resented their haughtiness. Some activists behaved like they existed on a higher plane than did the rest of the world. Catholic radicals didn't have a monopoly on morality and ethics, she thought. So at home she dug through some old philosophy books from college, preparing to fight fire with fire. She read St. Thomas Aquinas. She thought of the Book of Romans: "Rulers do not bear the sword for no reason." If defendants were going to enter the Book of Isaiah into evidence, a prosecutor could cite Romans.

Melissa didn't end up deploying Aquinas, even when she cross-examined a Y-13 defendant who was a philosophy teacher. The case wasn't about morals, after all. The case was about the law. She stuck to the facts.

Jeff and Melissa won. A jury convicted all 13 of misdemeanor trespassing. They were given a range of light sentences and fines.

"The government has no issue with demonstrations," Melissa said at one of the sentencing hearings. "The issue is crossing over that blue line."

The largest group arrest at Y-12 was in 1989, when 29 people were charged with crossing through the front gate. Arrests dropped off after 1990, when the local district attorney stopped pressing state charges. There used to be a catch-and-release policy at Y-12. Activists would cross the line into the arms of Oak Ridge police, and the city would process, fine, and free them in short order. After September 11, the country's humiliated national-security apparatus lurched in several new directions. The security conception of Y-12, which for most of its life had been considered a Soviet target reachable by ICBMs, was out of date. It was now a destination for suicidal terrorists on foot or in vehicles or aircraft. The laws were sharpened. The Department of Justice wanted stricter enforcement and prosecution.

Jeff was at his family cottage in western Michigan in late July of 2012. He liked to unplug during vacations, but he couldn't help noticing one particular e-mail from Melissa on Saturday morning the 28th.

"I don't want to bother you on vacation, but we have a situation."

THERE WAS A NEW TRESPASS CASE at Y-12 that went beyond trespass. Three people had gotten *way* inside, under the cover of darkness. This was no daytime catch-and-release. Jeff, without access to any of the media reports, asked if it could wait until he returned to Knoxville, but Melissa was insistent: This one was different.

At the detention hearing, Melissa argued for keeping the trio of activists behind bars as they awaited trial, calling them a "danger to the community," but they were granted release to await trial.

Back in the office the following week, Jeff absorbed the full weight of the break-in. It was stunning. An 82-year-old sister! How in the world could they have gotten to the secure area, which was protected

by a gauntlet of natural and man-made obstacles? He did some research and discovered that he could charge these people with more
than just trespassing. That would be the right thing to do. The trio
had put the safety of Y-12 workers at risk. They'd put *themselves* at
great risk. This type of crime, however peaceful it seemed, could
have caused great harm.

The U.S. attorney's office hit Transform Now Plowshares with
trespassing and both destruction *and* depredation of government
property over the amount of $1,000 in damage.

Next were the pretrial motions and hearings, and the tedious filing of paperwork by both the prosecution and the defense. This, too,
was part of a Plowshares action. While Megan, Michael, and Greg
were free on their own recognizance, their lawyers were continuing
the civil resistance in court. On the same day in November, the defense team filed for a motion to dismiss the charges and the prosecution filed a motion to prevent them from using certain defenses in
court.

Because Y-12 makes weapons that are so powerful that they cannot distinguish between military and civilian populations, the defense wrote, the site serves the planning of war crimes. The members
of Transform Now Plowshares *had* to act, because the mere existence
of nuclear weapons constituted an imminent harm perpetrated in
their name by a government out of compliance with international
laws and treaties.

"If these three people took this action in Iran, the U.S. government would praise them," the defense's memo said. "But in Tennessee, the U.S. government prosecutes them."

The U.S. attorney's office, meanwhile, asked the judge to prevent
the defendants from arming their arguments with international law,
the First Amendment, the U.S. government's nuclear-weapons policy, and religious, moral, and political beliefs. In their memo, Jeff and
Melissa cited a 1971 decision by future Supreme Court justice John

Paul Stevens on a case involving 14 men who stole and burned 100,000 draft records in Milwaukee. The men had been inspired by the Berrigan brothers and their Catonsville Nine trial.

"One who elects to serve mankind by taking the law into his own hands thereby demonstrates his conviction that his own ability to determine policy is superior to democratic decision-making," Stevens wrote in the decision. The "professed unselfish motivation, rather than a justification, actually identifies a form of arrogance which organized society cannot tolerate."

This was not a matter of right and wrong, the government was saying. This was a matter of reckless arrogance.

Jeff, during a November 20 hearing, told the judge that the defendants were asking the court to rule on a political question, which was out of bounds in a courtroom. He argued that they were misusing the Nuremberg principles, which absolve a citizen from obeying directives that violate international law. There was no international law against the possession or the use of nuclear weapons, he said.

"They say if they didn't act, that they are somehow complicit in this illegality," Jeff said, and that would mean every citizen who hasn't done the same is complicit in war crimes, "which is a ludicrous argument."

Bill Quigley, the lead defense attorney for the trio, was up from New Orleans, where he was a professor at Loyola University. Bill, bald and bespectacled, was a crusader for social justice, having worked on cases involving public housing, voting rights, and civil disobedience. He had represented Michael and Greg when they'd dressed as clowns and vandalized an ICBM site in North Dakota. His clients wanted their latest court date to be the first trial to litigate the mere *possession* of nuclear weapons.

"The effort to preclude necessity, international law, nuclear policy, God, conscience, history" is "inconsistent with our search, our mutual search for truth," Bill said. This trial is not just about a break-in. It's about "the survival of humanity."

Judge C. Clifford Shirley Jr. bristled. As a Knoxville magistrate, he had overseen previous cases involving activists at Y-12. "I'm having a little bit of a disconnect," Shirley said, "in understanding how the trial of essentially a trespassing case will affect the literal survival of humanity, regardless of outcome. So, I guess I would ask you: Which result will cause humanity to survive? Guilty or not guilty?"

"History develops one little knot in the string at a time," Bill replied. "The direction in which it goes is in part decided by this case."

In the meantime, Jeff offered a bargain to Megan, Michael, and Greg: Plead guilty to destruction of government property and get less than a year in prison. Don't plead guilty and we'll add more charges.

The trio refused. They didn't believe they were guilty. They wanted a trial.

On December 4 the prosecution handed down a new indictment: "intent to injure, interfere with, and obstruct the national defense of the United States." The charge, from the sabotage chapter of the U.S. code, carried a maximum of 20 years in prison. It was rarely leveled against civilians in the United States.

This meant that Megan, Michael, and Greg would not really be tried for their actions, which they had already admitted to. The trial instead would be about their *intentions*, about the *purpose* of the break-in. A battle was brewing between morality and legality, and it would now be fought in open court.

THE OLD MAN took his seat in the witness box. He was dressed in a navy suit with a white shirt and navy tie. His eyes were deep-set but bright, his silver hair combed back. He had been the attorney general under Lyndon Johnson, when Michael Walli had been deployed to

Vietnam. He had prosecuted activists who had organized resistance to the draft. Now, a week before the jury trial for Transform Now Plowshares, 85-year-old Ramsey Clark sat in front of Michael to support his defense.

Clark also had been the attorney general when the United States signed the Nuclear Non-Proliferation Treaty, which the defendants claimed was being violated at Y-12. After leaving the White House in 1969, Clark turned against the Vietnam War and defended Phil Berrigan when he and six others were charged in 1972 with conspiring to kidnap Henry Kissinger. Since then, Clark had defended all manner of unsavory characters in court—African dictators and Nazis, Saddam Hussein and Slobodan Milošević—and earned a certain reputation because of it. But he believed that the rule of law should govern all people, peace activists to warmongers, no matter how inexplicable their actions. He had come to Knoxville to testify that Michael, Megan, and Greg's beliefs were reasonable and that their actions did not harm the national defense.

After the former attorney general was sworn in, Bill Quigley asked him if it was reasonable that the defendants believed they had no legal alternative to breaking into Y-12.

"Attention has to be paid," Clark said. "And attention *isn't* paid. And [an act of civil disobedience] calls attention to it. That's about all a person can do, an individual, to try to cause our government and our public to pay attention to something that threatens life on the planet."

Jeff Theodore cross-examined Attorney General Clark.

"I mean, the democratic process *does* work, don't you believe?" Jeff asked.

"Well, it hasn't worked," Clark responded. "And they have devoted a big part of their lives to try to save ourselves from ourselves. . . . Our militarism seems to have grown steadily. Our nuclear-weapons policy seems to have grown steadily. I haven't seen any improvement in it."

"And you're not aware that there's been a reduction in the actual nuclear warheads?"

"Not in the destructive capacity."

Clark's testimony reminded Sister Megan of Psalm 34: *The righteous cry out, and the Lord hears them.*

The magistrate decided not to admit Clark as a witness for the trial, which was set for May 6, 2013, with a federal judge from Kentucky named Amul Thapar. Born in Detroit to Indian immigrants who were culturally Hindu but not devout, Thapar grew up in Toledo, Ohio. His grandfather, a great storyteller who lived with the family, extolled Gandhi's ability to drive out an occupying empire without spilling a drop of blood. At Boston College, a Catholic university, Amul studied economics and philosophy, read Aristotle and Dostoyevsky, and extended his investigation of moral codes into law school at the University of California at Berkeley. He worked in private firms and in U.S. attorney's offices in Ohio and Washington, D.C. In 2007 Thapar was nominated by George W. Bush to the Eastern District of Kentucky, where he heard a wide range of cases, many drug-related, and the occasional coal-mining lawsuit. He took pride in showing mercy to drug addicts, helping to rehabilitate them through the court system.

This Plowshares case, for him, was something new and very different. When all was said and done, he would view it as one of the more challenging cases he'd tried.

SIXTY-SIX POTENTIAL JURORS lined up to go through security at the courthouse in downtown Knoxville on the morning of Monday, May 6, 2013. They were joined by a parade of 75 activists, who had marched down Market Street with signs that said, "Transform Now!"

The main action was in courtroom 1A, a medium-size gallery with wood-paneled walls and ten benches for spectators. There was an overflow courtroom with a closed-circuit television of the proceedings. Both rooms were full of activists, prospective jurors, and members of the media.

On the right side of the main courtroom, next to the jury box, was the prosecution: Jeff Theodore and Melissa Kirby, who was six months pregnant. They greeted some of the spectators they'd prosecuted in previous trespass cases.

On the left side of courtroom was the defense, seated behind desks arranged in an L shape. There was Sister Megan, Michael, and Greg. There was Bill Quigley, the point man from New Orleans. Michael's attorney was Chris Irwin, who ran his own law firm in Knoxville. Greg was representing himself, though he retained a young public defender named Bobby Hutson as an adviser. Sister Megan's attorney, Francis L. Lloyd Jr., was straight out of a John Grisham novel: a short man with a big presence, a quiet but deep voice, an accent flavored by the Shenandoah Valley. He was eloquent and preacherly. He pronounced "statute" as "sta-TOOT," and always pulled a rolling briefcase with his files. His heroes were the legendary Clarence Darrow, who defended Darwinism in the Scopes "monkey trial," and the theatrical Jacques Vergès, whose clients included Carlos the Jackal and Nazi gestapo chief Klaus Barbie. The defendants of Transform Now Plowshares referred to him as "St. Francis." He was a proud member of Amnesty International, and wore its pin on his lapel, but considered himself a lawyer with clients, not a lawyer with causes. This was his 32nd year practicing law, and he had been fascinated by Sister Megan's case from the day he got the call to represent her. Debating motives in court and arguing right and wrong were as essential to democracy as the right to vote, he believed, and this case offered a compelling chance to do so. Over the course of his career, though, he saw judges increasingly constrain certain arguments, like the necessity and justification defenses. He was troubled by the narrowing of debate, the attempt to strip moral discussion from crimes of conscience, and he saw it happening in the pretrial hearings. The focus was solely on the facts, to the detriment of philosophy.

Francis had argued that the government could not charge a crime that mentioned an "intent to injure" but then prevent the defendants from talking about the *nature* of their intent. He argued that the new sabotage charge was prosecutorial overreach, that it set a disturbing precedent, that the underpinning law was designed for wartime scenarios. Y-12 was not a military installation. It did not have full-scale weapons that could be launched or damaged. It was run not by the government but by private contractors.

"I don't believe Congress, in enacting this early statute, had in its mind the prospect of an executive branch which might, without a declaration of war, declare war to exist everywhere," Lloyd had argued, "and which might determine as part of its policy-making that the national defense encompasses every contractor, subcontractor and sub-subcontractor who bears some relationship to military activities."

Was this charge under the sabotage chapter, Francis wondered, a symptom of an America that saw war everywhere, that viewed any threat as villainous and indivisible?

JUDGE THAPAR ENTERED the room in a black robe and took his seat below the state seal of Tennessee mounted on the wall behind him. The seal depicted an eagle, one claw clutching an olive branch, the other gripping a bundle of arrows. Weeding through the 66 prospective jurors, each with his or her own number, was both a grinding and illuminating process. The judge and the lawyers tried to ferret out bias toward or against law enforcement, the military, the media, Catholic sisters and priests, and Oak Ridge itself. Though the prospective jurors were pulled from counties outside the Oak Ridge area, the connections to the city were clear.

Juror 218's grandfathers, grandmothers, aunt, and uncle had retired from the Department of Energy in Oak Ridge. Several jurors had sons-in-law who worked for DOE subcontractors, or brothers-in-law who worked at the K-25 site, or ex-husbands who did engineering and machining at Y-12. Two jurors had pastors who had asked their congregations to pray for the people who work at Y-12. One woman conducted a handbell choir that included an Oak Ridge security chief. One man sold and serviced elevator parts at the DOE sites. A couple had great-grandfathers who had worked on the Manhattan Project and told stories about wearing pins that detected radiation.

"My dad actually works in Oak Ridge right now, but it wouldn't affect me," said juror 234 at one point.

"Do you know what your dad does there?" Judge Thapar asked.

"No," 234 said. "He's been there for 34 years, and he's never been able to tell me what he does."

"My father was in the Army and retired from K-25," said juror 249.

"What did he do at K-25?" Judge Thapar asked.

"I really don't know," said 249.

"Where is his office in Oak Ridge?" Judge Thapar asked juror 258 about her husband's workplace.

"I have no idea," 258 said. "You have to have a badge to get into wherever it is, so I've never been there."

"Have you ever talked to him about his work at Oak Ridge?"

"No. He doesn't say anything."

"Have you ever had any conversations with him about it?"

"No. His work is very separate from his family."

In the afternoon, one after the other, prospective jurors approached the bench to talk about their concerns in private with the judge and lawyers.

"If three senior citizens can break into a federal facility, our security is severely lacking," said juror 233. "And I really think it's absurd" to jail them "when they actually kind of pointed out problems."

"If you incarcerate them, you'll make them a martyr for the cause, good or bad or whatever," said juror 3, who worked at Y-12's central training facility for the guard force. "I do not want to see this spill out of control, a debate on nuclear arms or the good or bad of it."

In the fourth hour of jury selection, Judge Thapar asked the room if anyone had strong views about nuclear weapons.

None of the prospective jurors raised their hands.

The lawyers dismissed them by the dozen. By 7 p.m. they had bargained their way down to 12 jurors and 2 alternates, among them a nurse, a bus driver, a social worker, an engineer, and a teacher. They were given instructions to report by 9 a.m. the following day, at which point the defense would try to convince them that three repeat offenders—who admitted to their criminal actions—were, in fact, *not* guilty.

SMOKY FOG HAD ROLLED INTO Knoxville from the mountains overnight. It veiled another parade of activists, who drummed their way toward the courthouse on the streets of downtown. At one point they actually found themselves at the intersection of Church and State streets.

Michael wore a T-shirt that said END TORTURE. Greg wore a T-shirt that said LOVE. Sister Megan wore a lilac-colored hoodie, jeans, clip-on sunglasses, and a shirt that said I WISH TO LIVE WITHOUT WAR. A Buddhist monk in saffron robes chanted at the front of the parade.

"This is Criminal Action 3-12-CR-107. United States of America versus Michael Walli, Megan Rice, and Greg Boertje-Obed."

The jury was sworn in and seated. Both courtrooms were again at capacity. In the audience were Greg's wife, Michele, and other Plowshares veterans, including Father Carl Kabat, who was part of the first action in 1980, jackhammered the concrete cap of an ICBM silo in

Missouri in 1984, and had dressed up as a clown with Greg and Michael to deface a silo in North Dakota in 2006.

There was Father Louis Vitale, a Franciscan priest who had been arrested a few hundred times and who had co-founded the Nevada Desert Experience, the community in Las Vegas that organized resistance against the Nevada Test Site and had hosted Sister Megan for several years.

Also present were a dynamic duo of Catholic sisters: Carol Gilbert and Ardeth Platte. In 2002 Carol and Ardeth had cut through two gates around an ICBM site in Colorado and, after hammering on the silo cover, painted the sign of the cross on it with their own blood. They were charged with the same crime as was Transform Now Plowshares: intending to endanger the national defense. Their case would come up several times during this trial.

Sitting nearby were previous Y-12 trespassers Sister Mary Dennis Lentsch and Jesuit priest Bill "Bix" Bichsel, who after a 2009 visit to Hiroshima joined the Disarm Now Plowshares action that had inspired Sister Megan to seek out Greg. Steve Baggarly, whose testimony in this very court had moved Jeff Theodore, was present, too.

Melissa Kirby opened for the government. In her soft Tennessee twang she described the broad actions of July 28, 2012. The break-in shut down the site for two weeks, she said, and a shipment of material had to be diverted.

"The defendants actually did interfere with our national defense," she said. "Deliverables had to be rescheduled the day of the incident and subsequent days, too."

Whether "deliverables" was a euphemism for "secondaries"—the part of the bomb that amplifies its power—remained unclear, as did the ironic possibility that the trio had interrupted the dismantlement of weapons that they wanted to eliminate.

Chris Irwin, Michael's lawyer, opened for the defense. "What you'll find informative is what they did and what they did *not* do," he said. "You'll hear no evidence that they tried to blow a hole in the side of the building. You'll hear no evidence that they even tried to get in."

Greg gave his own opening statement, in which he described his and Michael's roots in Catholic Worker houses and Sister Megan's service in Africa.

"I believe our lives—before the action and during the action— demonstrate what is *real* security, what is *real* defense," he said in his meek and measured voice. "We believe that the work at Y-12 con- tributes to false security. Nuclear weapons are an *illusion* of security. They are designed to terrorize and kill civilians."

His parting words to the jury were bold and direct, and he had said them in court before: "You are the conscience of the community."

Francis Lloyd focused mainly on his client's biography. "At an early age, she was troubled by the fact, even as a child, that a neighbor of her parents, who it turns out was working on something related to the Manhattan Project, could not even discuss at his home, with his own wife, what he did," Francis said. "Later, she learned from an uncle who actually, in military service, had been posted to Nagasaki after the dropping of that bomb, what that officer saw while there."

The government's first witness was Steven Erhart, who managed both the Pantex Plant and Y-12 for the National Nuclear Security Administration (NNSA). He had been transferred from Amarillo to Oak Ridge just ten days before the break-in. Melissa asked him about Y-12's history, its uranium for the Hiroshima bomb, its current role in contributing to the nation's nuclear deterrent, the mechanics of a modern two-stage thermonuclear explosion. Several jurors' eyes glazed over when he started talking about hydrogen isotopes and X-ray energy, and one began to nod off. Melissa steered Erhart back toward the function of Y-12 and why its disruption harmed the national defense. This was precisely what Megan, Michael, and Greg wanted to be heard in open court: that Y-12 was not so much a "national security site" as a weapons factory.

It's a "one-of-a-kind" production facility, Erhart said. Without Y-12, "you don't have a secondary and, therefore, you don't have a nuclear weapon. And without the nuclear weapon deterrent being strong, you lessen our national security."

"In what other ways has the defendants' breach harmed Y-12 operations?" Melissa asked.

"Credibility is related to the deterrent," Erhart responded. "It affected our credibility at Y-12. We certainly have a lot of people that were affected by that, and the circumstances around it, and then the actions that had to be taken after that. So it affected a lot of people, a lot of lives."

Bill Quigley cross-examined him, aiming to get Erhart to admit that it was the government itself whose lax oversight endangered the national defense, that the activists triggered an *improvement* in security.

"Would you agree that there was a sense of complacency among the security personnel that has been changed as a result of this incursion?" Bill asked.

"I believe a better word would be—or a better term would be 'normalization of the deviation from the optimum,'" Erhart said, to scoffs from the audience. The dozing juror was now fast asleep.

Francis Lloyd cross-examined Erhart next, bringing up a couple of nuclear incidents over the years, including the mistaken bomber flight of six unaccounted-for nuclear weapons from North Dakota to Louisiana in 2007.

"So it is possible, given our fallibility, our mutual fallibility," Francis said, "that a mistake could create the same sort of extensive harm Professor Quigley was asking you about?"

"Well I guess everything to some degree is possible," Erhart said.

"I will say the probability—if we're talking about an inadvertent nuclear detonation, a full-out weapon—is extremely improbable."

Francis had him where he wanted him, but his tone was as supple and sunny as ever. "Before July 28, 2012, would you have said that it was extremely improbable that three people, including an 82-year-old nun, would end up standing next to a highly enriched uranium manufacturing facility?"

Erhart shifted in his seat. "As I stated before, I was quite surprised, yes, sir."

AFTER AN HOUR FOR LUNCH, Melissa was back up for a redirect of Erhart. She began to re-litigate a debate from 68 years prior.

"What event ended World War II?"

"I believe the bombings that we spoke of earlier," Erhart said. "Hiroshima and Nagasaki, I believe, are primary to that."

"Do you have any idea how many American lives were saved by the use of the bomb in that particular instance?"

"I've heard various estimates as to—"

"Objection, Your Honor," Francis said, standing. "Speculation."

"Sustained," Judge Thapar said.

The government then called the two men who first responded to the scene: Kirk Garland and Sergeant Chad Riggs. While Riggs was on the stand, Jeff played portions of the grainy, black-and-white security video from Y-12's protected area. The soundless video, portions of which were redacted with blackouts, showed three tiny black dots moving like ants in the gray distance. The courtroom watched Kirk arrive, address them from his SUV, exit the vehicle, call for backup, wait as the intruders fetched candles from their backpacks. Then Riggs arrived with urgency.

Jeff asked why Riggs drew his gun.

"I felt in danger," Riggs said.

"You didn't use deadly force against them?" Chris Irwin asked Riggs during cross-examination.

"No, sir, I did not."

"You didn't believe it was necessary."

"No, sir, I did not."

Kirk then took the stand in a navy polo shirt. It was now about nine months since he'd been fired from Y-12.

"You had dealt with peace protesters before?"

"Correct. I've arrested quite a few of them. . . . I mean, I understand a peace protester when I see one."

"So you were authorized to use lethal force, though?"

"Correct."

"But through your training and experience, you chose not to?"

"Well, I'm authorized to use deadly force when my life is being threatened or somebody else's life is being threatened, or in other situations. None of those situations was present."

"Were they passive?"

"They were passive."

Next on the government's witness list was the man in charge of all security at Y-12. Brigadier General Rodney L. Johnson arrived at Y-12 four days after the break-in to assist with "recovery." The government called him to prove that the damage caused by the defendants exceeded $1,000. Jeff went through an itemized list of repairs—mending fences, scrubbing and repainting the HEUMF—which totaled $8,531.67. When Francis cross-examined Johnson, he determined that the cost was less than $1,000 when the cost of labor was subtracted.

For the first time, Greg rose to ask his own questions. "I have a special interest, because I'm a house painter," he said. ". . . It looks like you purchased 100 gallons of paint. Is that correct?"

"Yes, according to the receipt," Johnson replied.

"And do you know if there was any paint left over?"

"No, I don't."

"Because it seems to me that's quite excessive. So have you ever painted a room or hired somebody to paint a room in your house?"

"Yes, I have."

"Do you recall about how much paint it took to cover one room?"

"No."

"I can suggest perhaps it takes about a gallon."

Melissa rose. "Objection, Your Honor," she said, but Greg's point was made.

The government then played the audio of the defendants making phone calls from Blount County jail and a video of a TV interview, with Greg saying, "We take responsibility for what we did."

The government rested its case at 4:45 p.m.

The defense, for its first witness, called Sister Megan to the stand. She was ready to be a bit unruly.

THE CLERK BEGAN: "Do you solemnly swear or affirm—"

"If that also includes the Constitution of the United States, the truth," Megan said softly.

Judge Thapar looked up from his laptop, where he was taking notes. "She has to take the oath," he said. "Ma'am, I'm sorry, can you hear me?"

"Yes, sir."

"Did you hear the oath?"

"I just wanted to ask if it includes the Constitution of the United States, the truth. If you'll accept that as the truth."

"Well, the United States accepts it as a binding document," the judge said, "but do you swear to tell the truth?"

"Yes," Megan said. Francis then asked the sister about her upbringing. She called herself "a Depression baby." She talked about how her father taught his medical students to minister to the poor, how her mother studied slavery and its abolition, how they lived by the Columbia University physics building, how her next-door neighbor couldn't tell his family about his work, how her uncle Walter was sent to Nagasaki, how she learned to use radioactive tritium in college to study cell division. Francis's line of questioning brought the court through her decades in Africa, her trips to the Nevada desert during Lent in the 1980s, the early-morning hours of July 28, 2012.

"Did you expect to encounter security personnel?" Francis asked.

"I was keeping my mind clear," Megan said. "I sort of had this intuition that for 70 years you can't keep up 24/7 hours of observation. So I thought very possible, you know, that people don't have that energy to do this kind of thing. I really believed, anyway."

"In one of the clips that the government played of you being interviewed, I thought I heard you say 'we were led.'"

"Clearly we were led. Certainly. I mean, physically, Greg was in front of us, but I didn't think Greg knew where he was going. I mean, there was no path. I mean, we're struggling—all we were trying to do was get inch by inch through that densely bushed wooded area. So clearly we were led. Yes."

"Led by whom, Sister?"

"A spirit within us and around us."

SISTER MEGAN was back on the stand the next day, May 8, in the same clothes, at 9 a.m. sharp. Melissa Kirby, wearing a black blazer and a strand of pearls, was ready to cross-examine her. Unlike the sister and her supporters, Melissa wore no outward signs of her faith. On a social media page of hers, though, was a Latin prayer to St. Michael the Archangel, her patron saint. The prayer had allegedly been written by Pope Leo XIII in the 1880s after he had a vision of demonic spirits invading Rome. It began:

St. Michael the Archangel,
Defend us in battle.
Be our defense against the
wickedness and snares
of the Devil.

The task at hand was less biblical and more procedural. The government witnesses on day 1 had testified that Y-12 was crucial to national security, and now Melissa had to get Sister Megan to admit that she wanted to halt operations at Y-12.

"Good morning, Sister Rice."

"Good morning, Miss Kirby."

A strange reversal for the former Catholic schoolgirl.

"What do you think about what they do at Y-12?"

"I feel that they're making a huge amount of money. Of the people's money."

"Why did you pick Y-12 as a place to go on to and commit these acts of damage to property?"

"I was conscious that there are many places, and I was hoping that we could bring truth to this—one of the initiators of the Manhattan Project."

"So basically you picked Y-12 because it was a nuclear-weapons production facility?"

"Yes."

"Do you want Y-12 to stop their nuclear operations?"

"With all my heart."

"So basically you chose Y-12 because of the impact your intrusion there would have on the nuclear weapons program and the national defense?"

"I was aware of every moment being an imminent threat to the life and the harmony of the planet. . . . And I had to do it. My guilt is that I waited 70 years to be able to speak what I knew in my conscience. I've never been there to say that. I've never tried to help and heal Y-12."

"Why does Y-12 need healing, forgiveness and the imminent empowerment that you spoke of a moment ago?"

"I think everyone can answer that question. As I say, it is manufacturing that which can only cause death."

"So you obviously believe that using atomic bombs in World War II was wrong?"

"I believe it was—"

"Objection," Francis said. "Relevance."

Hiroshima and Nagasaki had again found their way into the courtroom.

"All right," Judge Thapar said. "Sustained."

Melissa re-tacked. She asked Sister Megan why she'd never protested at nuclear-weapons sites in Pakistan, India, Russia, or North Korea.

"I don't have the money," Megan said. "I don't have the time. I don't have the energy. I'm an individual among the seven billion people on the planet, and we are all equally responsible."

"Do you consider yourself an American?"

"Actually I consider myself a citizen of the world. I believe that all boundaries are arbitrary."

The defense called Michael to the stand. There was the usual trouble with the oath.

"You said the whole truth," Michael said to the deputy clerk. "To the extent I am permitted, I do agree."

Judge Thapar suppressed a sigh and turned to the defense attorneys. "He's got to take the oath, or he's not testifying," he said. "He's got to swear to tell the truth. I'm not sure what he means by that. Do you want to ask him about it?"

"You swear to tell the truth, don't you, Mr. Walli?" Bill Quigley said from the defense table.

Michael was still standing, his jaw set and brow furrowed. "With the understanding that the government qualified the oath when it said 'the whole truth,'" he said. "If I am permitted to tell the whole truth, I'll give that a shot."

The judge, wincing slightly, turned to Jeff and Melissa. "Is the government satisfied with that?"

Jeff stood. "I don't think so, not with those conditions, Your Honor. I think that he needs to take the oath as given, accept it and affirm it."

The judge turned and looked down at Michael. "Do you swear to tell the truth and nothing but the truth?"

Michael had made his point, whatever it was. "The whole truth, yes I do, Your Honor."

"You can be seated."

"Please state your name for the record, sir," said the deputy clerk.

Michael leaned into the microphone. "Testing, testing. Matthew, Mark, Luke, John. My name is Michael Robin Walli."

Bill asked Michael to give the jury some biographical information. He talked about growing up on a farm, about dropping out of high school, about the draft, about deployment to Vietnam.

"I obtained employment as a terrorist for the United States government in the U.S. Army," Michael said, adding that he heard the news of Martin Luther King Jr.'s assassination while in Vietnam and that he devoted his post-Army life to following in the footsteps of Jesus and opposing nuclear weapons.

"Would you tell the jury a little bit about what the Catholic Worker is about?" Quigley asked.

"Well the essential point of my own activities at Y-12 and my participation in Catholic Worker activities is a followership of the head of the church, Jesus Christ," Michael said. "And I note following in a particularly distinctive way the life choices of Dorothy Day, who founded the Catholic Worker movement. This is the anniversary month of her founding of the Catholic Worker movement in 1933, when capitalism failed once again and the Great Depression was going on."

And why did you trespass at Y-12?

Michael was getting worked up, and stumbling through run-on sentences. "I decided, basically, because since Dorothy Day, a great prophet, had condemned nuclear weapons and since these criminal activities are persisting at Y-12, despite the condemnation of this prophetical woman, Dorothy Day, and Dr. Martin Luther King also condemned them. There was a need to institute the rule of law and to comply with my legal obligations under the Nuremberg principles to oppose the crimes of my own government."

Bill asked about the meaning of their banner that quoted Isaiah.

"It means that God's will was reflected approximately 2,600 years ago by a great prophet of God who introduced the notion of total global demilitarization into the world. We did not invent—the three of us—God's will. We were mindful of God's prophets and God's will in doing the will of our heavenly father."

"Do you want to harm the United States? Harm the defense of the United States?"

"I have benign intentions and desires for all of my fellow human beings."

"Mr. Walli, do you have a net worth?"

"Yeah, I get a small stipend. And if people are nice to me, I try to be co-equally nice to them. This court recognizes the fact that I can be characterized as being indigent."

"Do you own a car?"

"No."

"Do you own a house?"

"No."

"Do you have a savings account?"

"No."

"Do you have any stocks and bonds?"

"No."

"When you planned, did you think you were going to get all the way to wherever you ended up getting in Y-12?"

"We took it to the Lord in prayer, knowing that the Lord can and has used frail vessels. I guess it was an answer to prayer, and a miracle. God wanted the work done, and we were the three manual laborers who accomplished the mission."

Jeff cross-examined Michael. "You referred to the Y-12 National Security Complex as a terrorist site," he said. "Is that right?"

"Yes."

"Do you believe they're engaged in terrorist activity there?"

"Yes."

"Have you ever gone to another country to protest nuclear weapons there? Have you ever gone to China or Russia, Pakistan, anyplace like that?"

"I'm an indigent person, and I feel I must bloom where I am planted. A citizen of heaven. But by accident of birth, I was born in the neighborhood here, and I try to do what I can with the scanty resources available to me."

"I noticed that in your testimony, you compared—you lumped together the Klan, KKK, al-Qaeda, and the United States together. . . . You feel they're all basically kind of all the same, in a way?"

"They're all murderers. Terroristic factions in noncompliance with the rule of law."

"You also mentioned in your testimony that you compared Y-12— you said it's the equivalent of the Auschwitz concentration camp the Nazis ran?"

"Yes, indeed."

Bill Quigley had the redirect. He asked if Michael believed in the Eisenhower quote that was on a strand of cloth wrapped around the ball-peen hammer: "Every dollar that is spent on armaments is a theft from the poor."

"Yes," Michael replied. "As part of my personal intentions, see, I am indigent, as the court knows. I've been a homeless person in at least ten different states here in the United States. I'm a victim of the misuse of these resources, just as Dwight D. Eisenhower said."

AFTER A BREAK, Greg took the stand at 11:21 a.m. His adviser, Bobby Hutson, asked him to describe his background. Greg talked about his Army days, when he was trained "to fight and supposedly win a nuclear war." Hutson then asked him questions to substantiate that nonviolence was their goal, even though it was undertaken at night and in secret. Despite the use of hammers and bolt cutters and blood, Greg said, their only aim was to bring peace and transformation to Y-12.

"I believe that it was very clearly a miracle that we were able to go from that church parking lot over the ridge and directly to the HEUMF building," Greg said. "There's no other way that I could explain it."

Hutson asked about the uninterrupted time they had inside the secure zone.

"Well, we didn't know how much time we would have," Greg said. "We go into these—" he quickly pivoted himself away from the Plowshares movement's parade of crimes "—this action with faith, founded on faith, believing that if we are allowed to do what we intended, it would be because it is God's work."

"Were you trying to destroy Y-12, the facility?" Hutson asked.

"No."

"In your mind, at the time that you went in to this facility, were you going there in peace?"

"Yes."

"Greg, in fact, were members of your group actually thanked by Congress for your actions in this case?"

"Yes."

Jeff rose for cross-examination. This was the government's last chance to prove, using the defendants themselves, that Transform Now Plowshares was not some miracle granted by God, that it was a misguided felony committed by misguided agitators who wanted publicity for a cause that belonged in politics, not court. Jeff, who was wearing a Catholic medallion underneath his dress shirt, decided to speak the language at hand.

"Do you feel that it's sinful or evil what they do at Y-12?"

"The making of nuclear weapons is putting your trust in a false God," Greg said.

"Okay. So you're not just talking about *using* nuclear weapons. You think even just possessing and having them, a nation having them, that that is [sinful]?"

"Yes."

Sister Megan "believes the people at Y-12 were psychologically or are psychologically damaged," Jeff said. "Do you believe that? People who work there?"

"Yes," Greg said.

"How so? What do you mean by that?"

"From my experience in the military, being trained to fight and win a nuclear war, I believe that is acting according to blindness. And that is a form of damage, to be blind."

Jeff asked him if he expected and desired a response from Y-12.

"Yes," Greg said. "We wanted a transformation response."

"Okay," Jeff said. "And you were hoping that that would somehow change the way Y-12 operates?"

"To stop the work that causes an epidemic of cancers all around the world, and especially the workers who are dying from the work."

Jeff brought up one of Greg's calls from jail, in which he mentioned the planned Uranium Processing Facility. He asked Greg why he mentioned it.

"I don't know if the jury is aware," Greg said, "but the UPF is a new nuclear bomb factory that the U.S. is planning to build right next to the HEUMF."

"And you're hoping to stop that?" Jeff asked, trying to tighten the connection between impeding Y-12 operations and weakening America's national security.

"We, along with many activists around the country and the world, are hoping that the U.S. will not continue to build nuclear-weapons factories."

"Do you believe that the United States should, on its own, eradicate, get rid of all its nuclear weapons regardless of what other countries do?"

"I believe the U.S. should follow the treaties it has signed, including the non-proliferation treaty, which says we should negotiate with other nuclear nations and end the producing of nuclear weapons at an early date," Greg said.

Jeff asked about Hiroshima and Nagasaki, hoping to contain their horror to World War II, but Greg wouldn't take the bait. He brought up the depleted uranium used in bombs in Iraq and Afghanistan. He brought up the hundreds of nuclear tests conducted above ground in Nevada and the Marshall Islands.

"Do you have any remorse for what you did on July 28, 2012, at Y-12?" Jeff asked.

"No."

"Are you glad you did it?"

"Yes."

Bobby Hutson briefly redirected. He asked Greg why they didn't plead guilty in exchange for lesser charges and lesser punishment.

"Because," Greg said, "I believe that we are not guilty."

Jeff asked for one more question.

"*One* question," the judge said.

Jeff rose. "Isn't it true the actual reason is you wanted publicity for your cause?" he asked.

"Absolutely not," Greg said.

And with that, the main part of the trial was over. The court broke for lunch before closing statements. The activists had already achieved one victory: The prosecution and the judge himself stated multiple times that Y-12 was a "nuclear-weapons production facility," which is a far more specific designation than "national security site." Now it was time to seal the second victory: acquittal through the hearts and minds of the jury.

FOUR PEOPLE GAVE CLOSING ARGUMENTS, one for the government and three for the defense. Jeff was up first, and he used the overhead projector to display evidence of the intrusion: the severed fencing, the biblical graffiti, the streaks of blood.

Jeff, in a dark navy suit, reminded the jury that he didn't have to prove that the defendants had injured the national defense; he only had to show that they *intended* to do so. Nevertheless, there was clear evidence of real harm: the two-week shutdown of operations, the diverted shipment of nuclear material, the blow to Y-12's credibility even though its security was not 100 percent.

"Do you excuse what the burglar did because the homeowner was maybe a little lax on their security?" Jeff reasoned. He then talked about the dual forces of law and democracy. "There's ample opportunities for them to express their opposition to nuclear weapons, to rely on the democratic process," he said. "Things do get changed. We live in a constitutional democracy. You can change things through the democratic process. But no. They don't want to do that. They don't want to rely on that. It's not going to happen fast enough. You can't just take law into your own hands, force your will on other people. That's not what our country is based on."

The defense had three closing statements. Bill Quigley went first. One of his goals was to soften the image of Megan, Michael, and Greg. Despite their equipment, their boldness, and their successful intrusion, they were just peace protesters who didn't think they'd make it over Pine Ridge.

"Now, these folks may not be the most popular folks in town," Bill said, "and some of you may and some of you may not agree with their positions about nuclear weapons or disarmament or that. You may think they're spiritual. You may think they're socialist. You may think they're idiots. You may think they're prophets. That's not what it's about at this point." Reasonable doubt was the issue at hand, he said, and it was the threshold for taking away the defendants' freedom. "Do you feel so strongly about their intent to injure the United States—the national defense of the United States of America—that you would make one of the most important decisions of your life based on that?" Bill argued that the real harm was the clumsy security apparatus at Y-12. "Three senior citizens showing up with a backpack and a couple of banners is a threat to the United States of America, to this country that we believe in? *That* threatens us beyond a reasonable doubt? I don't think so. . . . Every single person said that Y-12 is safer today, less likely that nuclear weapons are going to get loose or be misused. Safer today than it was the day they showed up."

He motioned to the defense table. "We're here to protect freedom." Then he pointed to the prosecution. "They're here to protect Y-12."

After a ten-minute recess, starting at 2:49 p.m., Greg closed by putting the facts into the framework of two well-known parables. One was the Gospel story of the Good Samaritan, who ministers to an injured man on the side of the road.

"We see victims of nuclear weapons and victims of the U.S. empire at the side of the road in great multitudes," Greg said.

The second story was Hans Christian Andersen's "The Emperor's New Clothes." The U.S. government, in Greg's mind, was the emperor.

"How it relates to us is that we have exposed that the emperor does not have effective fences," he said. "The emperor does not have real security. Nuclear weapons do not provide real security. Nuclear weapons are instruments of terror and killing, and they have killed massive numbers of people. There is one expert that has said tens of millions of people have died from the making of nuclear weapons and the testing of them. So we would say that our actions were promoting *real* security, and they were exposing the false security."

Francis Lloyd was the last to speak.

"I have to admit I'm not much with the PowerPoints," he said to the jury in his refined drawl. "My wife gets concerned when I even approach the wheelbarrow."

After two whole days of tension and tedium, the jury and audience laughed. Francis smiled, his first goal accomplished. His second was to turn the tables on the government.

"The shortcomings in security at one of the most dangerous places on the face of the planet have embarrassed a lot of people," Francis said. "I would submit to you that because they've embarrassed a lot of people, because contracts have been lost, you're looking at three scapegoats behind me. There's a great many things that are right about our government, but I'll tell you one thing that's wrong about our government. The man who, based on his own experience, recognized—who recognized peace protesters when he saw them, who dealt with them appropriately—is the individual who doesn't have his job today. The individual who put these three people—whom Professor Quigley described as almost certainly qualifying for senior-citizen discounts—the man who put them facedown on the ground and handcuffed them with tight plastic cuffs still has his job. Figuratively speaking, the ·government is asking you to again put these people facedown on the ground and handcuff them. I ask that you resist the call of your government to do that."

WHEN THE JURY RETIRED to deliberate at 3:34 p.m., the defendants and dozens of their supporters gathered in a tight circle in the hallway outside the courtroom. Plowshares veteran Art Laffin, the patriarch of the Dorothy Day Catholic Worker house in D.C. where Michael lived, motioned for people to join hands.

"Lord, we ask you to send your wisdom and your courage to the jury," he said, and the singing began again.

"Peace is flowing like a river," they sang in two-part harmony. In subsequent verses, they substituted "truth" for "peace," then "love" for "truth," then "hope" for "love."

"I thought this was a courthouse, not a church," a nearby bailiff said to himself.

The jury deliberated for just under two and a half hours. The foreman was a goateed man in his early 40s named Keith Graybeal. He was a teacher and bus driver in Sevierville, birthplace of Dolly Parton, at the foot of the Smokies. He had served on a couple of juries for open-and-shut cases, when there was no moral or legal ambiguity, no talk of what America was or wasn't, or should or shouldn't be. He had never seen a trial begin with a peaceful parade through the streets. He had never seen defendants come across as sacrificial lambs. He was a Christian who went to church every week, and he believed in miracles. He had seen people overcome cancer. But was getting into the Fort Knox of Uranium a miracle?

Ten jurors were ready to vote guilty and two were ready to vote not guilty. One refused to convict a nun. Another said the defendants seemed like they were part of a cult. Another thought Sister Megan was being exploited to court sympathy and get publicity. Some jurors went back and forth with what–ifs: What if they had been a decoy and there was a small army of insurgents behind them in the woods?

A juror named Kathy Starr, a 66–year–old retired nurse who lived on a cattle farm 80 minutes away, had made up her mind before entering the jury room. Y-12 was a nuclear facility. There was a serious break-in. It was black and white. It didn't matter if a shipment was turned away; what if the United States had been attacked and the nuclear arsenal wasn't ready because Y-12 was shut down? It didn't matter that the defendants were motivated by religion; Kathy was a Baptist and believed that laws were meant to be followed. It didn't matter that her husband got skin cancer after working a dozen years as a machinist at Y-12; the plant was crucial to the defense of the country.

The jurors went through slides of evidence. They splayed maps of Y-12 over the table. They listened again to the defendants' phone calls from jail, and Keith found them eerie. There was such calmness and certainty in the voices of the sister and the housepainter, and such fervor in the veteran's. Again, the what-ifs clouded the deliberation: What if they had been al-Qaeda? From what the jurors had learned about Y-12 during the trial, this breach was shocking and dangerous no matter who was responsible.

There were holdouts who believed the activists did not intrude in order to harm anything or anyone. That was the sticking point for Keith. The charge was *intent* to endanger, to damage, to obstruct. They clearly wanted to stop nuclear weapons, he thought, but they weren't there to endanger anyone—which is what made convicting them so difficult.

THE JURY FILED into the room and sat down at 6:01 p.m. Keith Graybeal handed a single sheet of paper to the bailiff, who handed it to Judge Thapar, who asked the defendants to rise. Megan, Michael, and Greg stood up, with their lawyers. Megan was smiling.

"Guilty on all counts," the judge said.

Sister Megan continued smiling. She turned her palms upward, as if to say, *This is what will be.*

"Ladies and gentlemen, this concludes your service in this case," the judge said to the jury. The jury stood, turned away from the audience, and began to file out of the box to the back door of the courtroom. The defendants' supporters sang softly toward them from their pews.

"Love, love, love, love. People, we are made for love."

A Quaker peace song. Supporters raised their hands at the jury as if imparting a blessing.

As he reached the door, hearing the quiet singing behind him, the foreman felt the hairs on the back of his neck stand up.

As the defendants were led, one after the other, out a rear door into custody, supporters wiped away tears and called out their gratitude.

The veteran was handcuffed—"Thank you, Michael!"—and then was gone.

The housepainter gave a wave—"Thank you, Greg!"—and then was gone.

The sister blew a kiss—"Thank you, Megan!"—and then was gone.

THE LAWYERS were left to discuss the potential release of the activists while they waited for their sentencing hearing. There was some confusion.

"We believe that this offense, under the Sabotage Act, constitutes a crime of violence," Jeff said, meaning that detention was mandatory. The violence, in this case, was against property.

The defense objected. Judge Thapar wanted time to study the law and statutes. He suggested they all meet again the following morning to determine if the activists' nonviolent action fell under Congress's definition of "violence."

Outside the courthouse, supporter Ellen Barfield, a designated spokeswoman for Transform Now Plowshares, was addressing the media. "It's pretty obscene but not terribly surprising, to slam them into jail for total nonviolence," she said. "The real crime? Nuclear weapons."

The players were in the courtroom by 9 a.m. the following morning. Megan, Michael, and Greg had spent the night in the Blount County jail, where they'd first been taken after the break-in ten months earlier. They were now dressed in orange Crocs and beige jumpsuits with FEDERAL INMATE stamped on the back. Their ankles and wrists were shackled.

For 90 minutes the judge and both legal teams tangled themselves in relevant case law and subsections of the U.S. criminal code. Jeff said that breaking into a national-security site is the same as breaking into a home, and that burglary equals force and that force equals a crime of violence. Bill Quigley referenced Antonin Scalia's definition of "violence" from a 2010 case before the Supreme Court: "extreme physical force," as in "murder, forcible rape, assault and battery." No way did Transform Now Plowshares fall into this category, he said, especially when their intent was *nonviolence*.

Congress "gave us no liberty to distinguish between terrorists and peace activists," Judge Thapar said, troubled by the rigid nature of the laws in question. "Al-Qaeda could have done the same thing and come in, and you could have stopped them at the fence. Let's say you arrested them, and they got convicted. You would agree with me that they're in no different procedural posture, at that point, than peace activists?"

Yes, said Jeff.

"Your Honor," Bill said, "that's where I think the opinion of Justice Scalia does, in fact, give you the ability to interpret that."

The outlook wasn't good. The prosecution reminded the judge that Greg had failed to show up for a hearing after a Plowshares action in the '80s. Michael had trespassed at Y-12 just three years earlier. Megan had at least two previous convictions of trespassing on federal property. They were unlikely to flee while they awaited sentencing, Jeff said, but they were "incorrigible" recidivists who might act again. Judge Thapar was clearly unhappy with his predicament. The law required him to treat these pacifists like they were true enemies of the state.

The audience began singing "Down by the Riverside" as the judge retired to his chambers and Megan, Michael, and Greg were led away.

Back outside the courthouse, Greg's wife, Michele, stood in the shade of an oak and watched supporters mingle with the media. This wasn't the first time she'd seen her husband disappear into the prison system, his sentence and fate undetermined. Their roles had been reversed several times before. Her heart hurt, but it was also strengthened by this latest Plowshares episode.

"There is a gigantic mountain that people have been trying to move since the beginning of time," she said. "That mountain is held together by greed, corruption, and fear—human traits that don't show our better selves. That mountain manifests in different ways: corporations, weapons of mass destruction, institutions, and systems."

She paused. It was a beautiful spring day. There was an upside here.

"The judge didn't have to fight as hard as he did," Michele continued, admiring Thapar. "Justice and the law: the judge struggled hard to bring them together. When you can do that, you get a better shot at moving the mountain. The trial exposed these things. The circle continues to grow. The mountain is still there, but the circle that goes at that mountain continues to grow."

The following day, the judge formally denied the defendants' request for release. Their offenses constituted a "federal crime of terrorism."

FOR THE FOLLOWING EIGHT MONTHS, home was a county detention center on Cotton Drive in Ocilla, Georgia, ten miles from where Jefferson Davis was captured by Union cavalry. Their fellow inmates were mostly illegal immigrants in legal purgatory. There were 50 to 70 in a pod. The aura in the men's wing was mean-spirited and unpredictable. Fights were common. Being an inmate in the U.S. prison system consisted mostly of waiting. Greg kept his nose in a Bible. In the women's block, the food was too starchy and the air-conditioning was too high. Sister Megan tried to stay warm by wearing two pairs of long underwear beneath her jumpsuit. It was a constant battle to get refills of her heart medication. Otherwise the experience reminded her of her summer camp in the mid-1940s in Maine, where she first heard about Hiroshima. She saw a parallel injustice in Ocilla, nearly 70 years later: an inhuman system that operated almost automatically in the service of profit and conflict. Daniel Berrigan had written her a letter when she was in jail in 1998, telling her to make the most of her time "under federal scholarship." Even in prison, she remained a student of the quantum theory of physics. She felt connected, not isolated, because her fellow inmates were opportunities for love and consolation.

Even after the media attention faded, the letters from the outside world kept coming, faster than the three could answer them. "Thank you," people wrote. The letters said stay strong, keep the faith, the sacrifice will bear fruit.

"Gratitude" was how Sister Megan, now 83, signed her responses.

"Your respectful servant" was how Michael signed his.

"With hope for the coming justice" was Greg's signature. His daughter, Rachel, turned 19 while he was away. His wife had begun the process of opening a new Catholic Worker house in Duluth, Minnesota, to serve women who had been trafficked.

In January 2014, 18 months after the break-in, the trio was shipped back to Knoxville by U.S. marshals in a little van with a metal grate separating them from the driver. Again they found themselves in the Blount County jail, on the eve of their sentencing hearing, which would also establish how much they owed Y-12 for the damage they caused. They knew they would be given one last chance to speak for the record in court. Michael planned to read another indictment of the United States. Greg was more open to divine inspiration. He was thinking of the Gospel of Mark: "Whenever you are arrested and brought to trial, do not worry beforehand about what to say. Just say whatever is given you at the time, for it is not you speaking, but the Holy Spirit."

Bill Quigley visited the men the day before the hearing and assured them that their action stoked the anti-nuclear movement. "We don't know when it's going to boil, but it will," Bill said. "There are so many people who are inspired and activated."

About 200 of those people gathered at the Church of the Savior in Knoxville that evening. Some had traveled from as far away as California and Alaska. There were speeches.

"They can jail the resistors, but they can't jail the resistance," Bill said.

"The work they're doing now will cast a shadow on the next century," Sister Mary Dennis Lentsch said of Y-12, where she had been arrested with Michael in 2010.

"We are born with this little voice," said Sister Ardeth Platte, speaking to nascent Plowshares activists. "The passion is within us. Take that one extra step beyond your comfort zone."

THE NEXT MORNING, January 28, 2014, the security line snaked around the lobby of the courthouse and doubled back on itself. The activist and folk singer Pete Seeger had died the previous day, so the supporters sang "If I Had a Hammer" as they waited to pass through the lone metal detector. Courtroom 1A was once again filled by 9 a.m. Sister Megan, wrists shackled, had trouble pouring herself a glass of water.

The government's first witness was a repeat from the jury trial: Brigadier General Rodney Johnson, Y-12's security chief. He was called to testify to the monetary value of the damage, so that restitution could be imposed on the defendants. That number, which was around $8,500 during the trial, was now about $53,000, after the contractors factored in overhead costs and additional expenses—deploying canine units on a weekend at a cost of $13,000, videotaping 16 miles of fencing at a cost of over $7,000, paying a "systems" planner $49.65 an hour to do undefined work.

"From a security perspective, what other concerns did you have looking forward?" Jeff Theodore asked Johnson at the end of his questioning. "Did you have any concerns about other events, other things occurring afterward?"

The week before this hearing, unbeknownst to most of the courtroom, 20 grams of highly enriched uranium was found aboard a laundry truck on its way out of Y-12. A careless technician had left two vials of HEU in the pocket of his coveralls. There was no reason for Johnson to mention this incident.

"No," said Johnson, who was dressed in his Army uniform. "I mean, my—my one concern, honestly is simply, you know, Y-12 had a reputation as the Fort Knox. . . . The mystique, if you will, is gone. And I would be concerned of other folks viewing Y-12 as some—as an appealing target, that they may not have looked at it before."

Francis Lloyd rose to cross-examine Johnson. The attorney got the brigadier general to admit that he didn't know if the contractors' payment had already been docked by the government; that he was confused by the lines of authority between Y-12, the NNSA, and the Department of Energy; that although the five carpenters deployed to make repairs were each paid $45 an hour, the contractor charged the government $114 an hour per carpenter.

"I assume B&W Y-12 was there to make a profit?" Francis asked about the Y-12 contractor.

"Yes," Johnson said.

Was part of the contractor's job "to keep these three people outside the perimeter of Y-12?" Francis asked.

"Yes, it was."

"All right. But they got in, didn't they?"

"Yes, they did."

And then they "charged you and me and the other taxpayers over $26,000 to do what they needed to do because these people got in?"

"I believe they charged for hours they worked, yes."

"Were they paid?"

"I don't know."

After an hour and 43 minutes of arguments, the judge ruled that the defendants owed the government $52,953. This was a moot exercise, because the defendants had no means to pay.

Outside it started to snow.

The courtroom shifted to sentencing, which hinged partly on the defendants' remorse and the likelihood that they would commit similar crimes again. Jeff said that Greg and Michael had used the same unsound arguments about international law during their last Plowshares action, in North Dakota.

"I think it shows that they're not being sincere," Jeff said, to groans from the audience.

Quigley compared his clients to abolitionists and suffragettes.

"People break laws to illustrate the injustice that the law is protecting," he said. "The status quo today is that these weapons are totally legal in the United States. That is the status quo. They object to that. They think they are wrong *now*. They think it's *been* wrong, and they are fairly confident that there will be a time when even the status quo will recognize that these weapons, like mustard gas . . . were, in fact, illegal and immoral and violated international law."

The defense then called its first character witness, Kathy Boylan, to speak on behalf of Michael. Kathy, a grandmother, had lived in the Dorothy Day Catholic Worker house in D.C. for 20 years and had taken part in five Plowshares actions. In 1989 she swam, with a hammer tied around her neck, to a Trident submarine docked in New London, Connecticut. Now she took the witness stand to assist the latest Plowshares action.

Michael's attorney, Chris Irwin, asked Kathy to tell the court about Dorothy Day and the Catholic Worker movement, and Kathy concluded her explanation by saying Michael was the personification of both. Day called nuclear weapons gas chambers without walls, and Kathy's rhetoric matched.

"Gas chambers and ovens have become nuclear weapons, and those gas chambers without walls are being readied for use at Y-12," she said forcefully in her Bronx accent. "The whole world has been turned into a concentration camp. Humanity is trapped by these omnicidal weapons, and incineration is our fate unless we transform now, unless we disarm now." Her voice rose. "Michael Walli is trying to save our lives." She turned to the players. "*Your* life, Judge Thapar. *Your* life, Mr. Theodore. And all our lives. Please listen to him."

Jeff, in his cross-examination, asked if she would discourage Michael from future actions.

"No," Kathy said.

Francis Lloyd then called Mary Evelyn Tucker, a senior lecturer at Yale who had known Sister Megan all her life. Tucker's grandparents were close friends with Megan's parents in New York. Tucker's grandfather advised Megan's mother on her dissertation on the Catholic opinion on slavery, and Tucker had been born on Claremont Avenue and educated by the Sisters of the Holy Child Jesus.

"She is a person of love," Tucker said. She is "in a great lineage of

Gandhi, who transformed a nation, of Mandela, who we just cele- brated around the world in his death moment, of Martin Luther King. She is in a lineage, clearly, that is transformative."

Megan slipped on a coat and scarf. The chill from Ocilla hadn't left her. Outside the snowfall was increasing.

Bill Quigley called the final character witnesses, Wilfred "Andy" Anderson and John LaForge, who had driven together from Du- luth to testify. They knew Michael and Greg from Catholic Worker houses. Anderson enlisted in the Navy in 1944 and was on a destroyer in the Pacific that was hit by a Japanese torpedo and kamikaze plane. In the crazed aftermath, he sat on the stern and held one of his friends as he died.

"I came home a different person, and I hope I've been a different person ever since," Anderson said from the witness chair, before call- ing Michael and Greg "terrific human beings."

LaForge had worked for an environmental justice group called Nukewatch for 22 years. The previous summer he had protested at a German Air Force base because it hosted 20 American B61 nuclear warheads, a class of weapon scheduled for refurbishment at Y-12. Greg rose to ask his own questions. Suddenly the end of World War II was being litigated again.

"Could you briefly give your understanding of perhaps why the dropping of the first atomic bomb was not really the reason that the war ended?" Greg asked.

At the defense table, Jeff gripped the arms of his chair, ready to rise in objection, even though his co-counsel had asked a version of the question during the jury trial last May.

The war was basically over by the time Hiroshima was bombed, LaForge said, and the only sticking point was the United States' re- fusal to accept anything but an unconditional surrender by the Japa- nese. The Soviet Union's entry into the war that week was both the true cause of Japan's surrender and the strategic reason the United States used the bombs.

Jeff was nearly hovering off his seat, ready to object, but didn't rise until it was time for his cross-examination.

"Do you think that they should not have done what they did when they intruded on Y-12?" he asked LaForge.

"I think they committed an act of crime *prevention*," LaForge answered.

"If they were back in the community, you certainly would not discourage them from engaging in this type of activity again, would you?"

"Well, I take the view of the late Philip Berrigan with regard to that," LaForge said. "He was one of the founders and the first actor in the so-called Plowshares movement, and he always said, 'Well, we *need* to discourage one another from doing these sorts of demonstrations.' In fact, if you could be talked out of it, then you're not ready to handle it. So yes, I would discourage them."

At 1 p.m. the court took a 15-minute recess, during which the judge got word that the court was closing at 2:30 because of the snow. The court still had to hear final statements from each defendant, so the judge suggested they resume at a later date. The spectators, many of whom had traveled from out of town, murmured with disapproval.

Sister Megan turned to Francis. "It's *done*," she whispered sharply, slicing her hand in the air with finality. "Everything's been said."

The lawyers and the judge agreed to reconvene on February 18. As the defendants were led out of the courtroom to do more waiting, someone called out "Happy birthday, Megan!" She would turn 84 in two days. The audience began to sing "Keep Your Eyes on the Prize."

"This is still a courthouse," a bailiff said, "and you're not allowed to do this."

———————

THE HEART OF the American peace movement was crammed into courtrooms 1A and 1B on a bitterly cold mid-February day for the delayed finale of *United States v. Michael Walli et al.* Before the judge entered, Sister Ardeth Platte found herself chatting with her old friendly foe at the railing that separated spectators from the attorneys.

We're praying for you, Sister Ardeth told Jeff Theodore.

Jeff thanked her. He told her that he was on his knees the night before, praying for Megan, Michael, and Greg.

Ardeth smiled. TRUTH was emblazoned on her long-sleeve shirt. "I hope someday you walk with us," she said.

When Megan, Michael, and Greg entered, their supporters stood and held out their hands in a silent blessing. Megan, surprised by the volume of the crowd, flashed a peace sign and bowed, the shackles on her wrists jangling.

Even with the unplanned three-week recess, Judge Thapar was still not comfortable with the criminal statute and sentencing guidelines that applied to the case. The guidelines for the trio ranged from roughly 6 to 9.5 years, which was far lower than the 30-year maximum but still overkill, the judge thought, especially for nonviolent offenders, one of whom was now 84. He had been inundated with thousands of letters from the defendants' supporters, who asked for lenient sentences. Some supporters wrote that they wished they had committed the action themselves, a sentiment the judge had never encountered. Part of his duty, as prescribed by law, was to impose sentences that deterred criminal conduct.

But how do you deter the undeterrable?

These activists and their supporters, especially those in the Plowshares movement, were repeat offenders who committed the same crimes even after serving years in prison. At some point, the judge thought, the law had to command respect. There were lawful ways to redress grievances, and yet these defendants were continually committing crimes to use the court system as a soapbox. They celebrated the breaking of the law, were cheerleaders at one another's trials, but then pleaded for lenient sentencing. There was an illogic to it, even a hypocrisy. Still, Judge Thapar could not arrive at a sentencing number that felt right, that landed between deterrence and mercy. Sentencing, for him, was the worst part of the job, regardless of the case.

The criminal statute and sentencing guidelines seem "not to distinguish to me between the saboteurs that truly intend harm and the peace protesters that truly intend change," the judge said after the hearing began. How do you take—by all accounts—very good people and deter them from very bad acts?

Engaging in nonviolent disobedience is not a danger to society, said Michael's lawyer, Chris Irwin.

"You know, I'm a Catholic myself," Jeff Theodore said. "I have a lot of respect for their commitment to their cause, but they're not above the law. . . . They may be nonviolent but it doesn't mean that they're not dangerous."

Irwin told the court that there was a clear distinction between acts of protest in peacetime and acts of sabotage during wartime, and the Sabotage Act applied only to the latter.

"This country is under a state of emergency right now," Jeff countered. "There are several executive orders, even renewed by President Obama yearly, with respect to 9/11. We are still under a state of emergency."

Some members of the audience turned to one another and shook their heads.

A brief recess was then ordered before their final statements.

"Bless you, Michael," Art Laffin called out. "The Holy Spirit is at work."

———

AT 4:20 P.M., the activists of Transform Now Plowshares finally had a chance to say whatever they wanted in open court. It was now nearly 19 months since they had hiked Pine Ridge. Michael stood at the central rostrum, facing the judge, his supporters behind him. His hair was longer. He wore a charcoal-colored jumpsuit. He was ready to speak for the ages.

"I make no apology," he said in his strained voice. "I'm not remorseful. I have no sense of guilt or shame. I would do it again. I am the face of tomorrow, the face of total global demilitarization and the vindication of the prophets Isaiah and Micah, who foretold 2,714 years ago total worldwide demilitarization."

He brought up the Nuremberg principles, the Nuclear Non-Proliferation Treaty, the depleted uranium used in drone strikes, the United States' plan to modernize its weapons and delivery systems so they last through 2080—topics forbidden during the jury trial.

"The ongoing building and maintenance of Oak Ridge Y-12 constitute war crimes," Michael said, speaking off the cuff. "We are required by international law to denounce and resist known crimes. For the sake of the human family threatened by nuclear weapons, and for the sake of our planet Earth, which is abused and violated, we indict the Oak Ridge Y-12 nuclear-weapon facility and all government officials, agencies, and contractors as responsible for perpetuating these war crimes! I'm finished."

Greg was next. He spoke softly. He quoted "Hymn to the New Humanity," a poem by Daniel Berrigan, his mentor from 30 years before, when he had just left the Army. The verse was about nuclear weapons, but never mentioned them by name.

> There is a rare gun, a gun of dark rumor.
> The ultimate gun, the gun named god. Like god,

it has never been seen; in virtue of the
invisibility, it must be believed in.
Somewhere, no one knows where, whether on land or sea or
in the air, this gun is sequestered, stroked, nourished
by the hands of servitors. [. . .]
This is a metaphysical gun. It renders all other guns,
together with their makers and uses, redundant.
It is aimed at the heart of history, the secret wellsprings of life.

Greg had brought a copy of it with him over Pine Ridge. Their weapon on that hike was also metaphysical. They had it with them as they cut their way into the lethal-force zone. Greg had it with him now, in the courtroom. He bent the microphone closer to his mouth, prepared to deploy it.

"There's been a lot of talk about promoting respect for the law," he said. "It's my belief that the U.S., if it would abide by the Nuclear Non-Proliferation Treaty, it would promote respect for the law. Right now, people all around the world are aware that we are not abiding by that treaty. . . . President Obama went to Europe and gave a speech. It was a very significant speech. He said, 'We want to sign this treaty with Russia and we want to reduce nuclear weapons to zero.' People were happy. He comes home, comes back to the U.S. He explains later that in order to get this treaty signed in Congress he has to agree to fund and build three nuclear weapons factories—one of them in Oak Ridge—in order to get the votes to pass it. And these new factories will continue building weapons for 70, 80 more years, and that is a clear violation of the law. That's all."

Sister Megan was last. She was in a beige jumpsuit. She gripped the edges of the rostrum to steady herself. It was 4:43 p.m. on February 18, 2014, and she had been working her way to this moment for 75 years, from Manhattan to Harvard to Africa to Nevada to Oak Ridge.

She spoke for 30 minutes straight, starting all those years ago on Claremont Avenue.

"The secrecy began in 1943, when worker women—probably 6,000 at least—could not even tell their fellow workers or family what they were doing," she said. "Still now, secrets are kept between workers, officials, and managers. The secrecy prevailed to try relentlessly to turn these United States into a superpower, an empire, as Germany tried to be under the Third Reich. When I was growing up—to our generation, these were very evil terms. Has any empire or aspiring superpower not declined, not fallen apart from exceptionalism into decadence? So we had to come to this facility to call it to transformation. Thank you for revealing these kept secrets as evidence."

She decried the fallout from "misspending" trillions of dollars on nuclear weapons for 70 years, from the "constant unending war making by a military-industrial complex," from the income gap in a "debt-ridden" America, from a prison system that puts profit first—down to the $15 that's charged for every prison call she made from Tennessee to Washington. She thanked the judge, the jury, the attorneys on both sides, and the "prophetic peacemaking remnant" that sat behind her in the audience with tears in their eyes.

"So please have no leniency with me," she said to the judge, her voice swelling beyond her slight frame. "To remain in prison for the rest of my life would be the greatest honor you could give me. Thank you. I hope it will happen."

Then it was the judge's turn to give his own statement.

"As judges, we judge actions, not viewpoints," Thapar said. "And the actions—there is no question in this court's mind—transgressed the laws of the United States. . . . I don't have the wherewithal to judge God's will, as Mr. Walli said. I'll leave that to God. I don't have the wherewithal to determine if your viewpoints are right or wrong. I will leave that to the future."

The judge's tone was resigned, compassionate, a little mournful.

"Courts are not a place for judges to disregard the law, or we will truly have anarchy, and we'll have the very systems you all profess to hate," he continued. "In our country, I firmly believe that breaking the law is not the answer; rather, the political process is the answer. . . . I can't help but think, as I listen to your allocutions, that if all that energy and passion was devoted to changing the laws, perhaps real change would have occurred by today. . . . But today we sit here in a very sad case where the court can say it's generally distressed at having to place what I perceive—and continue to perceive—as good people behind bars. . . . I continue to hold out hope that a significant sentence will deter the defendants and others from this type of conduct and lead them back to the political process I fear they have given up on."

Judge Thapar gave Greg and Michael prison terms of just over five years each, followed by three years of supervised release. "Both are very good people that made a lot of bad decisions," the judge said.

He then turned to Megan. "Sister Rice, I know you want a life sentence and I just can't accommodate that request," he said. "Not only am I confident that you will live long past any sentence I give you, but I am sure that you will continue to use that brilliant mind you have. I only hope you'll use it to effectuate change in Washington rather than crimes in Tennessee."

He gave her two years and 11 months.

Before he disappeared to his chambers, Judge Thapar looked at Megan, Michael, and Greg. "I wish you the best of luck, and I do appreciate your good works," he said. "And I hope you will continue them."

ON THE SAME COLD DAY, in the same courthouse one floor above, Kirk Garland and his wife were at their bankruptcy hearing. As the activists expressed no remorse for their actions on the first floor, Kirk and Joann waited on the third floor to see if any creditors would show up to object to their filing. Kirk declared his worldly assets at $41,475—about $10,000 less than the cost of cleanup and repairs at Y-12. After their bankruptcy meeting, Kirk and Joann decided not to get in front of the news cameras that showed up for the activists.

Kirk was working as a corrections officer at the Morgan County Correctional Complex, a medium-security prison for a few thousand inmates in Wartburg, Tennessee, a 30-minute drive northwest of Oak Ridge. This work was tougher than the Y-12 job, and it paid a quarter of what he earned at Y-12. Ironically, he was in more constant danger surrounded by 100 volatile inmates in a single wing than he had been patrolling a site containing a huge store of fissile material.

His rent was $1,100. His last utility bill was $345. The math had been ruthless since he was fired from Y-12. After 30 years of working in nuclear security for the Energy Department's private contractors, he was a 53-year-old who had to rely for a time on food stamps and checks from his mother.

Kirk appealed his termination, but in the days before his scheduled arbitration, his speech began to slur, he lost muscular control of his right hand, and he was diagnosed with multiple sclerosis. He read articles online about possible causes, which included stress and exposure to toxic chemicals.

He thought of his father, Ronald, his brother, Kevin, his uncle Jim.

He was trying to buy a plot of land in Sunbright, a whisper of a township farther north, for a mobile home and a barn. Something to approximate the American dream. He had plenty of time to think on his 40-minute commute to and from the prison in Morgan County, past mangled roadkill and Confederate flags on the side of the road, past Baptist church after Baptist church, past the signs that said, "Pray for Our Country," all the way to the crop of short granite-gray buildings wreathed in concertina wire, nestled between ridges crowned with fog.

Kirk thought about the government, seemingly immune from consequence. He thought about the private contractors, insulated by profit. He thought about the activists, comforted by a devoted network of supporters. And then his thoughts drifted the only direction they could: upward. He reminded himself: *God's got something planned for us.*

PART III

RELATIVITY/ UNCERTAINTY

Truth is not that which can be demonstrated by the aid of logic. If orange-trees are hardy and rich in fruit in this bit of soil and not that, then this bit of soil is what is truth for orange-trees. If a particular religion, or culture, or scale of values, if one form of activity rather than another, brings self-fulfillment to a man, releases the prince asleep within him unknown to himself, then that scale of values, that culture, that form of activity, constitute his truth. Logic, you say? Let logic wrangle its own explanation of life.

ANTOINE DE SAINT-EXUPÉRY,
Wind, Sand and Stars (1939)

9.

THE MODERN PARADOX

In the beginning was the Creator, and the Creator made the people and the people's land. The land was a great basin of wide desert valleys and narrow mountain blocks, running north to south, crowned with juniper and rich in minerals. Deer and antelope pranced across meadows and alkali flats. The people called themselves "Shoshone," and the Creator commanded them to be in harmony with one another. Over thousands of years the Shoshone built trade routes across the land and developed agriculture, astronomy, and government. In the 17th century, nonnative tribes of white men began encroaching on the land, searching for a future in the west, cobbling together what would become the United States.

In the autumn of 1863, the Shoshone signed a peace agreement with the United States: the Treaty of Ruby Valley, which stated that white men could travel unmolested through the territory and use it for purposes of mining, transportation, and settlement. In return, the Shoshone would be awarded monetary compensation for the inconvenience. The treaty did not transfer ownership of the land to the United States, although the following year it made the territory an official state of the union called "Nevada." Just shy of a century later—after the Shoshone and other American Indians were corralled onto reservations, after the Hoover Dam was wedged into the Black Canyon, after the neon city of Las Vegas sprang from the dusty basin floor—the United States began testing atomic bombs on the people's land.

The Marshall Islands in the Pacific were too far away to test weapon designs efficiently, so to eliminate lag time the Nevada Test Site hosted 928 full-scale tests from 1951 to 1992, some above ground and most underground. Hotel roofs on the Vegas Strip were prime viewing spots for guests who wanted to sip a nightcap and watch the colors on the horizon. In 1955 the military built houses, populated them with mannequins, put up signs that said "Elm Street" and "Main Street," called it "Survival Town," and then detonated a bomb that had twice the yield of Hiroshima's. U.S. soldiers were ordered into trenches for the blasts and then told to march toward the mushroom clouds, to train for a nuclear battlefield. The shock waves murmured through the suburbs, sometimes more than once in a 24-hour period.

"This is the valley where the giant mushrooms grow," said the narrator of an Air Force promotional video. "The atomic clouds. The towering angry ghosts of the fireballs."

It is also the valley where activists camp. Every Holy Week since 1982, the year that a million anti-nuclear demonstrators marched through Manhattan, activists have gathered in the desert across the road from the Nevada Test Site. But first, they walk the 56 miles from Las Vegas on foot.

PALM SUNDAY. The Vegas Strip. April 2014. Two months after the sentencing of Transform Now Plowshares.

Two dozen walkers began at the National Atomic Testing Museum on East Flamingo Road. They ambled their way up escalators and across pedestrian bridges, struggling to stand out from the noise and bling of the city. Their banners said IMAGINE PEACE and NO NUKES! NO DRONES! The walkers included Code Pink women, Veterans for Peace, Catholic Workers, alumni of Occupy Wall Street, the dutifully employed, the delightfully adrift. Only a few were under the age of 40. They slipped through the front plazas of the Palazzo and the Venetian, rounded fountains and mounds of white carnations, passed by Fendi, Dior, and Burberry. At a side street called Cathedral Way, the leader of the walk stood at the corner in a lava-colored tunic, pointed north, and shouted cheerily to passing cars.

"Nuclear weapons, 60 miles that way! Happy Palm Sunday!" said Marcus Page-Collonge, who lived on a Catholic Worker farm in California and frequently wore a black T-shirt emblazoned with an image of Dorothy Day holding a cigarette, like a holier version of Barbara Stanwyck, saying, "Don't call me a saint."

Fremont Street, the halfway point of the first day of the walk, was lined with outdoor daiquiri bars and beggars with handwritten signs.

"Parkinsons. Down on my luck. Just need a little help please."

"26 FLAVORS."

"Stranded. Please help."

"BIGGEST AND BEST BUFFET."

The walkers circled up outside a casino and performed modest choreography to a song called "We Shall Be the Peacemakers."

The epithet "hippies" was used by passing tourists.

The walkers stopped to pray at the National Nuclear Security Administration's North Las Vegas facility, a tall and silent structure surrounded by a chain-link fence and barbed wire.

"Anybody got some blood?" said an activist named Robin. "Where's Sister Megan?"

Megan was two months into her formal prison term at the Metropolitan Detention Center in Brooklyn, but for a few years after her return from Africa, she had lived in Vegas, in one of the barracks of the Nevada Desert Experience (NDE), which organizes the Sacred Peace Walk. The NDE was an activist community bent on stopping all kinds of nuclear testing, even the subcritical tests at the newly named Nevada National Security Site. Those subcritical tests shocked bits of plutonium with high explosives but stopped far short of causing a chain reaction.

The walk concluded its first day at a Martin Luther King Jr. statue in town. The first night was spent back in the barracks, but for the rest of the journey all the walking and sleeping would be done on the side of Route 95.

The four-lane highway shoots northwest out of Vegas, skirting Red Rock Canyon National Park, and its asphalt shoulder was the footpath to the destination. The Sheep Mountains were to the right. The Spring Mountains were to the left. The walkers spent the next five days out in the horizontal vertigo of the desert, covering 10 to 15 miles a day and pitching tents on the rough caliche soil on the side of the highway, among yellow creosote bushes and magenta prickly pear blossoms. The only evidence of the animal kingdom were white moths and the occasional blur of a jackrabbit. A couple of support cars motored up and down 95, hauling supplies, providing water and meals, towing a portable toilet perched on a trailer at a precarious angle. The shoulder was littered with shredded tires and cans of Bud Light. Semis whooshed by, trailing the dissonant blast of their horns. Sometimes the walkers got a peace sign from a passing driver. Sometimes they got a middle finger.

The desert is a drawing salve. It strips away distraction. Time and space flatten. You lose scale. It's a perfect setting for a campaign like this, the walkers said. With each step, the infinite becomes surmountable. Each step was a vote, a way to put skin in the game, a way to state for the cosmic record that not everyone signs off on war making. The walk was a way to feel part of something in a country that was very good at isolating, at cordoning off, at ignoring. The number of

American servicemembers deployed in combat zones was at its lowest level in more than a decade, yet Congress was forever raising the Pentagon's war budget. Forty cents of every dollar earned by an American taxpayer went to military spending in some form. The antiwar movement had receded in this new century of perpetual war, and the Sacred Peace Walk was one way to recapture the feeling of destiny, of the arc bending toward something, anything.

"A walk is something I can *do*," said Darcy Leo Thika Ike, 71, a gangly former anthropology instructor who had lost his right ring finger during a mortar attack in Vietnam. "It's going to bring all of us—you, me, all of us—somewhere else together. It's shoestring morality."

"I was 35 and I'd never thought about nuclear weapons," said Felicia Parazaider, an interfaith pastor from Berkeley, California, describing her first walk a few years before. "I was freaking after my first visit to the test site. I felt a sense of shame because I'd never spent any time and didn't care about the issue. Younger people think activism is passé. They look at you like you're from Mars."

"If everyone who was against war would occupy a military base once a month, we could stop this," said Toby Blome, a retired physical therapist and full-time Code Pink activist from El Cerrito, California. "It's not that much work. People have a lot of power. They're just not using it."

On day three they stopped outside High Desert State Prison, now 40 miles into the walk, for a ceremony of remembrance. They circled up. They burned sage. They turned as a group and lifted their hands toward the prison.

"I ask for peace, for my brother, who's incarcerated there," said Vera Anderson, 25, a Vegas musician who quit her job as a waitress three weeks earlier.

"For Sister Megan," Marcus said. "For Greg and Mike."

"A 16-year-old boy killed in Pakistan," Toby said, referring to a Waziristan native named Tariq Aziz who was driving with his cousin at the time of the 2011 strike. "A 16-year-old American boy killed by our missile."

Six more miles down the road, they had lunch and discussed what they would do when they reached Creech Air Force Base, from which the United States pilots its armed drones overseas. Creech is a mirage of squat, dust-colored buildings on a bend in 95, just short of a natural oasis of 100-year-old cottonwood trees, about 15 miles from the nuclear test site. The base was originally a training camp built after the attack on Pearl Harbor to prep airmen for combat in World War II. In 2005 the base was given its current name and its current mission: fielding unmanned aerial vehicles, or UAVs, that either provided surveillance in combat zones or dispatched Hellfire missiles to assassinate suspected and confirmed terrorists in places like Afghanistan, Yemen, and Somalia. Civilians were occasional collateral.

Protesting drones was a natural prelude to protesting nuclear weapons, the walkers believed. If you give psychic permission to the most dangerous weapon on Earth—the taproot of evil, as Father Richard McSorley had called them—then all manner of bloodshed was not only possible but also permissible: from mass shootings with handheld automatic weapons to targeted assassinations from remote-controlled robots at 25,000 feet.

The walkers decided they would deliver an indictment to the base commander the next morning, charging the government with war crimes.

They'd have to get past a staunch patriot named Phil first.

AT 6:30 THE NEXT MORNING, Phil Frank was in his position near the entrance to Creech, on a median between Route 95 and the access road to the base's front gate. He had his camping chair, his big American flag, a tan sweatshirt with "USA" on it, and his large free-standing sign.

HOME OF THE FREE
BECAUSE OF YOU

He waved to base employees as they turned off 95 in their SUVs, headed for a day's work. Phil, nearly 70, had served six years in the Navy and retired from construction work to live here in Indian Springs, population 900-something, a 40-minute drive north of Vegas. There was one casino, with a $6.99 steak-and-eggs special, and one motel, with rooms for $19.99 a night, and one Air Force base. When Code Pink started trotting out fabricated child-size coffins several years ago, Phil began his occasional vigil to offer a counterweight.

"Keep up the good work out there, fellas," Phil called out, a one-man drive-thru of encouragement. "You're keeping my grandchildren safe. Everybody makes a difference."

The peace walkers set up across the highway with signs.

DRONES:
STATE-SPONSORED
TERRORISM

The objects in question buzzed a few thousand feet up, on practice missions. There were two types of them, Predators and Reapers, and they sounded like giant insects but glided like tiny jets. They landed from the east. They took off toward the west. Predator. Reaper. Reaper. Predator. The Reaper, newer and slightly larger, delivered a bigger payload.

"We are part of you," said Robert Majors, 26, of the Vegas Catholic Worker. He was three days into a fast, carrying a "Green Jobs Not War" sign over by Phil.

"You are not a part of me at all," Phil said.

Robert held out conscientious-objector forms to passing cars.

Phil held out his American flag to block him.

A Shoshone Indian entered the median. This was Johnnie Bobb, chief of the Western Shoshone National Council. In preparation for the walkers' trespassing onto the test site, he had issued them Shoshone permits to be on the people's land: "For non–Western Shoshone citizen to enter the Southern Zone of the Western Shoshone Nation (aka the Nevada Test Site)."

"Hey, those are my horses," Johnnie said, making a wry joke about colonialism, as three mounted police officers from Vegas idled by Creech's gate. Johnnie began beating a drum as the walkers organized for their action.

Police on foot marched two by two, in paramilitary fashion, waiting for the activists with bouquets of plastic hand ties.

"Once you pass that small metal gate, you're trespassing," an officer told a group of nine walkers who were beginning their short march.

"We're not here to commit a crime," said Brian Terrell, a bearded walker from Iowa. "We're here to stop a crime."

The walkers tucked copies of the indictment into the chain-link gate. It read in part:

> Extra judicial killings, such as those the U.S. carries out by drones, are intentional, premeditated, and deliberate use of lethal force to commit murder in violation of U.S. and International Law. . . . We appeal to all United States citizens, military and civilian, and to all public officials, to do as required by the Nuremburg Principles I-VII, and by Conscience, to refuse to participate in these crimes, to denounce them, and to resist them nonviolently.

They were arrested but processed and released in time to return to the base at 3:30 that afternoon, to make a scene for employees on their way home. Phil was there again with his wife, daughter, and grandson. Around 4 p.m. a digital tone signaled from the PA system on the base. A chintzy instrumental recording of the national anthem began playing. It sounded like it was coming from everywhere, from inside the brown hills, from out of the light-blue sky. Phil removed his ball cap and placed his hand over his heart. Darcy Ike removed his fisherman's hat, adorned with wildflowers, and held it against his heart with the hand that was missing a ring finger. Cars stopped. Drivers emerged from their vehicles, looking toward the base. Everyone, activists and drone pilots alike, was frozen in place, saluting the same country.

A couple of minutes after the anthem ended, a white Tiburon SUV screeched past, its driver calling out the window at the activists: "They're saving your fucking lives, you assholes."

"We all have the same idea," Phil said to Toby afterward, a man in red, white, and blue next to a woman in pink. "Just a different philosophy on how to get there."

THE PEACE WALKERS ate dinner on the grounds of the Temple of Goddess Spirituality, an oasis for pagans, wiccans, and activists up the road from Creech. At dusk a visitor arrived in his SUV, with its bumper stickers that said, "Don't Forget Benghazi" and "9-11-01 Never Forget." Phil Frank took a seat next to Marcus in a circle of activists. Over the course of an hour, they faded into silhouettes. They talked about the philosophy of nonviolence, the conundrum of conflict, the guiding principle of religion.

Nearby cottonwood trees murmured in the night breeze as Phil told a story about a break-in at his home several years ago. He described how the intruder attacked him. How he readied his gun to shoot in self-defense. How he broke out in a cold sweat when the intruder let go of him and the situation was resolved without violence. How he praised God that he didn't have to do the unthinkable.

"Would it have been better to have a robot then?" Marcus asked. "To have a robot kill someone who might kill you?"

"Absolutely," Phil said.

"So I understand why you think technology can save us," Marcus said. "You'd save yourself the suffering of having killed someone."

The conversation meandered and doubled back and tied itself in knots, eventually arriving at a cordial "good night" instead of a clean resolution.

"I just came by," Phil said as he left, "to let you know who I am."

THE ROCKY EXPANSE across from the test site was once host to thousands of protesters, encamped in joy and anger against underground nuclear explosions during the 1980s. They stayed in makeshift sweat lodges. They were chased over the creosote by helicopters. Their leader was Corbin Harney, a Shoshone healer and an anti-nuclear activist who died in 2007 at age 83. "We are one people," he reportedly said on his deathbed. "We cannot separate ourselves now." In red marker Sister Megan had written his name next to her uncle Walter's on the hammer she used to chip away at the Highly Enriched Uranium Materials Facility at Y-12.

Now, with explosions kept to a subcritical level inside steel spheres, two dozen walkers pitched tents as the hot desert wind whipped through the camp site. They had made it, all 56 miles, without mishap or injury other than bloody, blistered feet. Johnnie Bobb was there, drumming the walkers into the finish line, where the test site was a smudged streak of light along the hills.

"There's blood in this land," Johnnie said. His people had been driven north, and slaughtered if they couldn't keep pace. Now at least he was back, drumming a heartbeat toward the test site.

The site was used for more than subcritical plutonium tests. The government conducted all kinds of emergency scenarios there. There was really nowhere else in the United States, for example, where you could safely stage a chlorine spill. More than 200,000 first responders from across the country had trained on-site, but nuclear weapons were still a major part of operations. A new $200 million underground facility was being built there to handle more subcritical tests. The repository inside Yucca Mountain, under 1,000 feet of rock on the edge of the site, was ready to receive nuclear waste as soon as Congress approved it. The land was good for nothing else, some local-government officials believed. About $15 billion had been spent on the Yucca repository since its construction was greenlighted in 2002, but Sen. Harry Reid (D-Nev.) had fought its opening. As the number of warheads on the planet decreased over the decades, and as nuclear power proliferated, the amount of fissile material increased. There was somewhere between 1,500 and 2,000 tons of plutonium and highly enriched uranium on the planet at the end of 2012, and every year the amount of plutonium in the world increased by a volume that would furnish 740 nuclear warheads. So in total there was enough fissile material on the planet to furnish more than 100,000 nuclear weapons, and the excess and waste had to go somewhere.

There were powerful members of Congress who envisioned scenarios in which testing should be resumed in Nevada. "You don't know how a car performs unless you turn the key over," said Rep. Mac Thornberry (R-Texas), chairman of the House Armed Services Committee, who was against the ratification of the Comprehensive Nuclear-Test-Ban Treaty. "Why would we accept anything less from a weapon that provides the foundation for which all of our national security is based on?"

At sunrise the next morning, Good Friday, the walkers held hands around a fire. Johnnie Bobb burned cedar and sage. "We need to keep gathering," he said. "We need to do this out here while they do that in there." He pointed to the lights across the highway.

Over a breakfast of oatmeal and leftover chicken, the walkers wrote messages in cards to Sister Megan, Michael, and Greg. Robert from the Vegas Catholic Worker wrote in green pen, "You are a light to us all." An enlarged photo of the trio, holding the TRANSFORM NOW banner they had carried into Y-12, was laid on the windshield of a support car for inspiration. Then it was time for the nuclear Stations of the Cross, a progression on foot from the camp to the property line of the test site. They carried photos of war victims from Hiroshima and Nagasaki and Vietnam.

The group stepped around baby rattlesnakes, into dried creek beds and passed under 95 through two concrete culverts, which were scribbled with graffiti from earlier Sacred Peace Walks. There were swirly hippie doodles, handprints in paint, and quotations and peace signs, some messages faded or lost, like ancient cave paintings. There was that great platitude from Margaret Mead in gray lettering: "Do not think that a small group of citizens cannot change the world. Indeed it is the only thing that ever has."

They emerged on the other side of 95 and walked along rusty barbed wire and then onto the entrance road to the test site. Strung along the property line were the same yellow No Trespassing placards from the Department of Energy that bordered the Y-12 site. Johnnie Bobb, wearing a necklace of animal teeth, was drumming. Waiting at the property line were police officers from the Nye County sheriff's office and special police officers from WSI, the same security company that had staffed Y-12 until the break-in. They had German shepherds at the ready.

"You guys taking care of us, and the animals?" Johnnie Bobb asked them, nodding to the horizon, standing on one side of the white line.

"We're trying," said a guard in desert camouflage.

"What about up at Yucca Mountain?"

"Don't know anything about that."

Johnnie turned to face two walkers from Vegas named Ming and Laura-Marie, who were going to get married before trespassing. The bride held a bouquet of rosemary, mint, yarrow, and pink roses.

"This is the day they're going onto Shoshone land," Johnnie said, before officiating the brief ceremony.

The vows were short and sweet: "I'll always be your friend. I'll always love you. I'll stay with you through hard times. I'll hold you as my dearest incarnation of God."

The newlyweds were the first to cross the line, heading toward the officers, the dogs, the scrubby hills of the people's land. The others followed. The dogs barked and strained against their leashes. The Sacred Peace Walk—a spiritual quest to establish a happy moral order before it was too late—ended in a chain-link pen, where each walker received a $637 citation for trespassing on federal property.

Six days after the Sacred Peace Walk ended, another small group of people connected to Nevada took its own bold step—not in the desert, but from the ocean.

THE LARGEST LAND MAMMAL in history, a hornless cousin of the rhinoceros that stood 18 feet tall, started lumbering around Asia about 30 million years ago. About the same time, bats proliferated, roosting in caves around the world, their guano fossilizing over eons into phosphate deposits that would eventually be mined for fertilizer and cosmetics. And in the Pacific Ocean, atolls were forming. Coral gathered around islands and volcanoes over tens of thousands of years. Over millions more, they expanded into circular reefs as the landmasses subsided into rising seas loosed by glacial melt. Around 2,000 years ago, during a period of falling sea levels, a sprinkle of atoll islands surfaced just north of the equator, nearly equidistant from what would become Hawaii, Australia, and Japan. The islands sat atop these ancient reefs, creating lush lagoons on the interior while the ocean lapped on the outside. Native Pacific peoples, who commanded the vastness of Micronesia in outrigger canoes, fought one another to the death for those scarce wisps of land and built a civilization in the middle of nowhere off the bounty of the sea and the mastery of celestial navigation. Their way of life continued for a mini-epoch, until the islands were converted to Christianity by missionaries and occupied by a succession of foreign empires: the Spanish, who named them the Marshall Islands after a British explorer, then the Germans, then the Japanese, and finally, after fierce battles during World War II, the United States, which considered the islands a perfect site to test nuclear weapons.

The first peacetime nuclear test was conducted on Bikini Atoll in the Marshalls not even a full year after Hiroshima and Nagasaki. On a Sunday after church in February 1946, a U.S. Navy commodore met with the people of Bikini Atoll and told them that they were like the Israelites, a chosen people, and that perfecting the atomic bomb was "for the good of mankind," that it would "end all future world wars."

"We are willing to go," said Juda, the Bikini chieftain. "Everything is in God's hands."

Within one month of that conversation, the Bikinians had boarded American ships for relocation to a sparser atoll 125 miles east.

In July 1946 two nuclear tests were conducted in a military operation called Crossroads. The first bomb was plastered with a picture of Rita Hayworth, dropped from a B-29, and exploded 518 feet over the Bikini lagoon with a blast that was hotter than the surface of the sun. The second, an underwater shot, instantly lifted two million tons of lagoon a mile into the sky. A fleet of sacrificial naval vessels sank.

That autumn, the Bikinians wondered when they might go back to their atoll. The U.S. military explained that their village and plants were gone, that the water and fish would be unhealthy for a long time.

"Oh," said the Bikinians' interpreter, a Marshallese man named Pillip. "We very sorry to hear this."

The following year, through the United Nations, the Marshall Islands became an American "trust territory." The United States agreed to usher the islands out of the ashes of World War II and toward self-determination. Instead it used Bikini and Enewetak atolls to conduct 65 more nuclear tests, including the world's first thermonuclear detonations, which erased entire islands and left mile-wide craters.

In the late winter of 1954, shirtless military men toiled in the heat to set up a 12-ton bomb called Shrimp in a large shed on an islet in the northwest corner of Bikini Atoll. The device, designed by the Los Alamos lab in New Mexico, would detonate in two instantaneous stages. The explosion of the primary—a sphere of plutonium undergoing fission—would create enough heat to prompt a fusion reaction in the secondary, which was a cylinder of a hydrogen compound encased in uranium and made in Oak Ridge. In other words, the splitting of heavy atoms would trigger the fusing of light atoms.

At 6:45 a.m. local time on March 1, those parts worked together to produce the largest man-made explosion to date, and the largest U.S. test ever.

At that moment, a nine-year-old boy named Tony deBrum was fishing for scad with his grandfather in the shallows off Likiep Atoll, 300 miles southeast of Bikini. The flash came first, silent and brighter than the sun, from a 4.5-mile-wide fireball beyond the horizon. The sky turned red, like God had placed a glass bowl over the island and poured blood on it. Then the wind roared through. Tony was as far away from the blast as Washington is from Cleveland, and yet it was a traumatic experience.

If detonated in Times Square, the Bravo test would've flattened most of Manhattan, much of Brooklyn, Queens, and Hoboken, and caused third-degree burns as far away as Scarsdale and the Jersey Shore. From Bikini, it hurled into the sky ten million tons of pulverized and radioactive coral, which drifted eastward in a poisonous plume and fell like ashy snowflakes on the people of Rongelap and Utirik atolls. Several days after Bravo, after children had played with and eaten the ash, American servicemen and several hundred Marshallese residents were evacuated from Rongelap and Utirik. The yield of the Bravo test was 15 megatons, which was nearly three times as powerful as expected. Its flash was seen from Japan, 2,600 miles away. Its radioactive fallout was later detected in cattle in Tennessee.

The following month, the Marshallese filed a complaint with the United Nations. "Land means a great deal to the Marshallese," the complaint said, adding: "Take away their land and their spirits go also."

The United States replied, "No stone will be left unturned to safeguard the present and future well-being of the Islanders." Tests continued over four more years. U.S. military men were exposed during and after the tests. Marshallese from the two test atolls and the two fallout atolls were shuffled around to different islands. They had become exiles in their own country, specimens to be studied. The U.S. government viewed the 1957 resettlement of Rongelap Atoll as an opportunity to monitor the effects of radioactivity on subjects, who, while uncivilized, were "more like us than mice."

Testing in the Marshall Islands was expensive and time-consuming for the United States, so from 1958 onward, detonations were confined to the Nevada desert. The damage in the Pacific was done though. If the combined explosive power of the detonations at Bikini and Enewetak were parceled evenly over the 12-year period of testing, it would equal 1.6 Hiroshima-size detonations per day.

One and a half Hiroshimas. Every day. For a dozen years.

And so when it became clear, in the following century, that the United States was not eliminating all its nuclear weapons—that it was instead spending a trillion dollars to modernize its arsenal—the boy from Likiep decided to sue.

EVEN 61 YEARS LATER, Tony deBrum gets "chicken skin" when sharing his memories of Bravo.

"We pause today to remember the victims of the nuclear-weapons testing program," Tony said, standing before a couple of hundred people seated in a convention hall in Majuro, the capital of the Republic of the Marshall Islands.

It was March 2, 2015, Nuclear Victims Remembrance Day, and the boy from Likiep was now the foreign minister of the Marshall Islands. He wore a white shirt, shiny black shoes, and a necklace of seashells. He is a quiet man. His indignation, though, was booming.

The victims of the tests "have been taken from us before their time," Tony said in his gravelly voice, so that Americans could learn more about the "effects of such evil and unnecessary devices."

Behind him was a banner depicting the underwater test at Bikini. In front of him were Marshallese elders who endured burns that reached to the bone, forced relocation, nightmarish birth defects in their babies, cancers in the short and long term. Beside them were Marshallese young people who inherited a world unmade, remade, and then virtually forgotten by Washington. The bald and lanky U.S. ambassador to the Marshall Islands, Tom Armbruster, sat a couple of rows back in a suit.

The remembrance ceremony went on for hours. Dancers reenacted the explosions using green and magenta glow sticks to represent radiation. Three women from Rongelap were asked to stand so that they could be applauded for their suffering and endurance. A senator from Bikini gave a tribute in Marshallese and twice used an English term that indicated a modern crisis instead of a past one: "climate change."

A woman named Lemeyo Abon sat on an aisle in an orange dress with a crown of orange blossoms on her head. She was 75 years old and had been through all this before, every year around this time: the remembrances, the speeches, the applause. All because of that one morning on Rongelap when the sun rose in the west, an impossibly bright light followed by terrible thunder. Then came the evacuation, the resettlement, the miscarriages, her father's death from stomach cancer, her thyroid removal, another evacuation. She sometimes visited classrooms, where she'd deliver her memorized testimony: "We didn't know we were like guinea pigs." She now lived in Rita, a crowded slum in Majuro, and longed for her land in Rongelap, where she used to walk freely. "The land is part of us," she said after the ceremony, but there was no going back at this point.

Later that afternoon Tony set up a fan on the concrete veranda of his home on the edge of the Majuro lagoon. A blue tarp draped off the roof for shade. It was hot. Water crept up his nearby boat slip and retreated. Tony had just turned 70. As foreign minister he'd traveled the world. Raising hell in Peru about climate change. Raising hell in Vienna about nuclear weapons. And now raising hell in the American court system and the International Court of Justice.

A couple of years earlier, he and the California-based Nuclear Age Peace Foundation partnered with a U.S. law firm to draw up a lawsuit against each nuclear power. The plaintiff was the Republic of the Marshall Islands (RMI). The charge was breach of the Nuclear Non-Proliferation Treaty. The evidence was the worldwide slowdown in disarmament, the reinvestment in arsenals, and the failure to pursue negotiations "in good faith" to disarm "at an early date," as the treaty requires. The suits were filed in each nation's court system and in the International Court.

The complaint listed the National Nuclear Security Administration's life-extension programs for warheads. It listed the Navy's planned fleet of new submarines, which would be operational into the 2080s. It listed the "grand bargain" of the treaty: that nuclear nations would eliminate their nuclear weapons in exchange for other nations not pursuing their own. When the treaty was signed, there were five nuclear powers. Now, nearly 70 years into the nuclear era, there were nine.

The lawsuit wasn't seeking damages. The United States, upon granting the RMI its independence in 1986, issued a "full and final" settlement of $150 million. By accepting this sum, the Marshallese withdrew all pending lawsuits and forfeited an easy path to obtaining more damages in the future.

Tony's lawsuit was dismissed by the Federal District Court in San Francisco a month before Nuclear Victims Remembrance Day 2015. His goal, though, was to try to appeal it all the way to the Supreme Court.

People called it a stunt. A waste of time. A squandering of whatever goodwill remained between the United States and the Marshall Islands, whose present relationship was in many ways as fraught as their past relationship.

"We have a mandate because of our history, and we think that nuclear weapons are a terrible thing to have," Tony said, tugging at his white undershirt to cool his chest. The breeze off the lagoon was hot. "And I think that should be sufficient reason to file the damn thing."

A quarter mile down the road from Tony's home was the office of an American nicknamed Bikini Jack, who thought the lawsuit was a distraction from the real issue at hand: money.

BIKINI JACK'S OFFICE was like an icebox, the air-conditioning on high, the door shut but labeled with a handwritten sign that said,

"Don't Knock Just Please Come In." His green Audi was parked outside Bikini Atoll Town Hall at a yellow curb labeled with the word LIAISON. Bikini Jack is Jack Niedenthal, a Pennsylvania man in charge of administering the Bikini people's trust funds, which were created by the United States as a perpetual apology—an "I'm sorry" dispensed in quarterly checks.

A knock at the door.

A heavy woman peeked inside Jack's office, her face met by the chilled air. Jack was at his desk, toothpick in his teeth. He beckoned her, and she shuffled in, baby on hip, and said, "Where's my check?" Jack flipped through paperwork, plucked out a slip of paper worth $147, and handed it over. Splayed across Jack's desk were some of the checks, cut from a trust fund administered by a division of M&T Bank in Baltimore, for 5,258 Bikinians. It was payday at the town hall, a teal-colored building in Majuro.

Jack arrived with the Peace Corps in 1981 and lived on a remote island that was reachable only by boat. He endured bouts of famine and drought with his Marshallese cohabitants, who never panicked because their society had been based for millennia on sharing and on living in harmony with nature. What Americans consider welfare, the Marshallese consider normal historical function: Fish, coconuts, and other perishables were given to the chief to distribute promptly and fairly, to avoid waste and to keep the peace. Then America, with its deep pockets, became the de facto high chief in 1986, when the countries signed a compact of free association. The islands became the Republic of the Marshall Islands, an independent nation, and the United States issued its $150-million settlement, established four trust funds, and continued to provide for much of the RMI's yearly operating budget. Plenty of treasure had already been lost in the clumsy merger between a Western economy of cold hard cash and a feudalistic society in which traditional chiefs and landowners hold sway.

Jack, meanwhile, married a Bikinian, built a life in Majuro, had children and grandchildren. In the 1990s, declassified documents from the Atomic Energy Commission were released by the Department of Energy. They showed how Americans treated the Marshallese as test subjects instead of as patients. They revealed that the fallout from the testing was not limited to the four atolls with trust funds. In 2001 an independent tribunal awarded the RMI $2.3 billion in health and property damages, but there was no mechanism to force the United States to pay it. Washington did not consider itself liable beyond the original settlement of $150 million and pointed to the additional tens of millions of dollars it granted every year to environmental, food, and health care programs.

And now the annual U.S. grants are decreasing until 2023, when they will expire with the compact. A new trust fund is being capitalized by the United States at a rate of $12 million to $16 million a year, to provide a life jacket for the RMI economy after 2023. But this fund would be just as vulnerable to hasty distribution as existing trusts, which have been siphoned at times by the Marshallese and frittered away.

As the trust liaison for the Bikini people, Jack manages the money. And he dogs his fellow Americans back in Washington, 7,000 miles away.

"Washington—and this is just my personal opinion—I think they're going out of their way to wash their hands of the Marshalls," Jack said in his office during the week of Nuclear Victims Remembrance Day. "You look at what they spend on Iraq and Afghanistan, and it's billions upon billions. For four bullets into a tree in Iraq, they could fix this entire place."

The place is huge and tiny at the same time. The Republic of the Marshall Islands is 29 atolls composed of 1,225 individual islands that all together look like bracelets dropped in the ocean. The RMI's land area is equivalent to D.C.'s, but it's spread out over a chunk of ocean the size of Mexico. The RMI was once called the most contaminated place on Earth, yet it has the dizzying beauty of a mirage. Wealthy foreigners spirit themselves to surfer paradise, past islanders living with sky-high rates of diabetes and thyroid abnormalities. In a place where the United States has sunk billions, children play in landfills. The Marshallese couldn't exist without the ocean, but now sea-level rise attributed to global warming has begun to imperil their homes and lives.

Bikini Atoll Town Hall in Majuro is actually 500 miles from Bikini Atoll, which remains mostly uninhabited. Majuro, home to the majority of the Marshallese population, is a town of 31,000 on a 30-mile ribbon of land that's never more than 2,000 feet wide. In almost every corner of Majuro you can either hear or see the ocean or the lagoon. You can feel the isolation in the U.S. dollars, soft and faded from recirculation, passed back and forth on taxi rides up and down the island. You can see its commercial importance in the lagoon, where tuna ships and cold-storage freighters drop anchor.

When the local yacht club packs a bar for its weekly roustabout, Majuro seems like Margaritaville, with boisterous Kiwis, Australians, and Americans telling tales of the high seas. They dream of snorkeling in the 15-megaton crater at Bikini. They recall elderly Marshallese who've interrupted their travels with comments like "You Americans have ruined our country," and it's impossible to argue otherwise. The nuclear tests unraveled Marshallese society, scattering the residents of four atolls to the wind, and an imported Western economy has reconstructed it as a tropical dystopia. In Majuro, families crowd into tin-roofed shanties above a water system contaminated by decomposing bodies from adjoining burial plots. Giant leftover shipping containers lurk along the roads. Fruits and vegetables are scarce. Imported starches and sugars abound. The tuna freighters pollute the lagoon. The Marshall Islands, 70 years after the first detonation at Bikini, is that old cliché: a paradise lost.

The Marshallese culture is rooted in a history of resource sharing, of ecological balance, of an intimate knowledge of how the winds blow, how the waves break, how the stars slip across the sky. Over the past 70 years, though, victimhood, corruption, and dependency have produced a different kind of fallout.

"We have basically destroyed a culture," said Glenn Alcalay, an anthropology professor at Montclair State University who took part in Greenpeace's second evacuation of Rongelap in 1985. "We've stolen their future. When you take the future from a people, you've destroyed them."

THE FUTURE of the Marshall Islands was dressed in blue jumpers and seated in pews at the Cathedral of the Assumption in Majuro. Sixth graders at the adjoining school took turns at the pulpit, below a projection screen showing images of burned children and deformed babies, and gave voice to stubborn, unhealing wounds.

"We are made in God's image and no one has the right to take our life."

"Castle Bravo is an example of arrogance."

"We are all victims."

After this commemoration service, the students scampered outdoors for their annual nuclear science fair, held the Friday before Nuclear Victims Remembrance Day.

Sophomore Limbuk Ackley, 16, whose mother is Marshallese and father is American, stood near a heap of origami peace cranes. "It's hard to take in what my mom's ancestors had gone through and what my dad's ancestors had done to inflict problems," Limbuk said, as students ran around in the muggy heat.

There are no permanent oncologists in the RMI, no ability to perform cancer treatments like chemotherapy, and no true consensus between the Department of Energy and the Marshallese about the effects of exposure, both during and after the tests.

There's no health risk to the current generation of inhabitants from radioactive contamination, according to a 1994 study commissioned—and then rejected upon completion—by the RMI government. But cancer and birth defects are the modern connections to the past. There are still radiation-related cancers that have yet to develop or be diagnosed in the population of Marshallese who were on the islands between 1948 and 1970. Everyone seems to have a relative whose cancer falls on the DOE's list of ailments traceable to radiation.

In many ways the cultural fallout is more insidious. Some Marshallese are either nervous to marry people from the exposed atolls, for fear of passing genetic mutations to offspring, or are keen to do so, because it means tapping into trusts. There is tension between members of the trust-fund atolls and the rest of the islanders, who view the United States as delinquent on a $2 billion IOU from the claims tribunal.

The other 364 days of the year, young Marshallese confront problems more emergent than those of the past: rampant alcohol abuse, schools that don't provide lunches, and one of the highest suicide rates in the world. U.S. food aid comes in the form of processed items like chicken and white rice, which have contributed to an epidemic of obesity and diabetes, the No. 1 cause of death here. Cancer is No. 2.

"The Marshallese are convinced that there is sufficient evidence—based on their own observations of changes to their reproductive functions—of intergenerational harm caused by radiation fallout," said a 2012 United Nations report, which also noted a "deep fissure" between the U.S. and the RMI governments.

The major perk of the compact with the United States allows Marshallese citizens to work indefinitely in the United States without a visa, and the most promising students often immigrate or enlist in the U.S. military and rarely return. They settle in Hawaii, on the West Coast, or in northwest Arkansas, where Marshallese expats congregated over the years and make up as much as 38 percent of the workforce at major poultry producers like Tyson Foods.

Students afford college in the Marshalls through Pell tuition grants. The Pell eligibility will expire with the compact in 2023, and there is growing anxiety about what will happen afterward to higher education in the Marshalls.

But at least one major agreement between the countries will endure long past 2023: the U.S. military's lease of 11 islands in the northern Kwajalein Atoll. There, in the name of national security, the Army operates a missile test range.

KWAJALEIN WAS KNOWN as "Execution Island" during World War II, when the Japanese used it as a POW camp. Louis Zamperini, the subject of the book and the film *Unbroken*, was held there for 42 days and tortured. Today, his name is on the U.S. dining facility on Kwajalein, which hosts a U.S. Army garrison and a ballistic missile test site named after Ronald Reagan.

The garrison is referred to as "Kwaj." It's just over 2,100 miles west-southwest of Hawaii. About 1,300 American servicemembers, contractors, civilians, scientists, and their families live there in bungalows and two-story barracks. There's a golf course and a yacht club. It's a bike-or-walk community, boring as hell but not unpleasant. Kwajalein Atoll surrounds the biggest lagoon in the world, which makes it perfect for target practice.

The atoll is a key staging ground for American missile activity. When an unarmed intercontinental ballistic missile is launched from Vandenberg Air Force Base in California, it sometimes plunks down near Kwajalein. In a military situation, the missile would carry a nuclear warhead that would deliver 20 times the payload of the Hiroshima bomb. Sometimes a test missile is launched from Kwaj toward

California and intercepted by another missile from Vandenberg. With Kwaj, the United States can practice launching or deflecting nuclear attacks, provide a territorial bulwark against China, detect any launch out of Asia, and offer a rocket-launch apparatus to civilian companies like SpaceX.

"Remote Pacific location is ideal for permissive safety and environmental constraints," says an Army brochure for commercial customers.

Though the garrison has been downsizing since the 1980s, the Department of Defense's lease doesn't expire until 2066; the rent (more than $15 million per year, depending on inflation) goes to a small group of land-owning Marshallese families, some of whom live abroad. About 900 Marshallese work on Kwaj—flipping burgers, maintaining the grounds, working in the carpentry or electrical shops—but they live a 20-minute ferry ride away, on a squalid sliver of purgatory called Ebeye.

More than 10,000 people are crammed into a tenth of a square mile of livable space on Ebeye. The island is crawling with children. A third of its residents are unemployed, and more than half are under 20 years old. Government buildings stand on crumbling stilts with exposed rebar, the concrete spalled away by a constant salty wind off the ocean. Raw sewage pools in the streets.

Ebeye, which is also a Rongelap resettlement, has been known as the "slum of the Pacific" for decades, but people live here for the country's highest hourly wage: Workers at the U.S. garrison make $10 to $12 an hour. The minimum wage in Majuro is $2 an hour.

Decent pay in squalid conditions is more appealing than living on Rongelap—a remote setting that has the aura of contamination, even though the U.S. government has okayed resettlement, paved roads, and built homes. And that is the conundrum wrought by the bomb, even decades later. It doesn't need to detonate to do damage.

"We'd have better living conditions in Rongelap," said Kenneth

Kedi, one of that atoll's senators, "but what is underneath the houses, the grass, the pandanus, the papaya, the coconut trees? . . . As a leader I'm caught between here and there. I want to go back to Rongelap now, but at the same time I'm not going to bring my family, especially the young children. It's a dilemma."

THE THING ABOUT the RMI is that most of it is absurdly beautiful. Ebeye and Majuro are plagued with problems—they host nearly three-quarters of the in-country population—but they are just two pieces of a scattered puzzle. The private island of Enemanit is 20 minutes from Majuro if you travel by Jerry Kramer's boat for one of his Sunday barbecues. Kramer is sometimes referred to as the Donald Trump of the Marshall Islands. On one particular Sunday in 2015, the 61st anniversary of the Bravo test, he seemed dressed for a Jimmy Buffett concert.

"I get Charles Schwab's son, the GoPro guy," Jerry said, listing guests whom he allows to anchor just offshore. "Larry Page sends a jet just to get something he wants to eat."

Off the port side of Kramer's boat, the Google co-founder's yacht looked like a spaceship. It was thin, sleek, and reportedly 240 feet long and worth $45 million. Page may or may not have been aboard. He may have been surfing in Ailinglaplap Atoll, where silky waves break on an aquamarine Eden. Jerry Kramer runs the construction company Pacific International, the second-largest private employer in the Marshall Islands. He owns 100 apartments, a couple of hotels, and the buildings that house the embassies of Japan, Taiwan, and the United States. He arrived in the Marshalls as a missile technician in 1961, back when all travel in the islands was restricted by the U.S. military. He fell in love with a local woman, raised a family, and built an industrial empire in Majuro. Kramer's passengers on this particular Sunday included his grandchildren, a few dozen visitors from Taiwan, a U.S. State Department official and his family, and chihuahuas named Buster and Snooki.

He saw endless economic opportunity in the beauty of the Marshalls, but quickly listed the obstacles: a native workforce still wary of illness, a regional airline that is often grounded, a government riddled with corruption and graft. Bikini tourism "could be a billion-dollar industry," Kramer said, sitting on the transom of his boat. "It could finally be something that makes amends." Divers would pay top dollar to inspect the china still sitting in the captain's quarters of the USS *Saratoga*, an aircraft carrier purposefully sunk by the Baker test in 1946. Bikini's last fledgling scuba operation flamed out in 2008 with the global economy. Today about half a dozen people live there: a few from the Bikini Projects Department and a few from the Department of Energy. There are a couple of houses, a garage, a generator, a reverse-osmosis unit for drinking water, a gazebo on the beach, and all that steel memorabilia from World War II at the bottom of the lagoon.

There is already a billion-dollar industry in the Marshalls though: tuna. Majuro Atoll's lagoon serves as a transshipment hub for foreign purse seiners who pay $8,000 a day for fishing rights. Cold-storage motherships ferry the "blue gold" to ports around the Pacific rim. But still the nuclear legacy creeps into modern-day concerns: What if old deposits of contaminated soil were disturbed and released into fishing waters?

The Runit Dome is a large concrete cap on Enewetak Atoll that covers 110,000 cubic yards of radioactive soil buried in a 350-foot-wide test crater. The United States constructed the dome in 1980, after 4,000 American servicemembers finished cleanup operations. The capped soil, sown with plutonium, will be dangerous for thousands of years. The dome, which would fail a landfill inspection if it were in the United States, is already showing signs of structural instability as tides nibble away at the concrete. But any release of the dome's contents would pale in comparison with the volume of contamination that's already in Enewetak's lagoon sediment, according to the DOE's Lawrence Livermore National Laboratory in California.

Enewetak has been partially resettled by several hundred Marshallese, though the American servicemembers who handled its cleanup are still fighting to get health care and compensation for cancers and other ailments linked to contamination. In 2015 a bill was introduced in the U.S. House of Representatives to classify them as "radiation exposed veterans." Similar bills have been introduced over the years, to no avail.

The perils and travails of Bikini and Enewetak are out of sight and out of mind on Jerry Kramer's island. Enemanit is carefree bliss: a cup of rosé, a leg of grilled chicken, a setting that's almost too idyllic, like a screen saver on a Windows 95 desktop computer. A 45-minute flight away, though, 500 Bikinians are struggling on the rocky island of Kili, where they've eked out a living since an older generation was moved there. A ship bearing food and diesel arrives every three months, if the weather behaves. The yearly king tide sometimes washes completely over the island, fouling freshwater reservoirs. The residents of Kili were exiled once by nuclear testing. Now they were staring down a second exile by sea-level rise.

"We can't be living like this," says Lani Kramer, Jerry's daughter-in-law, on the boat ride back to Majuro as the sun set on the Bravo anniversary. "We need to create jobs and find a way to put more money into our trust fund. But it's not just about money. It's about human rights. And it's sad because most of the people who are exposed are gone."

"NUCLEAR ISSUES ARE FOREVER."

Tom Armbruster became the U.S. ambassador to the RMI in 2012. Outside his office window was a balcony with a peach-colored balustrade, beyond which the ocean lapped over crushed coral on the outer edge of Majuro.

"A lot of these people are living with those ghosts," said Armbruster, bald, lanky, and considered by many Marshallese to be savvy and empathetic. "It's part of our shared history. Part of our Cold War. We're not going to go back and try to understand the decisions. But there are things we can do now."

He listed them: encouraging the resettlement of Rongelap, sending a couple of Marshallese students to California to study nuclear issues, building drinking-water catchments, strengthening disaster-management plans. The U.S. embassy considers the Marshall Islands to be on the front lines of climate change, which manifests most dramatically during the late-winter king tides. In March 2014, 1,000 people evacuated Majuro as the surge pulled homes into the ocean.

"Climate change is my nuclear experience," said Mark Stege, who grew up in Majuro, studied at Columbia University, and is now director of the Marshall Islands Conservation Society. "I can see a lot of connections at the emotional level and the community level, at the individual family level. The same questions are relevant in both situations. There's this really deep sense of loss."

On the afternoon of Nuclear Victims Remembrance Day, Ambassador Armbruster hosted the unveiling of a U.S.-funded memorial at an outdoor basketball court near the college. The court was named after Solomon Sam, the only Marshallese citizen to die in Iraq while serving in the U.S. military. Painted in white text on a blue wall was a written tribute to the Marshallese who had helped the United States in some form over the past 70 years: scouts who gathered intelligence during World War II, families whose land and livelihoods were poisoned by testing during the Cold War, and young generations who served in Iraq or Afghanistan.

Most of the white plastic chairs at the unveiling were empty. Present at the ceremony was a Marshallese man who had served in the

U.S. Army and deployed to Baghdad. He was a combat engineer who focused on explosive-ordnance disposal. In other words, he helped protect American troops from bombs. He thinks the memorial is a fine gesture from the United States.

"We're biting the hands that feed us," he said of remarks like Tony deBrum's. "We're sending out the message that this happened and we're supposed to be pissed, and that's been going on for 61 years. Why not change the tone? It's really depressing."

Tony was not present. He was on his terrace, 500 feet away. He didn't need to see another memorial.

"We're suffering the result of climate change and of the nuclear legacy, and we have had nothing to do with either," he said. "In either case, people have to *choose* to end this world, this universe. You can either do it slowly with climate change, or you can press a button and blow it up. And neither is justified."

In two and a half months, he would take his crusade to the United Nations.

10.

GOOD FAITH

She remembers it as a pinpoint of light streaking across the black sky, taking her imagination with it. Her father carried her out into their front yard to explain what Sputnik was and why it mattered. She was five years old and fascinated. When the Soviets launched the satellite, the satellite launched thousands of careers in the United States. Rose Gottemoeller's was one of them.

She was able to study Russian in high school in Columbus, Ohio, which prepared her to major in Russian language and linguistics at Georgetown University in 1971. A year later were the Strategic Arms Limitation Talks, a watershed moment of diplomacy between two superpowers that had been locked in a race to the apocalypse. The détente electrified Rose, who had wanted to become an interpreter but now yearned to be directly in the negotiator's chair. She wanted to wrestle with opposing forces and transform them into progress. While at Georgetown she read Pope John XXIII's *Pacem in Terris*, which, in the wake of the Cuban Missile Crisis, was a prophetic call to diplomacy.

We are hopeful that, by establishing contact with one another and by a policy of negotiation, nations will come to a better recognition of the natural ties that bind them together as men. We are hopeful, too, that they will come to a fairer realization of one of the cardinal duties deriving from our common nature: namely, that love, not fear, must dominate the relationships between individuals and between nations.

Inspired by the collaboration between the USSR and the United States on the Apollo-Soyuz space program, Rose entered the science and technology policy graduate program at George Washington University in 1978. After graduate school she had an offer for a full-time government job—a chance to start the slow but secure climb through civil service—but she decided to take a part-time job at the RAND Corporation. Cloistering herself in the think-tank world would be irrational, she thought to herself, but the RAND job sounded more challenging.

She moved to the Soviet desk at the State Department just before the Berlin Wall fell, then worked on the National Security Council staff during the Clinton administration. In her first two years on the council she helped persuade Ukraine, Belarus, and Kazakhstan to return thousands of Soviet nuclear weapons to Russia for disposition. It was a triumph of post–Cold War denuclearization. Her negotiation skills had helped to make the world safer.

In 1997 she moved to the Department of Energy to work on nonproliferation. While at the DOE she frequently quoted the ancient Chinese maxim "In chaos there is opportunity," and there was certainly chaos: the flurry of reports about DOE's "cynicism" and "managerial neglect," the Wen Ho Lee scandal, the creation of the National Nuclear Security Administration within but apart from the DOE, and the Senate's failure to ratify the test-ban treaty—a defeat cheered by

Texas governor George W. Bush, who was four months into his campaign for the presidency.

A career in government could feel Sisyphean, like a civil servant's job was to forever push a giant rock up a hill that never peaked. Rose felt this way about her work in arms control and nonproliferation—that it was, at times, hamstrung by partisanship and chauvinism and weighted by futility. What kept her going was faith. Faith rooted in her Catholicism, nourished by a Jesuit education that encouraged inquisitiveness. Faith in the possibility of accomplishment. Faith in process: a chain of incremental actions toward lower numbers of weapons, each step building on the last, in concert with other military powers.

She had faith in the State Department, in diplomacy. Rose was interested in achievable and realistic goals, not wishful thinking. There was no way to skip to a nuke-free world and forgo the hard work of responsible disposal, verification, and compliance. Peace and security couldn't be summoned by snapping one's fingers or agitating for immediate abolition. It was gradual. It was work.

She spent 2000 to 2009 at the Carnegie Endowment for International Peace, as the Bush administration swept away arms-control expertise from the White House and the Pentagon. She reentered government in Obama's first year as an assistant secretary for State's bureau of arms control, verification, and compliance. The office next to hers was once occupied by General Leslie Groves, the director of the Manhattan Project.

"There are very beneficial ghosts in this whole office suite," Rose told the *Columbus Dispatch*. "I find it a tribute to American ingenuity: We can both develop the bomb, and we can also look for ways to reduce and eliminate them." In this role she was the chief negotiator of New START, the latest arms-control pact between the United States and Russia.

With its modest requirements, the treaty should've needed only a gentle push. It turned into one of the heaviest rocks of her career.

The first problem was time. The existing START expired at the end of Obama's first year in office, and with it the crucial verification measures that allowed the United States to monitor Russian forces. The second was the Republican Party, which stymied the White House at every turn and thought Obama's vision for a nuke-free world was naive and reckless. A new treaty was a high priority for Obama, who had thrown down the gauntlet with his Prague speech, and he was personally involved in shepherding it.

Rose was a formidable presence at the negotiations in Geneva. Fluent in Russian, she spoke with care and firmness. She favored crisp blazers, assertive collars, and cuff links. She wore her silver hair short. She was unflappable. Colleagues said she knew Russian psychology better than the Russians themselves. This new deal was what Rose had been working toward her entire career, from the moment she saw Sputnik above Ohio.

The treaty was negotiated in a roller-coaster 12 months, a miraculous achievement, and it lowered the ceiling for deployed warheads from 2,200 to 1,550 by 2018 and made way for crucial weapons inspections. Then the treaty hit the buzz saw of Congress.

The Senate held hearings in the summer of 2010. Sen. Jon Kyl (R-Ariz.) said he would whip enough votes to ensure ratification of the treaty if Obama guaranteed $90 billion to modernize the nuclear-weapons complex over the next ten years. The White House needed nine Republican senators to join Democrats in voting yes.

"I think there's about a $10 billion gap," said Sen. Bob Corker (R-Tenn.), between Obama's proposal for modernization funds and the amount that was needed for existing plans. The cost of the Uranium Processing Facility at Y-12, in Corker's state, had risen from $3.5 billion to $5 billion that year. It would reach $6.5 billion by November, and its ballooning cost estimate ($11 billion by 2013, $19 billion by 2015) would serve as an inspiration for the Transform Now Plowshares activists. In the short term, though, it was a bargaining chip in the treaty process.

Over the summer and fall of 2010, the State Department was on the Hill regularly to assuage senators who were anxious about the treaty's impact on missile-defense systems. Rose and her team answered nearly 1,000 questions for the record. They enlisted the help of religious organizations, which helped cast a "yes" vote as a moral imperative.

In November, after the midterm elections, Senator Kyl withdrew his support because he thought the process was too rushed for a lame-duck session. After one of her nearly two dozen briefings for members of Congress, Hill staffers told Rose that she was not going to get New START across the finish line. Two days later, on December 22, the Senate consented to ratification of the treaty by a vote of 71 to 26. The consent resolution included amendments that encouraged the modernization of the nuclear-weapons complex. Senators Corker and Lamar Alexander of Tennessee, satisfied with a funding commitment that would benefit Oak Ridge and Y-12, joined 11 other Republicans in voting yes.

"My only concern in consideration of this treaty has been the safety and security of the American people," Corker said in a statement after the vote.

"It leaves our country with enough nuclear warheads to blow any attacker to kingdom come," Alexander said.

Since the 1972 bilateral talks, arms treaties between Moscow and Washington also included a tacit agreement between the State Department and the Pentagon: The military would back the treaty in exchange for a reinvestment in U.S. forces. So with a pact to preserve the nuclear triad, the Senate amendment on modernization, and the president's Nuclear Posture Review, which pledged to maintain a safe, secure, and effective stockpile, the Obama administration's foreign-policy victory with Moscow was also a victory for Cold War nostalgia and the status quo.

Rose didn't see it this way, though. New START prolonged Washington's ability to monitor the Russian stockpile, and only through verification could the number of weapons safely come down. And if the weapons weren't disappearing tomorrow, the responsible thing was to adequately fund their safety and security.

"As the nuclear arsenal shrinks, we're going to still need to take care of it," Rose said the day after the vote, "and we need to have a smaller infrastructure but a very efficient and effective one. So building some new facilities on a smaller footprint, I think, makes a lot of sense. That goes for the [Uranium Processing Facility] in Tennessee that has been much under discussion, and also some improvements, for example, to the Pantex Plant where we do weapons maintenance in Texas."

In 2012 Rose was nominated by Obama to be undersecretary for arms control and international security, the State Department's top arms control official. Republicans, who were concerned about funding levels for the nuclear weapons complex, held up her confirmation for two years.

Her office at State was known as the "T" bureau, and she kept a gag gift on an end table by her desk: a Manhattan Project board game, in which players competed to become the world's dominant superpower by enriching uranium and building bombs. In her new role she traveled to the Marshall Islands on the 60th anniversary of the Castle Bravo test, a month before Tony deBrum filed his lawsuit. She went to Hiroshima and made several trips to meet down-winders in Utah, where radioactive fallout had drifted from the Nevada Test Site. This "depression tour" irritated folks at the Department of Energy and the NNSA. Rose, undeterred, made overtures to Catholic groups and the Vatican to trumpet the U.S. approach to disarmament. She knew that if the government turned its back on abolitionists, people might wind up in the streets like in 1982. The outreach was also part of a public-relations effort to acknowledge the humanitarian consequences of nuclear weapons while projecting a firm commitment to maintaining an arsenal—a natural extension of Obama's "Prague agenda." Rose continued to oversee her bureau's annual "Generation Prague" conference, which brought young people to State to ponder the complexities of nuke policy. The event was also an attempt to coax people into civil service. About half of Rose's staff would be eligible for retirement by the 2020s, and the U.S. government needed fresh recruits who were passionate about nuclear weapons even though the Cold War had ended before they were born.

There were steady achievements in arms control and nonproliferation during the Obama years: More than a dozen countries, including Ukraine, had surrendered their highly enriched uranium since the Prague speech, and the United States had helped install hundreds of sensors at ports and borders to detect nuclear material.

Dark clouds were rolling in, though. Putin's return to the presidency in 2012 began a new ice age in U.S.-Russia relations. In 2014 Putin annexed Crimea, a move that much of the world saw as an invasion and occupation, and in the process violated the Intermediate-Range Nuclear Forces Treaty, according to the State Department's lawyers.

The world "should always keep in mind that Russia is not to be messed with," Putin said as he moved forces into Crimea. "I want to remind you that Russia is one of the largest nuclear powers. This is a reality, not just words; moreover, we are strengthening our nuclear deterrence forces."

There were more than 400 Russian incursions in NATO airspace in 2014. Putin said he would not participate in the last of Obama's nuclear-security summits, in 2016. Russia broke off a nuclear-security agreement with the United States that Rose helped implement while at DOE in the '90s. Former senator Sam Nunn (D-Ga.), one of the four horsemen of the nuclear apocalypse, said this would increase the chances of nuclear terrorism. In early 2015, Russia made plans to move nuclear-capable bombers into Crimea and deploy nuclear-capable missiles to the borders of Poland and Lithuania. Former Russian president Mikhail Gorbachev declared that the world was on the brink of another cold war.

At the same time, the anti-nuclear movement, long dormant, was beginning to awaken abroad. A coalition of non-nuclear nations, tired of waiting for disarmament, hosted conferences on the humanitarian impact of nuclear weapons in Norway in 2013 and Mexico in 2014. The organizers were not only fringe activists; they were also state officials who wanted to retake the narrative from China, France, Russia, the United Kingdom, and the United States—the nuclear-armed nations that had signed the Nuclear Non-Proliferation Treaty in the previous century but were now modernizing their stockpiles. None of the P5 nations had attended these conferences, but Rose sensed a swell of energy that could imperil the careful step-by-step process. The Mexico conference was bigger than Norway's, and it was now apparent that Vienna, the site of the upcoming third conference, would be bigger still. America needed to get inside and work the room, particularly in advance of the United Nations' Review Conference of the Nuclear Non-Proliferation Treaty in the spring of 2015. After a confab between State, the NNSA, and other agencies, it was decided: The United States would officially attend the Vienna Conference on the Humanitarian Impact of Nuclear Weapons in December 2014.

"I don't know if other P5 representatives are going—some are not too happy [with our decision]," Rose said a month before the conference. "I don't mind being the big elephant in the room."

THE CEILING OF Vienna's Hall of Sciences is a vast golden frieze of angels cavorting among clouds and peering down from billowing pink drapery. Red lights from behind the stage illuminated the logo of the International Campaign to Abolish Nuclear Weapons (ICAN), a young crusade to outlaw the possession and use of nukes. Five hundred young people ebbed through the aisles. ICAN's civil-society forum, the precursor to the more formal Vienna conference, began with a snazzy video set to buoyant music. The video compared the push for abolition to the struggles against apartheid, Jim Crow, and the disenfranchisement of women.

"We can do this without the nuclear-armed states," said ICAN executive director Beatrice Fihn from the stage. "The key actor is *not* the U.S. or Russia or China. The real superpower in the world: you."

Beatrice, a Swede in her early 30s, got into this line of work by accident. She studied political science and was captivated by poverty and climate change—"real" issues with irrefutable consequences that were unfolding before the eyes of the world. A position at ICAN opened up, she took it, and, like other young people drawn to anti-nuke work, found herself staring down a vexing and mighty foe: a weapon that was abstract in most people's minds, that hadn't been used in generations, that had fewer and fewer victims who were alive and capable of sharing their stories. This was a weapon that some countries insisted was integral to their security while claiming their goal was to get rid of it. ICAN's mission was to help make nukes taboo, to establish a moral norm that the P5 states would respect if not officially endorse. The blueprint was the Ottawa Treaty, which in 1997 banned land mines even though more than two dozen countries—including China, Russia, and the United States—did not sign the outcome document. If the world could craft conventions banning chemical and biological weapons, surely it could do the same for the most dangerous weapon on the planet. This "legal gap" had to be closed.

"Armed nations are probably quite worried about what we're doing this weekend," Beatrice told the attendees, who were as energized as Baptists at a revival. "They will say it's impossible. Don't let anyone convince you that making nuclear weapons illegal is impossible."

The weekend was packed with lively panels on stage and quiet strategy meetings in nearby cafés. There were Afghans who learned of Kazakh survivors of the Soviet Union's testing program and felt the solidarity of living under an oppressive regime. There were Kenyans who were fighting the uphill battle to make Africa care as much about nuclear weapons as it did about maternal health and sanitation. There were Americans who were trying to resurrect the stateside campaign through groups like Global Zero, a celebrity-backed movement in favor of eliminating nuclear weapons by the year 2030. There were number crunchers who determined that 411 financial institutions from 31 countries invested $402 billion in 28 companies—two-thirds based in the United States—that produced nuclear weapons. There were representatives of victims as well: *hibakusha*, the Japanese word for bomb victims, and Tony deBrum from the Marshall Islands. Their words on stage were sharp and graphic.

"Perhaps the most frightening sight was that they were carrying their own eyeballs in their hands," said Setsuko Thurlow, who was a 13-year-old student in Hiroshima on August 6, 1945. "And they collapsed onto the ground, and as they did their stomachs burst open. . . . This is something we want to prevent. We have to stop it. We have to ban all these wicked, wicked, evil bombs we have. . . . We have squandered money to produce 17,000 of them. It's a crime against humanity."

This new humanitarian movement began in the spring of 2010, when the International Committee of the Red Cross released a statement that said there was no way to respond to a nuclear detonation. Evacuation, triage, and aid would be unrealistic, given the totality of destruction. Within a month, Norway, Austria, Ireland, and New Zealand introduced language about the "humanitarian consequences" of nuclear weapons at the 2010 review conference of the Nuclear Non-

Proliferation Treaty. That summer, European officials and activists had an under-the-radar meeting in Amersham, a hamlet northwest of London. It was clear that the pace of the disarmament process would not match the intensity of Obama's rhetoric, especially with stockpile modernization plans. The strategy was to fund ICAN, to cast disarmament as a humanitarian imperative, to depoliticize the weapons by focusing on their horrifying effects, to wrest away the narrative from P5 powers who used techno-strategic language as a sleight of hand. They would launch a diplomatic process based on a series of conferences on the humanitarian impact, starting in Oslo. The players would bring governments into the fold and build year by year toward a ban, regardless of what the P5 did or did not do. "Prohibit, *then* eliminate" was the mantra. The status quo needed to be shaken. The movement was called the Humanitarian Initiative. And it was on a collision course with Rose Gottemoeller and the U.S. government.

THE ENERGY FROM ICAN's forum funneled Monday morning to the main event, the third Conference on the Humanitarian Impact of Nuclear Weapons. The setting was Vienna's Hofburg Palace, which was built as a medieval fortress in the 13th century and expanded over centuries into a 2,600-room seat of democracy. On the first day of the conference, actors in hazmat suits mock-screened attendees for radiation. Then, in the same building in which the Vienna congress met 200 years prior to balance power in Europe following the Napoleonic Wars, Austria's 28-year-old foreign minister took the stage.

"In the world after the Cold War in which I grew up, most people seemed to stop worrying about nuclear weapons," said Sebastian Kurz, wearing a sharp black suit, his hair slicked back. "They were seen as a relic from the past, only an abstract danger which didn't matter very much. But this is fundamentally wrong. The fact is, over 16,000 nuclear warheads still exist, distributed among 14 countries and throughout the oceans, many of them on high alert and ready for use on short notice. And we have to be clear: As long as nuclear weapons exist, the risk of their use—on purpose or by accident—remains real."

The vast ballroom was uncomfortably full. There were delegations from more than 100 nations plus an army of activists sitting under crystal chandeliers, between statues of cherubs and murals of white-wigged men frozen in the act of decision making. Between delegations from the United Kingdom and Uruguay sat the two U.S. officials dispatched by Rose: Anita Friedt, a veteran of the State Department and a key player in the New START negotiations, and Ambassador Adam Scheinman, Obama's special representative for nuclear non-proliferation. The media, especially photographers from Japan, were arranged like a firing squad around them and their British counterparts. The whole conference, in fact, would be conducted as a slow-motion shaming of the United States and the United Kingdom, speech by speech, panel by panel.

"How much longer can we allow the nuclear-weapons states to continue threatening all life on Earth?" Setsuko Thurlow said from the stage, after retelling her Hiroshima story.

Archbishop Silvano Maria Tomasi, reading a message from Pope Francis, chastised the philosophy of nuclear deterrence and asked attendees to be "prophetic voices" of peace.

If India and Pakistan each exchanged 50 nuclear bombs in a regional war, the smoke and fallout would trigger a global famine that would kill two billion people, said American atmospheric scientist Michael Mills.

The most arresting presentation was given by a small woman named Michelle Thomas, a 62-year-old survivor of breast and lung cancer, confined to a wheelchair since childhood by an autoimmune muscle disease. She had grown up in St. George, Utah, downwind of the Nevada Test Site, and watched from her backyard as pink mushroom clouds blossomed on the horizon. The radioactive iodine released into the air was enough to cause cancer in as many as 75,000 Americans.

Michelle introduced herself as a survivor of the Cold War, drafted into service while in the womb.

"Imagine the dissonance of being asked by your government to build bomb shelters in your homes to protect you from any air raids by Khrushchev," she said, toying with her turtleneck, "while your own country was bombing the hell out of you, day after day after day."

Her eyes welled with tears, but she maintained her sardonic tone as she talked about childhood cancers and deformed lifeless babies.

"I wanted to make peace with my country for what they've done to me, my family, my friends, my community," she said, gripping a tissue. "It's hard to do that. . . . You know, every four years we have an election and it's always about 'pro-life.' Pro-life. 'We mustn't let women have a choice of what happens to their babies.' Oh, really. You're *that* pro-life are you, and yet you won't sign to do away with bombs? You won't fight the biggest pro-life issue of all? You say, 'Oh, women can't have abortions.' You *caused* spontaneous abortions to us. It isn't fair to speak one thing and do another."

A diplomatic snafu followed. From the stage, the moderator announced that it was time for questions from the delegations. The United States was called on first. Ambassador Scheinman, caught off guard and confused by the procedure, did not have a question. He had come out of Cornell in the late 1980s, when Carl Sagan was talking about the notion of nuclear winter, so the substance of the presentations was not new to him. He and his colleagues in the State Department were well aware of the catastrophe of a nuclear detonation, so Scheinman reacted in the moment by reading the U.S. government's prepared six-paragraph statement.

"The United States recognizes the environmental and other impacts of nuclear testing," he said, but "does not support efforts to move to a nuclear-weapons convention, a ban, or a fixed timetable for elimination of all nuclear weapons."

This was not what the crowd wanted to hear, especially after the dramatic scientific presentations and the heartfelt testimony of survivors. Scheinman's statement was met with boos from the activists.

"Not enough!" one shouted.

THE PRESENTATIONS at the Vienna conference were by turns arresting and ponderous.

A presentation on the online vulnerabilities of nuclear facilities hushed the ballroom. Over the preceding four years, the National Nuclear Security Administration had been hacked 19 times.

"Maintaining a nuclear peace is a hard enough problem in itself, and what you do *not* need is a layer of cyber confusion on top of this," said Camille François, a fellow at Harvard Law School's Berkman Center for Internet and Society.

"The nine countries possessing nuclear weapons today are fielding new types of weapons, they're shortening the time needed to employ those weapons, and they're dispersing them more widely on ever-higher states of alert," said Bruce Blair, co-founder of Global Zero and a former launch control officer for ICBMs. Nuclear powers "are preparing for the unthinkable, and in preparing they risk causing it."

The single strategic war plan of the United States has been changed to a family of plans that are more flexible and suited for a wider range of scenarios, said Hans Kristensen of the Federation of American Scientists, presenting nonclassified but protected information that made Pentagon staffers back in D.C. raise their eyebrows.

The detonation in downtown Washington of a ten-kiloton nuclear device—two-thirds the yield of the Hiroshima bomb—would cause 45,000 immediate deaths, said Micah Lowenthal of the National Academy of Sciences, Engineering, and Medicine.

The program of speakers was arranged to entwine the scientific with the philosophical.

"Law stands on hollow ground where solid moral conviction is absent," said Nobuo Hayashi of the University of Oslo, and "a gap in law is often just a mirror through which we are impelled to gaze into our own ambivalent souls."

The U.S. delegation listened but couldn't get past the obstacle of verification. It's fine to argue for zero, but how do you *verify* that everyone's at zero? The process of verification increases in complexity as stockpile numbers decrease, particularly because no nation wants to expose its design secrets in the inspections process.

If the mood in the ballroom was any indication, much of the world was moving on from this cautious attitude. The blast waves of Hiroshima and Nagasaki were still reverberating, still compelling people to push for a world without nukes. The inherent morals and ethics were still radiating, searching for stability among paradoxes and unknowns. While Sister Megan, Michael, and Greg sat in separate prisons, the punished foot soldiers of old-school resistance, a new school was taking attendance at the Hofburg Palace, and it was working within the political process.

THE SECOND DAY of the conference was hobbled by an epic parade of statements by delegations, most of them dry and redundant affirmations of abolition. The voices of caution came from the United Kingdom, the United States, and their allies. One side was repeating, "The time to act is now," while the other's touchstone words were "practical," "realistic," "step by step."

This conference shows political will, Ambassador Scheinman acknowledged, but "we must have a practical way to do it."

Civil-society members were allowed to make statements as well, and an Australian activist named Richard Lennane swung for the

fences. He was seated with a silver laptop behind the official delegations. He began his statement by quoting the prophet Isaiah: "How
long, oh Lord, until the cities are wasted without inhabitant, and the
houses without people, and the land lies utterly desolate?"

And then he addressed the non-nuclear powers: "You can negotiate, and adopt, and bring into force a treaty banning nuclear weapons.
This is something you can *do*. It is something you can do *now*. The
alternative is to sit, passive, impotent, while the nuclear-armed states
continue as they always have, risking your security—along with all of
human civilization—in a misguided attempt to protect theirs."

His speech was met by 30 seconds of applause throughout the ballroom. The Americans and the British reacted with silence and the
slightest of head shakes.

The conference was closed by Alexander Kmentt, Austria's director of the Office of Disarmament Affairs. A tall and soft-spoken man,
Kmentt thought that this rebellious conference might cost him his
job, but he pledged that Austria would work to "stigmatize, prohibit,
and eliminate nuclear weapons." He would bring the conclusions of
the conference to the United Nations in five months' time. The Nuclear Non-Proliferation Treaty review conference was always a procedural battle, but now it would feature a new moral crusade.

ACROSS FIRST AVENUE from the United Nations is a granite wall
that curves along a staircase leading up to East 43rd Street. Incised
into the wall are the words of Isaiah:

> THEY SHALL BEAT THEIR SWORDS INTO
> PLOWSHARES. AND THEIR SPEARS INTO
> PRUNING HOOKS. NATION SHALL NOT LIFT
> UP SWORD AGAINST NATION. NEITHER
> SHALL THEY LEARN WAR ANY MORE.

From there, the granddaughter of Dorothy Day began the 500-foot walk to the headquarters of the U.S. mission to the U.N. Martha Hennessy was nearly 60 years old, her white hair tied in a ponytail, her purple shirt reading, "No Nukes Begins with U.S." Across the street, it was the second day of the monthlong Review Conference of the Nuclear Non-Proliferation Treaty, referred to by attendees as "the RevCon." Walking with Martha were a few dozen activists, mostly of a certain age, including Sacred Peace Walkers from Nevada, Art Laffin of the D.C. house named after Hennessy's grandmother, and Sisters Carol and Ardeth, who, with John LaForge, carried a banner-size map of ICBM locations spread across the northern Great Plains like chicken pox. There were also people who had walked, run, or biked the 700-plus miles from Oak Ridge over the previous four weeks.

The all-star cast of activists bunched up in front of the revolving door of the U.S. mission, its glass facade reflecting the morning sun. Visible inside the lobby were framed portraits of President Obama and Secretary of State John Kerry, who a day earlier had addressed the General Assembly at the start of the RevCon. In front of 191 delegations, Kerry had talked of learning about nuclear warfare as a new recruit in the Navy. The insane nuclear arms race of the mid-20th century had been supplanted, he said, by "a steady march in the direction of reason toward the promise of peace," a phrase that was a masterpiece of statecraft semantics.

"Nuclear weapons should one day be eliminated," Kerry said.

"Today," Sister Carol whispered, seated with other activists in the balcony of the hall.

"Today," repeated Sister Ardeth, at her side.

After Kerry came Tony deBrum, from the Marshall Islands.

"I wonder how many in this room have actually witnessed a detonation of a nuclear weapon," he said from the elevated rostrum.

He paused a moment, waiting for a show of hands that he knew wasn't coming.

"I have," deBrum continued. The Marshallese "still carry a burden which no other people or nation should ever have to bear."

Back to the present: Martha and the activists were now blocking the entrance to the mission with a long banner that said SHADOWS AND ASHES: ALL THAT REMAIN. They began singing "Down by the Riverside" and "Keep Your Eyes on the Prize." Officers from the New York Police Department awaited commands. A couple of police vans were ready to go on First Avenue. Pedestrians bobbed and weaved through the clot, cradling their Dunkin' Donuts iced coffees, pausing momentarily to take an iPhone photo of the retro-pacifist scene.

"This is a restricted area: No standing activity is permitted," an NYPD lieutenant said into a bullhorn, holding a laminated script headlined "Disorderly Conduct: Pedestrian Traffic."

Activists took video of the police officers who took video of the activists. As the officers began cuffing those blocking the entrance, supporters chanted, "Arrest those who wage war, not those who wage peace!" Sister Carol, as she was being led to a police van, chatted up an officer about the ongoing racial unrest in Baltimore and Ferguson, Missouri. Silent, and with her head bowed, Martha was loaded into a van, in the same fashion as her grandmother had been 70 years prior.

Four days later, at the end of the first week of the RevCon, 50 young anti-nuclear activists snacked from silver platters of baked Brie on the second floor of the French-Gothic Presbyterian Building in the Flatiron District. This was the first "action lab" organized by Global Zero, which launched in 2008, won the endorsement of both Obama and then-president Dmitry Medvedev, and enlisted celebrities like Matt Damon, Naomi Watts, and Michael Douglas to speak in favor of a nuclear deal with Iran and against the trillion-dollar reinvestment in the triad. Global Zero's 2015 initiative, compelled by the RevCon and the 70th anniversary of Hiroshima and Nagasaki, was an action corps "to mobilize all-star activists across the country to help us tackle the single biggest security threat of our generation."

These all-stars sat at round dinner tables in the small auditorium of a meeting space called Civic Hall, designed for tech entrepreneurs. Queen Noor of Jordan was the first speaker.

"Complacency is a powerful foe," the queen said from behind a transparent plastic rostrum. "The public is still largely asleep on the nuclear issue. When people think of nuclear weapons, if they think of them at all, it's usually in the narrow confines of Iran or North Korea. Most would be surprised to learn there are still more than 15,000 nuclear weapons on Earth. . . . Yours is the generation that must insist that we solve this problem, and soon."

The next speaker was Ward Wilson, a senior fellow at the British American Security Information Council. He gave a PowerPoint presentation on the myths of nuclear weapons. He declared that humanity was in a race between destruction and elimination, especially because of terrorist groups like the Islamic State and sources of bilateral tension like Ukraine.

A University of Oregon student named Brian asked if there was any alignment between nuclear weapons and climate change.

"If you assume climate change is real, which it is—if it will lead to greater conflict, which I think it will—then climate change is probably going to lead to a greater risk of nuclear war," Wilson said. "Most water for Pakistan comes from the Kashmir glacier. Those glaciers will be reduced by 50 percent by 2035. Hunger is an existential crisis for a country." The implication was that India and Pakistan, nuclear-armed neighbors with a history of conflict, would become even more volatile as food and water sources became unstable.

A student named Jenny asked for Wilson's most effective argument against disarmament skeptics and supporters of deterrence.

"Look, human beings are fallible," he replied. "Nuclear deterrence depends on human beings. It's not a machine. Nuclear weapons are a faith. A religion. People who believe in them invest them with their emotional faith."

That night, in a bit of guerrilla theater, Global Zero projected the image of a rubber ducky in crosshairs onto the limestone side of the U.N. building. Underneath the ducky, in bold white letters beamed from a truck a few blocks north:

**WE'RE ALL
SITTING
DUCKS**

INSIDE THE United Nations was a carnival of diplomats and wonks and agitators, all colliding in the General Assembly building for the first time in five years. There were formal meetings, excruciating in their dullness, in the U.N.'s auditoriums. There was glad-handing over double espressos in the Europe Café, and backroom dealings in basement conference rooms. There were strategy confabs hosted by activists and nongovernmental organizations furious with the slow pace of disarmament. The Non-Proliferation Treaty was the planet's fundamental arms-control agreement, but it was apparent only occasionally that the fate of civilization was at stake. The RevCon was a clumsy social mechanism, a four-week procedural drama with too many commercial breaks and too many actors.

There was the P5, the original nuclear powers when the NPT was signed in 1968: China, France, Russia, the United Kingdom, and the United States, all of which were modernizing their nuclear arsenals.

There were the non-nuclear allies of the P5 that relied on the U.S. nuclear deterrent and were reluctant to rock the boat: South Korea, Japan, Australia, members of NATO like Canada, and those countries that hosted U.S. nuclear weapons on their soil (Belgium, Germany, Italy, the Netherlands, and Turkey).

There was the Non-Aligned Movement (or the NAM): mainly countries from Africa, the Persian Gulf region, and the Asian subcontinent, led during the RevCon by Iran. Their highest priority was establishing some kind of timetable for disarmament, which the P5 resisted.

There was the New Agenda Coalition (or the NAC): Brazil, Egypt, Ireland, Mexico, New Zealand, and South Africa, which had been trying collectively since 1998 to push disarmament while viewing the P5 states as foot-draggers. The NAC's priority was fleshing out the persisting vagueness of the treaty.

And there was the new Humanitarian Initiative, which was led by Austria and included the NAC and much of the NAM. During the RevCon, Austria slowly collected signatures on a pledge to close the legal gap in the NPT. In other words, a growing coalition wanted to outlaw the only type of weapon of mass destruction that wasn't explicitly illegal under international treaty.

The treaty, now 45 years old, was indispensable but imperfect. The perpetual source of trouble was its Article VI.

> Each of the Parties to the Treaty undertakes to pursue negotiations in good faith on effective measures relating to cessation of the nuclear arms race at an early date and to nuclear disarmament, and on a treaty on general and complete disarmament under strict and effective international control.

The article requires negotiations, not results, and imposes no conditions. Every country had different interpretations of "good faith" and "effective measures." Even the comma was a source of argument. Did it mean there were two exclusive obligations in this article? Were they to be coordinated in tandem? Did the text after the comma apply only to nuclear-armed states? The treaty envisioned a nuclear-free world, but it didn't require it.

The goal of the RevCon was to produce an outcome document—a list of accomplishments and pledges toward further implementing the goals of the NPT. The document had to be agreed on by all 191 delegations. If even one country dissented after four weeks of haggling, there would be no consensus, thus no document, thus no progress in moving the treaty forward. One world, or none.

No provision for nuclear disarmament existed beyond the expiration of New START in 2021. With the next RevCon not until 2020, a document with interim goals and guidelines for disarmament was crucial.

If this conference failed, it would put the treaty on ice for another five years. If it succeeded, the world would take another small step toward safety and stability.

The RevCon was also suspenseful for two outside reasons. One was the U.S.-Iranian negotiations over a historic deal to limit Iran's nuclear program. The second was the momentum of the Humanitarian Initiative, still energized from its winter conference in Vienna. Cables from Australia in the months since the Vienna conference noted the "bleak prospects" for arms control and a "growing concern" about Austria recruiting other countries to endorse the outlawing of nuclear weapons.

"Like the US, Australia is worried about the Austria Pledge" and its impact on the RevCon, said a missive from Australia's Department of Foreign Affairs and Trade.

For the first two weeks, official delegations appeared at daily 9 a.m. meetings of civil society to answer questions and endure withering criticism. Matthew Rowland, the U.K. representative at the RevCon, was the first P5 representative to sit in the hot seat in cramped conference room C, in the basement of the General Assembly building.

"Do you agree with Australia's position that the catastrophic humanitarian consequences is why deterrence works?" asked Tim Wright, an Australian staffer of the International Campaign to Abolish Nuclear Weapons.

"It's certainly clear the impact the weapons have ties to their function in our deterrence strategy, yes," answered Rowland. "But they are political weapons for deterring action, not fighting wars. We're very clear we will only use them in the most extreme circumstances."

Such as? Wright asked.

"We don't define that," Rowland said.

What are the extreme circumstances? Wright pressed.

"They're extreme. Certainly national survival would be one of them. We're deliberately ambiguous about what the conditions are."

"This is becoming a bit reminiscent of a *Yes, Minister* episode," said Wright, referring to the British TV satire.

Adam Scheinman, the lead U.S. representative at the Vienna humanitarian conference, was back in the same role at the RevCon— but with even more of an uphill battle. "An impossible task" was how other U.S. officials regarded Scheinman's predicament, which was to ensure an outcome document despite the rabble-rousing Humanitarian Initiative, internal P5 conflict over Russian transgressions and Chinese obfuscation, and the imbalanced situation in the Middle East, whose only regional nuclear power (Israel) had never signed the treaty.

Scheinman and other members of the U.S. delegation viewed their job as promoting a vision of the future while dealing with what was possible in the present. Their goals and tactics were just as humanitarian as the movement that was opposing them. Nevertheless, they faced the same impatient scrutiny the day after the U.K. delegation did. Activists wanted to know: Was the U.S. government lobbying NATO allies to refuse Austria's humanitarian pledge? There had been a news report that the United States was bullying states like Norway.

"We have an issue with a ban," Scheinman replied. "We have committed to reduce reliance, but we're not prepared today to *end* reliance on nuclear weapons."

"You're talking about your love for Article VI," said New York activist Alice Slater, who had met Sister Megan in her Occupy Wall

Street group and connected her to Ralph Hutchison in Oak Ridge. "How can you say in the same breath that you're relying on nuclear weapons? Where is the good faith? I'm an American and I'm really embarrassed."

"We've had an 85 percent reduction in the stockpile," said Robert Wood, the U.S. representative to the Geneva conference on disarmament, sitting to Scheinman's right. "It's hard to say we haven't had a good-faith effort."

Over the course of the RevCon, the United States repeatedly said that it was reducing the role of nuclear weapons in its security strategy, and therefore honoring its treaty obligations. The State Department had produced a one-page memo for the RevCon: U.S. nuclear forces were not on hair-trigger alert, there was no launch-on-warning policy, and all ICBMs were targeted on open oceans.

Yet this message was constantly undercut before, during, and after the conference. "The role of our nuclear arsenal is at least as important today as it was in decades past," Major General Michael Fortney of Global Strike Command had said a few months prior. Retaining and modernizing the triad is "the highest priority mission of the Department of Defense," the Senate Armed Services Committee wrote in an early draft of the 2016 National Defense Authorization Act during the third week of the RevCon.

Civil society was disgusted with the United States and the United Kingdom, whose delegations were, in turn, vexed that civil society wasn't going harder after Russia, which was accused of violating another arms treaty by developing and testing an intermediate-range cruise missile, or China, whose stockpile management was nowhere near as transparent as the U.S. government's was.

With Scheinman running the show day to day, Rose Gottemoeller was free to dip in and out of the conference over the course of the month. During the first week, she appeared on a high-level U.S. panel with NNSA administrator Frank Klotz. The pair made a convincing argument that the United States was doing its best to comply with the spirit of the treaty.

The United States has 4,717 warheads in its active stockpile, Rose said, which "is still too many weapons and we know it." But the numbers can come down only with a "willing partner" in Russia.

Activists pushed back. Couldn't the United States pursue unilateral reductions? Didn't the life-extension program for the B61 gravity bomb include new capabilities? The bomb was being modernized with a guidance tail kit and an adjustable yield—features that increased its accuracy and varied its destructive capacity, making it a more tempting option during conflict.

"We will not build new nuclear weapons," Klotz assured the crowd, and "we will not provide for new military capabilities."

Activists weren't the only outside actors influencing the process. Four nuclear-armed states were not party to the treaty at all. North Korea had signed it in 1985, dropped out in 2003, and then conducted the 21st century's only nuclear detonations. India, which had just tested a missile capable of reaching China, had never signed. Pakistan, which was deploying short-range nuclear weapons to the Indian border, had never signed. The fourth was Israel. Javad Zarif, Iran's negotiator in the unfolding nuclear deal with the United States, condemned Israel on the first day of the RevCon and demanded that it join the treaty. Israel was present at the U.N., but only as an observer—until the final day of the conference.

ABOUT SEVEN MILES AWAY, down the East River and alongside the Gowanus Canal, Sister Megan was busy writing at the shared computer in her cell block on the sixth floor of the Metropolitan Detention Center.

"Dear friends, promoters of ways to make real the energies of the social gospel in our midst," she began.

She was prisoner No. 88101-020 in the detention center, a forbidding warehouse-like structure in an area of Brooklyn defined by smokestacks, barbed wire, pizza joints, and shuttered porno shops. Her block was an overcrowded open room with bunk beds occupied by women who were serving time mostly for drug-related offenses.

"The need is urgent for local (retired) lawyers to be found who can assist inmates who need second opinions," Megan wrote, referring to fellow prisoners. "We are all equally responsible to do what we feel able to do: be informed, reflect, analyze, act."

She had been behind bars for nearly two years. There was no place to go outdoors, and the only glimpse of the outside world was a partial view of a brick alley. Megan wore thermal pants under her greenish-beige prison uniform to keep warm. She had a punctured eardrum. Her front tooth had come out in a chewy brownie a few months earlier, and there were no dental services at the detention center. She was keeping the tooth in a small box of batteries for her radio.

"Failing empires which follow mindless policies are oblivious of being guided by the values and principles of the social gospel," she typed, ending a letter to supporters by asking New Yorkers to join in protests around the RevCon at the U.N. "Blessings and gratitude for life as we 'spring forward' into this new growing season."

In her letters to the outside world, Megan asked people to oppose the Uranium Processing Facility at Y-12 and to sign a petition in solidarity with the Marshall Islands and its lawsuit. In her view, keeping up correspondence and sharing information was a way to build and maintain a community of resistance from behind bars.

There was plenty to complain about in the detention center, but Megan was not a complainer. Prepared meals, however tasteless and repetitive, were still more luxurious than her diet while teaching in Africa. Plus, there were ways to get creative. The thick pea soup, for example, could be livened up with a splash of boiling water and some grated pepper-jack cheese. If she pulled her mattress up, she could approximate the feel of a chaise lounge. Yes, there was no connection to the Internet at large, but at least she had access to e-mail, BBC Radio, and *Democracy Now!* The "mindlessness" of prison culture was everywhere though: Inmates' in-boxes could hold only 30 e-mails, the defective vending machines gobbled up money until you'd spent $8 to coax out a yogurt. But at least there was yogurt to have. In Megan's mind, the women on the block were not hardened depressives or volatile bullies; they were opportunities for learning and teaching. During meals Megan used a missalette to perform brief liturgies. "We are all priests, prophets, and kings," she told her fellow prisoners.

In March the legal team for Transform Now Plowshares had argued in Cincinnati that the trio's convictions should be overturned. Barring success in the appeals court, Sister Megan still had another year to serve.

The action at Y-12 was still popping up here and there—at the U.N. during the RevCon, at lunchtime panels on nuclear security in D.C.—as evidence of a precarious and complacent security apparatus. Megan had heard about the TV show *Orange Is the New Black*, set in a fanciful women's prison in New York state, and how one minor character was an anti-nuclear Catholic sister. She assumed the character was based on Sister Ardeth, who was attending every day of the RevCon with Sister Carol. The episode in question, though, featured a flashback scene of the Catholic sister and two men cutting through fences and spray-painting biblical graffiti on a big white building.

Megan's accomplices were in separate facilities. Michael was one of 1,400 inmates in the McKean Federal Correctional Institution, a medium-security prison in northwest Pennsylvania. He began his correspondence by referring to himself as "a prisoner for Christ's sake." He printed out news articles about John Kerry and the ongoing nuclear negotiations with Iran and annotated them in black pen: "The antichrist arrogant U.S. government continues to attempt to dictate human affairs outside of the rule of law." He wrote poetry about St. George fighting the dragon.

He received notes from college students staying at the Dorothy Day Catholic Worker house in D.C.: "Thank you for your dedication & your commitment to our freedom."

Slipping between cursive and printing, he wrote letters that invoked Hiroshima and Vietnam and Martin Luther King Jr.: "The person who stares back at me in the mirror is very much responsible for the world as it is. I am also responsible for helping to craft the world of tomorrow."

Greg was in Leavenworth, a penitentiary outside Kansas City, Kansas. His wife, Michele, was running a new Catholic Worker house in Duluth. His daughter, Rachel, was now 20 and had her own apartment and three part-time jobs. Leavenworth was the largest and most racially segregated prison Greg had ever been in. Violence was pervasive. In just his first five months, one inmate had been beaten to death by another. Another had been stabbed. The unofficial seating regimen in the 125-table dining hall was by home state, though there were also four tables set aside for Christians.

Greg lived in a two-man cell on a block with older men, which was a calmer environment. Greg played Scrabble with other inmates. His small Bible-study group met nightly. He remembered Dan Berrigan's teachings in New Orleans—how one's life in prison was similar to one's life outside prison, how on either side one must study the Bible, find fellowship and community, be of service to others. In this way, there were no bars, no guards, no captivity. In this way Greg was still free.

It was now two years since their conviction, and two months since their appeal was heard. Absolution could come at any moment, or not at all.

MANHATTAN WAS GORGEOUS the whole month of May. A gentle sun. A cool breeze off the East River. Delegates were stuck inside the U.N. though, arguing over the meaning of vocabulary in drafts of the outcome document. Treaty language was highly specialized and slightly absurd. "Takes note" had a very different meaning than "welcomes," for example, as did "calls for" versus "affirms." There were disagreements about the meaning of terms as simple as "nuclear warhead" and "nuclear strategy."

"A diplomat's job is not to save the world," said ICAN's Beatrice Fihn over lunch at a nearby French restaurant, during the second week of the RevCon. "Success to them is language."

The 2000 outcome document outlined "13 steps" to further implement the treaty.

The 2010 outcome document listed "64 actions."

The volume of language was increasing but warhead dismantlement had decreased. ICAN's goal for the remainder of the RevCon was to push non-NATO states to introduce language about the humanitarian consequences, to recognize the legal gap in the treaty, and to turn "effective measures" into concrete requirements—like demanding the ratification of the test-ban treaty. The next step, of course, was a ban on the weapons themselves.

By the end of the second week, 84 countries had signed Austria's pledge. The P5 argued that a ban would sabotage consensus, fracture the NPT, and upset the balance of power in an already dangerous world.

The third week of the RevCon was all about accepting and rejecting language in the evolving draft of the outcome document. France objected to the word "fully" in paragraph 32, in reference to nuclear-armed states' commitment to refrain from using nuclear weapons on non-nuclear states. New Zealand wanted to move up paragraphs 22 through 26, which were about the humanitarian consequences. Mexico lamented the document's omission of the upcoming 70th anniversary of Hiroshima and Nagasaki. China objected, saying that treating Japan as a victim showed insensitivity toward atrocities committed by the empire during World War II. Trinidad and Tobago wanted to insert "slow" to criticize the pace of disarmament. Costa Rica was concerned that the strong verb "urge" did not appear often enough.

Abdul Samad Minty, South Africa's representative, bemoaned the petty fixation on verbiage, which distracted from the core issue of fairness.

"If for security reasons the [P5] feel that they must be armed with nuclear weapons, what about other countries in similar situations?" asked Minty. "Do we think that the global situation is such that no other country would ever aspire to nuclear weapons to provide security for themselves, when the five tell us that it is absolutely correct to possess nuclear weapons for *their* security?"

In between sessions, activists lobbied delegates on the floor of the auditoriums, trying to get more signatures for the Austrian pledge, which was now being called the humanitarian pledge. The final draft of the outcome document wasn't printed and dispersed until 2 a.m. on the final day of the conference.

By then, 99 countries had signed the humanitarian pledge—more than half the delegations at the RevCon. If there was no consensus on the official outcome document, activists said, at least there was a pledge toward forward action by a majority of states. As the closing session approached that final Friday afternoon, the rumor was that everything hinged on language around a conference to establish a weapons-of-mass-destruction-free zone in the Middle East. The Arab states, led by Egypt, wanted to impose a March 2016 deadline to fulfill this requirement, even over the objection or absence of a regional actor like Israel.

Shortly before 2 p.m. on that last day, the embassy of Israel sent a statement to American media to try to apply public pressure on the U.S. delegation. The embassy cited a 2010 promise that a conference on a WMD-free zone would not be convened without the consent of all Middle East nations.

"There is great concern in Israel that the U.S. won't live up to its commitments to Israel concerning NPT 2015," the statement said. These "safeguards for Israel, backed by U.S. guarantees, are glaringly absent from the draft resolutions now under consideration in New York. . . . To live up to its commitments to Israel, the U.S. must oppose these resolutions."

Meanwhile, over a matter of hours, the number of countries that had signed the humanitarian pledge had risen to 107. As consensus around the treaty conference was breaking down, a new consensus was gathering a critical mass.

AT 5:10 P.M. on the final day of the conference, Rose Gottemoeller walked onto the floor of the General Assembly with Adam Scheinman and other U.S. officials. The balcony, full of activists, chattered about what her presence meant. Was she there to join in the victory of consensus? Or to show strength in the midst of the RevCon's collapse?

Rose was second to speak, after Tunisia gave a thumbs-up to the outcome document. Her tone was firm but gloomy. The word "unfortunately" finally appeared in the seventh paragraph of her prepared statement. Rose said that the United States was ready to endorse all aspects of the document except the language about the Middle East conference on weapons of mass destruction, which "did not allow for consensus" and "set an arbitrary deadline." She singled out Egypt, which demanded "unrealistic and unworkable conditions" and failed to show flexibility. Once again, rigid single-mindedness had squandered progress.

"We know that this treaty is more important than one idea or one person or one country," Rose said, and the balcony audience bristled. Hadn't one country—a country that had not even signed the treaty—upended the whole process?

The United Kingdom backed up the United States, saying that "an incremental, step-by-step approach is the only practical approach to nuclear disarmament." Canada also fell in line, and was the only dissenter to call Israel by name.

Deborah Barker-Manase, the Marshall Islands' deputy representative to the U.N., spoke next. "Our outcome today deserves no accolades," she said. "Preventing this outcome from going forward is simply not a constructive approach."

"We wish to express our deep disappointment and dismay," said Iranian delegate Hamid Baidinejad.

"We are blocked from strengthening the NPT and the goal for a world free of nuclear weapons by three delegations," said Egypt, referring to the U.S., the U.K., and Canada, who in turn blamed Egypt for resisting compromise.

Austria's Alexander Kmentt spent several minutes naming all 107 countries that had signed on to the humanitarian pledge. "There is a reality gap, a credibility gap, a confidence gap, and a moral gap," he said.

South African delegate Nozipho Mxakato-Diseko compared the rule-by-minority policy of the nuclear-armed states to apartheid.

Rose sat through closing remarks from two dozen countries, which delivered bitter rejoinders to the United States and its allies. She was crushed. The only other person in her position who had failed to shepherd a successful RevCon was John Bolton, the undiplomatic George W. Bush appointee. Breaking consensus was an excruciating task, but she knew it was the right thing to do. Progress on a WMD-free zone depended on the fair and equal cooperation of all countries, and the Arab states wanted to splinter the process. The stakes were too high, and the consequences too far-reaching, to accept that. The failure of the RevCon didn't roll back the treaty, Rose knew, but it didn't advance it. She would have to find progress another way, at a domestic level, in the final 20 months of the Obama administration.

Without a consensus document, Austria, ICAN, and the rest of civil society promoted the idea that the humanitarian pledge was the true outcome of the 2015 RevCon.

A ban on nuclear weapons was next, they said. It's coming.

SISTER MEGAN'S YOUNGER COUSIN, who was also named Megan, sat in a gray Ford Escort parked on the exposed cobblestones of Second Avenue in the Sunset Park area of Brooklyn. There were three Megans in the extended family, and Megan Tourlis was known as "Megan No. 2." On the windshield of her car was an "Atomic Veteran" decal, placed there by her father, Walter Hooke. To her right were abandoned cars, overgrown weeds, and a posse of stray cats. To her left was the Metropolitan Detention Center. The only signs of life were the squeaks of sneakers from an indoor basketball game between inmates.

It was the third Saturday of May 2015, overcast and sticky, the end of the third week of the RevCon up the river. The day before, as the P5 fought back against more than 100 countries that wanted to preclude the use of nuclear weapons "under any circumstances," Judge Thapar had ordered the immediate release of Megan, Michael, and Greg. Their sabotage conviction had been overturned by an appeals court that month, by a vote of 2 to 1.

The government mistook motive for intent, concluded Judge Raymond Kethledge in his opinion.

"The question, then, is whether the defendants consciously meant to interfere with the nation's ability to attack or defend when they engaged in" their intrusion at Y-12, Kethledge wrote. "No rational jury could find that the defendants had that intent when they cut the fences; they did not cut them and allow al Qaeda to slip in behind."

But the defendants testified that their intent was to impede the production of nuclear weapons, said the dissenting judge, Danny J. Boggs.

"Their intent to obstruct and interfere, however couched and however quixotic," Boggs wrote, "was thus something that a rational juror could find existed."

The only conviction that stood was the destruction of government property; their two years of prison time had more than paid that debt to society.

Sister Megan could walk out of the prison at any moment, so Megan No. 2 waited in her car with one of her cousin's friends, Eleanor Oakley, who had met Sister Megan during protests against the School of the Americas.

Outside the car, a prison officer was dumping shredded tuna into bowls for the feral cats.

"You here for Megan?" the officer asked.

"Yes," Eleanor said.

"God bless, God bless," the officer said, shaking his head. "That woman should have never been in here."

Megan No. 2 checked her phone. She squinted at the large sliding gates. The hours dragged by. She and Eleanor traded stories about Sister Megan, expressing admiration and exasperation. Megan No. 2 mentioned her husband, who had died just the year before; and her son Anthony, who had died nine years earlier; and her father, Walter, who had been her cousin's muse. Sister Megan had said during prison visits how Walter was with her on that hike over Pine Ridge, and Megan No. 2 couldn't help thinking that her father would not have wanted this—the risking of life and limb, the costly and frustrating trial, the imprisonment. The single-minded devotion at the expense of everything else.

Megan No. 2 mentioned that her son Tim's childhood friend, a kid named Lopez, worked as a corrections officer at the prison. That was her only personal connection to the facility. She had told her cousin, just in case. She wondered if the two of them had ever interacted. It might've been nice to have a friendly connection on the inside.

Then at 6:15 p.m., after six hours of waiting, in the distance, through the gate: an old woman in gray sweatpants and a gray sweatshirt. She was walking alongside an officer, who was pushing three boxes on a small trolley. The gate slid open. Out they walked. Eleanor popped out of the car and fell into Sister Megan's arms. Megan No. 2 stood by the car and exhaled.

"Look at his name tag," Sister Megan said, pointing to the officer.

Megan No. 2 leaned in and squinted.

Lopez.

Megan No. 2 looked up. "You knew my son," she said.

"Yes," Lopez said.

"Anthony," Sister Megan said, pointing to the sky.

Megan No. 2's mouth opened but no words came out.

"Good luck to you," Lopez said after loading the boxes into the trunk of the car.

"Small world," Megan No. 2 whispered, easing into the driver's seat, a tear sneaking down her cheek.

"Is this Uncle Walter's car?" Sister Megan said after settling into the backseat.

"It is," Megan No. 2 said. "With 88,000 miles."

"That's nothing," Sister Megan said. "In Nigeria we went over 100,000 in Peugeots. They last *forever.*"

Megan No. 2 couldn't get over the fact that Lopez was the one who escorted her out.

"Happenstance," her cousin said from the backseat, almost dismissively. "Serendipity. All these little things are signs and symbols." She had a bag of materials with her, including a book titled *Psalms for Praying*. A holy card of the scorched statue of Mary in Nagasaki bookmarked Psalm 34.

The Lord will rescue his servants;
No one who takes refuge in him will be condemned.

Then they were moving through the dying light in Uncle Walter's car, underneath the steel ribs of the Gowanus Expressway.

Then they were merging onto the Brooklyn-Queens Expressway.

"Oh, it's so nice to see the leaves," Sister Megan said.

Then, suddenly, out the window: Manhattan. Gray Manhattan, scraping the gray sky. Taller and richer than she had known it as a child, and with new features since she had entered prison.

"There's the Freedom Tower, as they now call it," Sister Megan said. "Although nobody's free." This was classic Megan, not allowing herself a moment's respite, using her release to remind everyone of their invisible shackles.

Her eyes wandered north, past the Empire State Building, and stopped on a towering new structure that was impossibly thin. In fact, it looked like it was the tallest building on the island, stabbing upward somewhere just south of Central Park.

"What is *that*?"

A new condo building on Park Avenue. Ninety-six stories. The penthouse sold for $95 million.

"People homeless down below in Central Park," Megan said, shaking her head, "and they're paying *that*."

For the next couple of months, Megan eased into the outside

world. She visited her religious order's mother house in Rosemont, Pennsylvania, to outline her post-prison life. There was another piece about her in the *New York Times*, which referred to her "rabble-rousing energy" and "atomic radicalization."

She got her missing tooth replaced.

And she prepared to return to the scene of her crime.

ON A THURSDAY MORNING that summer, the nuclear priesthood gathered in the third-floor banquet room at the National Republican Club of Capitol Hill. This was the annual nuclear-triad conference, titled the Enduring Value of Nuclear Deterrence in the 21st Century. It was sponsored by the chamber of commerce of Minot, North Dakota, whose Air Force base is near the geographic center of North America. It was from Minot that six nuclear-tipped cruise missiles were flown to Louisiana without authorization in 2007. It was at Minot that monthly pay for airmen had to be increased by $300 to retain a force that was willing to drive long distances in subzero temperatures to work 12-hour shifts in underground silos riddled with maintenance issues, to be ready to engage in World War III.

The triad conference was also sponsored by three top defense contractors: Lockheed Martin, which produced the nuclear missiles on U.S. and British submarines; General Dynamics, which had the $1.85-billion contract to construct a new fleet of those submarines that will be operational into the 2080s; and Northrop Grumman, which provided support for the subs' launcher system and operated the Nevada National Security Site. Another sponsor was Merrick and Company, which was designing parts of Y-12's Uranium Processing Facility. Remarks were direct.

"I think we can safely say the president's Prague vision is dead," announced Rep. Mike Rogers (R-Ala.), who had received more than $200,000 in campaign contributions from nuclear-weapons contractors during his career. "And I'll leave it to the Nobel committee to ask for its prize back."

The summer of 2015 had been a grim one for international security. Nuclear-capable Russian fighter planes were still buzzing NATO airspace. ISIS, which was roiling Iraq and Syria, reportedly seized 40 kilograms of uranium from Mosul University. Two days before the triad conference, North Korea confirmed that it had restarted plutonium production and was on its way to conducting another test explosion.

There was yet another concern to add to the list, said guest speaker Frank Miller.

"Let me wrap up by alerting you to one relatively new threat to our deterrent, one which many of you probably have never heard of."

Miller, who served for 22 years in the Department of Defense, looked around at the airmen in navy-colored dress uniforms pushing uneaten breakfast potatoes around their plates.

"There is a well-funded grassroots group called the humanitarian movement to ban nuclear weapons."

Miller didn't believe that the abolitionists, the Global Zero crowd, and the Humanitarian Initiative had a lock on morality. He had worked within the government as a broker between nuclear bureaucrats and political appointees whose time and expertise were often thin. He worked to bring stockpile numbers down to a responsible level while advocating for a continued deterrent, which he believed had prevented war between major powers since Nagasaki—and, in effect, saved millions of lives in the process. He and his brethren wanted nuclear weapons not for warfare, but for peace. And now, decades after the Cold War, this peace was a bargain: The cost of nukes was a fraction of the Pentagon's total budget. This reasonable investment would be necessary, he thought, until the very nature of man was transformed. And, given current events, that was not about to happen.

"According to their propaganda," Miller said of the Humanitarian

Initiative, "they have enlisted the support of 115 governments in a quest to create a treaty which bans nuclear weapons, based on the Ottawa Treaty campaign, which created a ban on land mines. This group is holding multiple conferences a year—conferences attended by government officials and peace activists—to gather support for drafting a treaty and obtaining endorsement for it from supportive governments. They would then present that treaty to the United Nations."

Miller took a breath.

"I find the notion that returning to the pre-1945 world is somehow humanitarian to be particularly galling and offensive," he continued. "Some ten million combatants died in World War I, as did another seven million noncombatants. An estimated 20 to 25 million combatants perished in World War II, along with 50 to 55 million noncombatants. Was that humanitarian? Is it humanitarian to assert that we should return to that world? These activists and their governments— shamefully including some allies who seek shelter under our nuclear umbrella—have no role in assuring global stability or halting aggression. They have no responsibility to deter war. Their crusade could create conditions *for* war, and for massive bloodshed. The real humanitarians, I believe, are in our missile silos, our [subs] and our bombers, and in the units and headquarters which support them. And it's about damn time that we had the courage to start saying that. And to expose the current effort to delegitimize and ban nuclear weapons as the dangerous and destabilizing effort that it is."

AFTER A FAILED NPT review conference, the State Department scored a victory in a nuclear deal with Iran, signed in July by the United States, the P5 plus Germany, and the European Union after intense negotiations involving John Kerry and Department of Energy secretary Ernest Moniz. The deal relieved economic sanctions on Iran in exchange for restrictions on uranium enrichment and plutonium production for 10 to 15 years. The deal lengthened—from three months to a year—the time it would take Iran to fabricate enough material for a nuclear bomb. It also placed strict monitoring requirements on Iran's nuclear activity. Supporters hailed it as the only workable way to block Iran's path to a nuclear weapon. Detractors raised hell about allowing billions of dollars to flow into a theocracy that funds terrorism.

A series of nuclear anniversaries was rolling in on the heels of the deal, which made the timing either auspicious or ominous, depending on one's worldview. July 2015 was the 70th anniversary of the Trinity test, and Los Alamos announced that it was inaugurating a new supercomputer named Trinity that would make 3-D simulations of nuclear explosions with "increased fidelity."

Rose Gottemoeller planned to commit her final year and a half in the Obama administration to drumming up support for the ratification of the Comprehensive Nuclear-Test-Ban Treaty. She returned to Hiroshima and visited Nagasaki for the 70th anniversary of the bombings.

She met with Japanese students and listened to elderly survivors tell their stories, praising them for helping the world understand the "dire and terrible consequences" of the weapon. It had been almost 19 years since Bill Clinton signed the test-ban treaty, and the average age of *hibakusha* was now over 80.

"I do think that it's very, very important that the word get passed down to the next generation," Rose said in Hiroshima, continuing to lay the emotional pathway to bring the test-ban treaty back to the Senate. "We don't want to see nuclear use happen again."

With a Republican-controlled Senate, a fractious relationship with Russia, unease about the Iran deal, and a U.S. stockpile undergoing painful modernization, much of Washington thought Rose was crazy to push the treaty.

It was certainly a heavy rock, and the terrain was uphill. But she had faith.

Congress didn't. The treaty was a nonstarter with many Republicans. Both houses of Congress passed legislation ordering the knowledge of the "nuclear weapons life cycle" to be passed on "from one generation of nuclear weapons designers and engineers to the following generation."

At the State Department's sixth annual Generation Prague conference in 2015, the commander of the North American Aerospace Defense Command—the organization that guards the homeland against threats from the sky—had some stark words for the college-age attendees who were exploring careers in arms control and diplomacy.

"I don't see us being nuclear-free in my lifetime," Admiral William Gortney said. "Or in yours."

EPILOGUE

This is a mission area where we as human beings are
challenged to be perfect. We are not perfect.

GENERAL KEVIN P. CHILTON, COMMANDER OF
U.S. STRATEGIC COMMAND (2007–2011)

S eventy years to the day that Oak Ridge learned the purpose of
its wartime effort, two dozen activists gathered before dawn
outside the Y-12 National Security Complex. Under overcast
skies, as Y-12 employees arrived for work, the activists took turns
reading aloud the names of people who had died in Hiroshima. It was
August 6, 2015.

Ralph Hutchison was there, of course. Sisters Carol and Ardeth
had taken a bus in from Baltimore. They had prepared to cross the
line that weekend and be arrested, but then Jonah House would have
had no one at the helm. For the second time in two years, a young
married couple that was going to assume leadership of the house had
instead decided to move out of town.

At a Knoxville church the following night, Sister Megan, Michael,
and Greg reunited for the first time since their release from prison. A

hundred people, including Megan's lawyer, Francis Lloyd, showed up to see them and talk about the weekend's anniversary activities in Oak Ridge. Some wore white T-shirts with "The fruit of justice is peace" written graffiti-style, as if with spray paint. Ralph, guitar in hand, sang a song about the break-in.

> When the guard finally arrived
> They met him with a bow.
> No gun was drawn. The guard could see
> There was no danger now.
> They offered him some bread to eat
> And they offered him their prayers.
> He radioed his bosses
> He had peace protesters there.

It was the guard's day off, and he was an hour north in Sunbright. He had lost his arbitration case exactly a year before, so the window had closed on back pay and, in his mind, justice. Kirk Garland was putting together a new life though. A new home. A steady but dangerous job at the county detention center that gave him health insurance, which he needed in order to afford the $5,000-a-month medication for his multiple sclerosis.

> They locked the Transform Plowshares up,
> For how long no one knows.
> But the seed of peace they planted there
> Has sprouted and it grows.

He had started a sick-worker claim, just as his mother and brother's widow had done before. That claim would be rejected, for lack of evidence.

Who knows what act will turn the tide
And pave the way to life.
It's the reason we're required to do
What we see is right.

Life had been harder since the break-in, but Kirk felt more blessed. Maybe he had taken money for granted when he was at Y-12. Now he and his family were living within their means, and they felt like they had more instead of less. It was all part of God's plan, surely, and Kirk would live by it.

You don't need all the answers,
May not know precisely how.
But ignorance is no excuse;
The time to start is now.

The NNSA was readying the removal of the last highly enriched uranium from both Uzbekistan and Jamaica. Five kilograms from the former would be sent to Russia, and one kilogram from the latter would be down-blended for use in Tennessee power reactors. The United States was dismantling an average of one retired warhead every day, but its active stockpile was given new life.

It started at Y-12 at night,
In Oak Ridge, Tennessee.
Somehow still a living thing,
it lives in you and me.

Nuclear warheads were getting fresh cables, valves, telemetries, and other components, plus refurbished uranium secondaries from Y-12, to the tune of $65 billion—a line item on the trillion-dollar price

tag to keep the arsenal ready to preserve or destroy future generations.

A dream, a vision, a prayer, a call
For all those who have ears.
Transform swords to plowshares please,
Make pruning hooks from spears.

After Ralph's song, Megan, Michael, and Greg took seats on the
altar to speak and answer questions. They were undaunted by their
slog through the criminal-justice system.

"The prophets of God, Micah, and Isaiah have been talking about
global demilitarization for over 2,000 years," said Michael, who was
back living in the Dorothy Day Catholic Worker house in D.C.

"We no longer have a democracy," Megan said. "We have 7,000
nuclear weapons under the control of one man. . . . I don't feel I'm
free. I'm not out of prison. None of us is out of prison as long as one
nuclear bomb exists."

"Maybe this is a sign that something good is going to come from
the universe," Greg said about their early release. "It's a first for the
peace movement. A sign."

The next day, they joined 100 activists in walking from Oak
Ridge's town park to Y-12. Megan, Michael, and Greg carried a banner that said HIROSHIMA NEVER AGAIN. They walked down South
Tulane Avenue past the American Museum of Science and Energy,
which housed a replica of an A-house from the days of the Manhattan
Project. They turned left on South Illinois Avenue, the main thor-
oughfare of the city, and that's when the heckling began.

"Nukes rule!" yelled a young woman from a black minivan.

"What about Pearl Harbor, you dumbasses?" shouted a man in a
navy SUV.

The activists walked along the busy boulevard. They passed over East Fork Poplar Creek, which flowed with the elements of nuclear activity past and present. They turned right on Scarboro Road, skirting Pine Ridge, and passed the old white guard towers from when Oak Ridge was a gated city. Sister Mary Dennis Lentsch was there, in the shadow of the imposing relic, handing out paper peace cranes.

Megan, Michael, Greg, and the other walkers now approached Y-12 from the front, in broad daylight. A small line of cars waited behind a police cruiser, which was clearing the way for the protest. In a blue Nissan was a commissioner for Anderson County who was wearing a pink polo embroidered with the atomic logo of the Y-12 Federal Credit Union.

"Get outta my town!" she called through the open passenger-side window as the march processed by.

The walkers passed the turn onto Bear Creek Road and the employee security gate. They passed the big green sign that featured the name of the site's latest contractor: Consolidated Nuclear Security, a conglomerate led by Bechtel, which was also part of the previous contractor group. The current contract was worth $22 billion.

Megan, Michael, and Greg walked parallel to the black metal fence that had been installed along the shoulder after their break-in, between the road and the New Hope Visitors Center. Their toes against the white line of the northbound lane, the demonstrators sang "Mary Don't You Weep." Michael and Greg set the HIROSHIMA banner on the ground. On Ralph's command, they all crossed the two lanes to the black fence. Guards in camouflage uniforms watched from the visitor center parking lot, next to their white SUVs. Beyond them was the plant itself, the two water towers the trio had passed coming down Pine Ridge, the uranium storehouse they had defaced, the relics from the Manhattan Project, the foundation of the new Uranium Processing Facility rising out of the mud and mythology. It all seemed impenetrable, out of reach, futile, hopeless. They knew this wasn't true. The next Plowshares action, whenever and wherever it came, would be another reminder.

The sun blazed overhead. Sister Megan, at the end of a long road, tied a yellow peace crane to the gate. The crane would be collected and scrapped by guards within 30 minutes, but right then, at that moment in time, it was all she could do.

AUTHOR'S NOTE

All dialogue within quotation marks is from an official document or transcript, or was heard firsthand by me, or was substantiated by multiple sources. In chapter 8, for the sake of brevity, clarity, and efficiency, I have liberally condensed and elided dialogue from the jury trial, as well as omitted several witnesses, while preserving the dynamics and nature of the proceedings, all of which I witnessed in person and checked against court transcripts.

ACKNOWLEDGMENTS

This book is a work of synthesis. I am not a historian, physicist, lawyer, diplomat, activist, or beat reporter, so I've depended on people who are. These sources are listed, with respect and awe, in endnotes and the bibliography. I am particularly indebted to the work of Richard Rhodes, Lawrence Wittner, and Frank Munger, whose name, in the fine print, appears more than any other's between the covers of this book. Frank has been the nuclear and energy reporter for the *Knoxville News-Sentinel* for more than 30 years. His work has been to East Tennessee what it has been to this book-writing process: an indispensable asset.

Over two and a half years I made seven trips to Oak Ridge, totaling about 32 days, and spent an equal amount of time reading about the city and talking to people who know it—and Y-12—far better than I do. No amount of time can make an outsider an expert, so I relied on Trina Baughn, Tom Beehan, Glenn Bell, Colleen Black, Lindsey Freeman, Anne Garcia Garland, Steve Gibbs, the Rev. Steven D. Martin, Thom Mason, Ted Sherry, Rose Weaver, the Oak Ridge Reading Room at the city's public library, and especially D. Ray Smith and Ralph Hutchison.

I've lived in Washington, D.C., for the better part of 15 years, but it still took many people to help me understand how it functions and malfunctions, particularly around the nuclear-weapons complex: Robert Alvarez, Norman Augustine, Alex Bell, Taunja Berquam, Barry Blechman, Linton Brooks, Joe Cirincione, Leland Cogliani, Elbridge Colby, Tom Collina, Tom Countryman, David Culp, Tom D'Agostino, Toby Dalton, Lydia Dennett, Anita Friedt, Rebecca Gibbons, Jonathan Gill, Rose Gottemoeller, Bradley Harris, Loraine Heckenberg, Laicie Heeley, Meredith Horowski, Peter Huessy, Terri Lodge, Josh McConaha, Joe McDermott, Carmen MacDougall, Zia Mian, Frank Miller, Neile Miller, Adam Mount, Diane Perlman, Bob Peurifoy, Dan Poneman, Kingston Reif, Ben Rhodes, Adam Scheinman, Ashish Sinha, Al Stayman, Peter Stockton, Rep. Mac Thornberry (R-Texas), Alexandra Toma, David Trimble, Jon Wolfsthal, and Stephen Young. My gratitude to them, however, should not be an indication of their endorsement of this book.

The guidance and wisdom of Hans Kristensen, Stephen Schwartz, and Amy Woolf was crucial to my education. Their careers are a public service.

Each nuclear-weapons site in the United States is monitored by a citizen watchdog group, and thank goodness. Thank you in particular to Jay Coghlan in New Mexico, Marylia Kelley in California, LeRoy Moore in Colorado, and Ralph H. again in Tennessee.

Tom Hundley and the Pulitzer Center on Crisis Reporting provided money and support for my trip to the Marshall Islands and my stay in New York for the Review Conference on the Nuclear Non-Proliferation Treaty. My respect and admiration to the folks at the National Security Archive at George Washington University; they are always trying to pry secrets from the U.S. government that belong to the people. Though they are capable of causing enormous frustration, government employees who work in Freedom of Information Act offices deserve a mention here.

For their help in disparate but crucial ways, thank you to Glenn Alcalay, Ellen Barfield, Courtney Bender, Kathy Boylan, Patsy Burns, John Burroughs, Helen Buzaid, Ben and Suzanne Chutaro, John Coster-Mullen, Tony deBrum, James Doyle, Anabel Dwyer, Beatrice Fihn,

Megan Finnerty, Joe Finnerty, the Garland family (Misti, Kim Easter, and especially Kirk), Sister Carol Gilbert, Sheila Glodowski, Erik Johnson, Giff Johnson, Cindy Kelly, Melissa Kirby, David Krieger, Art Laffin, Sister Mary Dennis Lentsch, Francis Lloyd, Paul Magno, Michele Naar-Obed, Thomas Nash, Jack Niedenthal, Steven Orzack, Sister Ardeth Platte, Ned Price, Bill Quigley, Phil Runkel at Marquette University, Eric Schlosser, Jim Secreto, Alice Slater, Susi Snyder, Judge Amul Thapar, Jeff Theodore, Megan Tourlis, Mary Evelyn Tucker, Jonathan Weisgall, Alex Wellerstein, Tyler Wigg-Stevenson, Jocelyn K. Wilk at Columbia University, and Jerry Zawada.

For every name listed here, there is another that must go unmentioned. The nuclear world and Washington in general are secretive realms. My thanks to those who shared their insight and knowledge anonymously.

I've spent a third of my life at the *Washington Post*, and I was able to write this book because of my colleagues. Dana Priest passed along news of the Y-12 break-in, and Nicole Arthur knew I'd be game to write about it. Liz Seymour, Tracy Grant, and Marty Baron allowed me to take a yearlong leave and gave me room to run. Ann Gerhart edited the feature story this book is based on and Hank Stuever offered vital suggestions on the manuscript; to me, they are the soul of the *Post*. Gene Weingarten, the gold standard, first brought my work to the attention of my editor and publisher, David Rosenthal, an uber-mensch. The name Carrie Camillo is synonymous with quality control, and I was relieved that she could vet the manuscript late in the game.

This book would not exist without Kuhn Projects and my agent, Lauren Sharp, who with patience and precision guided me through the proposal process, got me a deal, and served as a coach during the reporting, writing, and editing. Thank you to the team at Blue Rider Press: David, Aileen Boyle, Katie Zaborsky, and Maureen Klier.

Much love to Maria Rowan and Zara Snapp, my first readers and encouragers; Lauren Ober, my work buddy; my brothers, whose creativity I aspire to; my grandfather, who taught me generosity; and to my parents, who taught me how to work and play.

Megan Rice, Michael Walli, and Greg Boertje-Obed have always said that they want the spotlight for their issue, not for themselves, but they allowed me to plunder their lives for the sake of a good story. I do recognize that in doing so I myself became part of their plan. And now, having read this far, so have you.

NOTES

PROLOGUE

3 **light of head, heavy of heart:** This description of the mental state of Plowshares activists on the eve of action is taken from *Essential Writings*, by Daniel Berrigan. The description of this particular scene in Tennessee is from interviews with the activists; I also visited the house in question after the fact.

CHAPTER 1. MANHATTAN

8 **on a diet of Schopenhauer . . . and Spinoza:** Wald, 82.

8 **the Department of Agriculture . . . to raise money for graduate school:** "Selig Hecht: Frederick Ives Medalist, 1941," John N. Howard, *OPN Optics and Photonics News*, March 2012, p. 22.

8 **Jacques Loeb . . . "and belongs to you":** Wald, p. 85.

9 **Heisenberg wrote in 1927:** *American Prometheus: The Triumph and Tragedy of J. Robert Oppenheimer*, by Kai Bird and Martin J. Sherwin (Knopf, 2005), p. 64.

10 **as clear as it was fast:** Written remembrance by Hamilton Hartridge, 1948.

10 **In his first chapter Bridgman asked bracing questions:** Bridgman, pp. 30–31. Bridgman posed them to illustrate that meaningless or unanswerable questions actually prompted lines of thinking that could reach answers, and therefore achieve meaning.

10 **By 1932 half the city's factories were closed:** Lower East Side Tenement Museum, http://www.tenement.org/encyclopedia/ecodepress_greatdepression.htm.

10 **Selig and other professors signed a protest:** "175 Educators Sign Kentucky Protest," no byline, *New York Times*, March 3, 1932.

11 **"into the composition of an event":** "The Uncertainty Principle and Human Behavior," by Selig Hecht, *Harper's Monthly Magazine*, January 1935, pp. 247–248.

11 **"a partial view of the world":** Typewritten letter to Marcel Reboussin of West Point, New York, January 11, 1935, Selig Hecht papers, Columbia University.

12 **30-ton, seven-feet-tall . . . 25,000 miles per second:** "Columbia's Historic Atom Smasher Is Now Destined for the Junk Heap," by William J. Broad, *New York Times*, December 20, 2007.

12 **the most efficient way:** *The Manhattan Project*, ed. by Cynthia C. Kelly, p. 40, excerpting William Lanouette's *Genius in the Shadows*.

12 **in his diary that night:** *A Guide to the Manhattan Project in Manhattan*, Cynthia C. Kelly and Robert S. Norris (Atomic Heritage Foundation, 2012), p. 22.

12 **"Complementarity":** Bird and Sherwin, p. 274.

13 **seven days a week:** Interview with Donald B. Trauger, Atomic Heritage Foundation oral history, September 22, 2005, excerpted in *Guide to the Manhattan Project in Tennessee*, p. 14.

13 **"and it would all disappear":** Rhodes, *Making of the Atomic Bomb*, p. 275.

13 **Over iced tea:** *The Manhattan Project*, ed. by Cynthia C. Kelly, excerpting William Lanouette's *Genius in the Shadows*, p. 39.

13 **The secrecy was on:** Rhodes, *Making of the Atomic Bomb*, p. 345.

14 **like wayward coal miners:** Ibid., p. 333.

14 **Three out of four physicists:** "Science Is Hush-Hushed," *Time*, May 11, 1942, excerpted in Wellerstein, p. 71.

14 **a pledge of secrecy:** Wellerstein, p. 44.

14 **on Staten Island . . . labeled URANIUM ORE . . . African colonies:** Norris, pp. 325–326.

14 **the Optical Society . . . in the field of optics:** "2,000 Scientists Speed Defense: Dr. Hecht Honored," no byline, *New York Times*, October 25, 1941.

15 **attributed this success rate to his conservative belief:** L. Fermi, pp. 147–148.

15 **In the fall of 1942 Selig taught a course:** "Study Principles for Camouflage," no byline, *New York Times*, August 30, 1942.

15 **His plain speech and blunt wit:** Wald, p. 90.

15 **"been bad taste to ask where":** L. Fermi, p. 161.

15 **State control of knowledge . . . into self-imposed censorship:** Wellerstein, 32.

15 **"A conspiracy":** Wittner, vol. 1, p. 6.

15 **tearooms, Chinese laundries, and small grocery stores:** L. Fermi, pp. 141–143.

16 **"Well, Dr. Hecht understands the Einstein theory":** Author interview with Megan Rice, October 2012, in Rosemont, Pennsylvania. All excerpts from the Selig Hecht papers, Columbia University.

19 **"if mankind is to survive":** "Dear Professor Einstein: The Emergency Committee of Atomic Scientists in Post-War America," Oregon State University's Special Collections & Archives Research Center, http://scarc.library.oregonstate.edu /omeka/exhibits/show/ecas/committee-main/the-committee.

19 **"the probability of disaster":** "The Real Problem Is in the Hearts of Men," by Albert Einstein, *New York Times*, June 23, 1946.

19 **"people could destroy New York":** Bird and Sherwin, xiii.

20 **"reservoir of concentrated force":** Wells, p. 22.

21 **170 million electron volts:** Serber, p. 5.

21 **"will help make intelligent voters":** *Explaining the Atom*, Selig Hecht, xviii.

22 **"the mark of a true scientist":** "Selig Hecht: 1892–1947," by C. H. Graham, *American Journal of Psychology* 61, no. 1 (January 1948): pp. 127–128.

22 **had the power to both "authorize" *and* "appropriate":** Ackland, p. 34.

22 **"the state over the citizen":** "How Can We Prevent Atomic War?" by E. L. Woodward, *New York Times*, January 13, 1946, excerpted in Boyer p. 146.

23 **"and ordinary things like that":** Ackland, p. 40.

23 **ten trillion dollars:** A 2013 update of *Atomic Audit: The Costs and Consequences of U.S. Nuclear Weapons since 1940*, by Stephen I. Schwartz, June 29, 1998, http://www.brookings.edu/research/books/1998/atomic.

24 **The hustle and strain . . . aided the war effort:** Written remembrance by Hamilton Hartridge, 1947.

CHAPTER 2. THE FIELD

26 **whined like tripped alarms:** The atmospheric details of the initial path toward intrusion were gathered from extensive interviews with the activists over years and from the author's own in-person tracing of their walk during both the daytime and nighttime in June 2014.

26 **building up her endurance by going on long walks:** Testimony of Greg Boertje-Obed, Transform Now Plowshares jury trial, May 8, 2013, document 193, p. 112.

26 **19-mile:** Testimony of Steven Erhart, manager of the National Nuclear Security Administration Production Office, in the Transform Now Plowshares jury trial, May 7, 2013, document 192, p. 124.

27 **Upper-middle-class families . . . row houses on Amsterdam Avenue:** The Morningside Heights Historic District Committee, http://morningsideheights.org/historic-district/historical-significance.

27 **the conscience of the 1960s peace movement:** The Thomas Merton Center at Bellarmine University, http://www.merton.org/chrono.aspx.

28 **in a more democratic manner:** "Rev. George B. Ford, a Crusader for Civil Rights and Ecumenism," by Morris Kaplan in the *New York Times*, August 3, 1978.

28 **If anything radical needs to be done:** "Father Ford's Morningside Parish Takes Religion Out of Sanctuary, into Marketplace" by Douglas Eldridge in the *Columbia Daily Spectator*, February 24, 1956.

28 **a spirited, enriching landscape:** Physical and social details of Corpus Christi from *The Seven Storey Mountain*, by Thomas Merton (Harcourt Brace, 1998), p. 227.

29 **Margaret Mead was one of her classmates:** Nevada Test Site Oral History Project interview with Megan Rice, conducted June 22, 2005, by Suzanne Becker for the University of Nevada, Las Vegas.

30 **as five feet ten . . . "a pronounced stoop":** FBI report dated December 26, 1940, FBI Personality Files of Dorothy Day, box 34, section 1, p. 2., National Security Archive.

30 **"those generally accepted today":** FBI report dated October 24, 1941, FBI Personality Files of Dorothy Day, box 34, section 1, cover page, National Security Archive.

30 **nature of its very name:** FBI report dated October 24, 1941, FBI Personality Files of Dorothy Day, box 34, section 1, p. 4, National Security Archive.

30 **"We confess . . . more so":** "A Life of Exquisite 'Foolishness,'" by Colman McCarthy in the *Washington Post*, December 3, 1980.

30 **"Ambassadors of God":** Excerpt from "The Duty of Hospitality," http://www.catholicworker.org/dorothyday/articles/435.html.

31 **in the West Village:** Forest, p. 125.

31 **the tulip tree:** Handwritten correspondence between the author and Megan Rice.

31 **"Mahatma Gandhi":** Report by an FBI "Confidential Informant" dated January 16, 1943, FBI Personality Files of Dorothy Day, box 34, section 1, National Security Archive.

31 **110,000 by 1936:** Forest, p. 125.

31 **refusing to beat the drum:** Roberts, p. 132.

31 **urged young men:** Report by an FBI "Confidential Informant" dated January 16, 1943, FBI Personality Files of Dorothy Day, box 34, section 1, p. 2, National Security Archive.

31 **"I saw a bit of Germany on the west coast":** Issue accessed in the FBI Personality Files of Dorothy Day, box 34, section 1; article not bylined but written in the first person, National Security Archive.

31 **"subversive" behavior:** FBI report dated October 24, 1941, FBI Personality Files of Dorothy Day, box 34, section 1, p. 4, National Security Archive.

32 **"activities should be restricted":** Letter from J. Edgar Hoover to Special Agent in Charge, New York, N.Y., February 3, 1942, FBI Personality Files of Dorothy Day, National Security Archive.

32 **"doing Hitler's work"** . . . **"Freedom of the Press":** Handwritten letter dated February 12, 1942, sender redacted, to Hon. J. Edgar Hoover, FBI Personality Files of Dorothy Day, box 34, section 1, National Security Archive.

32 **Dorothy was a Russian spy:** Memorandum from J. Edgar Hoover to Assistant Attorney General Wendell Berge, dated January 26, 1943, FBI Personality Files of Dorothy Day, box 34, section 1, National Security Archive.

32 **be charged with sedition:** Ibid.

33 **"the castle":** "At Riverside Drive and 140th Street; Gothic 'Castle' to House Ex-Prisoners," *New York Times*, November 5, 2000.

33 **"actions not words":** The Sisters of the Holy Child Jesus pamphlet on Cornelia Connelly, http://www.shcj.org/our-story/cornelia-connelly.

33 **the first American sister of her order:** Obituary of Mother M. Laurentia Dalton by Martha Woodall in the *Philadelphia Inquirer*, January 9, 1996.

33 **wistful passion made a deep impression:** Details of St. Walburga's and the Holy Child sisters from interviews (written, in-person and by phone) with Megan Rice and her classmates Patsy Burns and Helen Buzaid.

34 **"just servitude":** *American Catholic Opinion in the Slavery Controversy*, by Madeleine Hooke Rice (Columbia University Press, 1964), p. 152.

34 **"I just can't wait until . . . the world is tan":** Nevada Test Site Oral History Project.

35 **for the rest of his life:** Letter from Walter G. Hooke to Reverend Robert F. Drinan, S. J., dated May 10, 1999, from the Dorothy Day–Catholic Worker Collection, Marquette University.

35 **it in every walk of life:** Letters from Walter G. Hooke to Ken Paff, dated February 22, 1991, and to the editor of the *Post-Star*, dated March 23, 1992, from the Marquette University's Dorothy Day–Catholic Worker Collection.

35 **he began to feel guilty:** Author phone interview with Megan Tourlis, Hooke's daughter, January 26, 2015.

36 *Harper's* **declared that:** Boyer, p. 213.

36 **37 percent . . . compared with 1 percent:** Hillenbrand, p. 315.

36 **at least half a million American lives:** Rhodes, *Making of the Atomic Bomb*, p. 592.

36 **"about cockroaches or mice":** Russell, p. 98.

37 **"soft-hearted and tired"** . . . **"power of the universe":** Wellerstein, p. 145.

37 **"our least abhorrent choice":** "The Decision to Use the Atomic Bomb," by Henry Lewis Stimson, *Harper's Magazine*, February 1947, http://www.columbia.edu/itc/eacp/japanworks/ps/japan/stimson_harpers.pdf.

37 **justify the expense:** Rhodes, *Making of the Atomic Bomb*, p. 697.

37 **"as weather will permit"** . . . **no record of formal authorization:** Ibid., p. 691.

37 **"one of non-interference":** Norris, *Racing for the Bomb*, p. 376.

37 **a long garbage can with fins:** Rhodes, *Making of the Atomic Bomb*, p. 701.

37 **Many Japanese citizens looked skyward . . . its swift retreat:** *Downfall: The End of the Imperial Japanese Empire*, by Richard B. Frank, via *The Manhattan Project*, p. 333.

37 **counted 43 seconds:** Cynthia Kelly, *The Manhattan Project*, p. 332.

38 **which meant organ decay:** Ibid., p. 732.

38 **"boiling dust":** Boyer, p. 5.

38 **gale-force winds raged for six hours:** "Hiroshima and Nagasaki," as cited in *The Fate of the Earth*, by Jonathan Schell (Stanford University Press, 2000), p. 37.

38 **they had died and gone to hell:** Lifton, pp. 25–29.

38 **141 pounds . . . two pounds:** Several trustworthy sources over the years have reported that a gram or less of uranium underwent fission, but this isn't correct. According to the dogged research and revisions of John Coster-Mullen, author of "Atom Bombs: The Top Secret Inside Story of Little Boy and Fat Man," the total uranium falling over Hiroshima was 64.1 kilograms (or about 141 pounds). Historian Alex Wellerstein says "about one percent" underwent fission; journalist John McPhee says "one percent"; the Atomic Heritage Foundation and Coster-Mullen say 1.38 percent, which is the number I went with: 1.38 percent of 141 pounds is 1.9 pounds.

39 **"a harnessing . . . in making it work":** "President Harry Truman announces the Bombing of Hiroshima." https://www.youtube.com/watch?v=FN_UJJ9ObDs.

39 **"For all we know . . . turned against us":** Boyer, p. 5.

39 **the Catholic military chaplain:** "I Was Told It Was Necessary," a Q&A with George Zabelka by Charles C. McCarthy, *Sojourners*, August 1980.

39 **the Mitsubishi factory that made the torpedoes:** Rhodes, p. 739.

39 **playing poker in their Quonset hut:** "Zero Hour: Forty-Three Seconds over Hiroshima," *Newsweek*, July 29, 1985.

40 **haunted by the image . . . seconds later:** McCarthy, with Zabelka.

40 **where parishioners were waiting to give confession:** Mitchell, p. 96.

40 **many were asking to be killed:** Phone conversation between General Groves and Lt. Col. Rea in Oak Ridge, August 25, 1945, via the National Security Archive, http://www2.gwu.edu/~nsarchiv/NSAEBB/NSAEBB162/76.pdf.

40 **no more bombs be dropped:** Robert S. Norris presentation at the Atomic Heritage Foundation's 70th anniversary event, June 3, 2015.

40 **"and for His purposes":** Boyer, p. 6.

40 **bloodiest, costliest:** There is debate about the exact volume and range of casualties and fatalities, but all reputable sources conclude that no conflict trumps World War II. I defer to the simplest source, though, which is *Encyclopedia Britannica*, which calls it "the bloodiest conflict, as well as the largest war, in history."

40 **"curious new sense of insecurity":** Boyer, p. 7.

41 **"The use of the . . . on the Vatican":** "Vatican Deplores Use of Atom Bomb," Associated Press, in the *New York Times*, August 8, 1945.

41 **the Vatican privately affirmed:** Wittner, vol. 1, p. 164.

41 **"are vaporized, our Japanese brothers . . . hills of Easton":** Roberts, p. 135.

41 **Glass windows shattered 17 miles away:** Schell, p. 37.

41 **"Conditions appalling . . . conditions beyond description":** Telegram from Fritz Bilfinger dated August 30, 1945, file G 8/76, ICRC Archives, via icrc.org.

41 **The U.S. military never told:** "Atomic Vet Seeks Government Recognition," by Bettina Boxall in the *Bennington Banner*, c. 1982.

42 **sang "Silent Night" in the cathedral:** From Greg Mitchell's blog, http://gregmitchellwriter.blogspot.com/2012/12/nagasaki-silent-night.html?m=1.

42 **a half mile away from the detonation:** Lifton, p. 309.

42 **"When we are alone . . . indeed beyond repair":** Ibid.

42 **It prohibited the publication . . . atrocities in Manila:** One *World or None: A History of the World Nuclear Disarmament Movement through 1953*, by Lawrence S. Wittner (Stanford University Press, 1993), p. 47.

42 **the *New York Times* reported that:** Boyer, pp. 187–188.

43 **"It occurred to me . . . they were and are":** *The Decision to Use the Atomic Bomb*, by Gar Alperovitz (Vintage Books, 1995), p. 516.

43 **Japan probably would . . . American air supremacy:** United States Strategic Bombing Survey summary report (Pacific War), submitted July 1, 1946, p. 26, https://www.trumanlibrary.org/whistlestop/study_collections/bomb/large/documents/pdfs/24.pdf.

43 **walk from deck to deck:** Walter Goodman oral history, conducted by Cindy Kelly for the Atomic Heritage Foundation's Voices of the Manhattan Project.

43 **"When the bombs . . . going to live":** Rhodes, p. 736.

44 **no medical follow-up:** *American Nuclear Guinea Pigs: Three Decades of Radiation Experiments on U.S. Citizens*, a report by the House Subcommittee on Energy Conservation and Power of the Committee on Energy and Commerce, November 1986, p. 28, via the National Security Archive (box 9, "Human Radiation Experiments").

44 **more plutonium in a bite of contaminated ham:** "Old Radiation Claims Hit U.S. Brick Wall," Jouzaitis.

44 **The Pentagon withheld its own radiation reports:** "Expert Cites Underestimated Radiation Harm," by Pamela A. MacLean of United Press International, October 28, 1987.

44 **findings that showed veterans were overexposed:** "Pentagon Says Radiation Exposure Was Slight," by Tim Ahern of the Associated Press, December 11, 1985.

44 **only 16 of 4,000 atomic claims:** "Court OKs Class-Action Suits by Vets Who Claim Nuclear Injury," by the Associated Press, April 29, 1986.

44 **destroying thousands of documents:** "Judge Says VA Destroyed Documents," by Bob Egelko of the Associated Press, September 27, 1986; "Veterans Agency Fined for Destroying Data," by Robert Lindsey of the *New York Times*, January 9, 1987.

45 **no more than 10 percent fulfilled:** "U.S. 'Atomic Veterans' Fight for Compensation, Information," by Julia Rubin of the Associated Press, July 20, 1992.

45 **Walter wished he could testify:** "Atom Bomb Victims Tell of Holocaust," by Sharon Voas in the *Columbia Daily Spectator*, September 28, 1987.

45 **one of the associations' most respected:** Author phone interview with Glenn Alcalay, lobbyist and scientific adviser for the National Association of Atomic Veterans, February 11, 2015.

45 **"I saw enough . . . struggle for peace":** Letter from Walter G. Hooke to the archbishop of Denver, May, 2003, from the Marquette University's Dorothy Day—Catholic Worker Collection.

45 **He could never get Nagasaki out of his mind:** In-person author interview with Hooke's daughter, Megan Tourlis, May 16, 2015.

47 **lead vest . . . samples of tritium:** Transform Now Plowshares jury trial, transcript of May 6, 2013, document 191, p. 249.

47 **who had opposed using the bombs:** Rhodes, p. 688.

47 **"Every gun . . . cold and not clothed":** "The Chance for Peace" speech, delivered by Dwight D. Eisenhower to the American Society of Newspaper Editors, April 16, 1953.

47 **"adapt it to the arts of peace":** "Atoms for Peace" speech transcript, December 8, 1953, http://www.presidency.ucsb.edu/ws/?pid=9774.

48 **Congress chose not to participate in the drill:** "Vast D.C. Area 'Obliterated' in Mock Raid," by William J. Brady and Wes Barthelmes in the *Washington Post*, June 15, 1954.

48 **The resolution requested:** Joint Resolution to amend the pledge of allegiance to the flag of the United States of America, Public Law 396, Chapter 297, http://www.gpo .gov/fdsys/pkg/STATUTE-68/pdf/STATUTE-68-Pg249-3.pdf.

48 **where 679 sirens . . . on June 15, 1955:** "City Streets to Be Cleared," by Peter Kihss in the *New York Times*, June 15, 1955.

48 **"We will not obey . . . We refuse to cooperate":** Marquette University's papers on Dorothy Day and the *Catholic Worker*. http://www.marquette.edu/library/archives/ News/spotlight/04-2009.shtml

48 **a total loss of life within a 2.3-mile radius:** "City Streets to Be Cleared," by Peter Kihss in the *New York Times*, June 15, 1955.

48 **"loyalty to God . . . a coercive state":** Dorothy Day–Catholic Worker Collection, Marquette University, http://www.marquette.edu/library/archives/News/ spotlight/04-2009.shtml.

48 **Hoover tried to get:** Wittner, vol. 2, p. 140.

48 **an Army general . . . for his branch alone:** *History of the Custody and Deployment of Nuclear Weapons: July 1945 through September 1977*, prepared by the Office of the Assistant to the Secretary of Defense (Atomic Energy), February 1978, p. 50, via the National Security Archive,

49 **"You can't have . . . off the street":** Rhodes, *Arsenals of Folly*, p. 101.

49 **22,600 kilograms . . . Iran and Pakistan:** "U.S. efforts to stem 'extreme threat to global security' far from complete," by Douglas Birch and R. Jeffrey Smith for The Center for Public Integrity, March 11, 2015.

49 **mothers pushing strollers:** Dorothy Day–Catholic Worker Collection, Marquette University.

50 **66 percent:** Wittner, vol. 2, pp. 142, 254, 261.

50 **cherry-red aurora:** *100 Suns*, by Michael Light. Description of the blast from photo no. 77; duration of aurora from corresponding end note.

50 **short-circuited streetlights:** "The 50th Anniversary of Starfish Prime: The Nuke That Shook the World," by Phil Plait in *Discover*, July 9, 2012.

50 **a flowing white veil:** From Rice family photos shared by Megan's niece Megan Finnerty.

50 **build her own biology lab:** Testimony from Megan Rice in Transform Now Plowshares jury trial, May 7, 2013, document 192, p. 252.

51 **"an overwhelming atrocity":** *Faith and Violence*, by Thomas Merton (University of Notre Dame Press, 1984), p. 87.

51 **"a bell tolling for the whole world":** Wittner, vol. 2, p. 455.

51 **"American policy . . . order impossible":** Merton, p. 110.

51 **"bureaucratization of homicide":** "Unchecked Political Question Doctrine: Judicial Ethics at the Dawn of a Second Nuclear Arms Race," by Daniel T. Rust, March 2015 (thesis for Vermont Law School), p. 16.

CHAPTER 3. THE PROPHET

54 **the last remaining full-scale production facility:** Speech by Ralph Hutchison of the Oak Ridge Environmental Peace Alliance at the Festival of Hope in Knoxville, Tennessee, January 2014.

54 **currently in every warhead:** "Work Begins to Modernize Oak Ridge Nuclear Weapons Plant," Associated Press, March 28, 2002.

55 **the largest single inventory:** In-person author interview with Robert Alvarez, senior policy adviser to the Energy Department's secretary and deputy assistant secretary for national security and the environment from 1993 to 1999, February 3, 2015.

55 **started to read a warning:** Testimony of Y-12 security police officer Christopher Seals during *United States v. Gump et al.,* May 10, 2011.

55 **"Y-12 is a . . . in the world":** Transcript of *Gump,* May 9, 2011.

57 **frustrating hurdles . . . self-contained homesteads:** "Oak Ridge, Tennessee: A Geographic Study," Dale Edward Case, August 1955 (thesis by submitted to the graduate council of the University of Tennessee), accessed in the Oak Ridge Public Library Reading Room.

57 **The Cherokee natives . . . in the valleys:** *A Guide to the Manhattan Project in Tennessee,* by Cynthia C. Kelly (Atomic Heritage Foundation, 2011), p. 11.

57 **a natural spring:** National Register of Historic Places Multiple Property Documentation Form, U.S. Department of the Interior and National Park Service, http://pdfhost.focus.nps.gov/docs/NRHP/Text/64500613.pdf.

58 **spooked her children:** Video prepared by the Y-12 National Security Complex and screened at its New Hope Center in November 2014.

58 **"And I tell you . . . earth will shake":** *The Oak Ridge Story,* by George O. Robinson Jr. (Southern Publishers, 1950), pp. 18–19.

59 **Telephone and radio service connected:** *Clinton: An Identity Rediscovered,* ed. Margaret Anderson and Robert Marlowe, p. 20.

59 **make parts for airplanes:** Tennessee Valley Authority website.

59 **he slugged the publisher:** "M'Kellar, 88, Dies; Senator 36 Years," obituary by the Associated Press, printed in the *New York Times,* October 26, 1957.

60 **"Well of course . . . locate this facility?":** Oral history of Senator Howard Baker, conducted on August 19, 2009, by Jim Campbell, Amy Fitzgerald, and D. Ray Smith for the Center for Oak Ridge Oral History.

60 **nearly 60,000 acres:** Rhodes, p. 486.

60 **not subject to state or local laws:** Freeman, p. 20.

60 **"It now appears . . . for war purposes":** *The Journals of David E. Lilienthal,* vol. 1, *The TVA Years,* entry dated September 26, 1942, p. 540.

60 **"Without TVA . . . impossible":** Ibid., Lilienthal journal entry dated October 10, 1942, p. 549.

60 **Men with survey rods began puttering:** *City behind a Fence: Oak Ridge, Tennessee, 1942–1946,* by Charles W. Johnson and Charles O. Jackson (University of Tennessee Press, Knoxville, 1981), p. 39.

60 **"The only difference . . . could shoot them":** Johnson and Jackson, p. 43.

61 **Curtis Allen Hendrix:** Information on the Hendrixes, including Curtis's poem, from D. Ray Smith's historical website, http://www.smithdray1.net/curt/biography.htm, which includes a biography of Curtis by Dennis Aslinger, December 2005.

62 **$2 billion:** The total cost depends on what agencies and operations you include and

over what time span. The total is around $1.9 billion if you calculate through the end of 1945, and $2.2 billion if you calculate through 1946, according to the Brookings Institution's "Atomic Audit," edited by Stephen I. Schwartz.

62 **5,600 distinct inventions:** Presentation by Alex Wellerstein at the Atomic Heritage Foundation's 70th anniversary event for the Manhattan Project, June 3, 2015.

62 **a half million citizens:** Atomic Heritage Foundation's Manhattan Project National Park press kit.

62 **hundreds of labs:** Wellerstein, https://twitter.com/wellerstein/ status/605184768372830208.

62 **behind the backs of all but seven congressmen:** Wellerstein, p. 84.

62 **a lofty quest to defeat fascism:** Bird and Sherwin, p. 220.

62 **"unless you turn . . . one huge factory":** "Evolution and History of the Department of Energy and the Office of Environmental Management," http://energy .gov/sites/prod/files/2014/04/f15/Evolution_History_DOE_042314.pdf.

62 **400,000 workers:** *Now It Can Be Told: The Story of the Manhattan Project*, by Leslie Groves (Harper and Row, 1962), p. 98.

62 **Kingston Demolition Range:** Wilcox, p. 8.

62 **A road was paved:** *A Guide to the Manhattan Project in Tennessee*, Kelly, p. 18.

62 **Barns became parking garages:** Ed Westcott photo taken February 23, 1943, via "The Government's Oak Ridge Inheritance," by Frank Munger, the *Knoxville News-Sentinel*, May 23, 2014.

62 **38 million board feet of lumber:** Kiernan, p. 106.

62 **unstable enough to break apart:** Rhodes, *Making of the Atomic Bomb*, p. 490.

63 **the only isotope found in nature:** "Governing Uranium," a project by the Center for Strategic International Studies, http://uranium.csis.org/ore_to_bomb.

63 **Neither the letter nor the number:** Robinson, p. 92.

63 **4,800 workers:** Rhodes, *Making of the Atomic Bomb*, p. 491.

63 **that they were manufacturing ice cream:** Author interview with Oak Ridge city commissioner Trina Baughn, whose grandmother worked at Y-12, June 18, 2014.

63 **remodeled into a machine-gun tower:** Rhodes, *Making of the Atomic Bomb*, p. 602.

63 **$30 million:** Groves, p. 18.

63 **$427 million:** *Handbook on Oak Ridge Operations*, U.S. Atomic Energy Commission, 1964, p. 15.

63 **More than half:** Around 63 percent, according to *Atomic Audit*, p. 60.

64 **9,000 workers:** "K-25 Plant: Forty-Four Acres and a Mile Long," by William J. Wilcox, in the Kelly anthology *The Manhattan Project*, p. 199.

64 **trying to find . . . boxing gloves:** Groves, p. 96.

64 **14 percent:** "A Manhattan Project Veteran Had a Unique View of Atomic Bomb Work," by James Barron in the *New York Times*, July 26, 2015.

64 **"Snob Hill":** Johnson and Jackson, p. 105.

64 **20 to 1:** Freeman, p. 48.

64 **16 feet by 16 feet:** Johnson and Jackson, p. 87.

64 **free to ride:** Freeman, p. 44.

64 **Two hundred:** Robinson, pp. 95–96.

65 **by the time they returned home:** Presentation by Rosemary Lane, who moved to Oak Ridge in August 1943 to be a nurse, at the Atomic Heritage Foundation's 70th anniversary of the Manhattan Project event, June 3, 2015.

65 **Catholic children started thinking:** In-person author interview with Colleen Black, who was a K-25 leak detector, November 9, 2014.

65 **barbed wire salvaged:** Freeman, p. 20.

65 **no names on the jerseys:** Ibid., p. 3.

65 **and universal health care:** Ibid., p. 44.

65 **more than 70 hours a week:** Johnson and Jackson, p. 109.

65 **no tangible result:** Wellerstein, p. 63.

65 **first sample of enriched uranium:** Groves, p. 110.

66 **a hand-off relay:** Rhodes, *Making of the Atomic Bomb*, pp. 602–603.

66 **that looked like green salt:** "The Oak Ridger," article by Karl O. Johnsson, February 8 1984.

66 **a new label: "top secret":** Wellerstein, p. 69.

66 **22,482 employees:** Wilcox, p. 18.

66 **stymied by Secretary of War Henry Stimson:** Rhodes, *Making of the Atomic Bomb*, p. 617.

66 **"I think it . . . highly secret matter":** Letter from Henry Stimson to Harry S. Truman, dated April 24, 1945, Harry S. Truman Library and Museum.

67 **100-foot:** Interoffice memo from R. W. Henderson and R. W. Carlson to K. T. Bainbridge, June 22, 1945, via Wellerstein, https://twitter.com/wellerstein/status/621849785809567744.

67 **John Donne . . . *Bhagavad Gita*:** Bird and Sherwin, p. 304.

67 **a temperature comparable to that of supernovas:** Schell, "The Fate of the Earth," p. 17.

67 **"blasted . . . pounced . . . bored":** *Science: The Center of Culture*, by I. I. Rabi (World, 1970), p. 138, via Rhodes's introduction to *The Los Alamos Primer*, p. xvii.

67 **"The enormity . . . end of the world":** "The First Light of Trinity," by Alex Wellerstein in the *New Yorker*, July 16, 2015.

67 **a bright purple cloud:** Bird and Sherwin, p. 308.

67 **"strong, sustained . . . to the Almighty":** Dower, p. 272.

67 **seen from El Paso:** Memorandum for the Secretary of War, by General Leslie Groves, July 18, 1945, p. 2, Harry S. Truman Library and Museum.

67 **from 5.7 miles out:** Bird and Sherwin, p. 308

68 **"Now we're all sons of bitches":** Ibid., p. 309.

68 **"I no longer . . . such a bomb":** Groves, p. 474.

68 **would validate its existence:** Rhodes, *Making of the Atomic Bomb*, p. 697.

68 **"I have been . . . in Fort Leavenworth":** Ibid., 686.

68 **Dozens of scientists:** Bird and Sherwin, p. 302; Wittner tallies the signatories at 68 on p. 248 of his first volume.

68 **"a nation which . . . a world situation":** Petition to the President of the United States, July 17, 1945, Miscellaneous Historical Documents Collection, Harry S. Truman Library and Museum.

69 **charge Szilard with espionage:** Wittner, vol. 1, p. 248.

69 **He delayed the petition's:** Bird and Sherwin, p. 303.

69 **Del Genio was instructed:** "From Us in Oak Ridge to Tojo: The Story of Lt. Nicholas Del Genio's Autographed Dollar Bill," by William J. Wilcox Jr., prepared for the American Museum of Science and Energy Foundation, June 15, 2000.

69 **six wide runways . . . two miles long:** Rhodes, *Making of the Atomic Bomb*, p. 681.

69 **"when Manhattan appears over their homeland":** Ibid., p. 688.

69 **steel:** Ibid., p. 701.

69 **"From us in Oak Ridge to Tojo":** Freeman, p. 94.

70 **crying, "Uranium!":** Kiernan, p. 262.

70 **"We know now . . . virtually anything":** Groves, p. 415

70 **"The effect of . . . private corporations":** *Journals of David E. Lilienthal*, vol. 2, *The Atomic Energy Years*, 1964, pp. 1–2.

71 **100,000 copies:** Wittner, vol. 1, p. 63.

71 **90 percent:** Ibid., p. 62.

71 **"We are trying . . . believe is right":** "The Great Inquiry: Testimony at AEC Hearings," the *Bulletin of Atomic Scientists*, August–September 1949, p. 230.

71 **31 grams of uranium go missing:** "The Loss of Uranium at Argonne," in the *Bulletin of Atomic Scientists*, August–September 1949, pp. 231, 234.

71 **cost $90 each?:** "Washington Notes," by Anne Wilson Marks, in the *Bulletin of the Atomic Scientists*, August–September 1949, p. 218.

71 **a mere contractor for the Pentagon:** Newhouse, *War and Peace*, p. 77.

71 **put into a long-term reserve:** Rhodes, *Dark Sun*, pp. 226–227.

72 **1,450 by 1947:** Freeman, p. 105.

72 **tiny white mushroom cloud:** Ibid., pp. 114–115; the ribbon-cutting took place March 19, 1949.

72 **even the amount of toilet paper:** "After Years of Secrecy, Nuclear Arms Plants Show Off Technology," by Bob Davis in the *Wall Street Journal*, December 4, 1990 (via Gusterson, "Nuclear Rites" p. 69).

72 **prompted Joseph Stalin:** Comprehensive Test Ban Treaty Organization website: https://www.ctbto.org/specials/testing-times/29-august-1949-first-soviet-nuclear-test.

72 **an open-ended purpose:** Freeman, p. 108.

72 **took the lead in separating:** Wilcox, p. 26.

72 **"burning the rocks" . . . "burning the sea":** "In Memory of Alvin Weinberg," by Carolyn Krause in the ORNL Review, Volume 40, Number 1, 2007, http://www .orau.org/weinberg/legacy.html.

73 **eight times as much energy:** Rhodes, *Dark Sun*, p. 248.

73 *This piece of paper . . . has ever existed:* "A Hundred Holocausts: An Insider's Window into U.S. Nuclear Policy," by Daniel Ellsberg, from his book *The American Doomsday Machine*," excerpted by Truthdig on September 10, 2009.

73 **"a nuclear sword . . . they abolish us":** Address by President John F. Kennedy to the UN General Assembly, September 25, 1961.

74 **"The ultimate limits . . . highly speculative":** Technical report on the Underground Test Program by the Division of Military Application of the U.S. Atomic Energy Commission, November 20, 1962, via the National Security Archive, box 35, "Nuclear Weapons Secrets, Hansen Collection."

74 **an overwhelming majority:** Wittner, vol. 2, p. 261.

74 **Let us "examine . . . we cannot control":** John F. Kennedy Presidential Library and Museum.

74 **2,500 . . . 28,133:** Declassified stockpile numbers from the Department of Energy.

74 **55 specialized machine shops:** Y-12 Plant Technology Brochure, via Wilcox, p. 37.

75 **wearing a green cape:** "Miss Mead Asks the Questions," by June Adamson for the *Oak Ridger*, May 15, 1964.

75 **"No . . . horrible creatures":** "Margaret Mead Chastizes [*sic*] Oak Ridge," by June Adamson for the *Oak Ridger*, May 18, 1964.

75 **10 percent:** PBS, "Dr. Teller's Very Large Bomb."

75 **16 percent:** Wittner, vol. 2, p. 447.

76 **at its bloodiest:** There were 16,899 fatalities in 1968, the most of any year of the conflict. Statistical information about fatal casualties of the Vietnam War from the National Archives.

76 **distant, unearthly roar:** The details of Michael's Vietnam story come from interviews conducted with him in person and via phone and mail over a three-year period. Secondary confirmations and fact-checks will be given their own citations where appropriate.

76 **solicit building materials:** Bay Area Medical Center history, http://www.bamc.org/about-history.html.

78 **They were praying:** "Draft Records Napalmed by 9," by William R. MacKaye in the *Washington Post*, May 18, 1968.

78 **"to make it . . . kill one another":** "9 Seize and Burn 600 Draft Files," no byline, the *New York Times*, May 18, 1968.

78 **helped choreograph the action:** Peters, p. 95.

78 **The archbishop of Baltimore rebuked:** "Cardinal Scores Berrigan for 'Damaging' Act," no byline, the *New York Times*, May 27, 1968.

78 **In private she distanced:** Peters, p. 128.

79 **"You hide behind words":** Peters, 120.

79 **"We pour it . . . 10,000 miles away":** "Priest Given 6 Years for War Protest," by Bert Barnes in the *Washington Post*, May 25, 1968.

79 **it eclipsed the civil rights:** Wittner, vol. 2, p. 455.

79 **would cow his foes:** "Nixon, Kissinger, and the Madman Strategy during Vietnam War," posted by William Burr and Jeffrey P. Kimball on May 29, 2015, in the Nuclear Vault of the National Security Archive.

80 **breach the perimeter from all sides:** Details of the assault on Fire Support Base Buttons are from press reports, J.D. Coleman's "Incursion," Walli's memoris, and the unpublished recollection "The Battle for Buttons," by Ty Dodge, written in 2004 and revised in 2006, http://songbe.8thmob.org/SupportTrop/Hart/Battle%20For%20Buttons_Ty%20Dodge.pdf.

80 **spotted the incoming ambush hours earlier:** Coleman, pp. 162-163.

80 **Two Americans were dead and 26 were wounded:** Ibid., p. 165.

80 **From helicopters he flung propaganda:** Memories of Fire Support Base Buttons from written author correspondence with Walli, February 22, 2015.

80 **"This time I believe our president has the answer":** "Hope Takes Troupe to Vietnam Troops" in the *Washington Post and Times Herald*, December 23, 1969.

80 **"Yes . . . here on Earth?":** "GIs Not Forgotten, Hope Tells Troops" in the *Washington Post and Times Herald*, December 26, 1969.

81 **lined with Vietcong sanctuaries:** "Saigon Flotilla Poised to Begin Drive in Cambodia," by Terence Smith in the *New York Times*, May 7, 1970.

81 **mowed down water buffalo:** "For G.I., It's War as Usual in Cambodia," by James P. Sterba for the *New York Times*, May 24, 1970.

81 **Nixon honored 22:** Medsger, pp. 25–27.

81 **"Let us treat . . . regardless of age":** This was in April 1971. Medsger, p. 278.

81 **1,000 . . . 200,000:** Wittner, vol. 3, p. 18.

81 **killed 9,658 enemy soldiers . . . 12,000 individual weapons:** "Cambodia Foray after a Month: From Arms and Rice to Buttons," by James P. Sterba for the *New York Times*, May 30, 1970.

82 **337 American dead and 1,524 wounded:** "Last Combat Unit Out of Cambodia after 2 Months," by Iver Peterson for the *New York Times*, June 30, 1970.

83 **"No one who . . . kingdom of God":** Luke 9:62, International Standard Version of the New Testament.

83 **he destroyed all his memorabilia:** Written author correspondence with Michael Walli, February 22, 2015.

84 **forged during his four-year detention:** Obituary of Richard T. McSorley, by Rusty Pray, the *Philadelphia Inquirer*, October 2, 2002.

84 **starved, tortured, and terrorized by mock executions:** "Remembering Richard McSorley, S.J.," by John Dear, http://www.fatherjohndear.org/articles/death.html.

84 **from a Special Forces handbook:** Riegle, *Doing Time for Peace*, p. 29.

84 **"The taproot of . . . minor in comparison":** From McSorley's article "It's a Sin to Build a Nuclear Weapon."

CHAPTER 4. THE MIRACLE

87 **about 20 feet:** Testimony of Rodney L. Johnson in the Transform Now Plowshares jury trial, May 7, 2013, document 192, p. 199.

87 **4:15 a.m.:** The timing of the intrusion can be reliably estimated by comparing the recollections of the three activists with the "Y-12 Protective Force Response Timeline," a declassified Department of Energy document compiled September 7, 2012, and obtained by a FOIA request.

87 **an avenue of small white rocks:** Physical descriptions of the Perimeter Intrusion Detection Assistance System (PIDAS) are from photographs taken by law enforcement and site officials the morning of the intrusion. Some descriptions of the HEUMF come from the author's drive-by during a June 2014 public tour of Y-12.

88 **50 finger-size bullets per second:** "Bring Out the Big Guns," by Frank Munger in the *Knoxville News Sentinel*, September 28, 2007,

88 **42 percent:** Department of Energy FY 2016 Congressional Budget Request, February 2015.

89 **stainless steel cases:** "Making Smart Security Choices: The Future of the U.S. Nuclear Weapons Complex," by Lisbeth Gronlund, Eryn MacDonald, Stephen Young, Philip E. Coyle III, and Steve Fetter for the Union of Concerned Scientists, October 2013, pp. 7, 16.

89 **at least 5,000 secondaries:** "U.S. Nuclear Forces 2010," by Robert S. Norris and Hans M. Kristensen in the *Bulletin of Atomic Scientists*, May–June 2010, p. 68.

89 **for the W76 warhead:** Testimony of Steven Erhart, manager for the NNSA Production Office, in the Transform Now Plowshares jury trial, May 7, 2013, document 192, p. 106.

89 **"patients . . . alive . . . better ways to heal":** "National Nuclear Security Administration (NNSA) Office of Defense Programs Independent Assessment of Life Extension Program (LEP) Phase 6.X Process," Aerospace report no. ATR-2012(5709)-3, June 29, 2012, p. 46.

89 **all good things against this one necessary thing:** This sentence is almost verbatim from chapter 5 of Daniel Berrigan's *Essential Writings*, p. 183.

89 **4:29 a.m.:** Times are from the "Y-12 Protective Force Response Timeline."

89 **the impact of a jet:** "Y-12 Celebrates Dedication of Uranium Storehouse," by Frank Munger in the *Knoxville News Sentinel*, March 23, 2010.

89 **every 100,000 years:** *Final Site-Wide Environmental Impact Statement for the Y-12 National Security Complex*, vol. 1, February 2011, pp. 5–92.

89 **was tied with strands of cloth:** Testimony of Ryan Baker in the Transform Now Plowshares jury trial, May 7, 2013, document 192, p. 226.

90 **Lewis and 14 others:** "Protesters Rally for Peace at Y-12," by John Huotari for the *Knoxville News Sentinel*, August 7, 2005.

91 **five small rectangular windows:** Descriptions of the HEUMF are from photos taken by the government after the incident and from the author's tour of the site in June 2014.

91 **a Chevy Tahoe SUV:** Testimony of Sergeant Chad Riggs during the Transform Now Plowshares jury trial, May 7, 2013, document 192, p. 136.

91 **The town of Pella:** *The Biographical Dictionary of Iowa*, from the University of Iowa, specifically the entry for "Hendrik Pieter Scholte."

91 **"city of refuge":** City of Pella website.

92 **an auction that raised $100,000:** Pella Historical Society, website.

93 **"Though less than . . . they had lost":** *The Effects of Nuclear War,* by Congress's Office of Technology Assessment (U.S. Government Printing Office, May 1979), p. 127.

93 **dismayed with the apparent timidity:** Wittner, vol. 3, p. 46.

93 **$240 billion:** "Anatomy of the Nuclear Protest," by Fox Butterfield for the *New York Times*, July 11, 1982.

94 **"The weapons programs . . . nuclear tripwire tighter":** "Call to Halt the Nuclear Arms Race," by Randall Forsberg, anthologized in *Thinking about Nuclear Weapons: Analyses and Prescriptions*, edited by Fred Holroyd (Open University, 1985), p. 208.

94 **still considered himself a man of the cloth:** "Berrigans See a Reawakening for Antiwar Activists," by William Robbins in the *New York Times*, December 13, 1980.

94 **wondered if their action:** Daniel Berrigan, *To Dwell in Peace*, p. 291.

95 **lashed them with blood:** "Swords into Plowshares," by Daniel Berrigan, in the *Catholic Worker* 46, no. 8 (October–November 1980); "Berrigan Brothers Arrested at GE Plant," *Washington Post*, September 10, 1980.

95 **"We commit civil . . . things to death":** "Swords into Plowshares," Daniel Berrigan.

95 **declined accordingly:** "Anatomy of the Nuclear Protest," Butterfield.

95 **"Now they say . . . have small beginnings":** "Berrigans See a Reawakening for Antiwar Activists," Robbins.

95 **"No wonder that . . . no thank you":** "Swords into Plowshares," Daniel Berrigan.

96 **She was 83 and:** "Dorothy Day Dies at 83, Oft-Jailed Activist Founded 40 Houses of Hospitality," by Colman McCarthy in the *Washington Post*, December 1, 1980.

96 **pine-box coffin:** "A Life of Exquisite 'Foolishness,'" by Colman McCarthy in the *Washington Post*, December 3, 1980.

96 **red rose:** "About New York: Drifters, Priests and Nuns Pay Respects to Dorothy Day," by William E. Farrell in the *New York Times*, December 3, 1980.

96 **three hours:** Domestic news brief, no byline, United Press International, July 7, 1982.

96 **Eight activists slipped into:** *Swords into Plowshares: A Chronology of Plowshares Disarmament Actions, 1980–2003*, ed. Arthur J. Laffin (Rose Hill Books, 2003).

97 **"I've had about . . . I do here":** "Sympathy Aside, 5 'Trident Nein' Activists in Jail for up to One Year," by Karen Markin in the *Day*, November 10, 1982.

97 **"Individual liberties are . . . internal civil order":** Wittner, vol. 3, p. 262.

97 **nearly half:** Ibid., p. 170.

98 **Reagan issued a presidential directive:** Issued October 19, 1981. See the directive at http://fas.org/irp/offdocs/nsdd/nsdd-13.pdf.

98 **"A nuclear war . . . never be fought":** Wittner, vol. 3, p. 264.

98 **a $4.3-billion program:** "Despite Foes and Skeptics, Administration Presses Ahead on Civil Defense," by Judith Miller in the *New York Times*, June 10, 1982.

99 **after one military exercise:** Recollections of his youth and military service are from author interviews with Boertje-Obed, starting in December 2012, and conducted both in person and via written correspondence.

99 **"One can get . . . atom bombs":** From "On Pilgrimage," by Dorothy Day, http://www.catholicworker.org/dorothyday/articles/5.html.

100 **at least 280 square miles:** Schell, pp. 47–48.

100 **if detonated at 30,000 feet:** Ibid., pp. 52–53.

100 **He argued that Heisenberg's uncertainty principle:** Ibid., pp. 76, 92.

100 **"Once the . . . and the biological":** Ibid., pp. 195, 173.

100 **People had walked on foot:** "Momentum Gains on Nuclear-Limit Rally," by James Feron in the *New York Times*, June 6, 1982.

101 **The two northbound marches:** Details from the march are from "New York Rally Draws Half-Million," by Joyce Wadler and Merrill Brown in the *Washington Post*, June 13, 1982; and "A Spectrum of Humanity Represented at the Rally," by Robert D. McFadden in the *New York Times*, June 13, 1982.

101 **the largest political demonstration in U.S. history:** "Anatomy of the Nuclear Protest," Butterfield.

101 **"We've done it . . . United States history":** "Rally Speakers Decry Cost of Nuclear Arms Race," by Robin Herman in the *New York Times*, June 13, 1982.

101 **"To those who . . . more secure world":** "Reagan Urges Strength Through Deterrence," by Lou Cannon in the *Washington Post*, June 10, 1982.

102 **"More nukes . . . We Shall Overcome":** "1,600 Are Arrested in Nuclear Protests At 5 U.N. Missions," by Paul L. Montgomery in the *New York Times*, June 15, 1982.

102 **the anti-nuclear crowd:** "Anatomy of the Nuclear Protest," Butterfield.

102 **"freezeniks":** Wittner, vol. 3, p. 198.

102 **Twenty-three state legislatures and 370 city councils:** Gusterson, p. 169.

102 **Rep. Ed Markey:** "Anatomy of the Nuclear Protest," Butterfield.

102 **in May 1983:** Gusterson, p. 169.

102 **Sen. Gary Hart:** "Hart Praises Freeze Efforts, Ending Swing in New Jersey," by Gerald M. Boyd in the *New York Times*, May 31, 1984.

102 **Former vice president Walter Mondale:** "Mondale's Unilateral Nuclear Proposal," by David Lawsky of United Press International, February 4, 1984.

102 **"Do not be . . . in sheep's clothing":** "Jackson, Stumping California, Rips Arms Race, Immigration Bill," by Doug Willis of the Associated Press, May 17, 1984.

103 **perceived the movement as:** Wittner, vol. 3, p. 254.

103 **"evil, godless":** Ibid., p. 260.

103 **"You know . . . we are":** Ibid.

103 **"the human quantum . . . set in motion":** *The Dark Night of Resistance*, by Daniel Berrigan (Doubleday and Co., 1971), pp. 4, 5, 9, 20, 21.

104 **Margaret Mead's work:** Ibid., p. 18.

104 **Thomas Merton's letters:** Ibid., pp. 180–181.

104 **J. Edgar Hoover's deceptions:** Ibid., p. 15.

104 **"It has to do . . . heart of man":** Ibid., pp. 27, 94.

104 **In the first minutes of Monday:** "I Had a Funny Feeling in My Gut," by David Hoffman for the *Washington Post*, February 10, 1999,

105 **inspired by Jonathan Schell's book:** "Jonathan Schell, 70, Author on War in Vietnam and Nuclear Age, Dies," by Margalit Fox in the *New York Times*, March 26, 2014.

105 **candlelight vigils were held:** "ABC Film Depicting Consequences of Nuclear War Stirring Debate," by Sally Bedell Smith in the *New York Times*, October 6, 1983.

106 **McAlister and Berrigan wanted to nurture a community:** Riegle, *Doing Time for Peace*, p. 53.

106 **its primary function:** Author phone interview with Michele Naar-Obed, January 7, 2015.

107 **"The true verdict . . . not by man":** "4 Convicted for Their Attack on a Minuteman Missile Silo," by United Press International in the *New York Times*, February 25, 1985.

107 **Woodson then filed an affidavit:** "Saga of an American Dissenter," by Mary McGrory in the *Washington Post*, April 15, 1986.

107 **"They are not in charge":** Author phone interview with Michele Naar-Obed, January 7, 2015.

107 **The push of conscience is a terrible thing:** Daniel Berrigan, *Essential Writings*, p. 189.

108 **Greg engraved:** Recollections of Greg's first Plowshares action are from a series of interviews, conducted both in person and via phone and mail, from December 2012 through February 2016.

108 **They brought with them:** Laffin, *Swords into Plowshares*, p. 26.

108 **They were all arrested:** "Six Arrested at Electric Boat in Quonset Point," United Press International, April 18, 1985

108 **Four jurors:** Laffin, *Swords into Plowshares*, p. 26.

109 **"Not like that":** Tourist quotes and some choice details of the action are from "Peace Warriors," a profile of Berrigan and his family by Gary Smith in the *Washington Post*, June 5, 1988.

110 **They took turns:** Author phone interview with Michele Naar-Obed, January 6, 2015.

110 **Dressed as circus clowns:** "Three Arrested after Protest at Missile Silo," by Blake Nicholson of the Associated Press, June 21, 2006.

110 **with a hammer:** Photos from the action are accessible via the Jonah House website: www.jonahhouse.org.

110 **Guards positioned them facedown:** A letter from the trio sent from Burleigh County Jail in Bismarck, North Dakota, to the *Nuclear Resister*, printed July 24, 2006.

111 **2,065 people were arrested:** Gusterson, p. 179.

111 **a full year of prayer and planning:** "Jury Finds Protestors Who Cut through Bangor Fence Guilty," by Maks Goldenshteyn in the *Kitsap Sun*, December 13, 2010.

111 **who did not report them because:** "Jury Finds Protestors Who Cut through Bangor Fence Guilty," Goldenshteyn.

111 **kept on the base for hours:** "Five Arrested for Breaking into Naval Base," by Ed Friedrich in the *Kitsap Sun*, November 3, 2009.

112 **"and the lives of others":** Dialogue from the Disarm Now Plowshares trial comes from the article "Jury Convicts Plowshares Disarmament Group," in the *Nuclear Resister*, December 20, 2010.

112 **urged her to keep quiet:** Author interview with Paul Magno, February 11, 2015.

CHAPTER 5. SECURITY

115 **"Something is not right in zone 63":** B&W Y-12 Show Cause follow-up (additional questions), November 16, 2012, p. 10.

115 **unless they had a Q clearance:** Testimony of Rodney Johnson in the Transform Now Plowshares jury trial, May 7, 2013, document 192, pp. 207–208.

115 **as part of a "human reliability program":** Court testimony of Ted Sherry in *United States v. Gump et. al.*, May 9, 2011.

115 **tiny font . . . cramped room:** Details about the central alarm station from Gibbs, 312.

115 **one second later:** All references to the timing of the intrusion and the security response, as well as the security nomenclature, are from the "Y-12 Protective Force Response Timeline," September 7, 2012.

116 **an average of 2,170:** Details of the security deficiencies at Y-12 come from the Response to Show Cause Notice, prepared by Babcock & Wilcox Technical Services Y-12, LLC, COR-Y12-8/27/2012-54506, September 10, 2012, pp. 3–20.

116 **guards were directed not to respond:** E-mail from Thomas D'Agostino to Steven Erhart, August 30, 2012.

116 **none of the cameras:** "Response of G4s Government Solutions Inc. to the Show Cause Notices issued by the NNSA and B&W Arising from the Intrusion of Protesters into the Protected Area at the Y-12 Facility," September 2, 2012, p. 24.

116 **Ten percent:** E-mail from Thomas D'Agostino to Steven Erhart, August 30, 2012.

116 **which they dismissed:** "Special Report: Inquiry into the Security Breach at the National Nuclear Security Administration's Y-12 National Security Complex," U.S. Department of Energy Office of Inspector General, DOE/IG-0868, August 2012, p. 2.

116 **they might have taken them out:** Testimony of Gregory H. Friedman, Federal News Service transcript of a hearing of the Oversight and Investigations Subcommittee of the House Energy and Commerce Committee—Subject: "DOE's Nuclear Weapons Complex: Challenges to Safety, Security, and Taxpayer Stewardship," Rayburn 2123, September 12, 2012.

117 **a 24/7 response:** Testimony of Brigadier General Rodney Johnson during the Transform Now Plowshares sentencing hearing, January 28, 2014.

117 **"Level 4 . . . camera coverage":** "Response of G4s Government Solutions Inc. to the Show Cause Notices . . . ," September 2, 2012, p. 20

117 **still housed the site's analytical chemistry labs:** "NNSA Deputy Administrator for Defense Programs Tours Y-12's Analytical Chemistry Labs," by Targeted News Service, January 11, 2012.

117 **a few thousand feet east:** Layout of Y-12 from a site map created by former site M&O contractor Martin Marietta, date unknown, accessed via the National Security Archive.

117 **his lieutenant said:** In-person author interview with Kirk Garland, February 4, 2013.

118 **steered the project to their state:** Ackland, p. 58.

118 **2,600 acres:** "Rocky Flats History," by Patricia Buffer, July 2003, via the Department of Energy's Office of Legacy Management.

119 **the community welcomed:** Iversen, p. 5.

119 **"In a matter . . . our own backyard":** Ackland, p. 62.

119 **black like coal and hot to the touch:** Gusterson, *Nuclear Rites*, pp. 135–136.

119 **seven to nine pounds each:** Ackland, p. 3.

119 **safe enough to locate:** Ackland, pp. 58–59.

120 **they blew southward:** Ibid., p. 61.

120 **Two creeks flowed out:** Map in ibid., p. 79.

120 **an elevated social caché:** Kristen Iversen's book *Full Body Burden*, about growing up in the shadow of Rocky Flats, is an excellent resource on the social and physiological impact of the plant; Len Ackland's *Making a Real Killing*, which also explains the science and the management at the plant, was my other valued source.

120 **the report stated:** *Deterrence and Survival in the Nuclear Age*, by the Security Resources Panel of the Science Advisory Committee, November 7, 1957, pp. 1, 12.

121 **in 30 minutes:** "Strategic Deterrence in the 21st Century," p. 33.

121 **a retroactive rationale:** Woolf, "U.S. Strategic Nuclear Forces: Background, Developments, and Issues," p. 2.

121 **population nearly doubled:** Ackland, p. 125.

122 **Little Washington:** Ibid.

122 **looked like both a hospital:** McPhee, p. 145.

122 **Only a handful:** Iversen, p. 17.

122 **The site was pocked:** Map in Ackland, p. 80.

122 **As early as 1959:** Buffer, p. 9.

122 **the costliest industrial accident:** Ibid.

122 **to beg Congress:** "A-Warhead Production Is Halted as Fire Destroys Plutonium Plant," no byline in the *Washington Post and Times Herald*, June 25, 1969.

122 **were able to cover up incidents:** Ackland, pp. 124–125.

122 **higher than in Nagasaki:** Iversen, pp. 59, 66.

122 **25 . . . 6,000:** Wittner, vol. 3, p. 26.

123 **hundreds of autopsies showed:** Iversen, p. 162.

123 **who sat on the train tracks:** "5,000 in Colorado Protest a Nuclear Weapons Plant," by Molly Ivins in the *New York Times*, April 3, 1978.

123 **Ginsberg recited his poem:** Iversen, p. 157.

123 **a 31-year-old worker:** "Federal Probers Sound Alarms: Rocky Flats—Boon Turns into Ecological Nightmare," by Tamara Jones and Dan Morain of the *Los Angeles Times*, June 20, 1989.

123 **The brain went missing:** "U.S. Government Uses Illegal Tactics in Beating Lawsuits Brought by Workers at Nuclear Weapons Factories," CBS News, January 13, 1991.

124 **They were raised:** Garland family details from interviews with Kirk Garland, his sister Kim Easter, and their sister-in-law Misti Garland, Kevin's widow.

124 **the B-25 bombers used:** History from Boeing's website: http://www.boeing.com/history/products/b-25-mitchell.page

124 **They were arrested as:** Buffer, p. 14.

125 **"You cannot take . . . face the consequences":** "2 Nuns to Spend Six Months in Prison for Nuclear Protest," by the Associated Press in the *New York Times*, November 23, 1982.

125 **Three months later:** Transcript of an October 28, 2006, event sponsored by the Maria Rogers Oral History Program and Rocky Flats Cold War Museum, http://oralhistory.boulderlibrary.org/transcript/oh1441t.pdf.

125 **12,000 demonstrators held hands:** Buffer, p. 14.

125 **sometimes as combative as possible:** Details on work and protests at Rocky Flats from in-person author interview with Kirk Garland, February 4, 2013.

125 **the special response team was dispatched:** Transcript of October 28, 2006, event sponsored by the Maria Rogers Oral History Program and Rocky Flats Cold War Museum,

125 **6,000 employees:** Ackland, p. 204.

125 **Every month there were dozens:** "Federal Probers Sound Alarms," by Tamara Jones and Dan Morain in the *Los Angeles Times*, June 20, 1989.

126 **the first and only time:** Mostafanezhad, p. 159, anthologizing "A Plutonium Tourism Ode: The Rocky Flats Cold War Museum," by Lindsey A. Freeman.

126 **the dumping of toxic waste:** "FBI Alleges Cover-Up at Rocky Flats," by Tamara Jones in the *Los Angeles Times*, June 10, 1989.

126 **Residents began digging ditches:** "Federal Probers Sound Alarms," Jones and Morain.

126 **A DOE memo surfaced:** "FBI Accuses Energy Dept. of Lying," by T. R. Reid and Bill McAllister in the *Washington Post*, June 10, 1989.

126 **Rockwell sued the U.S. government:** Ackland, p. 220.

126 **The philosophy in the nuclear-weapons complex:** "Health, Safety Given Priority at Arms Plants; Energy Department Puts Production 2nd," by T. R. Reid in the *Washington Post*, June 16, 1989.

126 **the biggest public-works project:** "Rocky Flats: The Price of Peace," by Mark Obmascik in the *Denver Post*, June 25, 2000.

126 **In 1992 Rockwell International pleaded guilty:** Ackland, pp. 232, 234.

127 **radiation experiments on humans over decades:** Ibid., p. 236.

127 **where subjects were injected with plutonium:** "American Nuclear Guinea Pigs: Three Decades of Radiation Experiments on U.S. Citizens," a report by the House Subcommittee on Energy Conservation and Power of the Committee on Energy and Commerce, November 1986, pp. 2–3, via the National Security Archive, box 9, "Human Radiation Experiments."

127 **"adverse effect . . . legal suits":** Letter from Colonel O. G. Haywood Jr. of the Army Corps of Engineers to Dr. Fidler at the Oak Ridge site of the Atomic Energy Commission, dated April 17, 1947, via the National Security Archive, box 9, "Human Radiation Experiments."

127 **70,000 plutonium pits over 36 years:** Many details on the violations at cleanup of Rocky Flats are from "Rocky Flats: The Price of Peace," by Mark Obmascik in the *Denver Post*, June 25, 2000.

127 **the nation's most dangerous building:** Ackland, p. 89.

127 **About 600 pits were sent:** "Rocky Flats," Obmascik.

128 **more than 8.5 miles away:** Ackland, p. 126.

128 **he spent 20 hours:** Ibid., p. 154.

128 **which cut corners on safety:** Ibid., p. 145.

128 **production at any cost:** Iversen, p. 267.

128 **"To have a . . . never be me":** Ackland, pp. 135, 137.

130 **at least 700,000:** The Cold War Patriots website: http://www.coldwarpatriots.org/about.

131 **16,000:** "The Perils of Pantex Hundreds of Workers Sickened at Texas Nuclear Weapons Plant," by Daniel Bernard in the Fort Worth Star-Telegram December 12, 2015.

131 **"gravel gerties":** Description of Pantex from photos from the Amarillo Area Office of the Department of Energy.

131 **Toxins had leached into aquifers:** "Pantex Celebrates 70th Anniversary," by Jacob Mayer in the *Amarillo Globe-News*, September 20, 2012.

132 **nourished one-fifth:** "How Long before the Great Plains Runs Out of Water?"
by Brad Plumer in the *Washington Post*, September 12, 2013.

132 **Nearly 14,000:** "U.S. Nuclear Forces 2010," by Robert S. Norris and Hans M.
Kristensen in the *Bulletin of Atomic Scientists*, May–June 2010, p. 68.

132 **"It made me . . . for other work":** "The Bishop at Ground Zero," *Life*.

133 **the mop heads were incinerated:** "The Budget and the Bomb: An Aging Arsenal,"
by Dana Priest in the *Washington Post*, September 16, 2012.

133 **50 years old:** "Modernizing the Nuclear Security Enterprise: NNSA Increased Its
Budget Estimates, but Estimates for Key Stockpile and Infrastructure Programs Need
Improvement," General Accounting Office report, GAO-15-499, August 2015.

133 **300-by-475-foot:** "New Y-12 Storage Site Nearly Complete," by Frank Munger in
the *Knoxville News Sentinel*, September 10, 2008.

133 **400 tons . . . 91,000 cubic yards:** "Fort Knox Is Nation's 'Y-12' for Gold," by
D. Ray Smith in the *Oak Ridger*, October 7, 2008.

133 **made of wood:** In-person author interview with Robert Alvarez, February 3, 2015.

133 **construction cost had doubled:** "New Y-12 storage site nearly complete," Munger.

134 **"Fort Knox . . . for gold":** "Fort Knox Is Nation's 'Y-12' for Gold," Smith.

134 **the only Tennessee congressman:** "Fort Campbell Brings Home Bacon in Bills,"
by Bill Theobald in the *Tennessean*, August 21, 2006, confirmed by the official
alphabetical list of the House of Representatives of the United States for the 110th
Congress, 2007–2009.

134 **for years sought extra funding:** "Y-12 Plant May Get $45 Million in Extra Federal
Funding," by the Associated Press, March 10, 2000.

134 **cost overruns and chaotic construction:** "Subcontractor Speaks Out on HEUMF
Dispute: 'This Has Put a Heck of a Hurt on Us,'" by Frank Munger on the Atomic
City Underground blog of the *Knoxville News Sentinel*, July 29, 2011.

134 **too small for the force:** Author phone interview with Steve Gibbs, former deputy
general manager of the pro-force, October 18, 2015.

134 **make nearly $100,000 a year:** Author interviews with Kirk Garland, February 4,
2013, and Steve Gibbs, October 18, 2015. I also spoke with other current and former
pro-force members who wished to anonymous. They helped paint a picture of life
onsite.

134 **passed countless trainings and courses:** Training reports from BWXT Pantex and
other sources, dated from 1988 to 2005, provided by Kirk Garland.

134 **and cynicism in the ranks:** Presentation by Jonathan Gill of the Government
Accountability Office at the Nuclear Deterrence Summit, February 20, 2015.

135 **"an endeavor of chilling monotony":** Joint statement by Major General C. Donald
Alston (Ret.) and Richard A. Meserve before the U.S. House of Representatives
Committee on Energy and Commerce, Subcommittee on Oversight and
Investigations, for the Hearing on DOE Management and Oversight of Its Nuclear
Weapons Complex, "Lessons of the Y-12 Security Failure," March 13, 2013, p. 3.

135 **17-hour shifts:** "Feds Say 2 at Y-12 Caught Napping," by Frank Munger in the
Knoxville News Sentinel, January 15, 2008.

137 **About once a year:** This is a rough estimation based on the fact there were
seven such incidents between 2000 and 2008, according to "Report: More Guards
Caught Napping," by Frank Munger in the *Knoxville News Sentinel*, January 17,
2008.

135 **"vulnerability assessment team":** B&W Y-12 Show Cause report (additional
questions), November 16, 2012, p. 16.

135 **Only parts of Y-12's fencing:** Joint statement by Alston and Meserve, p. 4.

135 **Termites chewed through wooden beams:** Letter from John Conway, chairman of the Defense Nuclear Facilities Safety Board, to Brigadier General Thomas F. Gioconda, acting deputy administrator for defense programs in the Department of Energy, May 29, 2001, cited in Robert Alvarez's report "Reducing the Risks of Highly Enriched Uranium at the U.S. Department of Energy's Y-12 National Security Complex," October 9, 2006.

136 **Toxic-waste drums were used:** Defense Nuclear Facilities Safety Board weekly staff report, October 22, 2004, cited in Alvarez, "Reducing the Risks of Highly Enriched Uranium at the U.S. Department of Energy's Y-12 National Security Complex."

136 **Employees were judged more:** "Management assessments were aligned more to paperwork compliance reviews than actual work performance," according to the Contractor Assurance System Effectiveness Review requested by Chuck Spencer and sent in writing to Steven Erhart, August 30, 2012; document 183 of FOIA 14-00244-R.

136 **the story of how:** "Y-12: Poster Child for a Dysfunctional Nuclear Weapons Complex," by Robert Alvarez in the *Bulletin of Atomic Scientists*, August 4, 2014.

136 **7,400 people:** Presentation by D. Ray Smith at the East Tennessee Preservation Conference at Y-12, November 6, 2014.

137 **$6.6 billion:** "Top 100 Contractors Report" for FY 2012 from Federal Procurement Data System.

137 **an inherent trust developed:** "Modernizing the Nuclear Security Enterprise: NNSA's Reviews of Budget Estimates and Decisions on Resource Trade-Offs Need Strengthening," by the Government Accountability Office, July 2012, p. 12.

137 **"faith-based management":** This is the Defense Nuclear Facilities Safety Board, from a 2000 report cited by former DOE senior policy adviser Robert Alvarez in "Reducing the Risks of Highly Enriched Uranium at the U.S. Department of Energy's Y-12 National Security Complex."

137 **ever-present instability:** Gibbs interview.

137 **"Department of Evil":** Gibbs, p. 32.

137 **far away psychologically:** Joint statement by Alston and Meserve.

137 **SPOs abandoned their posts:** Ibid., p. 9.

137 **Safety was considered "nonproductive" work:** Westbrook, pp. 1–6.

138 **"The fight begins at the skin of the MAA":** "Response of G4s Government Solutions Inc. to the Show Cause Notices issued by NNSA and B&W Arising from the Intrusion of Protesters into the Protected Area at the Y-12 Facility," September 2, 2012, p. 33 (p. 187 in FOIA HQ-2015-00979-F).

138 **cutting as many as 34 security police officers:** "About 50 Security Jobs to Be Cut at OR," by Frank Munger in the *Knoxville News Sentinel*, July 23, 2012.

139 **He withdrew candles:** Transform Now Plowshares jury trial, May 8, 2013, document 193, p. 118.

140 **BearCats and special response teams:** "Special Report: Inquiry into the Security Breach at the National Nuclear Security Administration's Y-12 National Security Complex," DOE/IG-0868, August 2012, p. 2.

140 **Additional guards:** Gibbs, p. 308.

140 **The activists sang:** Testimony of Greg Boertje-Obed, Transform Now Plowshares jury trial, May 8, 2013, document 193, p. 115.

140 **K9 tracking units:** Updated Y-12 situation report completed at 6 p.m., July 29, 2012, and e-mailed to management as a PDF by Stephen J. Macklin.

140 **would be power-scrubbed away:** Testimony of Rodney L. Johnson, Transform Now Plowshares jury trial, May 7, 2013, document 192, p. 200.

141 **merely a diversion:** Testimony of Steven Erhart, manager of the NNSA Production Office, Transform Now Plowshares jury trial, May 7, 2013, document 192. p. 75.

141 **until a few weeks later:** Testimony of Ryan Baker, Transform Now Plowshares jury trial, May 7, 2013, document 192, p. 227.

141 **until December:** "Unmended Fences: Months after Y-12 Break-In, Hole in Barrier Remains," by Frank Munger of the *Knoxville News Sentinel*, December 20, 2012.

141 **restrained with metal handcuffs, patted down:** Testimony of Ryan Baker, Transform Now Plowshares jury trial, May 7, 2013, document 192, p. 220.

141 **"And we went . . . to be alive":** Exhibit 66, a voice call by Greg Boertje-Obed from Blount County Detention Center made July 28, 2012, submitted as part of the government's evidence in the Transform Now Plowshares jury trial, May 7, 2013.

141 **"catastrophe":** Hearing held by the House Committee on Armed Services' Subcommittee on Strategic Forces, September 13, 2012.

CHAPTER 6. WASHINGTON

145 **"Appalling . . . Mind-boggling incompetence":** Federal News Service transcript of a hearing held by the Oversight and Investigations Subcommittee of the House Energy and Commerce Committee—Subject: "DOE's Nuclear Weapons Complex: Challenges to Safety, Security, and Taxpayer Stewardship," Rayburn 2123, September 12, 2012.

147 **"Congress reacts to . . . flew into buildings":** Fortenberry remarks at the Carnegie International Nuclear Policy Conference, March 24, 2015.

147 **Osama bin Laden had called for a Hiroshima:** "What Bin Laden Sees in Hiroshima," by Steve Coll in the *Washington Post*, February 6, 2005.

147 **"As unfathomable as . . . of mass destruction":** "Cheney Is Fulcrum of Foreign Policy," by Glenn Kessler and Peter Slevin in the *Washington Post*, October 13, 2002.

147 **the only serious penetration:** "Y-12 Intrusion Embarrasses the 'Fork Knox of Uranium,'" by Erik Schelzig of the Associated Press in the *Tennessean*, August 20, 2012.

148 **a blast of five to ten kilotons:** This scenario was posited by physicist Frank N. von Hippel in "Suicidal Nuclear Threat Is Seen at Weapons Plants," by Matthew L. Wald in the *New York Times*, January 23, 2003.

148 **within 40 miles:** "U.S. Nuclear Weapons Complex: Y-12 and Oak Ridge National Laboratory at High Risk," by the Project on Government Oversight, October 16, 2006.

148 **"Most students at . . . knowledge of war":** "Breaking the War Mentality," by Barack Obama in *Sundial* 7, no. 12, March 10, 1983.

148 **for which he got an A:** "Obama's Youth Shaped His Nuclear-Free Vision," by William J. Broad and David E. Sanger in the *New York Times*, July 4, 2009.

149 **made sense to Obama:** Remnick, pp. 116–117.

149 **his grandmother worked:** "Barack Obama's Grandma, 86, Dies of Cancer before Election," by Dan Nakaso in the *Honolulu Advertiser*, November 4, 2008.

149 **used to firebomb Japan:** Maraniss, p. 75.

149 **would make way for the treaty:** Author interview with Robert Alvarez, February 3, 2015.

150 **Y-12 was ordered to continue:** *Final Site-Wide Environmental Impact Statement for the Y-12 National Security Complex*, vol. 1, February 2011, pp. 1–32.

150 **no experience:** "Energy Nominee Unschooled in Nuclear Weapons Issues," by Thomas W. Lippman in the *Washington Post*, December 22, 1992.

150 **68 percent:** "Arms Control and Environmental Groups Say Next Energy Secretary Must Be Prepared to Redirect U.S. Nuclear Weapons Complex," by Peter L. Kelley for Fenton Communications, December 21, 1992.

150 **eight minutes:** "Cold-War Doctrines Refuse to Die," by David Hoffman in the *Washington Post*, March 15, 1998,

150 **59 counts:** *United States v. Wen Ho Lee* indictment via the Federation of American Scientists: http://fas.org/irp/ops/ci/docs/lee_indict.html.

151 **solitary confinement for nine months:** "The Making of a Suspect: The Case of Wen Ho Lee," by Matthew Purdy et al. in the *New York Times*, February 4, 2001; "The Prosecution Unravels: The Case of Wen Ho Lee," by Matthew Purdy with James Sterngold et al. in the *New York Times*, February 5, 2001.

151 **"a clear mission . . . and accountability":** *Science at Its Best; Security at Its Worst: A Report on Security Problems at the U.S. Department of Energy*, by the President's Foreign Intelligence Advisory Board, June 1999.

152 **"To set up . . . what I need":** "Effort for Separate Nuclear Weapons Agency Gaining Support," by H. Josef Hebert for the Associated Press, June 15, 1999.

152 **except to the secretary himself:** National Nuclear Security Administration Act, public law 106-65, 113 STAT. 953, Sec. 3281(1) and 3281(2), October 5, 1999.

152 **"a birth defect":** "National Nuclear Security Administration (NNSA) Office of Defense Programs Independent Assessment of Life Extension Program (LEP) Phase 6.X Process," Aerospace report no. ATR-2012(5709)-3, June 29, 2012, p. 47.

153 **Iraq was a dumb war:** Transcript from NPR: http://www.npr.org/templates/story/story.php?storyId=99591469.

153 **his top three priorities:** Alter, p. 33.

153 **munitions were splayed around:** "Obama-Lugar Proposal Targets Stockpiles of Conventional Weapons," by Jeff Zeleny in the *Chicago Tribune*, November 2, 2005.

153 **"Many of these . . . far too devastating":** Federal News Service transcript of the Council on Foreign Relations meeting "Challenges Ahead for Cooperative Threat Reduction," held at the Washington Club, November 1, 2005.

153 **had pondered using nuclear weapons in Vietnam:** "Nixon White House Considered Nuclear Options Against Vietnam, Declassified Documents Reveal," National Security Archive Electronic Briefing Book no. 195, edited by William Burr and Jeffrey Kimball, July 31, 2006.

154 **"new and dangerous nuclear era":** "A World Free of Nuclear Weapons," by George P. Shultz, William J. Perry, Henry A. Kissinger, and Sam Nunn in the *Wall Street Journal*, January 4, 2007, http://www.wsj.com/articles/SB116787515251566636 (accessed July 8, 2015).

154 **the person who commands the arsenal:** Elaine Scarry's book *Thermonuclear Monarchy* is a bracing argument against the constitutionality of imbuing one person with the authority to end all life on Earth.

154 **"just as grave":** Alter, p. 65.

154 **the foremost threat:** Ibid. pp. 351–352.

155 **a nuclear version of September 11:** *9/11 Commission Report*, p. 380.

155 **would set the tone:** In-person author interview with Ben Rhodes, June 23, 2015.

156 **"Today, the Cold War . . . without nuclear weapons":** Transcript from the White House.

157 **chiefly for his vision:** Norwegian Nobel Committee press release, October 9, 2009.

157 **a fundraising letter:** "Obama's Youth Shaped His Nuclear-Free Vision," Broad and Sanger.

159 **"a zoo of extremely wild animals":** In-person author interview with Robert Alvarez, February 5, 2015.

159 **an office of management and operations:** In-person author interviews with Neile Miller on July 16, 2014, September 18, 2014, and December 16, 2014.

161 **300 feet:** Vice Admiral Joseph E. Tofalo at Peter Huessy Congressional Breakfast Seminar, May 29, 2015; this unclassified number was also cited to me by D'Agostino himself.

161 **reducing the cost:** NNSA policy letter NAP-21, "Transformational Governance and Oversight," approved February 28, 2011, p. I-1.

162 **"unprecedented":** "Y-12 Halts Nuke Operations," by Frank Munger in the *Knoxville News Sentinel*, August 2, 2012.

162 **"The protesters put . . . did not occur":** E-mail from Steven Wyatt to Y-12 site managers, July 28, 2012. Post-incident correspondence and some details of the break-in were obtained via FOIA requests sent to the NNSA.

162 **if the system had worked properly:** Gibbs, p. 336.

162 **perhaps the most impenetrable building:** E-mail from Steven Erhart to Y-12 managers, July 28, 2012.

162 **No one thought:** B&W Y-12/WSI Causal Analysis for the July 28 Security Incident at the Y-12 Site, submitted August 1, 2012.

163 **were required to take refresher courses:** "Response of G4s Government Solutions Inc. to the Show Cause Notices issued by NNSA and B&W Arising from the Intrusion of Protesters into the Protected Area at the Y-12 Facility," September 2, 2012, p. 30.

163 **B&W and WSI operated on their own:** E-mail from Steven Erhart to Michael Lempke, August 12, 2012.

163 **routine for at least two years:** "Security Lapses at Nuclear Complex Identified Two Years before Break-In," by Dana Priest in the *Washington Post*, September 11, 2012.

163 **high marks in all performance categories:** "Government Heaped Praise on Security Contractor before Y-12 Breach," by Frank Munger in the *Knoxville News Sentinel*, September 14, 2012.

163 **For the previous two years:** Memoranda from Theodore D. Sherry, manager of the Y-12 Site Office, and Steven C. Erhart, manager of the NNSA Production Office, to Neile Miller, deputy administrator of the NNSA, in the autumns of 2010, 2011, and 2012.

163 **adopted a more paramilitary attitude:** "Y-12 Update" handout coded "YGG 12-0479" and dated October 2012, sent by e-mail between Y-12 site managers.

163 **"working people to death":** "Long Hours for Y-12 Security Police," by Frank Munger on the Atomic City Underground blog of the *Knoxville News Sentinel*, September 25, 2015.

163 **received a classified briefing:** The scheduling of the visit is from an e-mail from Wade Heck, B&W government operations staffer, to B&W staff on August 13, 2012. Classified briefing noted in an e-mail from Steven Erhart to site officials, August 14, 2012.

163 **concluded that human error was the culprit:** "Corker Visits Y-12: 'They're Making Multiple Changes to Ensure . . . This Never Happens Again,'" by Frank Munger in the *Knoxville News Sentinel*, August 14, 2012.

163 **contentious:** This word is from an e-mail by the NNSA's Douglas Fremont, who was present for the meetings, to contractors, August 5, 2012.

163 **Sen. Dianne Feinstein (D-Calif.) proposed:** E-mail from Katherine Croft, congressional affairs specialist for the NNSA, to NNSA and contractor officials, August 15, 2012.

163 **"deeply troubling . . . unacceptable":** "Security Contractor Brings in Fresh Leadership; Other Changes Under Way at Y-12," by Frank Munger in the *Knoxville News Sentinel*, August 6, 2012.

163 **"The committee is gravely concerned":** Letter from Rep. Michael Turner (R-Ohio) to Chu dated August 31, 2012, included in an e-mail from Jed D'Ercole to NNSA and site officials, September 4, 2012.

164 **was praised by WSI:** "Fired Y-12 Guard Seeks Vindication (and a Lot of Back Pay)," by Frank Munger on the Atomic City Underground blog of the *Knoxville News Sentinel*, May 26, 2014.

164 **sickened him:** Gibbs, p. 313.

164 **Darrel P. Kohlhorst:** Kohlhorst, the single point of accountability for the safe delivery of the $900-million-a-year contract at Y-12, declined to comment, as did many other current and former Y-12 officials, on both the federal and contractor side.

164 **"We must become . . . would be devastating":** Message from Chuck Spencer in an e-mail from Y-12 spokesperson Ellen Boatner to Y-12 employees, August 11, 2012.

165 **a workforce plagued by sorrow and denial:** Chuck Spencer in a speech at the Nuclear Deterrence Summit, February 21, 2013.

165 **Local talk radio and social media:** Gibbs, p. 317.

165 **retired after being relieved:** "The Y-12 Shakeup Continues: B&W Replaces Leadership at Oak Ridge Plant," by Frank Munger on the Atomic City Underground blog of the *Knoxville News Sentinel*, August 10, 2012.

165 **The top two guys at WSI:** "WSI Oak Ridge Announces Management Changes," no byline, *Oak Ridger*, August 8, 2012.

165 **were temporarily reassigned:** "Incident Response" of "NNSA Y-12 HEUMF Protester Incident on 28 July" prepared by NNSA for the White House August 6, 2012.

165 **Tom D'Agostino's multiple offers to resign:** Author interview with Daniel Poneman, March 29, 2015.

165 **"performance-based incentive":** Gibbs, p. 311.

165 **widespread cheating:** "Special Report: Review of the Compromise of Security Test Materials at the Y-12 National Security Complex," DOE/IG-0875, October 2012.

166 **"detected and caught":** E-mail from the NNSA's Joshua McConaha to Steven Wyatt and Clarence Bishop, August 2, 2012.

166 **Suspicions lingered:** Gibbs, p. 337.

166 **"Thank God Kirk . . . no-win situation":** "Union Contests Firing of Y-12 Security Guard," by Frank Munger on the Atomic City Underground blog of the *Knoxville News Sentinel*, August 27, 2012.

167 **Sister Megan, meanwhile, was telling the press:** "Fired Y-12 Guard Claims He's a Scapegoat for Security Breach," by Frank Munger in the *Knoxville News Sentinel*, August 25, 2012.

167 **"the new post 7/28 world":** E-mail from Steven Erhart to Michael Lempke, August 12, 2012.

167 **its most productive year:** "Y-12 Update" handout coded "YGG 12-0479" and dated October 2012.

167 **half a dozen incidents where:** "Response of G4S Government Solutions, Inc., to the Show Cause Notices Issued by NNSA," September 2, 2012, pp. 36–38.

167 **"The enemy of today . . . seeking to embarrass":** "G4S Ready to Move Past the 'Punishment Stage'; Security Firm's CEO Says 20 Minutes at Y-12 Wiped Away 20 Million Hours of Exceptional Service," by Frank Munger on the Atomic City Underground blog of the *Knoxville News Sentinel*, January 28, 2013.

168 **was suffering from chills:** "Sister Megan Rice's Condition," by Frank Munger on the Atomic City blog of the *Knoxville News Sentinel*, August 8, 2012.

168 **the nickname "Y-12":** "Protester Picked Up a Jailhouse Nickname," by Frank Munger on the Atomic City Underground blog of the *Knoxville News Sentinel*, September 19, 2012.

168 **released within the week:** "2 of 3 Y-12 Protesters out of Jail Tonight," by Frank Munger in the *Knoxville News Sentinel*, August 3, 2012.

169 **"and we will give peace a chance!":** The scene outside the jail is described—and the dialogue transcribed—from a video by Adam Brimer of the *Knoxville News Sentinel*.

169 **nun:** Author's note: I myself fell prey to the cachet of "nun" in the first story I wrote about the event, in April 2013, which served as the foundation for this book and is viewable at wapo.st/prophets. A nun lives a cloistered lifestyle; a sister, like Megan, is very much out in the world.

171 **FBI agents and DOE investigators started showing up:** Author interview with Paul Magno, corroborated by motion for discovery (document 46) submitted by Transform Now Plowshares defense attorneys William P. Quigley, Chris Irwin, and Francis L. Lloyd Jr., November 2, 2012, p. 5.

172 **about to win a $45 million Navy contract:** "Contracts for September 28, 2012," by Defense Department Documents and Publications, September 28, 2012 (via Nexis).

172 **"Embarrassment" . . . "The system is broken":** Federal News Service transcript of a hearing held by the House Committee on Armed Services' Subcommittee on Strategic Forces, September 13, 2012.

173 **"Time to break . . ." "Hopes!":** Written notes provided by Megan Rice.

173 **"A terrorist cell . . . was too late":** "The Risk of Nuclear Terrorism—And Next Steps to Reduce the Danger," testimony of Matthew Bunn for the U.S. Senate Committee on Homeland Security and Governmental Affairs, April 2, 2008.

174 **"mythology of anti-nuclear folks":** Remarks by Major General Garrett Harencak at the conference, September 16, 2014.

175 **"We must recognize . . . it might be":** Remarks by Ambassador Robert Joseph at the deterrence summit, February 18, 2015.

175 **The United States is in a race with itself:** Author interview with Hans M. Kristensen of the Federation of American Scientists, October 7, 2014.

175 **"will acquire weapons . . . in large numbers":** "New World Coming: American Security in the 21st Century," United States Commission on National Security/21st Century, September 15, 1999, p. 138.

176 **about 80 warheads:** A 2014 estimate by Hans M. Kristensen and Robert S. Norris for the Bulletin of the Atomic Scientists.

177 **$14 billion over ten years:** "Death Wears Bunny Slippers," by Josh Harkinson in *Mother Jones*, November–December 2014.

177 **to keep all ICBM silos regardless:** "U.S. Strategic Nuclear Forces: Background, Developments, and Issues," by Amy F. Woolf for the Congressional Research Service, September 5, 2014.

177 **80 pits a year by 2030 regardless:** "U.S. Plutonium Pit Production for Nuclear Weapons," by Nukewatch New Mexico, April 23, 2015.

177 **allows its contractors:** "Modernizing the Nuclear Security Enterprise: NNSA's

Reviews of Budget Estimates and Decisions on Resource Trade-offs Need Strengthening," Government Accountability Office report GAO-12-806, July 2012.

177 **there isn't money *for* the teardowns:** "Massive Nuclear Cleanup Hobbled by Funding Shortfall," by John R. Emshwiller and Gary Fields in the *Wall Street Journal*, November 1, 2015.

177 **Congress inserted an exception:** "The Trillion Dollar Nuclear Triad," by Jon B. Wolfsthal, Jeffrey Lewis, and Marc Quint for the James Martin Center for Nonproliferation Studies, January 2014, p. 7.

177 **higher than at any point in history:** "Billion Dollar Boondoggles: Challenging the National Security Administration's Plan to Spend More Money for Less Security," the Alliance for Nuclear Accountability, May 2014, p. 1.

177 **The share of Pentagon spending:** "The Trillion Dollar Nuclear Triad," Wolfsthal, Lewis, and Quint, p. 4.

177 **would peak at the same time:** Ibid., p. 26.

178 **$4 billion:** Rep. Chuck Fleischmann at the Energy Communities Alliance Peer Exchange at the Liaison Hotel in Washington, D.C., February 12, 2015.

178 **"Oak Ridge . . . is a special place":** Ibid.

CHAPTER 7. OAK RIDGE

181 **"We had this . . . painful to watch":** Author interview with Ted Sherry, former federal manager of Y-12, February 2014.

182 **"We haven't had . . . major safety incidents":** "A New Measure of Success," by Frank Munger on the Atomic City Underground blog of the *Knoxville News Sentinel*, July 1, 2014.

183 **second-largest employer . . . 24,000:** Y-12 Community Relations Council.

183 **7,400:** Presentation by D. Ray Smith at the East Tennessee Preservation Conference in Y-12's New Hope Visitors Center, November 6, 2014.

183 **from 28 counties:** Y-12 National Security Complex PowerPoint handout on "Y-12 Employees by County."

183 **to attract and retain skilled labor:** "National Nuclear Security Administration (NNSA) Office of Defense Programs Independent Assessment of Life Extension Program (LEP) Phase 6.X Process," Aerospace report no. ATR-2012(5709)-3, June 29, 2012, p. 79.

184 **in case of earth-bound asteroids:** "Nuclear Weapons: Actions Needed by NNSA to Clarify Dismantlement Performance Goal," Government Accountability Office, GAO-14-449, April 2014, p. 41.

184 **the largest federal construction project:** "Alexander: Congress May Not OK UPF Budget Funds at Requested Levels, but Says There's Bipartisan Support," by Frank Munger on the Atomic City Underground blog of the *Knoxville News Sentinel*, February 5, 2015.

184 **"This project is needed . . . will change here":** Testimony by William Lyons in a public meeting of the Defense Nuclear Facilities Safety Board in Knoxville, Tennessee, October 2, 2012, p. 161.

184 **"In our opinion . . . by the billions":** Testimony by Ralph Hutchison in a public meeting of the Defense Nuclear Facilities Safety Board in Knoxville, Tennessee, October 2, 2012, pp. 178–179.

184 **$19 billion:** "No News on the Uranium Processing Facility May Be Good News,"

by Lydia Dennett for the Project on Government Oversight, October 28, 2014.

184 **via hundreds of letters and e-mails:** Public comment from the *Final Site-Wide Environmental Impact Statement for the Y-12 National Security Complex*, vol. 2, Comment Response Document, February 2011, pp. 24 and 31.

186 **"It's hard for . . . to be prepared":** Author interview with Trina Baughn, June 18, 2014.

186 **the only NNSA site where:** Gerald Boyd, former Oak Ridge manager for the DOE, interviewed May 14, 2013, by Keith McDaniel for the Center for Oak Ridge Oral History, p. 19.

186 **hampers the city:** Westbrook, 12-9.

187 **million-dollar monthly electric bill:** Author tour of the Oak Ridge National Laboratory, June 2014.

187 **utopia on the frontier:** Freeman, p. 37.

188 **more than 10 percent:** 2009–2013 American Community Survey 5-Year Estimates, American Community Survey, U.S. Census Bureau.

188 **170 acres of federal land:** "Property Transfer for Oak Ridge Airport to Be Discussed during Info Session on August 18," by John Huotari in *Oak Ridge Today*.

188 **double that of Knoxville:** 2009–2013 American Community Survey 5-Year Estimates, American Community Survey.

188 **"We do know . . . get blank stares":** Author interview with then-mayor Tom Beehan, June 12, 2014.

189 **Oak Ridgers have become more blue-collar:** Author interview with former Oak Ridge councilwoman Anne Garcia Garland, November 2014.

190 **". . . slums that were deliberately planned.":** Kiernan, p. 301.

190 **12 miles:** Agency for Toxic Substances and Disease Registry, http://www.atsdr.cdc.gov/sites/oakridge/east_fork_poplar_creek.html.

190 **poisonous to humans:** "Y-12: Poster Child for a Dysfunctional Nuclear Weapons Complex," by Robert Alvarez in the *Bulletin of Atomic Scientists*, August 4, 2014.

191 **"You can find Oak Ridge in the Mississippi Delta":** Author interview with Ralph Hutchison, February 2013.

191 **fish-monitoring sites:** Environmental Monitoring Plan of the Tennessee Department of Environment and Conservation and the DOE Oversight Office, January through December 2014, p. 33.

191 **The DOE plans to build:** "Cleanup Progress: Annual Report to the Oak Ridge Community," by the Department of Energy, DOE/ORO-2467, 2013, p. 29.

191 **still above Tennessee guidelines:** Oak Ridge Site Specific Advisory Board FY2014 Annual Report, October 2013 to September 2014, p. 15.

191 **50,000 kilograms:** *Final Site-Wide Environmental Impact Statement for the Y-12 National · Security Complex*, vol. 1, DOE/EIS-0387, February 2011, p. D-31.

191 **$1.5 billion . . . 10,600:** Division of Energy Employees Occupational Illness Compensation Program (as of March 13, 2016), http://www.dol.gov/owcp/energy/regs/compliance/statistics/WebPages/Y-12_PLANT.htm.

191 **for medical reasons:** "We Believed What We Were Told," by Frank Munger in the *Knoxville News Sentinel*, September 4, 1996.

192 **warned against having any food:** "Information Bulletin #2" from J. R. Miller of the Industrial Hygiene Division of Reynolds Electrical and Engineering Company Inc.

to "Interested Personnel"—Subject: "Beryllium as a Health Hazard and Techniques for Handling," October 31, 1962.

192 **coffee and doughnuts were laid out every day:** PowerPoint presentation titled "Peeling the Onion from the Inside: ISMS for a Multiple Contaminate D&D Project," by David Kirby, certified industrial hygienist and certified safety professional, who prepared the presentation as a contractor/subcontractor for the U.S. government (provided by Glenn Bell).

192 **"I'm walking in . . . talking calculus":** "The Psychosocial Effects of Beryllium Sensitization and Chronic Beryllium Disease," by Jeff Miller, PhD, for the University of Tennessee Department of Public Health, January 10, 2013, pp. 19, 27.

192 **more than 40 percent:** Radiation dosage data from the Department of Energy, cited in Robert Alvarez's report "Reducing the Risks of Highly Enriched Uranium at the U.S. Department of Energy's Y-12 National Security Complex," October 9, 2006.

193 **sleep in shifts:** Colleen Black interview for Voices of the Manhattan Project, conducted August 13, 2013, by Cindy Kelly and Denise Kiernan.

195 **"You couldn't keep . . . we were told":** Colleen Black died March 19, 2015, in Oak Ridge at 89. She was a vibrant, thoughtful woman who was devoted to telling her story, however modestly she viewed it. A couple of days after I visited her in November 2014, she mailed me a Thanksgiving card with a collage of photos of our time together. She is a featured subject in Denise Kiernan's *The Girls of Atomic City* and in the Atomic Heritage Foundation's Voices of the Manhattan Project. Her obituary in the *Oak Ridger* called her a volunteer extraordinaire, an Oak Ridge fashionista, a talented columnist, and a world traveler. She is buried in Oak Ridge Memorial Park, near the Clinch River, less than half a mile from Y-12.

196 **hell-bent on exacting revenge:** "Friends: Suspect Had Two Sides," by Bob Fowler in the *Knoxville News Sentinel*, July 29, 2008.

CHAPTER 8. THE TRIAL

204 **"It is precisely . . . sin and death":** Transcript of *United States v. Gump et al.*, Case 3:10-cr-00094, May 11, 2011, document 325, p. 58.

206 **stopped pressing state charges:** "New security leaders appointed at Oak Ridge," by the Associated Press, August 8, 2012.

206 **The Department of Justice wanted:** Author interview with Jeff Theodore, February 14, 2014.

207 **"If these three . . . government prosecutes them":** Memorandum in support of motion to dismiss, by William P. Quigley, Chris Irwin, and Francis L. Lloyd Jr., November 2, 2012.

208 **who stole and burned 100,000 draft records:** Riegle, *Doing Time for Peace*, p. 33.

208 **The men had been inspired by:** Ibid., p. 87.

208 **"One who elects . . . society cannot tolerate":** *United States v. Cullen*, 454 F.2d 386 (7th Cir. 1971), via the government's motion to preclude defendants from introducing evidence in support of certain justification defenses (document 45), November 2, 2012, p. 13.

208 **"They say if . . . a ludicrous argument":** Transcript of proceedings, motion hearing before C. Clifford Shirley Jr., November 20, 2012, p. 58.

209 **"History develops one . . . by this case":** Ibid., pp. 93–94.

209 **a new indictment:** Superseding indictment (document 55), by Jeffrey E. Theodore and Melissa M. Kirby, December 4, 2012.

210 **"Attention has to . . . on the planet":** Motion hearing, *United States v. Walli et al.* April 23, 2013, pp. 21-32.

211 **one of the more challenging:** Author interview with Amul Thapar, November 13, 2015.

213 **"I don't believe . . . to military activities":** Motion hearing, *United States v. Walli et al.*, February 7, 2013, document 84, pp. 19–20.

215 **Church and State streets:** Author's note: "Church" is actually West Church Avenue, but I didn't want precision to get in the way of clearly communicating what was otherwise an evocative symbolic coincidence.

215 **"This is Criminal Action 3-12-CR-107":** All quotations from the trial are from the official court transcript by court reporter Lisa Reed Wiesman. Descriptions of the proceedings are from the author's own eyewitness.

216 **a few hundred times:** "Protesting Priest's Path Leads Repeatedly to Jail," by Richard C. Paddock of the *Los Angeles Times*, April 9, 2009.

216 **They were charged with the same crime:** Laffin, pp. 79–80.

216 **after a 2009 visit to Hiroshima:** Riegle, *Crossing the Line*, p. 303.

216 **remained unclear:** Author's note: Twenty-one months after I filed a FOIA request for details on this shipment, I was given 100 pages of forms that were 99-percent redacted. A log on page 63 of the FOIA response does confirm that the origin of the shipment was the Pantex Plant in Amarillo, which does not disprove the theory that uranium in some form was being conveyed.

220 **"recovery":** Testimony of Rodney Johnson in the Transform Now Plowshares jury trial, May 7, 2013, document 192, p. 208.

222 **$8,531.67:** Ibid., p. 206.

222 **The prayer had allegedly been written:** Wikipedia: https://en.wikipedia.org/wiki/Prayer_to_Saint_Michael.

233 **tens of millions:** Author's note: The exact death total is a matter of debate, and fluctuates depending on whether you count both historical cases of cancer/illness *and* estimated future cases. Chapter 7 of "Atomic Audit," published in 1998, estimates that anywhere between 140,000 and 1.6 million people worldwide have been fatally affected by fallout from U.S. and Soviet atmospheric tests (p. 395). The figure is actually 2.4 million, according to a 2003 report by International Physicians for the Prevention of Nuclear War. There have been additional illnesses and deaths among the 600,000-plus people who have worked in the U.S. nuclear-weapons complex since 1942. A 2015 investigation by McClatchy found that 33,480 nuclear-weapons workers have died since 1945, though the criterion was if they received compensation for their injuries, not if their injuries were definitively linked to exposure; since 2001, about 186,000 workers have been exposed to harmful materials, McClatchy found. Arjun Makhijani, president of the Institute for Energy and Environmental Research, says that "millions" of people around the world—both civilians and members of the military—have been affected by bomb production and testing. Is it "*tens* of millions"? Hard to say. At this point, anyway.

234 **Ten jurors were ready:** Author's note: Two jurors, Keith Graybeal and Kathy Starr, agreed to interviews. One juror declined. The other nine were either unreachable or did not respond to requests for an interview.

235 **the plant was crucial:** Author interview with Kathy Starr, November 12, 2015.

235 **what made convicting them so difficult:** Author interviews with Graybeal, November 11, 2014, and November 9, 2015.

238 **"federal crime of terrorism":** "Remanding decision" by Amul Thapar, Document 165, p. 2.

239 **"under federal scholarship":** Allocution by Megan Rice, February 18, 2014, document 334, p. 27.

241 **in the pocket of his coveralls:** "Inspection Report: Allegations Regarding Management of Highly Enriched Uranium," INS-L-15-03, U.S. Department of Energy Office of the Inspector General, September 2015; "20 Grams of HEU in the Wrong Place," by Frank Munger on the Atomic City Underground blog of the *Knoxville News Sentinel*, February 12, 2014.

242 **$114 an hour:** Author's note: The difference is the "incremental fringe rate," which are the added costs of bringing someone to work who is also accumulating pension and health benefits.

243 **In 1989 she swam:** Laffin, pp. 43, 62.

CHAPTER 9. THE MODERN PARADOX

257 **The land was a great basin:** "How to Kill a Nation: U.S. Policy in Western Shoshone Country since 1863," Western Shoshone National Council, by Peter d'Errico: http://www.umass.edu/legal/derrico/shoshone/pamphlet.html.

257 **the Creator commanded them:** "Circle of Stories: Corbin Harney," PBS, http://www.pbs.org/circleofstories/storytellers/corbin_harney.html.

257 **which stated that white men:** "United States Treaty with the Western Shoshone, 1863" via http://www.umass.edu/legal/derrico/shoshone/ruby_valley.html.

258 **to eliminate lag time:** Ackland, p. 55.

258 **Hotel roofs on the Vegas Strip:** Freeman, *Plutonium*, p. 161.

258 **"This is the valley . . . of the fireballs":** McPhee, p. 93.

261 **at its lowest level in more than a decade:** "How Pentagon War Funding Became a Budget Buster Washington Can't Resist," by Warren Strobel of Reuters, July 31, 2015.

261 **Forty cents of every dollar:** "Where do your 2014 income tax dollars go?" Friends Committee on National Legislation, April 2015, http://fcnl.org/assets/flyer/FCNL_Taxes13_final.pdf.

261 **Tariq Aziz:** "Bureau Reporter Meets 16-Year-Old Three Days before US Drone Kills Him," by Pratap Chatterjee for the Bureau of Investigative Journalism, November 4, 2011.

262 **The base was originally:** Creech Air Force Base history: http://www.creech.af.mil/library/factsheets/factsheet.asp?id=21924.

262 **psychic permission:** "Psychic numbing" is psychiatrist Robert Lifton's term for the diminished reaction to the abstract (but overwhelming) idea of mass destruction. See Wittner, vol. 1, p. 324, and Lifton's "Death in Life."

266 **"We are one . . . separate ourselves now":** "Circle of Stories: Corbin Harney," PBS.

267 **More than 200,000:** NNSA Strategic Vision, p. 7.

267 **between 1,500 and 2,000 tons:** 1,900 tons, according to Feiveson et al., p. 69; 1,730 tons, according to Evans et al., p. 197.

267 **740:** "Obama Curbs Nuclear Security Goals as Bomb-Building Budget Grows," by Douglas Birch for the Center for Public Integrity, July 29, 2014.

267 **more than 100,000:** Evans et al., p. 197.

267 **"You don't know . . . is based on":** "New Nuclear Weapons Needed, Experts Say,

Pointing to Aged Arsenal," by Ralph Vartabedian and W. J. Hennigan in the *Los Angeles Times*, November 29, 2014.

270 **"We are willing. . . is in God's hands":** Weisgall, pp. 106–113.

270 **the surface of the sun:** Weisgall, pp. 185–186.

270 **two million tons of lagoon a mile into the sky:** Ibid., p. 223.

271 **"We very sorry to hear this":** Bradley, pp. 162–163.

271 **If detonated in Times Square:** This rough estimation of the devastation of a 15-megaton surface detonation is from Alex Wellerstein's online tool Nukemap: http://nuclearsecrecy.com/nukemap.

272 **ten million tons:** "Castle Bravo: Fifty Years of Legend and Lore: A Guide to Off-Site Radiation Exposures," by Thomas Kunkle and Byron Ristvet for the Defense Threat Reduction Agency, January 2013, p. 52.

275 **The complaint listed:** Complaint for Breach of the Treaty of the Non-Proliferation of Nuclear Weapons, filed April 24, 2014, in United States District Court, in the San Francisco Division of the Northern District of California, Case 3:14-v-01885, p. 15.

280 **"The Marshallese are . . . by radiation fallout":** "Report of the Special Rapporteur on the Implications for Human Rights of the Environmentally Sound Management and Disposal of Hazardous Substances and Wastes, Calin Georgescu" to the United Nations Human Rights Council and General Assembly, September 3, 2012, p. 14 for the diabetes statistic, p. 16 for the "fissure" description.

CHAPTER 10. GOOD FAITH

290 **to return thousands:** "Ukraine Gives in on Surrendering Its Nuclear Arms," by R. W. Apple Jr. in the *New York Times,* January 11, 1994.

290 **While at the DOE:** Author interview with Rose Gottemoeller, April 24, 2015.

291 **the Bush administration swept away:** Dalton, p. 361.

291 **"There are very beneficial ghosts":** "Dragon Tamer" by Jack Torry for the *Columbus Dispatch*, July 7, 2011.

292 **the Republican Party:** Meese and Perle via Dalton, p. 354.

292 **a roller-coaster 12 months:** Briefing on New START with the Russian Federation via teleconference, December 23, 2010; transcript: http://www.state.gov/t/avc/rls/153700.htm.

292 **$90 billion . . . over the next ten years:** "Republican Senator Sets Conditions for Backing START," by Susan Cornwell for Reuters, August 5, 2010.

292 **nine Republican senators:** "Senate Ready to Talk about Renewing Arms Treaty with Russia," by Mary Beth Sheridan and Felicia Sonmez in the *Washington Post*, December 16, 2010.

292 **"I think there's about a $10 billion gap":** "Republican Senator Sets Conditions for Backing START," Cornwell.

292 **had risen from $3.5 billion to $5 billion:** "Corker Estimates Higher Cost Range for UPF," by Frank Munger of the *Knoxville News Sentinel*, July 27, 2010.

292 **$6.5 billion:** "Oak Ridge Likely to Benefit from Russian Arms Pact," by John Huotari in the *Oak Ridger*, December 24, 2010.

292 **$11 billion by 2013:** "Uranium Processing Facility: When You're in a Hole, Just Stop Digging," by Lydia Dennett and Peter Stockton for the Project on Government Oversight, September 25, 2013.

292 **$19 billion by 2015:** "Y-12 Drops the Ball on Security Upgrades," by Jacob Marx for the Project on Government Oversight, September 9, 2015.

293 **1,000 questions:** Briefing on New START with the Russian Federation via teleconference.

293 **They enlisted the help of religious organizations:** Eric Saap of American Values Network at Generation Prague, July 15, 2015.

293 **Senator Kyl withdrew his support:** "Kyl Statement Deals Serious Setback to Obama's Push for START," by Mary Beth Sheridan and Felicia Sonmez in the *Washington Post*, November 17, 2010.

293 **included amendments:** "New START Treaty: Resolution of Advice and Consent to Ratification," December 22, 2010, http://www.state.gov/t/avc/rls/153910.htm.

293 **Corker and Lamar Alexander . . . joined 11 other Republicans:** Roll call, http://www.senate.gov/legislative/LIS/roll_call_lists/roll_call_vote_cfm.cfm?congress =111&session=2&vote=00298#position.

293 **"My only concern . . . the American people":** "Corker Outlines Support for New START Treaty, Says It Should Be Called 'Nuclear Modernization and Missile Defense Act of 2010,'" statement via Corker's Senate office, December 22, 2010.

293 **"It leaves our . . . to kingdom come":** "Nuclear Arms Pact Is Poised to Pass," by Naftali Bendavid and Jonathan Weisman in the *Wall Street Journal*, December 22, 2010.

293 **a tacit agreement:** Dalton, p. 370.

294 **"As the nuclear . . . maintenance in Texas":** "Briefing on New START with the Russian Federation via Teleconference," December 23, 2010, via http://www.state .gov/t/avc/rls/153700.htm.

295 **"should always keep . . . nuclear deterrence forces":** "When It Comes to Nuclear Weapons, Words Are Deeds," by Alexei Arbatov of the Carnegie Moscow Center, February 9, 2015.

295 **400 Russian incursions:** "NATO Reports Surge in Jet Interceptions as Russia Tensions Increase," by Alberto Nardelli and George Arnett in *The Guardian*, August 3, 2015.

296 **increase the chances:** "Russia Ends US Nuclear Security Alliance," by Bryan Bender in the *Boston Globe*, January 19, 2015.

296 **Russia made plans:** "Russia Is Putting State-of-the-Art Missiles in Its Westernmost Baltic Exclave," by Vladimir Isachenkov of the Associated Press, March 18, 2015.

296 **Mikhail Gorbachev declared:** "Mikhail Gorbachev: World on Brink of New Cold War over Ukraine," by Chris Johnston in the *Guardian*, November 8, 2014.

296 **"I don't know . . . in the room":** Conference call with Rose Gottemoeller, November 7, 2014.

298 **411 financial institutions:** Presentation by Wilbert van der Zeijden at the Review Conference of the Nuclear Non-Proliferation Treaty, May 1, 2015.

301 **75,000 Americans:** "40 Years Later, Bomb Test Fallout Raises Health Alarm," by Curt Suplee in the *Washington Post*, October 2, 1997.

302 **hacked 19 times:** "Records: Energy Department Struck by Cyber Attacks," by Steve Reilly for *USA Today*, September 11, 2015.

303 **"Law stands on . . . own ambivalent souls":** The text of each presentation at the conference is on the website of Austria's Foreign Affairs Ministry, http://www.bmeia.gv.at.

304 **might cost him his job:** Kmentt statement at the Nuclear-Free Future Awards in the Rayburn House Office Building in Washington, D.C., October 28, 2015.

310 **Cables from Australia:** Ministerial submission from Peter Tesch to Ms. J. Bishop and Mr. Robb, Department of Foreign Affairs and Trade of the Australian Government, March 18, 2015, p. 59, of ICAN freedom of information request: http://www.icanw .org/wp-content/uploads/2015/09/FOI-DFAT-Sept2015.pdf.

310 **"Like the US . . . Austria pledge":** Ibid., p. 111.

312 **a one-page memo:** 2015 U.S. National Report to the Nuclear Non-Proliferation Treaty Review Conference.

312 **"the highest priority":** Section 1636 of the Senate Armed Services Committee's version of the FY16 National Defense Authorization Act.

313 **a more tempting option:** "B61 LEP: Increasing NATO Nuclear Capability and Precision Low-Yield Strikes," by Hans M. Kristensen for the Federation of American Scientists, June 15, 2011.

316 **he wrote letters:** Handwritten letter from Michael Walli to the author, dated May 8, 2015.

316 **He remembered Dan Berrigan's teachings:** Details on Greg's time in prison are from handwritten correspondence and from "Transformation Now Plowshares . . . Our Midwest CW Connection," by Greg Boertje-Obed in the July 2014 edition of *Via Pacis*, a publication of the Des Moines Catholic Worker.

322 **"The question, then . . . slip in behind":** Opinion of District Judge Jeffrey J. Helmick and Circuit Judge Raymond Kethledge to vacate the sabotage conviction, May 8, 2015, document 56-2 of Case 14-5220, U.S. Court of Appeals for the Sixth Circuit, p. 9.

322 **"Their intent to . . . could find existed":** Dissent of Circuit Judge Danny J. Boggs, May 8, 2015, document 56-2 of Case 14-5220, U.S. Court of Appeals for the Sixth Circuit, p. 14.

323 **It was at Minot that:** "Independent Review of the Department of Defense Nuclear Enterprise," conducted by General Larry D. Welch (Ret.) and Admiral John C. Harvey Jr. (Ret.), June 2, 2014.

323 **$1.85-billion:** General Dynamics website: http://generaldynamics.com/news/ press-releases/2013/01/general-dynamics-awarded-46-billion-submarine -programs.

323 **Merrick and Company:** Merrick and Company website: http://www.merrick.com/ Portfolio/Uranium-Processing-Facility.

323 **more than $200,000:** "Bombs versus Budgets: Inside the Nuclear Weapons Lobby," by William D. Hartung and Christine Anderson, Center for International Policy, June 2012, p. 16.

326 **buzzing NATO airspace:** "Behind Putin's Nuclear Threats," by Elisabeth Braw in *Politico*, August 18, 2015.

326 **seized 40 kilograms:** "Iraq Tells U.N. That 'Terrorist Groups' Seized Nuclear Materials," by Michelle Nichols for Reuters, July 9, 2015.

326 **as a broker:** Nolan, *An Elusive Consensus*, p. 43.

326 **a fraction of the Pentagon's total budget:** It was 3 percent of the Department of Defense's budget in 2015 and is expected to rise to 7 percent in the mid-2020s, as new delivery systems for the arsenal are built, according to the congressional testimony of Deputy Defense Secretary Robert Work in June 2015. In the Department of Energy in 2015, nuclear-weapons activities accounted for nearly 30 percent of the budget.

327 **The deal relieved:** "The Iran Nuclear Deal: A Definitive Guide," by the Belfer Center for Science and International Affairs, August 2015.

328 **"increased fidelity":** Los Alamos National Laboratory: "Trinity to Trinity," http:// www.lanl.gov/about/history-innovation/trinity-to-trinity/index.php.

328 **"I do think . . . use happen again":** "U.S. Diplomat: Hiroshima Atom Bombing Should Never Be Repeated," by Mari Yamaguchi for the Associated Press, August 7, 2015.

329 **"nuclear weapons life . . . the following generation":** NDAA FY2016.

EPILOGUE

331 **"This is a mission . . . not perfect":** Chilton was quoted by Sen. John Warner (R-Va.) in "Hearing: Air Force Nuclear Security," Senate Committee on Armed Services, February 12, 2008. Via Scarry.

331 **the activists took turns:** "Ceremony at Y-12 on Anniversary of Hiroshima," by Frank Munger on the Atomic City Underground blog of the *Knoxville News Sentinel*, August 6, 2015.

333 **readying the removal:** "NNSA Partnership Successfully Removes All Remaining HEU from Uzbekistan," press release from the NNSA, September 29, 2015.

333 **one kilogram from the latter would be:** "HEU Caribbean Has a TVA Twist," by Frank Munger on the Atomic City Underground blog of the *Knoxville News Sentinel*, September 28, 2015.

333 **an average of one retired warhead:** Remarks by NNSA deputy administrator Madelyn Creedon at the Peter Huessy Congressional Breakfast Seminar, April 24, 2015.

333 **$65 billion:** U.S. Nuclear Modernization Programs fact sheets and briefs, the Arms Control Association, December 2015. https://www.armscontrol.org/factsheets/USNuclearModernization.

334 **7,000 nuclear weapons:** Sister Megan said the United States had 7,000 nuclear weapons in 2015, while Rose Gottemoeller at the RevCon said there were 4,717 in the "active stockpile." Both are correct. Sister Megan combined the number of active warheads—meaning those usable by the military—with the number of inactive warheads awaiting dismantlement (about 2,500).

BIBLIOGRAPHY

BOOKS

Ackland, Len. *Making a Real Killing: Rocky Flats and the Nuclear West*. University of New Mexico Press, 1999.

Albanese, Catherine L. *American Spirituality: A Reader*. Indiana University Press, 2001.

Allison, Graham. *Nuclear Terrorism*. Henry Holt, 2004.

Alperovitz, Gar. *The Decision to Use the Atomic Bomb*. Vintage, 1995.

Alter, Jonathan. *The Promise: President Obama, Year One*. Simon and Schuster, 2011.

Anderson, Margaret, and Robert Marlowe. *Clinton: An Identity Rediscovered*. Clinton Courier-News.

Saint Augustine. *Confessions*. Penguin, 1961.

Bales, Stephen Lyn. *Natural Histories: Stories from the Tennessee Valley*. University of Tennessee Press, 2007.

Barker, Holly M. *Brave for the Marshallese: Regaining Control in a Post-Nuclear, Post-Colonial World*. Wadsworth/Cengage Learning, 2013.

Berrigan, Daniel. *The Dark Night of Resistance*. Doubleday, 1971.

———. *To Dwell in Peace: An Autobiography*. Harper & Row, 1987.

———. *Essential Writings*. Orbis Books, 2009.

———. *Isaiah: Spirit of Courage, Gift of Tears*. Fortress Press, 1997.

Bird, Kai, and Martin J. Sherwin. *American Prometheus: The Triumph and Tragedy of J. Robert Oppenheimer*. Vintage, 2006.

Boyer, Paul. *By the Bomb's Early Light: American Thought and Culture at the Dawn of the Atomic Age*. University of North Carolina Press, 1985.

Bracken, Paul. *The Second Nuclear Age: Strategy, Danger, and the New Power Politics*. St. Martin's/Griffin, 2012.

Bradley, David. *No Place to Hide, 1946/1984*. University Press of New England, 1983.

Bridgman, P. W. *The Logic of Modern Physics*. Macmillan, 1927.

Buffer, Patricia. *Rocky Flats History*. Department of Energy, Rocky Flats Field Office, 2003.

Cirincione, Joseph. *Nuclear Nightmares: Securing the World Before It Is Too Late*. Columbia University Press, 2013.

Coleman, J. D. *Incursion*. St. Martin's Press, 1991.

Coster-Mullen, John. *Atom Bombs: The Top Secret Inside Story of Little Boy and Fat Man*. Self-published, 2002.

Dower, John W. *Cultures of War: Pearl Harbor | Hiroshima | 9-11 | Iraq*. New Press/W. W. Norton, 2010.

Downton, James, Jr., and Paul Wehr. *The Persistent Activist: How Peace Commitment Develops and Survives*. Westview Press, 1997.

Feiveson, Harold A., Alexander Glaser, Zia Mian, and Frank N. von Hippel. *Unmaking the Bomb: A Fissile Material Approach to Nuclear Disarmament and Nonproliferation*. MIT Press, 2014.

Fermi, Laura. *Atoms in the Family: My Life with Enrico Fermi*. University of Chicago Press, 1954.

Ford, Kenneth W. *Building the H Bomb: A Personal History*. World Scientific Publishing, 2015.

Forest, Jim. *All Is Grace: A Biography of Dorothy Day*. Orbis Books, 2011.

Frank, Richard B. *Downfall: The End of the Imperial Japanese Empire*. Penguin, 2001.

Freeman, Lindsey A. *Longing for the Bomb: Oak Ridge and Atomic Nostalgia*. University of North Carolina Press, 2015.

Gallagher, Carole. *American Ground Zero: The Secret Nuclear War*. Random House, 1993.

Gibbs, Steve. *Behind the Blue Line: Protecting Our Nuclear Weapons Complex*. Gibbs Publishing, with Red Horseshoe Books, 2015.

Groves, Leslie M. *Now It Can Be Told: The Story of the Manhattan Project*. Da Capo Press, 1962.

Gusterson, Hugh. *Nuclear Rites: A Weapons Laboratory at the End of the Cold War*. University of California Press, 1998.

―――. *People of the Bomb: Portraits of America's Nuclear Complex*. University of Minnesota Press, 2004.

Hecht, Selig. *Explaining the Atom*. Viking, 1947.

Herzog, Rudolph. *A Short History of Nuclear Folly*. Melville House, 2012.

Hillenbrand, Laura. *Unbroken: A World War II Story of Survival, Resilience, and Redemption*. Random House, 2010.

Iversen, Kristen. *Full Body Burden: Growing Up in the Nuclear Shadow of Rocky Flats*. Broadway Books, 2013.

Jenkins, Brian Michael. *Will Terrorists Go Nuclear?* Prometheus Books, 2008.

Johnson, Charles W., and Charles O. Jackson. *City Behind a Fence: Oak Ridge, Tennessee 1942–1946*. University of Tennessee Press, 1981.

Johnston, Barbara Rose, and Holly M. Barker. *The Rongelap Report: Consequential Damages of Nuclear War*. Left Coast Press, 2008.

Kelly, Cynthia C. *A Guide to the Manhattan Project in Tennessee*. Atomic Heritage Foundation, 2011.

———, ed. *The Manhattan Project: The Birth of the Atomic Bomb in the Words of Its Creators, Eyewitnesses, and Historians*. Black Dog & Leventhal, 2007.

———, and Robert S. Norris. *A Guide to the Manhattan Project in Manhattan*. Atomic Heritage Foundation, 2012.

Kevles, Daniel J. *The Physicists*. Vintage, 1979.

Kiernan, Denise. *The Girls of Atomic City: The Untold Story of the Women Who Helped Win World War II*. Touchstone, 2013.

Krieger, David, ed. *The Challenge of Abolishing Nuclear Weapons*. Transaction, 2009.

Laffin, Arthur J. *Swords into Plowshares: A Chronology of Plowshares Disarmament Actions, 1980–2003*. Rose Hill Books, 2009.

LaForge, John M., and Arianne S. Peterson, eds. *Nuclear Heartland: A Guide to the 450 Land-Based Missiles of the United States*. Rev. ed. Nukewatch, 2015.

Lanouette, William. *Genius in the Shadows: A Biography of Leo Szilard, the Man Behind the Bomb*. University of Chicago Press, 1994.

Levi, Michael. *On Nuclear Terrorism*. Harvard University Press, 2007.

Lifton, Robert Jay. *Death in Life: Survivors of Hiroshima*. University of North Carolina Press.

Light, Michael. *100 Suns*. Alfred A. Knopf, 2003.

Lilienthal, David E. *The Journals of David E. Lilienthal*: vol. 1, *The TVA Years*; vol. 2, *The Atomic Energy Years*. Harper & Row, 1964.

Maddow, Rachel. *Drift*. Crown, 2012.

Maraniss, David. *Barack Obama: The Story*. Simon & Schuster, 2012.

McPhee, John. *The Curve of Binding Energy*. Farrar, Straus and Giroux, 1980.

Medsger, Betty. *The Burglary: The Discovery of J. Edgar Hoover's Secret FBI*. Alfred A. Knopf, 2014.

Merton, Thomas. *Faith and Violence*. University of Notre Dame Press, 1984.

———. *The Seven Storey Mountain*. Harcourt/Harvest, 1998.

Mitchell, Greg. *Atomic Cover-Up: Two U.S. Soldiers, Hiroshima & Nagasaki and the Greatest Movie Never Made*. Sinclair Books, 2012.

Mostafanezhad, Mary, and Kevin Hannam, eds. *Moral Encounters in Tourism*. Ashgate Publishing, 2014.

Moxley, Charles J., Jr, *Nuclear Weapons and International Law in the Post Cold War World*. Austin & Winfield, 2000.

Newhouse, John. *Cold Dawn: The Story of SALT*. Holt, Rinehart and Winston, 1973.

———. *War and Peace in the Nuclear Age*. Alfred A. Knopf, 1989.

Nolan, Janne E. *An Elusive Consensus: Nuclear Weapons and American Security After the Cold War*. Brookings Institution Press, 1999.

————. *Guardians of the Arsenal: The Politics of Nuclear Strategy*. Basic Books, 1989.

Norris, Robert S. *Racing for the Bomb: General Leslie Groves, the Manhattan Project's Indispensable Man*. Steerforth Press, 2002.

Peters, Shawn Francis. *The Catonsville Nine: A Story of Faith and Resistance in the Vietnam Era.* Oxford University Press, 2012.

Present, Thelma. *Dear Margaret: Letters from Oak Ridge to Margaret Mead*. East Tennessee Historical Society, 1985.

Remnick, David. *The Bridge: The Life and Rise of Barack Obama*. Alfred A. Knopf, 2010.

Rhodes, Richard. *Arsenals of Folly: The Making of the Nuclear Arms Race*. Vintage, 2007.

————. *Dark Sun*. Simon & Schuster, 1995.

————. *The Making of the Atomic Bomb*. Simon & Schuster, 1986.

Rice, Madeleine Hooke. *American Catholic Opinion in the Slavery Controversy*. Columbia University Press, 1944.

Riegle, Rosalie G. *Crossing the Line: Nonviolent Resisters Speak Out for Peace*. Cascade Books, 2013.

————. *Doing Time for Peace: Resistance, Family and Community*. Vanderbilt University Press, 2012.

Roberts, Nancy L. *Dorothy Day and the* Catholic Worker. State University of New York Press, 1984.

Robinson, George O. *The Oak Ridge Story*. Southern Publishers, 1950.

Russell, Edmund. *War and Nature: Fighting Humans and Insects with Chemicals from World War I to Silent Spring*. Cambridge University Press, 2001.

Sagan, Carl, and Richard Turco. *A Path Where No Man Thought: Nuclear Winter and the End of the Arms Race*. Random House, 1990.

Scarry, Elaine. *Thermonuclear Monarchy: Choosing Between Democracy and Doom*. W. W. Norton, 2013.

Schell, Jonathan. *The Fate of the Earth* and *The Abolition*. Stanford University Press, 2000.

————. *The Unfinished Twentieth Century: The Crisis of Weapons of Mass Destruction*. Verso, 2003.

Schlosser, Eric. *Command and Control: Nuclear Weapons, the Damascus Incident, and the Illusion of Safety*. Penguin Press, 2013.

Serber, Robert. *The Los Alamos Primer: The First Lectures on How to Build an Atomic Bomb*. University of California Press, 1992.

Sokolski, Henry D. *Underestimated: Our Not So Peaceful Nuclear Future*. Nonproliferation Policy Education Center, 2015.

Southard, Susan. *Nagasaki: Life After Nuclear War*. Viking, 2015.

Weisgall, Jonathan M. *Operation Crossroads: The Atomic Tests at Bikini Atoll*. Naval Institute Press, 1994.

Wells, H. G. *The World Set Free* (1914). Project Gutenberg eBook, 2006, 2012.

Wilcox, William J., Jr. *An Overview of the History of Y-12: 1942 to 1992: A Chronology of Some Noteworthy Events and Memoirs.* American Museum of Science and Energy, 2001.

Wittner, Lawrence S. *One World or None.* Stanford University Press, 1993.

———. *Resisting the Bomb.* Stanford University Press, 1997.

———. *Toward Nuclear Abolition.* Stanford University Press, 2003.

ARTICLES AND PAPERS

Case, Dale Edward. "Oak Ridge, Tennessee: A Geographic Study." University of Tennessee, August 1955.

Cockburn, Andrew. "Game: East vs. West, Again." *Harper's,* January 2015.

Cohn, Carol. "Sex and Death in the Rational World of Defense Intellectuals." *Signs* 12, no. 4 (Within and Without: Women, Gender, and Theory, Summer 1987).

"Dienekes." "Broken Promises: The White House, Special Interests, and New Start." Los Alamos Study Group, February 5, 2013.

Dillingham, Clay. "Debunking Six Big Myths About Nuclear Weapons." *National Security Science,* December 2014.

Dorothy Day–Catholic Worker Collection. Department of Special Collections and University Archives, Marquette University Libraries.

FBI Personality Files of Dorothy Day. Nuclear Weapons Secrets (Hansen Collection) and Human Radiation Experiments. National Security Archive.

Fussell, Paul. "Thank God for the Atomic Bomb." *The New Republic,* August 1981.

Graham, C. H. "Selig Hecht: 1892–1947." *The American Journal of Psychology* 61, no. 1 (January 1949).

Hecht, Selig. "The Uncertainty Principle and Human Behavior." *Harper's Magazine,* January 1935.

Kristensen, Hans M., and Robert S. Norris. "Slowing Nuclear Weapon Reductions and Endless Nuclear Weapon Modernizations: A Challenge to the NPT." *Bulletin of the Atomic Scientists,* June 20, 2014.

Lichterman, Andrew M. "Up from the Concrete: Making Connections and Building Coalitions for a U.S. Movement to Abolish Nuclear Weapons." Western States Legal Foundation, 2000.

Lyttle, Bradford. "The Flaw in Deterrence." Midwest Pacific Publishing Center, 1983, 2001.

Mauroni, [Albert J.]. "Discarding the Cold War WMD Construct." U.S. Air Force Counterproliferation Center, September 2013.

———, ed. "Deterrence in the 21st Century: AY14 Nuclear Issues Research Group." U.S. Air Force Center for Unconventional Weapons Studies, 2014.

McInnis, Kathleen J. "Extended Deterrence: The U.S. Credibility Gap in the Middle East." *The Washington Quarterly* 28, no. 3 (June 2005).

McSorley, Richard T. "It's a Sin to Build a Nuclear Weapon." *The Post-American*, February 1977.

Mount, Adam. "Making U.S. Disarmament Commitments Credible." *The Nonproliferation Review* 21, no. 3–4 (September/December 2014).

Norris, Robert S., and Hans M. Kristensen. "U.S. Nuclear Forces 2010." *Bulletin of the Atomic Scientists*, May/June 2010.

Schwartz, Stephen I. "The Cost of U.S. Nuclear Weapons." Center for Nonproliferation Studies, October 1, 2008.

Selig Hecht papers, the University Archives, Rare Book and Manuscript Library, Columbia University.

Stimson, Henry Lewis. "The Decision to Use the Atomic Bomb." *Harper's Magazine*, February 1947.

Toma, Alexandra I. "The Fissile Materials Working Group: Case Study of How a Civil Society Group Can Impact Fissile Material Policy." *Strategic Analysis*, March 19, 2014.

Voelz, George L., as told to Ileana G. Buican. "Plutonium and Health: How Great Is the Risk?" *Los Alamos Science*, no. 26 (2000).

Wald, George. "Selig Hecht 1892–1947: A Biographical Memoir." *The Journal of General Physiology* 32 (1948). National Academy of Sciences reprint, 1991.

Wellerstein, Alex. "The First Light of Trinity." *The New Yorker*, July 16, 2015.

Westbrook, Janet L. "Stepping off the Cliff: A Whistleblower's Story," February 2006. http://janetwestbrook.com/cover.pdf.

Woolf, Amy F. "Nuclear Force Posture and Alert Rates: Issues and Options," June 2009. http://www.eastwest.ngo/sites/default/files/events-downloads/Woolf,%20Amy.pdf.

THESES

Case, Dale Edward. "Oak Ridge, Tennessee: A Geographic Study." University of Tennessee, 1955.

Dalton, Toby F. "Armed for Arms Control? Presidents, Bureaucrats and the Role of Government Structure in Policymaking." Columbian College of Arts & Sciences, George Washington University, 2015.

Mount, Adam J. "Moral Norms and Nuclear Disarmament." Graduate School of Arts and Sciences, Georgetown University, 2013.

Rust, Daniel T. "Unchecked Political Question Doctrine: Judicial Ethics at the Dawn of a Second Nuclear Arms Race." Vermont Law School, 2015.

Whaley, Carah Lynn Ong. "Reaching Critical Mass: The Rise of Grassroots Groups and the Rise of Nuclear Accountability." Department of Politics, University of Virginia, 2015.

REPORTS

"Allegations Concerning Information Protection at Los Alamos National Laboratory." U.S. Department of Energy, Office of Inspector General, DOE/IG-0935, February 2015.

"Allegations Regarding Management of Highly Enriched Uranium." U.S. Department of Energy, Office of Inspector General, INS-L-15-03, September 2015.

"American Nuclear Guinea Pigs: Three Decades of Radiation Experiments on U.S. Citizens." House Subcommittee on Energy Conservation and Power of the Committee on Energy and Commerce, November 1986. Via National Security Archive, box 9, "Human Radiation Experiments."

"Atomic Audit: The Costs and Consequences of U.S. Nuclear Weapons Since 1940," edited by Stephen I. Schwartz. Brookings Institution Press, June 29, 1998.

"Billion Dollar Boondoggles: Challenging the National Nuclear Security Administration's Plan to Spend More Money for Less Security." Alliance for Nuclear Accountability, May 2014.

"Bombs Versus Budgets: Inside the Nuclear Weapons Lobby," by William D. Hartung and Christine Anderson. Center for International Policy, June 2012.

"Castle Bravo: Fifty Years of Legend and Lore," by Thomas Kunkle, Los Alamos National Laboratory, and Byron Ristvet, Defense Threat Reduction Agency, January 2013.

"Cleanup Progress: Annual Report to the Oak Ridge Community." U.S. Department of Energy, DOE/ORO-2467, 2013.

"CNS Global Incidents and Tracking Database." 2014 Annual Report, James Martin Center for Nonproliferation Studies for the Nuclear Threat Initiative, April 2015.

"De-Alerting and Stabilizing the World's Nuclear Force Postures." Global Zero Commission on Nuclear Risk Reduction, April 2015.

"Deterrence & Survival in the Nuclear Age." Security Resources Panel of the Science Advisory Committee, November 7, 1957.

"The Effects of Nuclear War." Nuclear War Effects Advisory Panel, May 1979.

"Enterprise Strategic Vision: Mission First/People Always." U.S. Department of Energy and National Nuclear Security Administration, August 2015.

"Final Site-Wide Environmental Impact Statement for the Y-12 National Security Complex." U.S. Department of Energy, National Nuclear Security Administration, Y-12 Site Office, DOE/EIS-0387, February 2011.

"History of the Custody and Deployment of Nuclear Weapons: July 1945 Through September 1977." Office of the Assistant to the Secretary of Defense (Atomic Energy), February 1978. Via National Security Archive.

"Homeland Defense: Greater Focus on Analysis of Alternatives and Threats Needed to Improve DOD's Strategic Nuclear Weapons Security." Government Accountability Office, GAO-09-828, September 2009.

"Independent Review of the Department of Defense Nuclear Enterprise," conducted by General Larry D. Welch (Ret.) and Admiral John C. Harvey, Jr. (Ret.), June 2, 2014.

"The Iran Nuclear Deal: A Definitive Guide." Belfer Center for Science and International Affairs, August 2015.

"Making Smart Security Choices: The Future of the U.S. Nuclear Weapons Complex," by Lisbeth Gronlund, Eryn MacDonald, Stephen Young, Philip E. Coyle III, and Steve Fetter for the Union of Concerned Scientists, October 2013.

"Mercury Releases from Lithium Enrichment at the Oak Ridge Y-12 Plant— A Reconstruction of Historical Releases and Off-Site Doses and Health Risks." Reports of the Oak Ridge Dose Reconstruction, vol. 2, Project Task 2, July 1999. Prepared by ChemRisk for the Tennessee Department of Health.

"Modernizing the Nuclear Security Enterprise: NNSA Increased Its Budget Estimates, but Estimates for Key Stockpile and Infrastructure Programs Need Improvement." Government Accountability Office, GAO-15-499, August 2015.

"Modernizing the Nuclear Security Enterprise: NNSA's Reviews of Budget Estimates and Decisions on Resource Trade-offs Need Strengthening." Government Accountability Office, GAO-12-806, July 2012.

"National Nuclear Security Administration: Agency Report to Congress on Potential Efficiencies Does Not Include Key Information." Government Accountability Office, GAO-14-434, May 2014.

"National Nuclear Security Administration (NNSA) Office of Defense Programs Independent Assessment of Life Extension Program (LEP) Phase 6.X Process." Aerospace report No. ATR-2012(5709)-3, June 29, 2012.

"National Security Strategy," by President Barack Obama, May 2010.

"A New Foundation for the Nuclear Enterprise," by the Congressional Advisory Panel on the Governance of the Nuclear Security Enterprise, November 2014.

"The New START Treaty: Central Limits and Key Provisions," by Amy F. Woolf for the Congressional Research Service, August 27, 2014.

"New World Coming: American Security in the 21st Century." United States Commission on National Security/21st Century, September 15, 1999.

"Nuclear Posture Review Report." Department of Defense, April 2010.

"Nuclear Security: NNSA Needs to Better Manage Its Safeguards and Security Program." Government Accountability Office, GAO-03-471, May 2003.

"Nuclear Security: NNSA Should Establish a Clear Vision and Path Forward for Its Security Program." Government Accountability Office, GAO-14-208, May 2014.

"Nuclear Weapons: Actions Needed by NNSA to Clarify Dismantlement Performance Goal." Government Accountability Office, GAO-14-449, April 2014.

"Nuclear Weapons: DOD and NNSA Need to Better Manage Scope of Future

Refurbishments and Risks to Maintaining U.S. Commitments to NATO." Government Accountability Office, GAO-11-387, May 2011.

"Nuclear Weapons: Technology Development Efforts for the Uranium Processing Facility." Government Accountability Office, GAO-14-295, April 2014.

"Nuclear Weapons: The State of Play 2015," by Gareth Evans, Tanya Ogilvie-White, and Ramesh Thakur, Centre for Nuclear Non-Proliferation and Disarmament. Australian National University, 2015.

"Nuclear Weapons Complex Reconfiguration Study." U.S. Department of Energy, DOE/DP-0083, January 1991.

"Nuclear Weapons Sustainment: Improvements Made to Budget Estimates, but Opportunities Exist to Further Enhance Transparency." Government Accountability Office, GAO-15-536, July 2015.

"A Perspective on Atmospheric Nuclear Tests in Nevada," prepared by H. N. Friesen, Holmes & Narver, for the U.S. Department of Energy's Nevada Operations Office, August 1985.

"Prevent, Counter, and Respond—A Strategic Plan to Reduce Global Nuclear Threats (FY 2016-FY 2020)." National Nuclear Security Administration, March 2015.

"Project Atom: A Competitive Strategies Approach to Defining U.S. Nuclear Strategy and Posture for 2025–2050," by Clark Murdock, Samuel J. Brannen, Thomas Karako, and Angela Weaver, with Barry Blechman, Elbridge Colby, Keith B. Payne, Russell Rumbaugh, and Thomas Scheber, for the Center for Strategic and International Studies, May 2015.

"Projected Costs of U.S. Nuclear Forces, 2015 to 2024." Congressional Budget Office, January 2015.

"Recommendations for the Nuclear Weapons Complex of the Future." Nuclear Weapons Complex Infrastructure Task Force and Secretary of Energy Advisory Board, July 13, 2005.

"Report on Nuclear Employment Strategy of the United States Specified in Section 491 of 10 U.S.C.," June 12, 2013. http://www.globalsecurity.org/wmd/library/policy/dod/us-nuclear-employment-strategy.pdf.

"Report of the Secretary of Defense Task Force on DoD Nuclear Weapons Management, Phase II: Review of the DoD Nuclear Mission," chaired by James R. Schlesinger, December 2008.

"Reducing the Risks of Highly Enriched Uranium at the U.S. Department of Energy's Y-12 National Security Complex," by Robert Alvarez, October 9, 2006.

"Resolving Ambiguity: Costing Nuclear Weapons," by Russell Rumbaugh and Nathan Cohn, Henry L. Stimson Center, June 2012.

"The Results We Need in 2016: Policy Recommendations for the Nuclear Security Summit," by the Fissile Materials Working Group. http://www.fmwg.org/FMWG_Results_We_Need_in_2016.pdf.

"Science at Its Best; Security at Its Worst: A Report on Security Problems at the

U.S. Department of Energy," by the President's Foreign Intelligence Advisory Board, June 1999.

"Security Improvements at the Y-12 National Security Complex." U.S. Department of Energy, Office of Inspector General, DOE/IG-0944, August 2015.

"Special Report: Inquiry into the Security Breach at the National Nuclear Security Administration's Y-12 National Security Complex." U.S. Department of Energy, Office of Inspector General, DOE/IG-0868, August 2012.

"Stand Up and Fight! The Creation of U.S. Security Organizations, 1942–2005," edited by Ty Seidule and Jacqueline E. Whitt, United States Army War College, April 2015.

Stockpile Stewardship and Management Plans, Fiscal Years 2015–2017. National Nuclear Security Administration, April 2014 and March 2015.

"Strategic Stability in the Second Nuclear Age," by Gregory D. Koblentz for the Council on Foreign Relations, November 2014.

"Too Close for Comfort: Cases of Near Nuclear Use and Options for Policy," by Patricia Lewis, Heather Williams, Benoit Pelopidas, and Sasan Aghlani, Chatham House, Royal Institute of International Affairs, April 2014.

"Toward Disarmament Securely: Clarifying the Nuclear Security and Disarmament Link," by Deepti Choubey, Foreign Policy Institute, Paul H. Nitze School of Advanced International Studies at Johns Hopkins University, 2015.

"The Trillion Dollar Nuclear Triad," by Jon B. Wolfsthal, Jeffrey Lewis, and Marc Quint for the James Martin Center for Nonproliferation Studies, January 2014.

"UPF Update: Red Team Report Is Recipe for Disaster," by Ralph Hutchison, Oak Ridge Environmental Peace Alliance, May 2014.

"U.S. Nuclear Weapons Complex: Y-12 and Oak Ridge National Laboratory at High Risk," by the Project on Government Oversight, October 16, 2006.

"U.S. Plutonium Pit Production for Nuclear Weapons," by Nuclear Watch New Mexico, April 2015.

"U.S. Strategic Nuclear Forces: Background, Developments, and Issues," by Amy F. Woolf for the Congressional Research Service, September 5, 2014.

ORAL HISTORIES

Baker, Howard. Interviewed by Jim Campbell, Amy Fitzgerald, and D. Ray Smith, August 19, 2009, for the Center for Oak Ridge Oral History.

Black, Colleen. Interviewed by Jim Kolb, February 20, 2002, for the Center for Oak Ridge Oral History.

Boyd, Gerald. Interviewed by Keith McDaniel, May 14, 2013, for the Center for Oak Ridge Oral History.

Goodman, Walter. Interviewed by Cynthia Kelly, 2005, for the Atomic Heritage Foundation's Voices of the Manhattan Project.

Graham, Thomas, Jr. Interviewed by Charles Stuart Kennedy, May 15, 2001, for the Foreign Affairs Oral History Project of the Association for Diplomatic Studies and Training.

Hooke, Walter G. Interviewed by Wayne Clarke and Mike Russert for the New York State Military Museum, April 14, 2004.

Kelly, James. Interviewed by Dorothy Ciarlo, December 10, 2003, for the Maria Rogers Oral History Program, Carnegie Library for Local History, Boulder Public Library.

Moore, Leroy, and other Rocky Flats activists. Interviewed October 28, 2006, for the Maria Rogers Oral History Program and the Rocky Flats Cold War Museum.

Rice, Megan. Interviewed by Suzanne Becker for the Nevada Test Site Oral History, University of Nevada, Las Vegas.

MISCELLANEOUS

National Nuclear Security Administration Policy Letter (NAP-21), "Transformational Governance and Oversight," approved February 28, 2011.

"The Psychosocial Effects of Beryllium Sensitization and Chronic Beryllium Disease," by Jeff Miller, PhD, for the University of Tennessee Department of Public Health, January 10, 2013.

"Status of U.S. Deterrent Warheads and Selected Infrastructure—Reduction and Modernization," by Don Cook, presented at the Workshop on Nuclear Forces and Nonproliferation, Woodrow Wilson International Center for Scholars, December 8, 2014.

Statement of C. Donald Alston and Richard A. Meserve to the House Committee on Energy and Commerce Subcommittee on Oversight and Investigations hearing on "DOE Management and Oversight of Its Nuclear Weapons Complex: Lessons of the Y-12 Security Failure," March 13, 2013.

Statement of Brigadier General Sandra E. Finan to the House Committee on Energy and Commerce Subcommittee on Oversight and Investigations hearing on "DOE Management and Oversight of Its Nuclear Weapons Complex: Lessons of the Y-12 Security Failure," March 13, 2013.

CREDITS

INDEX

ABOUT THE AUTHOR

Dan Zak is a reporter for *The Washington Post*. He has written a wide range of news stories, narratives, and profiles while on local, national, and foreign assignments. He is from Buffalo, New York, and lives in Washington, D.C.